2001

W9-DGV-470

Experience Marketing

Experience Marketing

Strategies for the New Millennium

by Ellen L. O'Sullivan and Kathy J. Spangler

UNIV. OF ST. FRANCIS
JOLIET, ILLINOIS

Venture Publishing, Inc.
State College, Pennsylvania

Production Manager: Richard Yocum
Design, Layout, Graphics, and Manuscript Editing: Diane K. Bierly
Additional Editing: Richard Yocum and Katherine Young
Cover Design and Illustration: Ion Design, Ruth Bielobocky

Library of Congress Catalogue Card Number 98-86937
ISBN 0-910251-98-3

For the guys, Gary and Jim, the important experience makers
of our lives

Contents

Acknowledgments

Experiences didn't just spring up overnight. There have been people out there who were way ahead on the experience marketing curve. We would like to acknowledge the influence and impact of individuals who pioneered the place and pursuit of experiences. Just a few of those pioneers are:

- P. T. Barnum,
- Dorothy Bagwell,
- John Dewey,
- Walt Disney,
- Amelia Earhart,
- Zaren Earls,
- Henry Ford,
- Jim Henson,
- Frederick Law Olmstead,
- Ted Turner, and
- Peter Uberoth.

Experiences, as you will come to find out, don't happen without people. This book didn't either. Special thanks to Diane Wishart for her "extra"ordinary effort. She reviewed every chapter and still considers herself a friend. A special note of thanks to Ruth Bielobocky of ION Designs for her "eye on" our work. We are also delighted to thank the following people for their insight, energy, and enthusiasm as they read, reviewed, and provided feedback for various chapters in this book:

Amy Carver, Dave Clifton, Lori Daniel, Annabelle Davis, Danner DeStephano, Ron Dodd, Jim Donahue, Tom Dooley, Bill Foelsch, Sheila Franklin, Margie Gruber, Robin Hall, Helen Harris, Cindy Heath, Sara Hensley, Amy Hurd, Jane Hodgkinson, Daphne Hutchinson, Chris Jarvi, Stew Leonard Jr., Andrea McGuire, Kathy Merner, Denna Niedzwiecki, Marcia Noyes, Ernie Nance, Steve Parker, Bob Peck, Robina Schepp, and Terry Trueblood.

Introduction

When approached to create a second edition of *Marketing for Parks, Recreation, and Leisure*, all it took was a quick conversation between collaborators and this book was born. After a combined 8,000 miles crisscrossing the country and some parts of the world, it became abundantly clear to us that while the service marketing model moved marketing into a new era, it didn't begin to explain either the current state or future of marketing.

That realization led to the birth of experience marketing. So we set upon a journey not to invent marketing but to collect and pull together what was already occurring in the marketing milieu but not recognized in any formal manner.

We are individuals who enjoy each other's minds and spirits and between us hold a variety of professional roles among them President of Leisure Lifestyle Consulting, Professor of Public Health at Southern Connecticut State University, Director of National Programs for the National Recreation and Park Association, and Fitness and Wellness Coordinator for the National Recreation and Park Association.

Leisure Lifestyle Consulting focuses upon innovations in marketing strategies related to consumer behavior, psychographic profiles, and trends in those areas. Activities pursued with the National Recreation and Park Association include new strategies for customer-centered approaches for that industry resulting in six corporate-sponsored programs that deliver to the grass roots; a repositioning of the public parks and recreation industry for the twenty-first century; and creation of a quarterly publication.

After all this time and all these miles, we came to the realization that experiences drive the market and the ways in which people choose to live, work, and play have resulted in a merging of leisure with lifestyle as a way to reach convergence. We hope this book provides a framework for some of that convergence.

We've tried to make the book instructive and conversant, reflective yet directed, and appealing to both sides of the brain. At best we hope that the book is insightful to the reader and engages the reader in a process of discovery to determine a preferred course for improved marketing approaches in his or her part of the world.

Experience providers who can manage to dive into the meaning of Walsh's quote regarding people's need for experiences and come up with a renewed vision of how people want to live, work, and most especially explore, engage, and energize themselves through

> It is your soul's only desire to turn its grandest concept about itself into its greatest experience.
>
> Neale Donald Walsh

play and leisure alternatives are sure to be the winners in the marketplace of the twenty-first century.

Remember: Leisure and lifestyle equal the opportunity for experiences and the marketing of those experiences are the means to arrive at that opportunity. The way to people's pocketbooks is through preferred experiences!

How to Experience This Book

How do you write a book that can be read by people who know a great deal about marketing and those who may not? How do you write any kind of book for people who want depth of information and people who just don't have that kind of time or patience? How do you write a book that appeals to those who like facts and those who prefer situations or scenarios within the same pages?

Well, we admit that we don't have the absolute answers to any of those questions, but we did want to tell you a little bit about the structure of this book so you can experience it in the way that meets your preferences and needs. We have created a number of categories and headings that appear repeatedly through the chapters as follows:

- **Flashback**—a concise overview of traditional marketing practices appearing at the beginning of most chapters as a quick catch-up for those without a marketing background.

- **TAG** (Tying Action to Goals)—a list of suggestions or things to think about as you read the chapter so you can take action after completion.

- **Fast Facts**—statistics, data, and pieces of information presented in a list rather than in text.

- **ExEx** (Experience Examples)—concise examples of marketing techniques and applications in a bulleted format.

- **Closeup**—experience examples with greater depth or specifics.

- **Slice of Life**—statistics or a picture of various types of lifestyles or consumer behavior.

- **Spotlight on Success**—a look at an individual, organization, or company who has used experience marketing successfully.

- **Signs of a Shift**—examples of ways in which consumer behavior, marketing, and delivery of goods, services, and experiences have changed over time.

- **Bottom Line**—statistics, data, and information found in the three industry application chapters attesting to the economic impact of experience marketing.

- **Action Agenda**—list of suggestions for application of marketing techniques and strategies placed at the end of each chapter.

- **Transition Tracking**—brief recap at the end of each chapter describing how traditional marketing and experience marketing differ.

Chapter 1

The Experience Industry

The very excitement aroused by the mushrooming growth of
the service sector has diverted professional attention from
another shift that will deeply affect both goods and services
in the future. It is this shift that will lead to the next forward
movement of the economy, the growth of a strange new sector
based on what can only be called the "experience industries."

Alvin Toffler

Was Toffler right when he predicted this strange new sector as providing the
economic momentum for the future? Was he correct that this emerging industry
he termed "experience" would be overshadowed or largely ignored? Consider for
a moment the ever-increasing and -evolving role that experiences and the marketing of those experiences play in today's world.

People don't just go out to eat anymore. They explore the outback of Australia or a tropical rain forest or frolic in Ronald McDonald's playland. Planning a
vacation requires a choice between "getting away from it all" or "becoming the
best you can be." A trip to the movies becomes an outing to an entertainment
center and a visit to the local health club becomes a social adventure. Premium
ice cream and exotic coffee serve as reward or relief from life's routine.

Wherever you look, whatever you buy, the experience industry is present.
The shift to experiences is more than on. It may have taken us decades to notice
its gradual, but persistent growth but the experience industries are indeed here.
Experiences have been introduced, integrated, and infused into all aspects of
consumption and existence.

Experiences: What Are they?

It seems fairly evident. From museums to zoos, from hospitals to hotels, the
experience industry is a significant part of today's economy. This evidence raises
the question as to what exactly is an experience? If you stop to think about it,
couldn't everything be considered an experience? Many products are incorporating an experience component into their consumer offering. Most segments of the

Products and Retail

* ❖ Chrysler took out a 12-page special advertising section in *Newsweek* featuring its Jeep Cherokee except that pictures of the Jeep were overshadowed by information on downhill thrills and open road adventures.
* ❖ Jordan's Furniture of Avon, Massachusetts, helps shoppers get in the mood to purchase furniture by providing them with a hint of pine and the sound of crickets as they stroll past the stone fireplace in the Raccoon Lodge or sail by the ocean sounds and suntan scents in the Vineyard Casual section of the store.
* ❖ Local music stores throughout the country are offering a five-week program called Weekend Warriors that helps rock star wannabes form a band, practice, and make an appearance in a local club.

Ad Campaigns

* ❖ Ads with a dreamlike quality interspersed with action scenes appear on youth-oriented programs including "Saturday Night Live" and "The Simpsons" extolling the Army's new theme: *"Prove What You're Made Of."*
* ❖ A recent Toyota campaign replaces in-your-face images of cars with moms driving kids to soccer games or an array of good looking people vowing to improve themselves. The theme is "Everyday People," and the ads are augmented by music of the same name.

Health

* ❖ Kapiolani Women's Medical Center in Honolulu resembles a spa and seems more like a place for people who are well, not sick, as it provides women with private changing and waiting rooms and plush cotton bathrobes.
* ❖ "Red Roses for a Blue Lady" emanates from the hidden sound box under the baby grand piano, a nearby small machine emits the aroma therapy scent of the day, framed artwork covers the walls, and a large resource center and library on holistic health are just part of the patient-centered model of healthcare at Griffin Hospital in Derby, Connecticut.

Events

* ❖ The annual Masters of Food & Wine takes place every February in Carmel, California, featuring top chefs and winemakers from around the world showcasing their culinary talents.
* ❖ San Antonio's Feliz Navidad celebration along its River Walk brings throngs of visitors hoping to recreate the spirit of the holidays with a distinctly Tejano style.

service industry include an element of an experience within its components. Experiences can be infused into a product, used to enhance a service, or created as an entity into itself. However, there are some factors that make an experience or the experience component of a product or service uniquely distinct. An experience involves:

Hotels and Restaurants

❖ The Royale Hospitality Group specializes in "mind travel" at seven pastoral Midwest locations featuring themed suites including a Roman villa, thatched jungle hut, sheik's tent, and space capsule. Careful at reentry!

❖ Hungry visitors to Manhattan can select from any number of dining experiences, among them Planet Hollywood, Hard Rock Cafe, Harley Davidson, Motown Cafe, or the Brooklyn Diner.

❖ Sheraton New York Towers built a combination fitness facility and sports bar called a club/bar adding athletic amenities such as a four-story climbing wall, a skydiving simulator, and a glass-walled basketball court.

Entertainment

❖ At the crossroads of two freeways in California, the Irvine Entertainment Center with a Las Vegas–type lobby, 21 theaters, and love seats is an example of the twenty-first-century movie experience.

❖ Watching a spectacular pirate fight, witnessing a volcano eruption, cruising the Nile, or watching statues come to life are just a few ways Las Vegas uses entertainment as a draw.

Travel

❖ Royal Caribbean cruise lines created Coco Cay, an island built to look like the paradise pictured in the brochure and to ensure a safe and sanitary visit.

❖ The brochure for the Disney Institute talks about "a chance to savor, participate, explore, and discover."

❖ Virgin Atlantic Airways opened its first U. S. airport beauty salon in Boston where Upper Class passengers get free massages, manicures, and aroma therapy at the Virgin Clubhouse lounge.

- the participation and involvement of the individual in the consumption;
- the state of being physically, mentally, emotionally, socially, or spiritually engaged;
- a change in knowledge, skill, memory, or emotion derived through such participation;
- the conscious perception of having intentionally encountered, gone to or lived through an activity or event; and
- an effort directed at addressing a psychological or internal need of the participant.

An experience is quite different from purchasing a product or arranging for a service. The level of involvement as well as the emphasis on personal needs differentiates an experience from other segments of the economy. This difference is due in part to the individualized involvement, reaction, and response to an experience. Taking your car to be repaired is a service, but it isn't an experience.

Experience Experiences

❖ The Museum of Science and Industry in Chicago features a Create-a-Crash section which lets visitors re-create a car crash using a live crash-test simulator.

❖ Paul Crute of Dallas, Texas, charges people $25 to ride in the back of an open-top limousine and drive through Dealey Plaza just like Jack Kennedy did in the last minutes of his life. The tour comes complete with taped sound effects including gunshots at the critical moments as the limo passes the famed School Book Depository.

❖ Over 100 men and women over the age of 35 venture to Fort Myers, Florida, in February to don authentic uniforms, get their lockers, and play a version of major league baseball side by side with their former Boston Red Sox heroes.

❖ Sleek black gondolas traversing the waters under a starlit sky to the strains of Verdi doesn't necessarily mean Venice, because it also happens in San Diego as authentic Venetian gondolas cruise past palm-studded landscapes while passengers sip vino from chilled glasses and soak up all the romance and ambiance they can handle.

❖ Warbird Rides of America tailors flights for first-time fliers or nostalgia buffs who want to fly the real Texan (Navy, SNJ/Air Force T6) just like the aces of the 1940s.

The car owner is not physically involved in the repair of the car. Staying at the Comfort Inn adjacent to the highway necessitates the physical presence and involvement of the consumer. It's a service but not an experience since the overnight stay does not necessarily meet a psychological or inner need. True, there may be cases of horror stories involving auto repair establishments or instances of dirty, unheated rooms where people learn from experience not to go there again, but it is not an intentional aim of that encounter.

An experience is different from other segments of the economy because experiences address what Toffler referred to as the psychic needs of a society. Toffler based his prediction of the rise of the experience industry on the premise that once members of a society had most of their basic and physical needs met they would turn their time, attention, and discretionary dollars to meeting psychological needs. In fact, Toffler coined the term "psychologization" to describe just this shift in need.

Players Within the Experience Industry

Who then are the players within this emerging and growing experience industry? A simpler question to answer might be who isn't. Saturn throws barbecues and a summer reunion for its customers. Hospitals sponsor "senior proms" to reach older members of the AARP set. The Palace of Versailles, the famed Louis XIV chateau outside of Paris, augments the $15 per person tour price tag by holding a New Year's Eve Party with original cuisine from the 1700s, music in the King's chapel, and a fireworks display viewed from the Hall of Mirrors. It appears as if just about everyone is a part of this mushrooming industry. This "psychologization"

As you read this chapter begin to create a mental list of the  products and services you've purchased and whether or not some element of an experience was a part of that package. Develop your own list of examples of how experiences are becoming part of our way of life.

pinpointed by Toffler leads us beyond "functional" necessity. It turns products whether they are cars or couches into pursuits of adventure or peace of mind. It transforms a hotel into a haven and a rental car into a rendezvous. It leaves few parts of the economy untouched by the society's psychic needs.

Essentially, there are three different and distinct segments of the experience industry. These segments can be designated as *infusers, enhancers,* or *makers.* Infusers are primarily purveyors of products who infuse elements of experiences into their products as a way of generating increased sales. Enhancers generally include most segments of the service industry who use experiences to enhance the viability or attractiveness of their service. Makers are naturally the providers of fun and good times such as the amusement, leisure, and entertainment industry segments plus certain segments of the hospitality industry.

As we begin to evolve into a world where there is less scarcity and greater emphasis on personal growth and fulfillment, we should not be surprised that these changes spill over into business and commerce. Our need for "psychologization" impacts all sectors of the economy as more and more products and services slide from being necessities to becoming discretionary. Think of the number of product and service choices we have before us that are truly discretionary in nature. We may have to eat but we have a multitude of choices about what, how, where, and why. We may require transportation from place to place but the "psychic" gratification of that transportation choice is somewhat discretionary. We may seek relaxation and entertainment in our free time but the proliferation of choices approaches exponential growth.

Discretionary needs and choices best describe the hordes of products and services being introduced into the marketplace. This marketplace growth that reflects psychic rather than essential survival needs and focuses marketing attention on experiential factors to distinguish products and services from their competitors serves to fuel the growth of the entire experience industry.

The initial category of player within the experience industry is the infuser. The infuser segment consists of that portion of the economy which manufactures products. Infusers incorporate experiences to connect their products with an experience that their consumers find desirable. These businesses jumped feet first into the experience industry by identifying psychic needs and

Three Segments of Experience Industry

❖ Infusers—manufacturers who infuse their products with experiences for marketability
❖ Enhancers—service providers who use experiences to heighten the satisfaction level of participants or to differentiate their service from competitors
❖ Makers—service providers who create experiences as the central core of their service

incorporating those needs into experiential elements within their marketing mix. Cars come equipped with vacation or mountain-climbing guides. Couches are advertised as bringing a touch of the old world or the beach to your home. Even the plastics industry has cleverly and correctly created a public awareness campaign that highlights the ways plastic products positively impact the health, happiness, and well-being of people and society. Infusers are turning up almost everywhere.

The second segment of the experience industry is labeled enhancers. For companies and organizations in this segment, the experience is not their core focus, but it can serve to enhance their services and make them more attractive to customers. Service providers who make a regular and concerted effort to incorporate elements of preferred experiences into the marketing mix of their service make up this segment. These players are quickly becoming a mainstay of this ever-expanding industry and include the more personalized segments of the service sector such as hospitals, airlines, shopping malls, planned communities, and churches. They use experiences to enhance the service provided to their customers.

Experience makers are those businesses or organizations whose mission is creating experiences for their customers. The contenders in this segment go to great lengths to create an experience that involves people directly while engaging their psyche in the process to make the right kind of thing happen for their customers. Longtime players in this segment of the industry include the myriad of providers of fun and good times such as the amusement, leisure, travel, hospitality, and entertainment industries. Some of these players have been around forever such as Disneyland and various cruise lines. Some are newcomers to the industry having successfully targeted emerging experiential needs such as indoor play spaces for children and virtual reality.

Experiences: Why Now?

As we proceed through the information age leaving the industrial way of life farther behind us, society is experiencing many changes. These changes run the gamut and include demographic shifts, technological advances, and societal changes as well as the resulting ripples from each of these factors. One such ripple effect is the rise of the experience industry as Toffler so accurately predicted in 1970.

Why are the experience industries so uniquely poised to become an integral part of the economy at the beginning of the twenty-first century? There's not a simple answer, but rather there are a multitude of factors and changes that are converging and leading the way towards an economy directed towards psychic gratification. The waning years of the twentieth century harbor a number of changes; changes that significantly impact upon the way we live, learn, work, play, and consume. An exploration of these changes is helpful for both creating an understanding and developing a framework for this emerging part of the economy. Changes that support or influence the growth of the experience industries include:

- science and technology,
- demographic changes,
- economics,
- lifestyle patterns, and
- value shifts.

These factors all support the rapid growth of what Toffler referred to as "psychic needs" that fuel the need for experiences.

Science and Technology

Consider the impact of technology and the role of scientific advancements in life changes that ultimately contribute to the growth of experiences. Recent achievements in these arenas impact on practically everything and everybody. It enables us to live longer and, often, more independently. It sometimes forces us to take up new types of work but then allows us to work almost anywhere. Computer technology allows us to custom order jeans and scientific advances allow us to customize the genes of future offspring. Life as we know it will be dramatically changed by such innovations.

Shopping for either groceries or an automobile can be accomplished from the comfort of your home (or couch) through catalogs, 800 telephone numbers, informercials, home shopping services, or the Internet. Almost instantly you can have that customized bathing suit or tonight's dinner delivered right to your door. Your next vacation complete with itinerary, boarding passes, and hotel confirmations are just an on-line nanosecond away.

Not only are we living and shopping differently due to technology, but we're working differently as well. People work at the office, at home, or in cyberspace. People are self-employed, employed by small businesses, or virtual corporations. Some work with information and technology while others toil in the growing service sector. Our employment patterns vary as well. People can be unemployed, underemployed, overemployed, temporarily employed as well as downsized and outsourced. The world of work, like other facets of modern life, will defy categorization leading to emerging needs and more variety within them.

Each of the aforementioned work variations fuel the growth of the experience industry. People laboring in isolation either in cyberspace or the home office seek socially connecting experiences to balance the solitude. Those overemployed with two or more jobs or the overworked with demanding schedules create a growth market for supportive services and experiences. Sabbaticals and contingency project employment necessitate the creation of still additional opportunities for added growth, learning, and fulfillment.

Demographic Changes

An additional change will be the demographic makeup of the United States. Not only will people live longer but such life extensions will create a society with multiple generations alive at one time. Demographics certainly influence the direction and momentum of the economy. The 76 million Baby Boomers join the

World War II and Depression-era folks in a long march to maturity creating a 50-plus group poised to become the largest and most affluent target market in the United States. The size of this affluence may be determined by the size of the inheritance of the Baby Boomers as well as the future of the economy.

While the sheer size and spending power of these aging Americans is important, an even greater point of interest is the accompanying life stage changes. Having moved through the acquisitive life stage of early adulthood, these folks are satiated with goods and are creating a shift from "buying to being." According to Wolfe (1992), as people age they turn their attention (and pocketbooks) to experiences designed to create fulfillment and meaning for them in this new life stage rather than continued purchasing and acquiring. Wolfe maintains that there are three stages of adult development: the possessive, the catered experience, and the being experience stage.

During the possessive stage, people, usually young adults, purchase and acquire all kinds of things including clothes, equipment of all kinds, cars, and houses. As people age they shift away from the need to own things and become more interested in doing things. The catered experience stage finds people going out to eat or taking trips. As people become even older and outgrow that acquisitive stage and the catered experience stage, they begin to seek out experiences that will facilitate their personal growth and development. The aging of the population with its accompanying shift away from things and towards experiences will impact and influence the experience industries significantly.

Another factor fueling the rise of the experience industry is the value shift of that cohort group that follows the Boomers known as Generation X. This group is somewhat disillusioned as to its prospects of "having everything," and it practices what Feather (1994, p. 74) calls "conspicuous minimalism," the nonownership of products flaunted by previous generations. Disgusted with previous patterns this group redefines "everything" to mean experiences, not things. This redefinition by this cohort group working in concert with the shifts of the aging Boomers will lead to sizable increases in the interest in experiences.

Age and cohort aren't the only demographic shifts creating change. Move over and make room for the new look of America. The predominance of the white, European-based citizenry is being augmented by greater racial and ethnic diversity. The increasing birth rate among African Americans and Hispanics paves the way for a younger, more diverse population. Increases in the number of Asian Americans contribute as well. Such changes in birth and immigration patterns lead to greater variety in everyday and major life events expanding the market for new and different experiences.

The "who" we are in the United States is not the only area of change. We are changing the way we live as well. The long gone Ozzie and Harriet households of the 1950s have been replaced by a variety of household patterns. Projections for the near future suggest increases in households consisting of married couples with no children, single parent households, people living alone, and what demographers refer to as nonfamilies. Different types of households produce different types of needs. As fewer households resemble one another, they produce a greater variety of inner needs impacting all areas of consumption from eating to vacationing.

Some of those needs may be similar to one another, but the way people seek to resolve those needs will vary substantially.

Economics

A substantial part of Toffler's premise for the growth of the experience industry related to economics. He maintained that as people earned enough money to better or more fully meet their basic human needs they would then turn to address less basic, inner needs. Even though people's perception of how well they are doing in the economy may work against this premise, an examination of the reality reinforces just how well the more basic needs of Americans are being met. People live in larger houses with more amenities and appliances. We are able to work fewer hours for more money and are able to use that extra time and money pursuing entertainment, travel, and leisure pursuits.

A comparison of economic changes between 1970 and 1990 and resultant benefits based on those changes was compiled by the Federal Reserve Bank of Dallas. This comparison offers some interesting insights related to how well people's material needs have been met. Some of those comparisons included (Stein, 1997, p. 13):

	1970	**1990**
Average square feet of new home	1,500	2,080
New homes with central air conditioning	34.0%	76.0%
Households with color TV	33.9%	96.1%
Households with two or more vehicles	29.3%	54.0%
Average hours in the work week	37.1	34.5
Paid vacation days and holidays per year	15.5	22.5
Americans finishing high school	51.9%	77.7%
Americans finishing four years of college	13.5%	24.4%
Median household net worth (real)	$24,217	$48,887

Perhaps rising expectations on the part of Americans cause a certain reality gap in relationship to perception as to how well-off people are financially, but the numbers suggest that financial well-being has increased. It is the increases in discretionary dollars that serve as a natural springboard for people to turn to meeting other types of needs, generally nonmaterial and experiential in nature.

Lifestyle Patterns

Such changes within society go well beyond age, household status, and work patterns. Lifestyle differences bloom, grow, and flourish in the rapid changes of today's world. The converging myriad of changes seems to encourage the proliferation of individualized approaches to the way we live, work, and play. These differences provide the impetus for a growing array of choices in products, services, and of course, experiences.

These lifestyle variations are the subject of extensive documentation and analysis. Even when we seem to have much in common with others who live or work nearby, we are actually quite different inside, and these inside differences lead to variations in needs and subsequent behaviors. Market research companies such as Claritas and SRDS analyze and compare purchasing behavior with census information. Claritas' PRIZM program has identified 62 different lifestyle clusters within the United States and is able to isolate the subtle, internal differences between groups with similar incomes.

PRIZM can pinpoint differences between groups with almost the same median household income and living in affluent suburbs. For instance, the "Executive Suites" cluster with a median household income of $58,028 plays racquetball and owns a video camera while the "Pools & Patios" cluster whose median income is almost the same tallying in at $57,780 attends live theater and drinks Scotch (Reardon, 1995, p. 17). Likewise many people would lump computer users together as well. SRDS's Lifestyle Market Analysis differentiates between the discretionary preferences of PC versus Macintosh users on such things as wine, travel, and tennis.

Such lifestyle market analysis highlights the diversity of patterns and priorities among us. The way products are developed and distributed and the way services are created and delivered have all changed according to the inner version of who we are as human beings. Such diversity of patterns and priorities coupled with technological advances creates a whole new way of buying and selling as well as new directions and methods of consuming and living.

Value Shifts

Think about it for a minute. *Homo erectus,* an early predecessor to humankind, spent the bulk of his days roaming the countryside in search of shelter, sustenance, and survival. Just living day-to-day was an experience for early man. While life for our forefathers in the agricultural era was much improved, they still spent the bulk of their time producing and consuming items related to their basic needs.

It wasn't until the dawn of the industrial era that we began to see a shift from *working to live* to *living to work.* People no longer toiled to build their own shelter and raise their own food but rather ventured to factories and corporations to create an ever-growing and -increasing variety of "things" for

Fast Facts

❖ A survey commissioned by the Merck Family Fund found that over the past five years, 28 percent of Americans have voluntarily made changes that decreased their earnings citing the need for balance in their lives, stress reduction, and desire to spend more time with family as reasons for making this tradeoff.

❖ The Wirthin Report found that when asking men and women about their top priority, 95 percent of them agreed that it was their "health."

❖ A Roper Starch Worldwide survey for Age Wave found that for Baby Boomers the American Dream no longer means a big house and the corner office but rather "being true to yourself" and "staying healthy."

❖ A Hilton Hotel survey found that 61 percent of Americans felt that earning a living today is so difficult that it makes it hard to enjoy life.

❖ A CNN poll indicated that 69 percent of Americans would like to slow down and enjoy life more.

people (including themselves) to purchase and acquire. This time in our history fostered a focus on growth and perpetuated the American dream for bigger, better, and more and on our emphasis (or obsession) with material things. With the beginning of the twenty-first millennium many people living in the industrialized world have bought and consumed just about everything and anything. Their growing lack of resources (time, money, space, interest) mitigates against the continuation of this acquisitive type of behavior.

Surveys related to the importance of work and leisure are conducted periodically by Roper Starch Worldwide. When asked what was more important to them, work or leisure, Americans placed work first in surveys conducted in 1975, 1980, and 1985, but in 1989 leisure led the importance list for the first time, and this finding was repeated in 1991 and 1993. However, results for 1995 indicate that 37 percent of Americans chose work first and 36 percent chose leisure revealing a growth in the number of people seeking a balance between work and play (Edmondson, 1996, pp. 4–5).

Other changes in values are often detected through psychographic research. Ever since psychographics was introduced by the Stanford Research Institute through their VALS (values, attitudes, and lifestyles) model, such research has served as a barometer for social change and shifts in values. Two studies that have implications for the experience industry were conducted by BrainWaves Group of New York City and American LIVES from San Francisco.

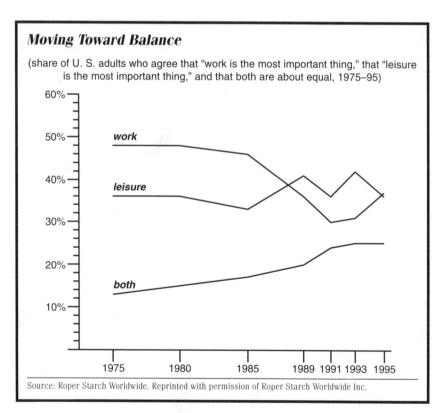

Moving Toward Balance

(share of U. S. adults who agree that "work is the most important thing," that "leisure is the most important thing," and that both are about equal, 1975–95)

Source: Roper Starch Worldwide. Reprinted with permission of Roper Starch Worldwide Inc.

A combination of extensive market research efforts conducted by BrainWaves revealed four distinct values subcultures within the United States. These four subcultures were labeled as Hard-Core Traditionalists, Family Values Boomers, Post Yuppies, and Self-Navigators. Some of the more important value spheres examined in this study were competence, empathy, belonging, and hedonism. These value spheres each have a number of specific concepts tied into them such as making the world a better place, having close friends, accomplishing goals, and enjoying life. The categories are described as follows (Walker and Moses, 1996, pp. 38–39):

- Hard-Core Traditionalists—18 percent of adults; tend to be older; value tradition and fitting in.
- Family Values Boomers—28 percent of adults; slightly more females; value relationships, tradition, and enjoyment.
- Post Yuppies—29 percent of adults; slightly more males; value achievement and developing as an individual.
- Self-Navigators—26 percent of adults; more than half under age 35; value close personal relationships, security, and fun.

The growing emphasis, particularly on the part of younger groups, upon relationships, personal development, and fun are signposts pointing the way to the continued growth of the experience industry.

The second study conducted by American LIVES revealed three different worldviews—Traditionalism, Modernism, and Cultural Creatives with beliefs and characteristics as follows (Ray, 1997, pp. 29–30):

- Traditionalism—29 percent of American adults; value tradition, nostalgia, God, and country.
- Modernism—47 percent of American adults; value consumerism, personal success, materialism, and technological rationality.
- Cultural Creatives—24 percent of American adults; value environmentalism, feminism, global issues, spiritual searching, and experiences.

There is particular interest within the experience industry regarding the trends in values and the direction those trends are taking. Ray believes that both the Traditionalism view which developed as far back as the 1870s and the Modernism view which could be summarized by the slogan "He who dies with the most toys wins" which surfaced in the 1920s are on the decline (Ray, 1997, pp. 32–34). Ray suggests that the Cultural Creatives first appeared on the scene in the 1970s and has grown significantly over the past decades. Ray believes that this group is "the prototypical consumers of the experience industry, which sells enlightening, enlivening experiences rather than things" (Ray, 1997, p. 34). He further indicates that this group of people are interested in experiences such as psychotherapy, weekend workshops, spiritual get-togethers, and all forms of authentic, personal growth opportunities.

When you combine the premise that Cultural Creatives are the leading edge of the new world-view and that the self-navigators identified by BrainWaves are younger consumers serving as the trendsetters for future patterns and preferences plus growth in the future marketplace, it becomes clear that values are fueling the current and future growth of the experience industries.

Growth of Psychic Needs

The collective changes, be they demographic, lifestyle, economic, or technological, have truly converged to significantly change the world, particularly the world of most Americans. On the brink of the twenty-first century confronted by economic challenges and prepared for the prediction of diminished expectations, the general change in the overall attitude towards life points in the direction of accelerated growth for the experience industry. Our values as a society are undergoing significant shifts. Frazier in his book, *Psychotrends,* suggested that Americans are shifting their goals from "being well-off" to "well-being" and are developing a new set of priorities that shun the consumerism of the past and embrace options for personal freedom and self-actualization as well as trading wealth for health (Frazier, 1994). In fact, author Amy Salzman even coined a term for this change in priorities, downshifting.

There are a number of additional trends in behavior and lifestyle patterns that support the growth in psychic needs. Faith Popcorn (1991), founder and chair of the Brain Reserve, originally cited 10 such behavioral trends with all of them implying a surge in the experience industry:

- cocooning in a new decade—people seeking shelter and solace within the home;
- fantasy adventure—desire for escape and entertainment;
- small indulgences—seeking little, often inexpensive rewards as sources of comfort and pleasure;
- egonomics—focus on self and inner feelings;
- cashing out—tendency to exchange monetary rewards for life quality and satisfaction;
- down-aging—redefining the roles and expectations of the maturing process;
- staying alive—concern and focus on health and wellness;
- the vigilante consumer—emphasis upon demands and expectations for value and personalization in the marketplace;
- 99 lives—prevalence of people to assume and attempt to balance too many roles and responsibilities; and
- S. O. S. (save our society)—interest and involvement in community, environmental, and societal concerns.

Popcorn (Popcorn and Marigold, 1996) went on to add an additional six trends to her original list that include:

- clanning—getting together with others with whom you share common interests;
- pleasure-revenge—rebelling against the "right" things;
- anchoring—connecting with a spiritual sense;
- femalethink—caring and sharing approach;
- mancipation—caring and sharing for men; and
- icon toppling—anti-big especially as it comes to business and government.

A review of Popcorn's list reiterates Toffler's initial supposition that we indeed are beginning to seek products, services, and experiences that address our psychic and inner needs.

Barry Feig, marketing consultant and author of *Marketing Straight to the Heart* (1997), has identified what he refers to as hot buttons that reflect current emotional and psychological needs that can be linked directly to buying behavior. Identified hot buttons include the following 15 factors (Feig, 1997, pp. 23–39):

- desire for control;
- revaluing;
- excitement of discovery;
- being better than others;
- family values;
- need for belonging;
- fun, novelty, stimulation;
- value of time;
- getting the best you can get;
- being the best you can be;
- continued interest in sexuality;
- nurturing;
- chance for a clean slate;
- perception of personal intelligence; and
- self-nurturance and the ability to stay ageless and immortal.

The variety and extent of the emotional and psychological needs that form the basis for this listing point towards the ever-growing desire on the part of people to address and fulfill needs that may have not surfaced previously.

One of Toffler's underlying premises in *Future Shock,* as indicated by the title, was that society would be so overwhelmed by the pace and extent of change that people would indeed be "in shock." Experiences provide an opportunity for people to maintain points of stability within their ever-evolving lives. Rites of spring, birthday parties, holiday traditions, and annual events can all be woven into the framework of our new pace of life to help people hold on to parts of the past and to normalize life as we know it.

Just as opening day of baseball signals the onset of spring and the World Series foretells the end of another carefree summer, events, rituals, pageants, and celebrations become strategies for sanity and survival. The strife over the baseball strike of 1994 that led to the cancellation of the World Series was experienced by nonfans of the sport as well. Facing fall without a World Series when the tradition itself had survived war and natural disasters created a sense of unrest and discomfort as a result of this nonhappening.

A framework for better understanding the values changes within our society that incorporates key demographic, economic, and social changes was developed by Wilson when discussing value-oriented lifestyles in the *Encyclopedia of the Future* (Wilson, 1996, pp. 569–572).

There are a number of different aspects of life included in SRI's view of the American Dream: the makeup of society, the United State's world position, the composition of family, trends in occupation, self-orientation, patterns of spending, and preferences related to possession. The movement from the Old American Dream to the New American Dream includes the shifts in those major life categories as follows (Wilson, 1996, pp. 569–572):

Life Aspect	From	To
Society	Melting Pot	Mosaic
World Position	Preeminence	Multipolarity
Family	Nuclear	"New Forms"
Occupation	Corporate	Own Business
Self-Orientation	Conformity	Self-Expression
Spending	Things	Experiences
Possession	Ownership	Rental

A review of some of these shifts indicates that people's needs have changed and will continue to change over time. As people begin to value experiences over objects and self-expression over self-orientation, changes in values suggest a movement from a more outer-directed conformity to a more inner-directed way of life where people's psychic needs will become increasingly a high priority.

As the world around us changes, people's individual personal changes cause human beings to acquire new personal and psychic needs. It's as if the psychological center of gravity in the United States is shifting. It only follows that consumer expectations will rise exponentially as people seek accommodations to these personal and inner needs. Taylor and Wacker identify four new freedoms available to people in today's ever-changing world—the freedom to know, go, do, and be. Each of these four freedoms reflects our growing access to information, global mobility, shift away from bureaucracies, and growth of individual reality (Taylor and Wacker, 1997, p. xviii). These authors also identify a new trend which they refer to as downward nobility:

> the decline in the value of formerly status-laden items and the simultaneous growth in the status value of just being satisfied. Self-affirmation will come by understanding incomes and exercising independence as consumers and workers, not by depending upon objects to establish worth. (Taylor and Wacker, 1997, p. 286)

❖ In 1996 the *Kiplinger Washington Letter* indicated that one-eighth of all consumer spending, a total of $640 billion, went towards leisure time, movies, travel, eating out, gambling, golf, pets, hobbies, sports, and exercise.

❖ According to the *1996 U. S. Statistical Abstract,* in 1995 Americans spent $25.2 billion on beauty shop expenditures, $5.9 billion on amusement park admissions, and $48.7 billion on sporting goods.

❖ A Wiese Research study conducted for Embassy Suites found that approximately 86 percent of adults have taken a minimum of at least one weekend getaway in the last year; preferred activities involved in this relaxing getaway included dining out, 97 percent; shopping, 75 percent; outdoor recreation, 72 percent; and sleeping late, 65 percent.

❖ Opinion Research Corporation for Budget Rent A Car reported that three of four Americans reported splurging on "small indulgences" when traveling to relieve stress.

❖ The Fitness Products Council and American Sports Data reported that fitness facility membership among people 55 years of age and older increased 145 percent to 2.7 million people between 1985 and 1995.

Downward nobility certainly reflects the pattern shifts outlined in the two different versions of the American Dream. The rise of the freedoms to know, go, do, and be will result in the proliferation of virtually limitless definitions of psychic gratification.

The proliferation of lifestyle patterns and choices accentuates the differences in how we define psychic gratification. Such differentiations cut through to the inner core revealing who we are, what we want, and our most inner or hidden needs.

Make way for the experience industry.

Evolution of Marketing Models: From Products to Services

Originally any and all marketing efforts were directed towards products. During this production era the clear focus was to increase output while reducing costs. There was also an emphasis on moving the product from the factory to a place where the customer could purchase it which explains "place" as a factor in the original marketing mix variables. Once the product left the factory, the marketing began. Actually the more accurate term for this activity in the production-era was selling. The role of marketing was to create a need to "push" the product on the consumer.

Eventually product marketing evolved to a stage where marketers became involved in both preproduction and postproduction phases. Identifying customer needs assisted with product development during preproduction while building brand awareness and trial product usage became a part of the postproduction efforts. Sales and promotional efforts remained an essential component of the marketing process as well.

The growth of the service industry caused certain aspects of marketing to be reexamined in light of this growing sector of the economy. Since much of marketing during the production-era centered on product features, distribution, and sales effort, how would marketing be applied to the newly emerging and rapidly growing service sector? Would there be differences that would dictate changes in the marketing process? Berry defined a product as an object, device, or thing and a service as a deed, performance, or effort (Lovelock, 1991, p. 7). Do the differences in these two definitions have an impact upon the marketing process? While it seemed at least on the surface that there were a number of similarities, it became readily apparent that there were some significant differences as well.

In spite of the surface similarities, Zeithaml, Parasuraman, and Berry detected differences between goods and services by isolating four factors characterizing services that set them apart from goods (Bateson, 1995, p. 9). They identified:

- intangibility,
- inseparability of production and consumption,
- heterogeneity, and
- perishability.

These four factors pinpoint significant differences related to the production, consumption, and marketing of goods and services.

Goods are certainly more tangible than services. People can see, feel, and touch cars, couches, and colanders, but it is far more difficult to do any of those activities with car repairs, swim lessons, or vacations. Notice the ways in which many service providers attempt to "tangibilize" their efforts. The auto repair shop returns replaced parts to you with your bill. The swim instructor hands out certificates or pins at the end of the lesson block, and people always drag home vacation souvenirs and mementos with them.

Another difference is the one between production and consumption. Goods are produced prior to sales while services are sold before production. It would be virtually impossible and not at all desirable for Proctor & Gamble to wait until there were dirty dishes in the sink or people waiting for a shower before they manufactured dish detergent or deodorant soap. Services do not have the same sense of control. Service industries are at the mercy of their customers since some involvement on the part of the customer is necessary for the service to be performed. This highlights a significant difference between products and services. Consumers don't have to be present or even involved while the dish detergent or car is manufactured but production of a service involves the consumer in a much more notable and personal fashion.

Closely related to the production-consumption cycle is the heterogeneity of services. There is greater variety among products today, and if you have any doubts about that variety check out the toothpaste section or cereal aisle at your local store. However, this level of variety really escalates when the myriad of differences inherent within services is added to the mix. For instance, the options for eating out—burgers versus health food, drive-through versus candlelight and all the varieties in between—illustrate the variety within just one segment of the service sector.

An additional difference cited is the perishability factor. Goods have a shelf life of days, weeks, months, or years while services can't be stored or warehoused like unsold kitchenware. Once a plane leaves the gate with empty seats, there is no way the airline can store those unused seats to be sold at a later time. If a client cancels a spa appointment 10 minutes prior to the designated hour, the chance of recouping that loss is fairly slim. These differences help to clarify why restaurants have started to charge for no-show diners.

These four factors characterizing the differences between goods and services created a basis for new ways of looking at marketing of services as well. Lovelock felt that in order to advance marketing for services a framework that both identified and analyzed the differences among the burgeoning service sector industry was needed. He developed questions to use within such a framework:

1. What is the nature of the service act?
2. What type of relationship does the service organization have with its customers?
3. How much room is there for customization and judgment on the part of the service provider?
4. What is the nature of demand and supply for the service? and
5. How is the service delivered? (Bateson, 1995, p. 9)

Incorporating Lovelock's framework into an examination of the service economy actually leads to the discovery of significant differences within the industry itself. In a number of instances it becomes difficult to pinpoint where the product ends and the service begins. All services are not created equal. When attempting to describe the actual nature of the service act, we encounter lack of clarity and overlap. While we may refer to goods and services somewhat interchangeably, the actual determination is made by "the extent that the benefits are delivered to the consumer by a service rather than a good" (Bateson, 1995, p. 8). For example, Lands End sells products but when the customer orders summer shirts and shorts from the Lands End catalog is he or she primarily purchasing the quality of the clothing or the ease and dependability of the service delivery or both? When a hungry lunchgoer stops at McDonald's, is he or she drawn by the Big Mac or the fast service and convenient location?

The examples are endless. As more products and services become discretionary in nature and as more services incorporate psychic needs into their marketing mix, it becomes more difficult to apply either product or services marketing to this new industry. The confusion between the products and services grows as more products create still more "service-oriented" benefits to attract and retain customers. Is Domino's Pizza delivery product or service? Is a night at an Omni Hotel service or experience?

An examination of Lovelock's framework including elements of customization, relationship with customer, supply and demand, as well as nature of the service itself demonstrates the need for a further evolution of marketing to incorporate the overlap between goods, services, and experiences. Begin to envision goods

Goods-Services-Experience Continuum

relatively pure good	good/ service hybrid	relatively pure service	service/ experience hybrid	relatively pure experience
car couch	fast food rental car	car repair painting	hospital restaurant	cruise movies

and services along a continuum with location on that continuum determined by the extent to which the benefits of the goods take precedence over the benefits of the service and the incorporation of elements of experience supersede the components of the service. The continuum can then be expanded to further distinguish services from experiences. Vacationing at Club Med: service or experience? Eating by candlelight in a romantic setting: product, service or experience?

Enter Experience Marketing

Just as it became apparent when the economy shifted from the manufacturing sector to the service sector that new approaches to marketing were necessary, the same is true as we shift gears entering this new economic thrust known as the experience industry. The original marketing mix developed for the production era included the 4Ps of marketing: product, place, price, and promotion. The revised marketing mix created for the services industry substituted service for product and included some additional marketing Ps called peripherals that incorporated personnel, other participants, and, of course, the customer service emphasis.

Purchasing a bottle of dish detergent off the shelf at the supermarket has little in common with finding a well-qualified, honest mechanic to service the family car. In the same way, taking your car to be serviced is not the same as taking a getaway weekend or taking a chance at skydiving. Experiences speak to those inner needs and desires of people. Experiences call out to people who want to become involved in such a way that they will take elements of that participation away with them either for the moment or a lifetime.

Action Agenda

❖ Review a list of items, services, and activities you've purchased or participated in over the past two weeks and identify elements of experience marketing that have been incorporated within the products or services.

❖ Consider ways in which you, families and friends, and participants in your experiences have changed their needs and values over the past few years.

❖ Identify ways in which your company, product, or organization uses experiences within its marketing plan.

Experience marketing is the next natural progression of the industry. It mirrors the emerging direction of the economy. It addresses the inherent differences between products, services, and experiences. It speaks to the increasingly diverse yet definitive nature of people's needs. It incorporates the heightened consumer preference for personalization as dictated by technology and rising expectations. It reflects the burgeoning competition within this segment of the industry.

Coming Attractions

What's ahead as we explore elements and aspects of marketing for the experience industries? This exploration of experience marketing begins with an examination of the 4Ps of experience marketing: parameters of the experience, people, peripherals, and PerInfoCom. Parameters of the experience replace the traditional P of product or service marketing orientation. People are incorporated into the marketing mix of experiences since experiences can't happen without them. The third P of the experience marketing mix, peripherals, combines many of the product, place, and price variables of traditional marketing. PerInfoCom is a newly created term to replace the fourth P, promotion, and incorporates emerging needs for personal communication that informs people.

The 4Ps of the experience marketing mix will give way to a number of aspects that are essential for organizations creating and delivering experiences. The need to create customer-centered organizations that continually infuse information internally and externally on an ongoing basis will be critical to success in the future of experiences. Emerging directions and changes in the marketing and management aspects and functions that are particularly important for the experience industry are included as well.

The third part of this experience marketing journey will include a spotlight upon the various players within the experience industries. Focus and applications

Transition Tracking

From	To
• Products and services	• Experiences
• Tangible benefits	• Inner needs
• From manufacturers and providers	• Infusers, enhancers, and makers
• Demographics	• Psychographics
• Standard of living	• Quality of life
• 4Ps of marketing: product place price promotion	• 4Ps of experience marketing: parameters people peripherals PerInfoCom

for experience infusers, enhancers, and makers are included. The journey ends with an exploration of how to sail your organization into the future.

Sources

Bateson, John E. G. (1995). *Managing services marketing* (3rd ed.). Fort Worth, TX: The Dryden Press.

Edmondson, Brad (Ed.) (1996, May). *The Number News.* Volume 16, Number 5.

Feather, Frank. (1994). *The future consumer.* Toronto, Canada: Warwick Publishing.

Feig, Barry. (1997). *Marketing straight to the heart: From product positioning to advertising.* New York, NY: AMACOM.

Frazier, Shervert H. (1994). *Psychotrends.* New York, NY: Simon & Schuster.

Lovelock, Christopher H. (1991). *Services marketing* (2nd ed.). Englewood Cliffs, NJ: Prentice-Hall.

Popcorn, Faith, & Marigold, Lys. (1996). *Clicking: 16 trends to future fit your life, your work, and your business.* New York, NY: HarperCollins.

Popcorn, Faith. (1991). *The Popcorn report.* New York, NY: Doubleday/Currency.

Ray, Paul H. (1997, February). The Emerging Culture. *American Demographics.*

Reardon, Patrick T. (1995, November 5). How place defines us or does it? *The Chicago Tribune Magazine.*

Stein, Charles. (1997, January 5). Things are better than you think. *The Boston Globe Magazine.*

Taylor, Jim, & Wacker, Watts. (1997). *The 500 year delta.* New York, NY: HarperBusiness.

Toffler, Alvin. (1970). *Future shock.* New York, NY: Random House.

Walker, Chip, & Moses, Elissa. (1996, September). The age of the self-navigator. *American Demographics.*

Wilson, Ian H. (1996). Lifestyles, value-oriented. In George Thomas Kurian & Graham T. T. Molitor (Eds.), *The encyclopedia of the future,* pp. 569–572. New York, NY: Macmillan.

Wolfe, David. (1992, September). Business's midlife crisis. *American Demographics.*

The first P in the traditional market-
ing mix variable is product. Traditional
marketing dictates that there are
three dimensions to every product: the
core, the tangible, and the augmented. The core dimension refers to
the most fundamental level of the product or service focusing on the
primary benefit being sought by the consumer. The second dimension
of product is tangible and includes such factors as styling, features,
quality, packaging, and brand name. The augmented dimension represents any and all additional services or benefits offered to the target
market including such things as installation, credit terms, or after-
sales service.

It is easy to ascertain how products relate to these three dimensions. The core level of orange juice is liquid nutrition. The tangible
level would be styling or feature choices such as whether the juice
was fresh or frozen, with pulp or without. The augmented dimension
could even include such things as brand name of the juice and whether
or not the container is recyclable.

While these three dimensions suit product marketing quite nicely,
they don't begin to address the challenges created by a service. Lovelock
developed a six question framework to describe the dimensions of a
service. From his point of view, the dimensions of a service were quite
complex and included a multitude of levels within dimensions. He incorporated questions such as (Lovelock, 1991, pp. 26–37):

- The nature of the service act:
    service is tangible or intangible;
    service directed at a person or a thing.
- The relationship with the customer:
    formal, informal, or arm's length;
    continuous or discrete transactions.
- The extent to which the services are customized and the use of
  judgment on the part of service personnel in the customization:
    mass-produced, choices, or individualized;
    degree of dependence on provider's judgment.
- The nature of the demand for the service:
    stable or fluctuating;
    demand accommodated easily or with difficulty.
- The method of service delivery:
    service goes to the customer or vice versa;
    one or multiple outlets for the service.
- The attributes of the service:
    level of importance of equipment, area, facility, or skill.

Continued on page 24

Chapter 2

The First P: Parameters of the Experience

Sundance is a place where one is meant to slow down and
take stock; it's not a resort—it's a lifestyle experience.

Robert Redford

There are five segments incorporated with the marketing P termed parameters of
the experience:

- the stages of the experience—events or feelings that occur prior, during, and after the participation;
- the actual experience—factors or variables within the experience that influence participation and shape outcomes;
- the need(s) being addressed through the experience—the inner or psychic needs that give rise to the need or desire to participate in an experience;
- the role of the participant and other people involved in the experience—the impact that the personal qualities, behavior, and expectations of both the participant and other people involved within the experience play in the overall outcome; and
- the role and relationship with the provider of the experience—the ability and willingness of the provider to customize, control, and coordinate aspects of the experience.

These five parameters represent not only the essential components of an experience but also hint at the balance and interrelatedness of the parameters within the experience. The factors inherent within each of these parameters can be represented as a continuum along each dimension assisting marketers to create a better understanding of the components and process within various types of experiences.

Flashback continued

Note that the dimensions of a service are far more complex and encompassing than those of a product. Consider the differences. A service such as haircutting that physically requires the involvement of the customer, not to mention the internal or invisible needs of that individual, requires a much different approach than convincing someone to purchase a can of soup. Does a bank have an arms-length relationship with its customers through ATMs or does it afford its better customers a preferred membership service relationship with personalized and customized services? Two people could be customers of the same bank and have or require far different interactions with the same service provider.

A patient certainly expects that a physician use good judgment when making a diagnosis and, of course, expects that such a diagnosis is one based on the patient's individual needs or concerns. Yet that same person wouldn't think anything of it if the order taker at McDonald's wasn't particularly interested in his or her preference for no mayonnaise or lacked input into the special ordering process. Peoples' patience wears thin while waiting in line for a table at a restaurant but are often not even aware that their car is made to wait at the car repair garage.

Another aspect of traditional marketing relates to how consumers make the decision to purchase a particular product or service. This process is often regarded as problem solving. The customer buys dish detergent or decides to have the house painted based on a perceived problem. This decision-making process does not take place in a vacuum and is a result of the interaction between a variety of factors. Essentially, this problem-solving process consists of six basic steps (Peter and Olson, 1994, p. 158):

- problem recognition,
- search for relevant information,
- evaluation of alternatives,
- decision,
- purchase, and
- postpurchase use and reevaluation.

These steps are primarily directed at the purchase of products and nonpersonal services and work well in that context. It is relatively easy to recognize that the need to purchase dish detergent and the time elapsed and effort involved between the search and postpurchase may be minimal. The decision to paint the house may be somewhat more time consuming because it occurs less frequently and usually involves a more substantial sum of money. In a similar fashion postpurchase use and evaluation would differ as well.

Even this quick overview of the framework questions developed by Lovelock gives the marketer a sense of the challenges within service marketing. A thorough understanding of the dimensions within service marketing enables the marketer to bring many insights along to the experience marketing process.

Stages of Experiences

Experiences are different. People don't easily identify or uncover the inner or psychic needs they have. Trying to relate dish detergent or house painting to the adrenaline rush and exhilaration of rising above the sunrise in a hot air balloon doesn't translate well. Experiences don't come neatly compartmentalized in separate and distinct steps; rather they can be best represented in a series of three, overlapping stages. These three stages, preexperience, participation, and postexperience, encompass ele-

---

Experience Stages

❖ Preexperience
❖ Participation
❖ Postexperience

---

ments that help us understand how an experience is perceived and compartmentalized by the consumer. These stages are closely connected with one another.

Preexperience

The preexperience stage refers to anything and everything involved prior to the actual participation in the experience itself. This stage incorporates three separate phases: need recognition, alternative search, and preparation.

How does need recognition take place? Sometimes the would-be participant isn't even consciously aware that he or she is involved in a process of any kind. At some point the inner need or desire begins to take shape and surfaces. The individual becomes conscious of either an unrest from within or an urge to reach out and address some previously unrecognized need or desire.

It's important to note that while need and desire tend to be used interchangeably, the two terms differ significantly from one another. A need is generally perceived as being genuine and necessary to maintain homeostasis while desire falls more into the category of being a strong preference somewhat discretionary in nature. For example, does someone really need to take a weekend getaway, or does he or she actually have a strong desire to do so?

Need recognition just like the need itself varies from person to person. Some people may just awake one morning and decide they need to go skydiving while in actuality they may have been considering it subconsciously for some time. For others the surfacing of a need may be caused by an internal or external event within their life. The advent of a significant birthday or retirement may do it for some folks. Watching a PBS television show on cardiac health, a live theater production, or oriental cooking can serve as an impetus for action.

During need recognition, the need or desire enters the consciousness of the individual leading to the second phase of this stage, search alternative. Search alternative, when related to experiences, is not necessarily as simplistic as it sounds. The length of time and the amount of effort expended in this phase varies greatly. It can be as instantaneous as recognizing that going to a movie will bring the participant a few hours of escape and relaxation, or it can be more exhaustive as people sometimes take that urge for relaxation or escape to mean a more significant shift in lifestyle and behavior.

The need recognition can be less apparent than the decision to go to the movies and may consist of a more gnawing feeling that something is missing from one's life causing a more exhaustive review of priorities and preferences. It is often difficult for people to make a connection between the feeling they have and the need that must be satisfied or resolved. Watching people become hooked on karaoke is an example of an inner need that may be difficult for people to either

Phases of Alternative Search

Need Recognition—first phase
(escape and relaxation)

↓

Generic Alternatives
(physical activity, entertainment, socialization)

↓

Specific Behavior Choices
(walking, bike riding, yoga)

↓

Experience Provider
(bike rental shops)

identify or express. In fact, many people were not even aware of an interest in being a "star in their own life" until karaoke arrived upon the scene.

One of the interesting subcomponents of this phase is the progression whereby the search to resolve the need goes from generic to specific. Having identified the need for escape and relaxation, the individual may mentally construct a list of the variety of general activities that may address this need such as entertainment, physical activity, or socialization. Having decided upon physical activity, the next level of the progression would lead the individual to explore the specifics within that generic category such as walking, bike riding, bowling, and yoga. Once that decision has been made, the person turns to the outside world and begins to weigh alternatives between the various experience providers.

The final phase of this initial preexperience stage is preparation. Like other phases in this stage, the phase can be brief or extensive. Some experiences necessitate extensive preparation activities while others appear to be nearly instantaneous as would be the case with an individual spontaneously deciding to go outside for a brisk walk contrasted with marathon runners known to train for years to get ready for a single 26-mile event. Likewise an individual planning a trip to the Third World may spend a great deal of time researching the area, searching out special necessities to pack, receiving the right immunizations, and perhaps even studying a new language. The amount of time and effort expended within this category varies significantly.

This preexperience stage of the experience should never be overlooked or discounted especially from a marketing point of view. The decisions that are made during this phase significantly impact upon the actual experience itself. In addition, many people report nearly as much enjoyment during this phase as they do with the actual experience itself. Planning the wedding is almost as exciting as the wedding day. Packing for the trip and reading about the destination is very much a vital part of some people's journeys.

Participation Stage

The second stage of an experience is the actual participation in the experience. The initial component of this stage is anticipation. The preparation and anticipation portions of the experience are closely aligned and serve as a natural

Preexperience

❖ Need recognition
❖ Alternative selection
❖ Preparation

bridge between the preexperience and the participation stages of the experience. The excitement and anticipation that can be raised prior to the experience actually become a part of the entire experience. Just as it is difficult to separate the augmented dimension of a product from its core, a similar phenomena occurs as the lead-up activities create an excitement or level of interest that either becomes a significant portion of the experience or significantly enhances the actual experience.

Disney is a master at building the anticipation. While waiting in line at Space Mountain one encounters signs advising against riding on this amusement if one is pregnant or has a heart condition. While these warnings may have some roots in legal liability issues, it heightens the apprehension and anticipation of those weaving their way closer and closer to the thrill and danger known as Space Mountain.

Think of all the hoopla preceding the Super Bowl every year. There are people who perceive the lead-up to this event as more exciting than the actual game, and they may well be right. The hype that precedes the release of new blockbuster films for the holiday or summer season is yet another example of how marketers play on and build the anticipatory phase of this stage.

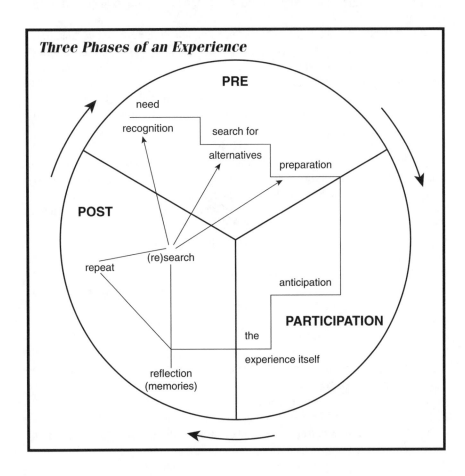

Three Phases of an Experience

PRE

need
recognition
search for
alternatives
preparation

POST

(re)search
repeat

anticipation

PARTICIPATION

the
experience itself

reflection
(memories)

When anticipation is at an all-time high, then and only then should the experience take place. Experience marketers note the great importance of this component and its ability to influence and augment the actual experience. The expectations and excitement (or lack of) set the stage for the experience and as such are very much a part of the individual's reaction to and evaluation of that experience.

Postexperience

It's not over when it's over. The last stage of an experience is the aftermath of the participation. The family van pulls in late Sunday night from an eventful camping trip and you can bet that dirty laundry and bug bites aren't the only things returning with the family. There are a variety of postexperience options that they may bring home with them including repeat, (re)search, and remember.

If the family members felt that this trip was the answer they had been looking for as respite from the pace of day-to-day life and the intrusions of modern technology, look for them to repeat this experience. If the family members enjoyed their first foray into the wild, they may decide to expand their horizons and look for a more adventurous piece of the wilderness. Look for them to explore ways to repeat this experience. In this case the repeat option may lead to the (re)search alternative.

If this particular outing wasn't this family members' definition of a good time, they are likely to begin the search process once again by looking for other alternatives for the fun or bonding opportunity they so desired. Of course, they may decide that they've experienced enough bonding and expand the search to address some other need. Naturally, there's always the possibility they enjoyed the camping but weren't particularly pleased with their destination or campgrounds and may begin the search for a new place or provider.

A third option or reaction is remembering—experiences form memories that people retain. Check the van because it's a good bet that whether the weekend was terrific or terrible there is likely a camera that recorded those moments as well as an assorted collection of T-shirts and tacky souvenirs to keep those memories alive. Outstanding or down right awful, you can be sure that this group will carry those memories with it. That's part of what makes an experience an experience and memories are an additional option within this last stage.

It's important to note that this last stage of the experience, postexperience, is not the same for all participants. People could have just returned from virtually the same Mother's Day Buffet at the same restaurant or the same cruise and have widely varying postexperience reports and reactions. The final selection from among the three options in this postexperience stage will depend on individual needs, preconceptions, and perceptions.

It is essential that experience marketers be both aware and cognizant of activities conducted within each of these three stages. During the preexperience, the experience marketer needs to be able to communicate with people perhaps before they've even recognized their internal needs. Positioning of the experience can play a critical role at this juncture. If possible the marketer becomes a part of the alternative search process providing people with information helping them clarify what they need and reminding them that his or her organization stands ready to address those needs.

The preparation for and anticipation of the experience serve as a bridge between the preexperience and the actual participation in the experience, and a link between the people and the provider is crucial to the eventual success of the experience. Trekkers into the woods will not have a good experience without the proper clothing and bug spray. The experience provider plays a major role in preparing these customers for just this experience. At the same time, if the provider of the experience is able to determine (or shape) the expectations of the customers, the greater chance for success for all involved. There is a significant link between the expectations built during anticipation and the evaluation during the postexperience phase.

Regardless of what the final outcome of the postexperience is, it's important to remember that an experience lasts forever, and its impact or stamp on the individual remains for life. The memories of the postexperience stage (good or bad) also present a host of marketing opportunities for the experience provider.

Understanding the Dimensions of the Experience Itself

The experience itself makes a natural starting point in our exploration of this first P of experience marketing. There are a number of variations related specifically to the experience that can be examined. Some experience variations relate to elements of the experience itself while others involve the interactive role between the participant and the experience and the type of outcome derived from participation in the experience. The following are a set of questions to help to create that dimension:

Elements within the experience itself:
- Is the experience natural or man-made?
- Is the experience real or virtual?
- Is the experience customized or mass-produced?
- Is the experience commonplace or unique?
- Does the experience focus on people, an attraction, facility, equipment, or performance?
- What is the level of authenticity within the experience?

Interaction between participant and experience:
- Does the experience consist of discrete or connected episodes?
- Is the experience self-directed or facilitated?
- Is the participant's role that of a spectator or participant?

Range of outcome due to participation:
- Does the experience create a change in people that is temporary or transforming?
- Does the experience result in pleasure versus preservation?

Dimensions Within Experience Portion of First P: Parameter

	Niagara Falls	Campground	Amusement Park	
Natural				Manmade

	Grand Canyon	Omnimax Theater	SONY Playstation	
Real				Virtual

	Spa Treatment	Museum Visit	Jungle Ride	
Individualized				Mass

	New Year's Party	Laser Tag	Wind Surfing	
People				Object

	Movie Theater	Day at Disney	Cruise	
Discrete				Continuous

	Movies	Vacation	Ropes Course	
Temporary Change				Transformation

	Wilderness Camping	Natural Zoo	Flume Ride	
Authentic				Created

	Miniature Golf	River Rafting	Cooking Class	
Self-Directed				Assisted

	Theater Attendee	Living History	Fantasy Camp	
Spectator				Participant

	Spa Weekend	Ecotourism	Archeological Dig	
Pleasure				Preservation

	Bungee Jumping	Adventure Movie	Yoga	
Rush (adrenaline)				Relaxation

	Daily Exercise	Road Race	Fantasy Camp	
Routine				Novel

Review this list of questions and embark on your own experience of analyzing experiences you've had and contemplating the impact of variations within these categories.

Elements Within the Experience

Let's examine the elements within the

Select three specific, discretionary experiences you have participated in recently and take a look at the various parameters of those experiences based upon your recollection of participation. Be sure to note similarities and differences.

experience itself. Does it make a difference whether the environment is natural or man-made? On the surface, this may seem to suggest differences between the Niagara Falls and the Eiffel Tower, but it can and does go far beyond that. Does the camping trip take place in a wilderness area or at a man-made campsite. The whole question of natural versus man-made is a significant one that substantially impacts the entire nature of an experience. For instance, when riding on a "high-thrill" attraction at any of the many Disney facilities, it never crosses the minds of most adults that they are in any real danger. A part of their brain reminds them that this flume ride or trip through the arteries is only "pretend" while Disney's sterling reputation for safety dances through their heads so it never occurs to them that Disney would put them in any "real" danger.

This dimension takes on a whole new meaning as simulated experiences are being created for a variety of settings. Interested in relaxing on a Caribbean island without being concerned with ports of call that don't measure up or beaches that are dirty or food that may not be safe? Then take a cruise to Coco Cay with Royal Caribbean. This cruise line purchased land in the Bahamas and built a replica of a Caribbean island complete with tropical decor, steel drums, and a ship wreck just waiting to be discovered by snorkelers.

A second and related issue to this dimension within the experience parameter addresses the role of real versus virtual. Are you really standing at the rim of the Grand Canyon or playing golf at Pebble Beach, or are each of these experiences coming to you via computerized simulation? Sometimes the sense of vertigo or adrenaline rush makes it difficult to distinguish. As technology continues to create an array of options for creating experiences that don't "really" exist, this factor creates a variety of responses from a marketing point of view.

Another element inherent within the experience is the degree of customization. Is the experience customized for each individual participant, or is it relatively mass-produced? The jungle ride at Disney may have a few variations in the script to ensure that the "pilot" doesn't mutiny but other than that it is essentially the same ride for everyone. However, a visit to a spa for personal training, massage therapy, and nutritional advice is by definition individualized. Consider these parameters as a continuum. It does not have to be one or the other. For instance, a self-directed stroll through the Getty Museum, while not personally individualized, certainly differs from an organized tour. The range within this particular parameter leaves potential possibilities for experience marketers.

Another element is the novelty or commonality of the experience. Is this an experience that is fairly common and considered run-of-the-mill, or is the experience unique or quite unusual? An experience such as bungee jumping can start out as being unusual and eventually become commonplace. This element influences the stages of the experience, especially as it relates to the length of time required to move through those stages. The status of participating or being involved in an event or experience that doesn't happen often or has restricted access for people can also be a part of this element.

Does the experience include and primarily depend on the interaction with people or with things (natural and man-made)? If going to a social event such as a party, people are most interested in knowing "who else will be there" while a visit to the Statue of Liberty or an afternoon at the opera would be similar because the experience is directed at nonhuman elements, an attraction and a performance. A rock-climbing expedition may be either or both. Was the climb motivated by a desire to see and climb a particular peak, or is the purpose to foster a sense of dependence and teamwork among those in the climbing party?

What about the role of authenticity within the experience? Camping along the Appalachian trail is a more authentic experience than pulling the RV up to the campground hookup. Sleeping in a parador in one of Spain's former castles is different from spending the night at a hotel chain. Attending a living-history reenactment of a Civil War battle is different from seeing a televised version. There is quite a range within this category. A road trip along the old Turquoise Trail in New Mexico with its remnants of bygone mining days differs from visiting Mystic Seaport, a replica of a seafaring community.

The elements within the experience itself provide marketers with a host of options and opportunities. Marketers can change or raise the level of authenticity and attract a new target market. They can customize the experience to encourage repeat participation. They can change elements within the experience to make participation unique as a way to differentiate their experience from those of their competitors. The elements within an experience provide a basis for nearly limitless experience marketing strategies.

Interaction Between Participant and Experience

A second category of factors related to the experience itself with significance to the participants and the experience marketer is the interaction between the participant and the experience. The role of the participant in the experience is a critical factor that shapes the experience. Attending a theater production is at the far end of the continuum when compared to being an actor in the play. Going to Fenway Park to watch a baseball game as a spectator is not the same as catching a fly ball while playing right field at the Red Sox Fantasy Camp in Florida. The differences between being a spectator and being a participant are far reaching.

The involvement of others in the experience makes a difference as well. People embark on self-directed hikes or museum visits all the time. Contrast those experiences with a cooking class or hang-gliding lesson where the involvement of the participant is supervised or overseen by others. If the painting teacher "fixes up" a participant's painting, how does that assistance impact upon the experience?

Does the experience consist of one discrete or separate activity, a series of discrete activities, or continuous action? How does the nature of this interactivity alter the participants' perception of their relationship with the experience provider? While visiting Sea World, participants may participate in a series of discrete encounters. They are instructed to park in distant lots while passing many vacant areas. They become breathless during the attraction and are disappointed when they don't get to touch a seal. They take in the otter show and purchase snacks and souvenirs. Even though these are all separate activities or encounters, participants define the entire collection of encounters as one. Experiences such as cruises or stays at all-inclusive or remote resorts are perceived by the participants as an all-in-one, continuing relationship with the provider.

Understanding how the consumer perceives the experience is important to the eventual success and outcome. A stop for lunch on the way home from a museum is a discrete transaction to the independent museumgoer but may be a part of the entire picture to the tour group participant.

Range of Outcomes

A final category of factors within the experience is the range of outcomes derived from participation in the experience. Does the experience create a sensation that is temporary or transforming in nature? Learning to pilot a hang glider on one's own for the very first time may very well be the sort of experience that has a transforming impact or lasting change on the participant while going to the movies may provide momentary diversion, relief, and/or enjoyment but may not have any lasting impact on the moviegoer. This category like the others does not stand alone. The range of transformation varies and is dependent on other factors such as the authenticity of the experience, the degree of challenge involved, as well as the individual's role within the experience.

The range of experience outcomes as they relate to the relationship between pleasure and preservation is an important one as well. Many experiences are embarked upon for the sheer amusement and enjoyment they bring while others are intended to maintain or preserve something people hold precious. Going to the movies or visiting the amusement park are clearly at one end of the continuum while participating in an archeological dig or working at restoring nature trails fall at the other end. Both of these categories of outcomes closely relate to the postexperience reflection and its impact on another key experience parameter, needs.

The dimensions and the differences of the experience all interact with one another to enhance the marketer's understanding of the actual experience and to enable him or her to identify opportunities that both attract and retain consumers of the experience.

❖ Boutique hotels are smaller, unique and more intimate facilities that have themes or approaches that make them distinctive such as the Casablanca Hotel in New York with rattan chairs, ceiling fans, a cigar-friendly bar, as well as Internet access, continental breakfast, and weekday evening wine and cheese for guests.

❖ The historic Durango & Silverton Narrow Gauge Railroad with its steaming black engine moving along the 236-mile San Juan Skyway takes people through one of the last true Western experiences including views of gold miners' ghost towns and prehistoric cliff dwellings.

❖ The Shady Dell RV Park & Campground is a vintage travel trailer park where people can stay in one of seven Airstream or Silver Streak trailers with chenille bedspreads and art deco radios tuned to swing music. Located in Bisbee, Arizona, an old copper mining town, Dot's, a 1956 diner, completes the picture.

❖ Within Yosemite National Park there are a variety of overnight experiences ranging from the 123-room Ahwahnee Hotel, a granite and faux-redwood 1920s landmark filled with Native American blankets and baskets, to white canvas cabins, a rustic alternative at the eastern end of the valley.

❖ The Back to the Future Ride at Universal Studios in Hollywood and Florida puts people in a DeLorean sitting in front of an Omnimax screen where they ride through time meeting up with dinosaurs, plummeting down volcanic tunnels, and floating over glacial ice fields.

❖ The Peabody Hotel in Memphis, Tennessee, features a twice daily duck parade with the quackers marching to the lobby fountain.

❖ Delaney's Pub in Hong Kong, complete with hanging Victorian lamps, weathered wooden floorboards, and an antique Guinness sign on the wall, is just one of more than 1,000 prefabricated pubs that have been established in 35 countries.

❖ The municipal pool in Urbandale, Iowa, is drained and filled with fresh water and 1,000 trout as residents—many without access to rivers and lakes—are provided with fishing gear for its annual "couch fishing" contest.

❖ The Richard Petty Driving Experience at Disney World lets a would-be NASCAR star put on a fire-retardant suit and helmet and drive at 100 M.P.H. in a real Winston Cup stock car at a one-mile track.

The Role of Need Within the Experience Parameter

A group of people assembled along the shoreline of the Colorado River prepares to embark on a four-day rafting trip through the Grand Canyon. On the surface, one could assume that even though they differ in age, occupation, or residence, the people are all fairly similar when it comes to their goals for floating down the river or reasons for shoving off on this adventure. This is not necessarily an accurate assumption. An experience may consist of the same components, but the actual needs addressed for the people involved in an experience are not necessarily the same. In fact, the needs being fulfilled may not even be all that similar. For this reason, the range of specific needs being fulfilled by a particular experience is an important part of this first marketing mix variable, parameters of the experience.

During an individual's search for self-development, personal fulfillment, or self-actualization, his or her psychic and inner needs, wants, and desires are both numerous and varying. In order to make some sort of sense out of these needs, wants, and desires for the purposes of examination and discussion the following five categories have been identified:

- sense of self,
- emotional,
- social and/or affiliative,
- spiritual, and
- mental and/or intellectual.

Sense of self can be interpreted as having both an internal and external focus. Exercising to improve stamina and overall well-being could be construed as enhancing one's internal sense of self while pumping iron to demonstrate one's prowess to others would fall more into the category of an external focus. The entire need area of self is actually quite extensive and can include such aspects as self-esteem, sense of accomplishment, locus of control, recognition, dominance, confidence, self-reliance, and just the overall testing of one's ability and skills against self, others, or something bigger than that.

While the sense of self category has much in common with the emotional category, there are some additional factors inherent within this second category. Challenge, excitement, escape, relaxation, pleasure, exhilaration, nostalgia, and reduction of sensory overload are just some of those needs that may be included within this category. A small group of people huddled together getting ready to parachute out of the aircraft may be seeking a variety of emotional releases. Some may have been drawn by the challenge of such an undertaking while others were attracted by the sense of exhilaration or focus necessitated by such a venture. Needs, especially psychic and inner needs, are so individual and often hidden that marketers can never make broad assumptions about what drew people to a particular experience.

The social category is quite extensive. Interpersonal relationships, friendships, companionship, fellowship, and affiliation all fall within this category, as do sense of belonging and community. Options for communication, just plain old social interaction, as well as avenues for awareness and sensitivity to others are found within this category. Consider all the ways human beings seek out the company of others. Middle-aged motorcyclists looking perhaps for the freedom and nostalgia of bygone days rally in Laconia, New Hampshire, or Sturgis, South Dakota, rather than taking to the open road alone. Singles within our society continue to generate revenue opportunities for bars, fitness clubs, and matchmakers.

While people need to connect with others, the other end of the social spectrum calls for people to disconnect as well. This need to disconnect from the mainstream of ongoing life often manifests itself in a spiritual manner. Be sure to note that spiritual and religious are not necessarily one and the same thing. People may have spiritual needs while not being religious and vice versa.

The spiritual component of inner or psychic needs is one that may defy exacting personal definitions, but it does hold some general categories with implications for people such as contemplation, reflection, renewal, aesthetics, appreciation, and altruism just to name a few. People are often drawn to sunsets, flowers, art, and natural beauty as a means of regenerating themselves. The summer vacationers toiling on the trails of the Cascades in Washington to rebuild hiking trails may be addressing their inner spiritual needs. The hundreds of thousands of volunteer hours logged in hospitals and schools attest to the need people have to both connect with and help their fellow human beings.

Although the final need category is termed intellectual, it should not be assumed automatically that this category is limited to those who may be perceived as being intellectual types because that is certainly not the case. Such things as the need for stimulation and exploration as well as avenues for creativity and problem solving, things that have value to all of us as human beings, fall within this category. For many people lifelong learning and growth is as necessary as oxygen to maintain their lives. The growth of opportunities afforded people through Elderhostel, the Disney Institute, and the myriad of "how to" programs attest to this need.

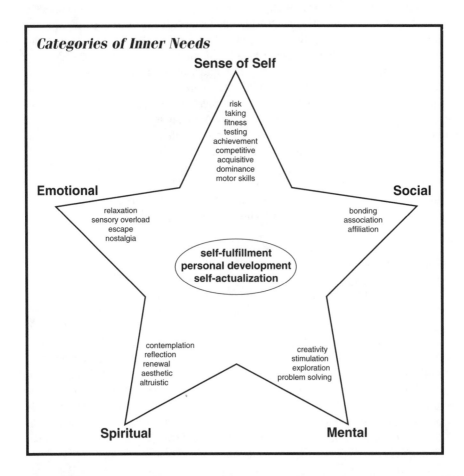

Recall that four-day Grand Canyon river-rafting trip mentioned at the beginning of this section. It serves as a good illustration of the importance and varied nature of the needs component of an experience. Standing on the riverbank ready to shove off may be people motivated by the sense of achievement or perceived risk taking found within the sense of self category as well as a group of family or friends traveling together seeking bonding time with one another. These folk will be sharing space in the raft with people possibly seeking the emotional release of relaxation, the spiritual need to commune with nature, as well as the intellectual desire for new experience.

Get ready to rock the raft because that's exactly the type of impact that the needs component has upon the marketing of experiences. Like the waters awaiting the raft, the hidden currents of marketing experiences can't always be seen, but one can certainly feel their impact when they cause changes in direction and focus of attention.

People: Their Place Within the Parameter

What role does the participant in the experience have within this pursuit? What impact does the presence of others involved with the experience (whether actively or passively) make? In what ways do the personnel employed by the

- ❖ Gen Xers have changed the look of the traditional bachelor parties or bridal showers as groups of friends now go on three-day sailing trips or nonstop games as last-ditch bonding opportunities.
- ❖ The Kripalu Center for Yoga and Health in Lenox, Massachusetts, set on 90 acres of a former Jesuit seminary, is booked steadily with people seeking relaxation and renewal through yoga, meditation, and relaxation techniques.
- ❖ Mountain Travel-Sobek, a large and well-established company selling adventure travel, has seen the demand soar for trips to experience inaccessible, less traveled destinations.
- ❖ Howard Schultz, the founder and CEO of Starbucks, envisioned weaving a sense of romance and community around the commodity of coffee (Balog, 1997, p. 4B).
- ❖ The Triple Bypass, billed as a single-day event that serves as "the original sprint adventure race," involves running, mountain biking, and kayaking for three-person coed teams that cover about 30 miles in four to six hours.
- ❖ According to a survey by Budget Car and Truck Rental, one-third of business travelers add some leisure travel to trips to reduce stress and 48 percent of those employees indicate their company is receptive to this practice (Carey, 1996, 1B).
- ❖ Bob Wood, Nike's vice president of American marketing, when asked about the company's switch to the new slogan, "I can," responded that "it reflects the deep emotional connection that people have with sports in feeling good about participating and setting personal goals" (Associated Press, 1997, p. 8).

*Clos*e*eup* InnerQuest, a wilderness adventure for body, mind, and spirit, offers three different wilderness experiences targeted towards varying needs of individuals. HeroQuest is described as a life and/or career renewal that is an advanced rite of passage. Pleasure-Quest is a playful wilderness adventure that lets people explore their senses through meteor showers, massage, hot springs, decadent desserts, and fragrant wildflowers. The Lovers Adventure, a romantic wilderness adventure for couples, allows couples to share a passionate, fun-filled, outdoor adventure while learning how to become better communicators and ecstatic lovers.

experience provider interact and make a difference in the experience? All of these are excellent questions that need to be addressed if one is truly to understand the experience.

Some factors that need to be taken into consideration are as follows:

- the role of the participant,
- the impact of the participant's competency or performance upon the experience,
- the presence or involvement of other participants, and
- the role of provider personnel.

The significance of the role assumed by the participant and its impact on the experience was previously mentioned. The potential impact can be further analyzed as the various roles of participants and potential impact upon the experience are considered. Imagine a little theater production of *West Side Story*. What are the participant roles within such an experience? The amateur thespian assuming the role of a gang member is thoroughly involved in this experience both physically and psychologically. What about members of the audience? Doesn't the involvement and participation of the average theatergoer differ from that of the parent whose child is making his or her debut on the stage?

Participant involvement in experiences is varied and complex. Since such participation is motivated by inner needs it is often difficult to detect the actual role or importance of such participation. If a simple night at the little theater can evoke so many different roles within one experience, just imagine the potential in other more encompassing types of experiences. Levels of participation can and do vary. Participants can be observers, passive performers, or active performers. Visiting a re-created historical attraction such as Sturbridge Village depicting colonial life in New England enables people to be observers of the past. However, people who choose to interact and dialogue with the resident actors of this village become part of the experience in a different way. People who tour dairy farms and look at the cows have a much different experience from those who choose to spend the weekend assisting with the daily farm chores.

There are endless experience marketing possibilities within this category. There is also the possibility of some drawbacks as well. What role, if any, do the

Slice of Life

Emotions

During the course, you will experience a full spectrum of emotional as well as physical demands. Living closely with the elements requires your best effort. The excitement and thrill of overcoming obstacles individually and as a group are invariably accompanied by moments of stress. Bring openness to change, adaptability and resourcefulness when you come. These qualities will add to the richness of your experience.

wording from Outward Bound brochure

skills, talents, and abilities of the participant play in the outcomes of the experience? There are some experiences where everyone succeeds. However, there are a whole host of experiences where the success and subsequent satisfaction with the experience is quite dependent upon the participant. Contrast the river ride through the Mexican pavilion at Epcot where all the riders are successfully transported to Mexico with golf lessons or cartooning classes at Disney Institute where the success in these experiences is directly related to both the efforts and talents of the participant. How does the provider explain to the participant that it wasn't the provider's fault but rather the participant's ineptness or lack of attention to directions that undermined the quality of the experience?

Children and adults alike drop out of sporting activities and recreational classes for a variety of reasons, but their own role in the experience may certainly be a factor. Climbing parties to Mount Everest have recently come under fire due to fatalities that some people suggest are due to the lack of preparation or inexperience of the people enrolled in the journey. Care needs to be given during the promotion and preparation phases of experience marketing to ensure that expectations do not exceed the success of the experience itself.

In what ways do the presence of others influence and alter the experience? Two golfers wait at the first tee anxious to get their game under way. One of the golfers looks around at the crowd waiting to tee off behind them and revels in the opportunity to have witnesses to his probable great shot. The other, a novice golfer, inwardly shudders at the thought of having to step up and address the ball with all these people standing around watching and witnessing the five-foot dribble shot off the tee. The experience of a couple celebrating a thirtieth wedding anniversary in an elegant restaurant will likely be shaped by the party of eight seated at the next table or the young couple who brought their toddler along with them for dinner. Woodswomen, an adventure travel company for women of all ages, confirms the fact that the presence of others makes a difference as participants attest to the energy and enthusiasm they drew from others in their travel group.

In certain instances, other people become secondary participants. For instance, parents are often required to spend time waiting for or watching their children in different play settings. Family entertainment centers that have created an environment where parents can sit, relax, watch television, read magazines, or check phone messages while keeping children in sight, have changed the experience significantly.

The number of people involved in the experience makes a difference as well. In a 10-year period the number of visitors to Venice increased from 400,000 to 2 million (Matchan, 1997, p. M20). Overcrowding at popular attractions or destinations impacts on the experience. Arches National Park in eastern Utah used a series of photographs showing a range of visitors at various sites to determine the number of trail encounters acceptable to park users (Manning, 1997, pp. 36-37).

Both active or more passive coparticipants form a powerful force within an experience, as do the employees of the experience provider. Recall the nature and significance of employees, otherwise known as experience personnel, as they relate to the actual experience of the participant. People stream into movie theaters without giving much more than a ritual glance at the ticket seller or ticket takers since our silent, passive experience of sitting in the theater will not directly involve them or their talents. Contrast that with people sending their children away to summer camp. Parents will be certain to inspect carefully the appearance, attitude, abilities, and credentials of those to whom they are entrusting the safety and well-being of their precious offspring.

The type of experience, the length of time, and the degree of risk involved or depth of the experience all contribute to differences related to personnel. People want a mountain-climbing guide who looks like he knows the ropes. People in more learning-oriented tour groups such as those sponsored by the Smithsonian Institute assume and anticipate that tour guides will be not only knowledgeable but also be considered experts in their field of study.

There are different strokes for different folks, and that holds true in the case of experience personnel as well. Some people respond better to the barking of a ski instructor who was a former Marine drill sergeant while others make more downhill progress in the company of the encouraging grandmother type. Some 60-year-old folk have more success learning to work a computer from a six-year-old while others much prefer having a peer as a teacher.

People are a powerful parameter of the experience and also the most difficult for the experience provider to program.

The Role of the Provider

The task of balancing the intricacies of the experience itself—along with the individual needs of the participants as well as the roles and talents of all the cast of characters involved in the experience—falls upon the shoulders of the provider. There are a number of factors in this equation such as:

- the ability and willingness to customize the experience;
- the ability to control or adapt to demand for experiences;
- the degree of control the provider has over the experience and its outcomes;
- the extent of coordination and cooperation required among providers;
- the ability and willingness to provide varying levels of an experience;
- the extent to which experience is planned by provider; and
- the extent of provider-participant contact prior to the participant phase of the experience.

Consider the ramifications of some of the factors within this portion of the experience parameter. The ability and willingness to customize is demonstrated in the ongoing McDonald's versus Burger King competition. One can turn out virtually identical burgers at unmatched speed while the other smiles and let's you have it your way but it takes longer. The same holds true for experiences. Gone are the days when chefs insisted their specialties could only be prepared their way regardless of the personal preferences or dietary needs of diners, and the travel agent worked extensively with clients to make sure that their itinerary worked better for the agent than the client.

People stand freezing in a lift line impatiently waiting to make use of their $60 ski ticket during a winter holiday weekend. Contrast that with the Outback Steakhouse whose waiting lines are legendary. Diners are provided with plenty of sitting and sipping space as well as beepers so they can wander while they complete their 90-minute wait for a table. The sign at the bottom of the Statue of Liberty indicates that the wait to reach the top is 47 minutes and the temperature at the top is 94 degrees. The National Park Service may not be able to control the flow of visitors, but it can allay any misconceptions about the experience.

The degree of control that the provider has over the experience varies extensively. Hot air balloon rides over the Napa Valley are canceled due to fog or wind conditions much to the chagrin of the balloon companies. Whale watches off the coast of San Diego almost always enjoy good weather, but the boat owner cannot guarantee a whale sighting. On the other hand, theater performances almost always go off without a hitch or glitch, and health clubs open their doors on time rain or shine. There are many variations within this factor. Disney World and MGM Studios have devised ways to modify stunts within shows so that the show can still go on regardless of weather irregularities.

For one taking an independent fly-drive European vacation, there are a variety of different travel providers including the airline, the car rental company, and the various hotels. The interchanges and exchanges with these individual providers aren't necessarily perceived by the customer as being just one big picture. So the two-hour delay for the rental car followed by the flat tire en route doesn't automatically impact upon the hotel providing respite for that evening. However, the participants of the group tour perceive everything from the lousy lunch to getting stuck in traffic as being the fault of the tour provider. The type and level of coordination and cooperation varies within experiences. The success of special events, whether they be the Summer Olympics or local fireworks, is dependent on the various providers such as food, transportation, signage, crowd control, rest rooms, and communication being in sync with one another.

Is the experience providing the same for everyone such as attending a live theater performance, or does the provider arrange for a smaller, more special experience such as meeting the actors backstage after the play for certain season ticket holders? Does the provider go even further and provide an option for an individual to assume a walk-on part in the production. Examples of varying levels of the experience being created and offered by the provider are the way guests staying on the property are allowed into the theme park one hour before the "general public" at Disney World or the opportunity for some guests to have breakfast with Mickey and Donald.

Customization and various levels of the experience provided often come with a price tag. The restaurant that goes out of its way to accommodate special seating arrangements or dietary preferences may do so at no additional cost. The cruise which offers an incredible variety of activities so that there is something to meet the needs of everyone appears to be customizing, but the customization does not match those of small cruise lines where people can dine at whim or arrange for unusual tours.

The two final factors are closely aligned with one another. How much of the experience is planned and controlled by the provider as opposed to the participant and how extensive was provider-participant contact prior to participation in the experience? These two factors significantly impact the experience. If you wander through Paris on your own, you may well have an interesting and intimate experience. If you are a member of a tour group visiting Paris, you are virtually guaranteed to see the major sights listed in the brochure and never encounter a language or cultural barrier. If you sign on with Abercrombie and Kent to go on safari in Africa, you can be reasonably assured of safe and pleasant accommodations, but they can't control whether or not the animals appear on cue. The Mount Snow Golf School in bucolic Vermont can provide you with daily lessons and videotaping of your game, but it can't overcome lack of physical aptitude.

Experience providers need to be clearly aware of their relationships in the planning and execution of their experiences as well as the aptitude, abilities, and attitudes of their participants. The interaction of these factors will subsequently determine the outcomes of the actual experience and clear expectations on the part of all involved prior to the participation is a plus. If an individual is touring Africa, the provider can forward him or her a list of needed clothing and supplies as well as a suggested reading list prior to the trip. These efforts are designed to enhance the participation in the experience. On the other hand, some experiences do not afford the provider with the luxury of previous contact. For example, visitors to the San Diego Zoo could benefit from suggested footwear and gear as well as prior reading material.

❖ Pan Aqua Diving of New York City offers unique underwater experiences that include diving around *Lizzy D*, a rumrunner that sank in 1922; *Iberia*, an old tramp steamer; and *Pinta*, a Dutch freighter that sank carrying lumber.
❖ The Ritz-Carlton on St. Thomas Island sends drivers to pick up guests at the airport to control the experience from the time they get off the plane until the time they reboard.
❖ To eliminate the need to cancel a performance the Indiana Jones show at Disney-MGM Studio in Florida has 12 different versions of the same show so that stunts can be varied based on changing weather conditions.
❖ When the restaurants of Epcot found that the number of diners during the evening hours was below profit projections, Disney responded by creating the Illuminations Show as a way to retain visitors in the evening hours.

View each of the elements or factors within these parameters of the experience as being a continuum where there is a wide range of options and choices. The continuum afforded providers related to the actual design, control, and implementation of the experience can enhance or detract from the experience itself as well as the success of the organization. Attention to this portion of the parameter would be time well-spent. The marketing implications are nearly endless.

Going for Flow

While the expression, "go with the flow" is often used as an antidote to stressful situations, the same slogan can be applied to experience marketing as organizations try to ensure that the quality of the experience meets the needs of participants and to encourage their repeat participation in the experience.

As it relates to experiences, esteemed research psychologist Csikszentmihalyi defines flow as:

> . . . the state in which people are so involved in an activity that nothing else seems to matter; the experience itself is so enjoyable that people will do it even at great costs, for the sheer sake of doing it . . . . (Csikszentmihalyi, 1991, p. 4)

If you can recall the last time you became so completely immersed in an activity that you simply lost all track of time, you were likely experiencing flow. Csikszentmihalyi suggests that flow occurs when we lose self-consciousness and awareness of self-construct.

Having spent the past 20 years looking into flow, the psychology of the optimal experience, Csikszentmihalyi differentiates between two terms closely related to flow, pleasure and enjoyment:

Close **Seup**

The city-state of Singapore is an incredibly clean, tightly regulated, financial center touted as having stopover appeal for comfort-craving tourists or business people traveling in the less developed countries of Asia. In an effort to preserve history in the Chinese, Indian, and Malayan neighborhoods, the government restores and updates historic buildings. An 1860s convent, CHIJMES, now houses restaurants, stores, and an Irish pub. The once grand hotel from the glory days of the British empire, Raffles, had fallen on hard times only to be taken over by the government and renovated from top to bottom. In an effort to bring order to the hundreds of food hawkers, Lau Pa Sat, a Victorian-era iron cast structure, has been recycled into a multiethnic food court. The most recent renovation targeted the homes and shops near the Sultan Mosque by turning them into art galleries, travel agencies, and souvenir stores.

The results of these extensive efforts is a balance for tourists who venture to the Far East in search of an exotic adventure while still seeking the creature comforts and safety of home. This strength also runs the risk of being its biggest potential turnoff due to this well-scrubbed, highly regulated veneer (Bly, 1997, p. 4D).

Action Agenda

❖ Recall successful or less than satisfactory experiences that you've had recently and identify parameters of the experience with possible impact on your reaction.

❖ Develop your own list of ways in which products and nonpersonal services are similar and different from experiences.

❖ Review the stages of the experience as well as phases within each stage and brainstorm a list of possible marketing opportunities for your organization.

❖ Analyze your own activities associated with the alternative search process within the stages of experience and suggest implications for the marketing of experiences.

❖ Identify which parameters of a common experience are under the control of the experience provider and those that are not.

❖ Recall a recent, successful experience in which you were personally involved and consider ways in which certain parameters of that experience could have been changed to detract or enhance that experience.

❖ Interview three different types of people awaiting participation in the same experience and attempt to discern similarities and differences related to their need to become involved in that particular experience.

❖ Recall a situation in which your own involvement in an experience contributed to the success or dissatisfaction with the experience.

❖ Identify specific people, either employees or fellow participants in an experience, and describe their impact upon your experience.

❖ Examine your role as a provider of an experience and suggest ways in which changes in your role could influence the experience itself.

Pleasure = Contentment
Enjoyment = Accomplishment

He maintains that pleasure is a feeling of contentment achieved when the expectations dictated by biological needs or social conditionings have been met. It's the way you feel after you've had an ice cold drink coming in from a round of golf on an especially hot day or the feelings of relaxation as you collapse on the couch at the end of a long day.

Csikszentmihalyi believes that resting at the end of the day while sitting mindlessly in front of the television or at the movies may be pleasant but that enjoyment is different. Enjoyment occurs when a person has not only satisfied a need but has gone beyond that and achieved the unexpected.

According to Csikszentmihalyi enjoyment is characterized by:

• forward movement,
• sense of novelty or newness, and
• accomplishment.

If one examines the concept of flow more closely, one may discover some hints as to why some people continue with an activity while others drop it almost immediately. The activity must help an individual approach flow by creating just the right balance between the challenge within the activity and the skill level of the participant.

Transition Tracking

From	*To*
• Product attributes: core, tangible and augmented levels	• Stages of experience: preexperience, participation, and postexperience
• Product line, depth, and width	• Experience dimensions: the experience itself; interaction with participants, range of outcomes
• Tangible benefits	• Inner needs

challenge   skill

            ▲

There are a number of implications for experience providers. When introducing people to new physical activities, one should be sure to take into consideration their physical, psychological, and social readiness as it relates to the level of skill required by the experience. Skill should be matched with the challenge level. People who don't experience some measure of success with an experience will not likely repeat it anytime soon. Once people are involved with the experience, the provider needs to vary the challenge of the experience based on the individual's increasing skill and familiarity with the experience. The provider should expose people to a variety of new elements within the experience or raise their goals and expectations within the existing experience.

Sources

Associated Press. (1997, December 31). Nike has a new slogan, "I can." *The Tampa Tribune.*

Balog, Kathy. (1997, October 9). Starbucks redefines hill of beans. *USA Today.*

Bly, Laura. (1997, April 7). Singapore rediscovers its past in push for tourists. *USA Today.*

Carey, Anne R., & Stacey, Julie. (1996, July 11). Adding pleasure to business. *USA Today.*

Csikszentmihalyi, Mihaly. (1991). *Flow—The psychology of optimal experience.* New York, NY: HarperPerennial.

Lovelock, Christopher H. (1991). *Services marketing* (2nd ed.). Englewood Cliffs, NJ: Prentice-Hall.

Manning, Robert E. (1997, October). Social carrying capacity of parks and outdoor recreation areas. *Parks and Recreation.*

Matchan, Linda. (1997, September 14). Trampling the legacies. *The Boston Globe.*

Peter, J. Paul, & Olson, Jerry C. (1994). *Understanding consumer behavior.* Burr Ridge, IL: Richard D. Irwin, Inc.

Flashback

People have always been a part of the marketing process although not specifically a marketing mix variable. The traditional "people" emphasis referred to as target marketing was separate and apart from the variables. Dimensions of target markets usually included geographic considerations (place of residence, place of employment, travel time and distance) as well as sociodemographic factors (age, gender, income, and education). These dimensions of target marketing were typically used to develop a promotional strategy intended to *push* a product toward customers.

In the earliest days of marketing, limited versions of a product were created to meet the needs of one large group, a mass market. Eventually products were designed and developed not for everybody but for certain groups of "somebodies." These products reflected the needs and preferences of smaller groups of people to *pull* them rather than push them to a particular product or service. This resulted in the creation of three target market strategies: undifferentiated (mass market); differentiated with specific subgroups of people targeted; and niche marketing with concentration on a small group of people with very specific needs or preferences.

When service marketing came on the scene, consumer behavior, personal preferences, participation practices and timing of participation were added as target market descriptors. This subsequent incorporation of psychographics and synchronographics enhanced the *pull* power of marketing.

Chapter 3

The Second P: People

Young adults are slower to leave the nest. Most marriages no
longer last for life, and older people are more likely to live alone.

Martha Farnsworth Riche

The Second P of Experience
Marketing: People

Target markets have always been an important and integral part of the marketing
process. When it comes to experience marketing, people and process aren't mutually exclusive. It's similar to that old adage about a tree falling in the forest with no
one to hear it. People are at the center of an experience. If there are no people,
there is no experience. This is not true for product or service marketing. A box of
cereal is a box of cereal before someone buys it. The train still pulls out of the
station on schedule even if there are no passengers. This just isn't so for experiences. People are fundamental to the experience, and, therefore, the "people part"
of experience marketing is front and center, an integral marketing mix variable.

A revised framework to more completely understand the needs of people is
required. Since experiences address people's inner needs, the need component
belongs at the center of this framework. Needs continually undergo change.
People's needs, especially in relationship to experiences, must be perceived as
fluid rather than constant. Inner needs can be likened to an ocean with variations
in depth, temperature, and chemical makeup relative to tide, seasons, weather,
or pollution.

The "people" descriptors surrounding this need component consist of 4Cs
completing this framework. The four coordinates are core, culture, choice, and
change. The core coordinate refers to central and unchangeable elements of individuals and includes age and stages of development, gender, race, and ethnicity.
The culture coordinate includes cohort grouping, household status, religion, EIO

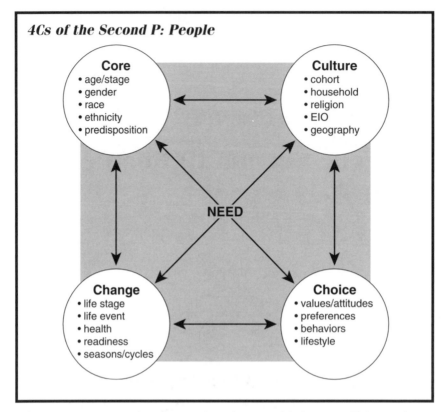

4Cs of the Second P: People

Core
- age/stage
- gender
- race
- ethnicity
- predisposition

Culture
- cohort
- household
- religion
- EIO
- geography

NEED

Change
- life stage
- life event
- health
- readiness
- seasons/cycles

Choice
- values/attitudes
- preferences
- behaviors
- lifestyle

(education, income, and occupation), and geographic location. This coordinate incorporates norms and behaviors precipitated by group affiliations and societal expectations. Elements within the choice coordinate include values and attitudes, preferences, behaviors, and lifestyles, and the change coordinate contains factors related to health, life stages, life events, and seasonal and cyclical influences.

At this point, consider making a list of the charac- **TAG** teristics, descriptors, factors, circumstances, situations, or events that either describe your current target market or possibly a potential target group and their motivation for seeking out your experience.

Make note of factors incorporated within the 4Cs of the people variable—core, cultural, choice, and change—to see if they help explain or support target market choices or patterns of participation.

While these four coordinates along with the elements within each of them are represented in the framework as being distinct from one another, the impact and influence that they have on one another are not. It is nearly impossible to separate core factors such as gender from the nearby coordinates of culture and change since both of these factors are shaped and influenced by the core characteristic. In a similar manner, it is inconceivable that the change coordinate would not be connected to the culture or choice coordinates since factors within each play a significant role in life changes. Constant and continuous vigilance to the subtleties and interrelationships between the four coordinates is a necessity for the experience marketer.

The Core Coordinate

What then are the core coordinates that define who we are and how we live our lives? Core elements, sometimes referred to as biographics, are those dimensions of our humanness that we bring into the world with us. Elements within the core coordinate include some of the more traditional target marketing factors such as age, gender, race, and ethnicity.

We are born in a particular year which establishes our age throughout our lifetime. We are born either male or female and with specific racial and ethnic characterizations. These biographics form the core of who we are. Take a look at what's known and what's not yet fully known about some of these biographic factors.

Age

It's no big surprise that age is a pivotal factor related to experiences. Whether one enjoyed drive-in movies or Omnimax theaters is in large part a function of when one was born. The timing of one's arrival in the world determines experiences available and popular during one's life span.

Age also influences the needs of people throughout their development with an almost predictable timing of those needs. Three- and four-year-olds have the urge to crawl through, under, and over any unusual object that catches their fancy while alternating this behavior with running from place to place. While this behavior is compatible with their needs at the time, it is almost incomprehensible to the teenager who finds such pursuits impossibly boring and wouldn't mindlessly race from place to place unless there was some compelling reason to do so. Human developmental stages have a significant impact on experience marketing because physical, motor, intellectual, mental, emotional, and social development vary over time.

Physical and motor development in infancy and childhood, as well as maturing years, dictate not only the kinds of experiences people are attracted to but also the range of experiences undertaken. Young children lack the stamina to hike for a full day and older adults may as well, but they are experiencing similar characteristics at different ends of the development spectrum.

Cognitive skills and intellectual interests are also dictated by such age-related stages of development. Recall how 10-year-olds thrive on a board game such as Clue. They can see the rooms, the potential suspects, and handle the weapons. These same children might become frustrated at more abstract scenarios of mystery and suspense because the context surpasses their cognitive stage of development.

Social and emotional development stages are critically important and are linked to needs underlying the marketing of experiences. Erickson's psychosocial stages of development outlined eight, age-related, stages of development. From infancy to childhood, he identified four tasks—trust, autonomy, initiative, and industry—while citing search for identity as being related to puberty and adolescence. Erickson believed in continual development throughout the life span and, therefore, divided adult development into three stages—intimacy, generativity, and integrity—to take people through young, middle, and late adulthood (Jolley and Mitchell, 1996, pp. 44–45). Such developmental stages help experience marketers understand why young adults crave the intimacy and connection of social situations while middle-aged adults might seek purpose and growth through volunteer work or continuing education.

The ability to play side by side as is the case of parallel play with preschoolers all the way along the continuum to the ability to play cooperatively or competitively are all part of social development. The different ages and various stages that humans go through from infancy to old age influences the need for experiences. Young children want to spend time with parents or adults while teens prefer being with their peers. Rites of social passage that coincide with these varying stages are also reflected in experiences from birthday parties to fiftieth anniversary celebrations.

It is important to note here that there is an interrelationship between stages of development and other coordinates within the people parameter especially change and culture. A sudden change in health status may precipitate an individual's move into the next stage of development. A more gradual change in societal practices may influence the nature of experiences that are deemed appropriate at various ages.

Gender

Is it true that men are from Mars and women are from Venus and that they are more different from one another than similar? Hard to tell, isn't it? As the number of female college graduates in this country surpasses the number of male graduates, and as women become engineers and men become househusbands, it may appear as if identification of need or interest related to gender might be moot. However, the jury isn't in just yet.

It is particularly difficult to differentiate between biology and sociology as the cultural influences within this category construe these findings. Did growing girls of the past choose ballet over basketball for biological or cultural reasons? Do women value close friends while men need buddies for reasons related to biology or sociology? Should gender be considered purely a biological element within the people dimension of experience marketing, or should it be placed within the cultural coordinate? Gender serves to reinforce the interrelationship and fluid nature of the coordinates of target marketing for experiences.

The demographic profiles of males and females have changed particularly as the profiles relate to education, income, and occupation. Market research has further revealed differences in men's and women's attitudes about a variety of activities such as housework, shopping, birthdays, and religion just to cite a few. Experience marketers need to keep current and watch closely the emerging information related to gender. Some of the research relates to biological functioning while other information includes demographic shifts or cultural reinforcement of gender differences.

Brain research indicates that the right and left hemispheres of the brain have different functions. Use of the right brain lends itself to more intuitive, holistic, and imaginative responses, and the left brain is responsible for the more logical, analytical, and computational abilities. There is some evidence to support that brain function is segregated in males while females use both sides of the brain in cognitive tasks. Some researchers believe that these sex differences account for women's verbal superiority or men's spatial superiority. Since these differences become more pronounced during adolescence and the onset of puberty, some scientists believe that these differences must be hormonal (Hyde, Fennema and Lamon, 1997, pp. 139–155.)

On the other hand, many of the more traditional cultural influences among the sexes have been substantially eroded. Women receive more college degrees than men, and a variety of career options have opened to them. Participation rates and patterns in sports and recreation pursuits have shifted to incorporate the newly found freedom for both sexes to participate in activities that were once gender specific. If Rosie Grier could take up needlepoint and Rosie Ruiz could get caught cheating in the Boston Marathon, an apparent role reversal in experiences is a part of today's society.

Physiological differences between the two genders are also narrowing as evidenced by the shrinking gap of athletic records such as the Boston Marathon (Women of the Future, 1996, p. 36):

Boston Marathon Winning Times

	1897	1974	1984	1994
Women	—	2:47:11	2:29:28	2:21:45
Men	2:55:10	2:13:39	2:10:34	2:07:15

Gender is likely to continue to grow in importance for experience marketers. Whether the influence is primarily biological or cultural or whether the group under study is males or females, the role this element will play in experience marketing will change and escalate.

- The National Center for Educational Statistics reported that women received more than half of all the degrees awarded in 1996. However, at the same time it also indicated that the majority of doctoral or professional degrees went to men.
- Mediamark Research and *American Demographics* predict that by 2000, one in three American households will have a male homemaker.
- The National Foundation for Women Business Owners reported that by the mid-1990s, more than 7.7 million women-owned businesses generated $1.4 trillion in revenue.
- According to the Women's Sport Foundation, in 1972 one of every 27 high-school girls played varsity sports compared with one in three in 1997.

Fast Facts

Race and Ethnicity

While we may use the terms race and ethnicity somewhat interchangeably, there is a difference and that difference is becoming the subject of growing attention and importance. Tiger Woods, the boy wonder of golf, maintains he is "Cablinasian," a term he coined as a child to combine his Caucasian, black, Indian, and Asian backgrounds. The Association of Multiethnic Americans has brought pressure to bear on the U. S. Census Bureau to implement project RACE (Reclassify All Children Equally) in response to the 1990 Census that listed only four major racial groups: white, black, Asians and Pacific Islanders, and native Americans. These four major categories don't allow for Americans of Latin or Spanish origin to designate themselves as Hispanics which is considered an ethnic or heritage category, and they create difficulties for people of mixed racial background.

As a result of increasing diversity within the United States and the pressure being brought by various groups, the federal government has made some changes in its policy related to this issue. Mixed-race Americans are now able to check off more than one racial category when providing information for the census, school registration, or mortgage applications.

The simple ability to track one another based on race and ethnicity only compounds the interrelatedness of biology and sociology. Genetic makeup based on race or ethnic origin often creates a predisposition for certain groups of individuals to develop specific diseases such as sickle cell anemia or Tay-Sachs. However, other diseases, including certain forms of cancer or heart disease, appear to be attributable to the interaction of genetic predisposition in certain racial groups with certain lifestyles.

The blurring between the genetic characteristics and societal influences continues to mount in a similar way as the gender differences which were cited earlier. The nature of race or ethnicity and its subsequent impact will continue to move to the forefront and become more important for marketers. There are a variety of factors contributing to the influence of these elements including increases in non-Caucasian births, growth of interracial marriages and immigration, and growing global influences. Younger Americans will increasingly be African American, Hispanic, or multiracial. Ethnic groups such

❖ During the 1990 census approximately 10 million people refused to describe themselves as white, black, Asian, or American Indian (Sandor, 1994, p. 36).

❖ According to the U. S. Census Bureau, the Hispanic population reached 27.4 million in 1995 and predictions indicate Hispanics will be the largest ethnic group by the year 2010 with 41 million people.

Fast Facts

❖ The U. S. Department of Education indicated that college enrollment by racial and ethnic minorities in the United States increased by 29 percent between 1980 and 1993 with Hispanic, Asian, and Pacific Islander responsible for most of the increase.

❖ The U. S. Census Bureau reported that Hispanics and Asians will account for 61 percent of the population growth between 1995 and 2025.

as Hispanics or Asians can't be placed in one category under the assumption that there are no differences between people from Mexico or Columbia or people from Korea or Vietnam. More recent immigrants to the United States often place greater value on family or group needs over the traditional American emphasis on the individual.

The interrelationship between age and ethnicity will be interesting in the next few decades. We will likely become a nation that is old and white and young and diverse as the numbers of maturing Americans who happen to be Anglo will increase while a rapidly increasing number of young Americans will be black, Hispanic, or Asian. In *An America Changed: Population Change and the Future of the United States,* demographer Steve H. Murdock, applied age and race specific participation patterns to 16 types of outdoor recreation pursuits (Edmondson, 1996). His analysis revealed that the only outdoor activity where the number of participants will grow faster than the total population is bird-watching, an activity primarily favored by white, older Americans. The three activities with slowest growth will be backpacking, tennis, and golf due to low levels of participation by younger members of minority groups.

Strolling Through the Park

(millions of people who participated in selected recreational activities at least one day in 1990, and projected percent change in participation, 1990–2050, by race and ethnicity)

	1990 participation	percent change 1990–2050			
		total	Anglo	black	Hispanic
walking	206	52.2 %	5.6 %	94.1 %	257.7 %
bird-watching	81	58.5	11.4	102.0	280.6
freshwater fishing	81	35.9	−1.5	97.3	235.5
camping	79	31.3	−9.4	83.3	220.5
bicycling	70	38.6	−8.9	74.1	206.2
hunting	54	33.6	−0.8	86.6	229.4
backpacking	50	23.1	−11.8	75.4	201.1
jogging	46	45.8	−12.9	74.7	207.3
softball	39	41.2	−13.7	74.7	207.3
basketball	34	42.9	−13.3	70.2	196.8
nature studies	30	41.1	3.9	94.3	242.7
tennis	29	27.2	−11.5	66.1	205.4
saltwater fishing	26	51.6	−1.4	106.3	240.5
golf	26	29.7	−1.1	119.9	243.3
football	22	43.0	−13.6	72.0	193.0
baseball	21	49.3	−12.0	76.2	197.6
total change	n/a	57.4	8.9	93.1	291.1

Note: Anglos are non-Hispanic whites; blacks are non-Hispanic; Asians and other races are not included.

As the United States changes its demographic makeup, the new immigrant groups help to create a salad bowl rather than a melting pot, and the entire world becomes more global in nature, the significance of racial and ethnographic factors and the role such factors will play within experience marketing will change.

Predisposition

Rarely a day goes by without science and technology releasing new or additional information about human genetic makeup and how such makeup has the potential for shaping one's life. If there ever was an area of exploding information, genetic predisposition would be so designated. Genes that cause Parkinson's disease or colon cancer and genes that suggest a predisposition for risk-taking activity are being uncovered at a rapid rate.

Psychologists have also joined the search for new information related to behavior and preferences. Goldman's theory of emotional intelligence overviews levels of maturity that influence human behavior as well as preference for treatment and interaction with certain types of experiences. Another example of such theory is Gardner's theory of multiple intelligence. This theory suggests seven categories of intelligence: linguistic, musical, logical-mathematic, spatial, bodily-kinesthetic, interpersonal, and intrapersonal (Dacey and Travers, 1996, pp. 226–227). Theories such as this one and others hold great promise for experience marketing. They may help explain why some people wouldn't miss the World Scrabble Championship while others are drawn to fantasy baseball camps.

The Culture Coordinate

While it's a challenge to separate core factors such as age, race, and gender from the influence and impact of culture, it is a necessary part of this new framework. We may be born with certain unchangeable attributes, but a variety of societal factors from the decade of our birth to the level of education we attain come together and shape the "who we are" which influences the needs we develop.

Cohort

Twelve is twelve and seventy is seventy, but then again maybe not. Just listen to grandparents compare (or protest) the amount of money spent on their grandchildren or the ways in which today's parents seem to coddle their offspring and you can begin to realize that childhood today is quite different from childhood in the 1950s or the 1970s or even the early 1990s.

While age has always served as an important indicator within marketing, a substantial impact of age is likely to be cohort groupings. The experiences that people have while growing up last throughout their lifetime. The commonality of those shared experiences among each generation or cohort group lead to the development of certain attitudes and behaviors that are critical to experience marketers. Of particular significance is the "coming of age" factor which suggests that events occurring during the passage to adulthood (both economic and

sexual) affect lifelong attitudes and behaviors (Meredith and Schewe, 1994,
p. 24). The cohort group dubbed the Depression Era refers to individuals who
came of age during the depression, not

> Men more closely resemble the
> times than they do their fathers.
>
> an old Arab proverb

those born during that time. This "coming of age" factor helps explain why the
Baby Boom cohort is subdivided into two groups, those who grew up during Vietnam and those who came of age during the period of Watergate.

There are a number of frameworks for identifying and designating cohort
groups within the United States, and one such typology involves cohort groupings
as follows (Meredith and Schewe, 1994):

- *The Old Guard:* the approximately 4 million Americans over the age of
  85 born between the turn of the century and the early teens. They remember World War I, and their current consumer behavior is dictated
  primarily by physical limitations and health needs.
- *The Depression Era:* the 13 million Americans who came of age during
  the Depression. Currently retired, their memories of rationing still influence the way they live and consume.
- *The WWIIers:* this group of 11 million were unified by a common enemy
  and they may be the last generation familiar with delayed gratification.
  They are currently at or approaching retirement.
- *The Eisenhower Generation:* the 41 million Americans who came of age
  during the social well-being and economic growth of the postwar. Most
  are still in the workplace with some at peak earnings while others have
  been pushed into early retirements.
- *The Early Boomers:* the 33 million members of the "never trust anyone
  over 30" generation who came of age during the Vietnam conflict and a
  time of political assassinations. They are currently in or approaching
  middle age.
- *The Late Boomers:* the 49 million younger members of this sometimes
  lumped together cohort who came of age after Watergate and whose
  economic outlook has not been as rosy as their older siblings.
- *The Busters:* the 41 million young adults currently 20 or 30 something
  often referred to as Generation X. They are the first latchkey cohort
  whose cynicism and independent alienation may be related to social and
  economic upheavals of their childhood.
- *The Mature Boomlet:* the larger wave of adolescents born between 1977
  and 1982 who reflect the growing diversity within the country as well as
  gaps between indulgence and basic survival related to child-rearing practices.
- *Coming Attractions:* the babies just keep on coming, and this new cohort
  tied to the years 1983–2000 will be reared on computers and technology and experience greater parental attention on the basics of health,
  safety, and family togetherness, and will truly be the generation of the
  new millennium.

The aforementioned categories for cohort groups are fairly well-accepted as such. However, Strauss and Howe (1991, pp. 247–335) in their book, *Generations: The History of America's Future 1584 to 2069* take a different approach. They begin the generational count at every 22 years from the beginning of the history of America. It is on that basis that they identify the following as generational groupings for today's society:

- Lost: born between 1883 and 1900; experienced Great Depression and World War II in midlife.
- G. I.: born between 1901 and 1924; came of age during Great Depression and World War II.
- Silent: born between 1925 and 1942; experienced Great Depression and World War II as youth.
- Boom: born between 1943 and 1960; experienced the great societal upheaval as young adults.
- Thirteenth: born between 1961 and 1981; unprotected during the cultural changes and adult self-discovery of their youth.
- Millennial: born between 1982 and 2003 with a return to parental and societal focus.

Strauss and Howe are strong proponents of the importance of common age location in history and its impact upon who people are, what they need, and how they behave. They remind us that 75-year-olds had no Woodstock and 35-year-olds had no D-day (Strauss and Howe, 1991, p. 48). A difference in their approach to the cohort-generation categorization is their premise that the study of the American generations reveals that there are four recurring "peer personalities" that follow one another in a fixed order. The four "peer personality" cycles are idealist, reactive, civic, and adaptive; each with different outlooks and approaches to life. Taking these cycles into account, the current cohort groups would then be categorized as follows (Strauss and Howe, 1991, p. 35):

- The Old Lost: reactives;
- The Senior G. I.: civics;
- The Midlife Silent: adaptives;
- Adult Boomers: idealists;
- Coming of Age 13ers: reactives; and
- Baby Millennials: civics.

Each of these four cycles of peer personalities relate to different experiences in youth, coming of age, adulthood, midlife, and old age for each generation.

What does this cohort information mean for experience marketers? The insights are plentiful and can be gleaned from the subtleties of the shared experiences of these groups. Which cohort group pastes the "I'm spending my children's inheritance" bumper stickers on their vehicles as they set off to enjoy retirement? That would be the young World War IIers not following the careful spending patterns practiced by their elders, the Depression Era cohort. Who in their right mind is paying big bucks for repackaged Beatles' CDs? It's the early Baby Boomers.

Newman's Own (as in Paul Newman's) line of high-quality, homemade items that includes salad dressings, salsa, pasta, popcorn, and lemonade began in 1982 and has subsequently donated all $68 million of its profits to charity. A big surprise is that the company has never advertised. It just didn't need to do so since its initial customers were drawn to the blue-eyed, famous actor. Enter Generation X. These folk don't have a clue as to who Paul Newman is or was. Talk about a threat to the company; so much so that the company turned to marketing students at Fairfield University in Connecticut. The students created alternatives for establishing a new generation of customers. Among their suggestions were posters of Newman on campus and Paul Newman film festivals. As a side note the posters stated clearly the policy of all profits going to charity, a positive among the 20-something crowd. This is just an example of customers from different cohort groups purchasing the same items but for different reasons (Weizel, 1996, p. 26).

It's important to note that just because Baby Boomers are turning 50 doesn't mean that they will suddenly become Glenn Miller fans. It just doesn't work that way. Examination of cohorts and their inclinations are excellent signals pointing the way to the kinds of experiences desired by each group as well as preferences about how, when, and why they spend their money.

Household

If you were constructing a questionnaire and included a checkoff category for marital status, just how many boxes would be needed? If you were attempting to label all the family groups within this variable, how many different designations would be required? Gone are the days when single, married, divorced or widowed did the trick for everybody. Gone also are the days when starter families versus empty nest families had clear meaning for marketers as well.

If there was ever a factor that helped marketers understand discretionary use of time and money, it was marital status and/or family designation. Martial status and family are legal definitions. Family refers to two or more people living together with blood or legal ties. Households can be one person or many people living under one roof without the legal or blood ties of families. But hold the checkoff boxes for just a minute. Who exactly is today's young family? Is it that 17-year-old single mother with a newborn or the 40-something couple just starting a family? Which box do people check off for marital status if they're recently divorced (again), or they're in a 10-plus years relationship with a significant other?

The United States reached 100 million households in early 1996 with some surprising revelations. While the number of households nearly doubled over the past 40 years, the size of these households became smaller, and during that same time period the share headed by married couples decreased while the share headed by nonwhites increased (The 100 Millionth Household, 1996, p. 15).

Households aren't what they used to be, but then neither are families. The Baby Boomers are fueling a baby boom of their own, but even as they do so they don't seem headed to a return to what was considered the traditional family.

Family lifestyles are changing and these changes subsequently influence needs and preferences for experiences. The U. S. Census Bureau uses a nine category system for delineating households as follows (Boutilier, 1993, p. 6):

- dual earner married couples with children;
- other married couples with children;
- childless married couples with householders under age 45;
- childless married couples with householders aged 45 to 64;
- childless married couples with householders aged 65 and over;
- single parents;
- childless singles under age 45;
- childless singles aged 45 and older; and
- other multiple-member households.

Take a look at television. While we don't want to confuse television shows with reality, the families portrayed on television today go well beyond the Nelsons' and the Cleavers' version of family:

- Married couple with children and one earner: "The Simpsons"
- Married couple with children and two earners: "Roseanne"
- Single working mother: "Cybil"
- Blended family: "Step by Step"
- Other nonfamily: "Golden Girls" or "Friends"

Some combination of the family-household category better reflects the realities of today's world by making room for single parents of either gender as well as people living alone and new families consisting of substitute families or collections of people living together. If a widowed, 72-year-old grandmother shares a residence with two friends just like herself, does she check off the same household box as a recent college graduate, who splits the rent on an apartment with a couple of people he seldom sees and barely knows?

Experience marketers need to arrive at a blend of households and family designations that seem to work well for their particular segment of the industry. Household and family patterns clearly speak to the amount of discretionary resources people have for experiences as well as the type and depth of need for experiences as well.

Fast Facts

❖ The number of married couples in the United States increased a mere 2 percent from 1990 to 1994 to 54.3 million, but the number of households reporting an unrelated adult living with them as an unmarried partner rose 19 percent to 5.3 million.

❖ The median age at first marriage in 1994 was 24.5 for women and 26.7 for men as compared to 20.1 for women and 22.5 for men in 1956 (Edmondson, 1996, p. 2).

❖ More than one-fifth of 25-year-old Americans live at home with their parents (Mogelonsky, 1996, p. 26).

Religion

Religion is another one of those elements where marketers can inquire as to whether it should be designated core, cultural, or choice and a case could be made for any of those designations. Some ethnic groups blend ethnicity with religious affiliation almost making it a biological factor. Choice is a consideration since some people are raised in one religion and at some point select a different one. The blending and interrelationship among the four coordinates of the people parameter continues with this element.

The impact of religion on needs and experiences is mixed. Similar to other growing differences within the United States, the element of religion is on that same widening continuum. While people indicate that religion is more important to them today, attendance at formal religious observances is declining. While Christian fundamentalists seek to influence society related to what children should learn in schools and where gambling casinos should be located, there are many Americans who consider themselves something other than Christian.

According to the National Opinion Research Center in Chicago, nine out of ten Americans believe in God or a higher power with more than half saying they pray every day. While four out of five called themselves Christians, the way in which they express their faith is varied and goes beyond the traditional going to church on Sunday morning in a white-steepled church (Grossfeld, 1996, p. 24). The proliferation of nondenominational churches blending concert performances with neighborhood block parties attests to such changes.

Not only is religion being practiced differently today, there is a rapid growth in what would once have been considered "nontraditional" religions within the American culture. There are 1,100 mosques in the United States today as compared with 104 in 1960 with predictions that sometime soon after the year 2000 the number of Muslims could outnumber the six million Jewish-Americans, making Islam the second largest religion in the country (Feather, 1994, pp. 41–42.).

There are other factors changing this landscape as well. The increased rates of immigration from Asia fuel an emphasis and growth of Eastern religions. The Eastern religions have a different point of view as to how to live and how the world functions. Such changes erode and reshape religious practices and preferences in the United States.

There is little doubt that religion or spirituality, regardless of how one defines it, can have an impact for experience marketers with a virtual unending array of implications. The proposals for new theme parks such as Bible Land coexist with referendums for additional gaming establishments. Meditation and herbs share the designations as either spiritual expression or alternative health treatments. Religion is one such element that will influence behavior and subsequent choices of experiences.

EIO

There was a time when education, income, and occupation formed a marketing triangle. If marketers were able to determine one of these elements, they had a fairly good handle on the others. Those were the days. While these three factors remain inextricably tangled with one another, they don't hold the certainties that they once did.

Education does still predict future earnings. There are rather substantial income differences between a white male who completes college compared to a white male with only a high-school degree. The differences are even greater when gender and race are factored into the equation. Level of education as a factor within experience marketing is not just limited to income. Behavior preferences and patterns are also related to educational attainment. People with a college degree are more likely to attend theater and art exhibits and spend time and money gardening.

Occupation just isn't what it used to be either, and that's especially true as a marketing descriptor. In the past, the marketer could determine general range of income as well and work patterns based on occupation but not anymore. Remember the days when engineers and attorneys were people who commanded high salaries while people who serviced or fixed things didn't? Forget those days. The shift from the industrial to the infotech era has juggled the income hierarchies and guarantees. The early retirement options proffered by corporate America has also changed the age assumptions we can make about prime earning years.

There are other changes within the work world that influence need for experiences. People who spend significant amounts of time commuting have different needs from people who telecommute in their bathrobes from the home office down the hall from the bedroom. People who provide services for other people will have differing experiential needs from people who work with machines all day. People who work part time or by contract will also come forward with different psychological needs as well as different resources. Some people will have the time for experiences but not the money while others will have the money but not the time and a full range of variables in between.

Geographic Location

Where does geographic location fit within this second P of experience marketing? Which people coordinate provides the best fit for this element? In traditional marketing, geographic location was a separate target market descriptor and generally referred to proximity between where the customer was located and where the product was made. Geography, specifically actual location, still remains a factor in the people equation especially as it relates to those experiences that occur on a daily or regular basis. Shopping malls realize that proximity is a factor when targeting markets. Fitness clubs recognize that travel time and distance is a factor when selecting a location for their operations. Fast-food establishments boast of being "E-Z" on and off the highway. Whenever it's an experience where convenience or expediency plays a role as it might be with a trip to an emergency room or a frequent stop for takeout food, geographic location, even down to the accessibility of the driveway, is important.

However, given current circumstances, the role of geography and its implications for experience marketing is evolving. Mobility, economics, education, media, and technology all play a role. Geographic location is no longer the permanent designation that it may have been in the past. People are more mobile and this mobility impacts on where they live, work, learn, and play. They don't necessarily spend their entire lives within one neighborhood or geographic area. Variations in education, occupation, and income influence physical location of work. Indoor soccer facilities and climbing walls afford people from all geographic locations, regardless of climate or terrain, to participate at will.

Geographic location is often subject to certain cultural influences. People in the Northwest region of the United States tend to eat less fast food and participate in more outdoor activities. People living in the South have a reputation for warmth and hospitality. Specialty food items in different regions of the country reflect food items traditionally associated with that area, climatic considerations, and ethnic mix and traditions of the region. The same is true of certain experiences. For example, Colorado is associated with skiing and New Orleans with Mardi Gras.

Climatic considerations create social mind-sets and practices as well. People in climates with varying seasons often gear up for the coming season when they can participate in favorite experiences such as gardening or snow skiing. Retirees living in Michigan head to Florida or Arizona for the winter months and people living in Las Vegas and Phoenix rush to the mountains or the seashore for cool air in the heat of July and August. Christmas celebrations occur in December, but the traditional practices vary based on the climatic differences between the northern and southern hemispheres.

There are a variety of other cultural influences related to geography and location. Population density has a role. People in more rural communities often perceive travel time and distance differently from those accustomed to the lengthy urban-suburban commute. People who live in highly concentrated urban centers often feel the need for open space more strongly than those in more rural areas. Age, gender, race, and ethnicity play a role as well. There are older people who won't leave the house after dark or women who might feel uncomfortable going to certain travel destinations alone.

Geography as a factor can reflect demographics as well. Tulsa, Oklahoma, reflects the average American demographic profile but not necessarily American attitudes and values. Communities with larger than average numbers of young adults will be more likely to have higher than average rates of expenditures on clothing and entertainment while communities whose demographics skew older will tally higher on healthcare and medical expenditures.

Media and technology have done a great deal to change the role and definition of geography as well. CNN has changed the world as global teenagers in Newark, New Zealand, and Nairobi are all interested in "Melrose Place" and Michael Jackson. In this instance, cultural differences based on geography are eroded. In some cases, geography hardly matters at all. People who shop the Internet are often unconcerned about location of the company and in some instances, the Internet enables shoppers to access products that would have been physically out of reach for them previously.

All of these factors related to geographic location are changing. Experience marketers will look for new ways to incorporate and address needs based on the evolving definition and parameters of geography.

The Choice Coordinate

Doctors don't necessarily take Wednesdays off to play golf. Steelworkers don't all go bowling. Some families never miss a Sunday at church, and for others a church is not part of their frame of reference. Many millionaires fly coach while some people "between jobs" set off on an extended world tour. Some people choose to live in Idaho while others can't be pried away from the smog and pace of Los Angeles.

Why? They have choice, that's why. If there is one thing that the United States prides itself on, it is individualism. This individualism coupled with changes in social norms, technology, and economics has given rise to more choices than people have previously imagined. There is no one set pattern, no one American way of life, and certainly no consensus on the definition of the American dream anymore. We are a nation with our hand on the remote control of life, punching in our preferences as fast as humanly possible.

How does one explain the well-groomed, designer-clothing-garbed matron stuffing cartons of generic paper products purchased at the local warehouse store into the trunk of her Mercedes? Whatever possessed hundreds of Deadheads to follow Jerry Garcia around the country for decades? No easy answers but the simplistic one is choice. The choice coordinate includes values, attitudes, and preferences that result in certain lifestyle choices people make.

Values develop slowly over time and address the important things in people's lives. Some suggestions for use of values in target marketing include (Ray, 1997a, p. 34):

- values usually don't follow demographics—two households with identical demographics may have two very different sets of values;
- values don't predict all purchase behaviors but are best used for symbolic and lifestyle-defining activities such as clothing, vacation, travel, books, and media use; and
- values are context-specific—people attach different values to differing behavior situations.

There are a number of value frameworks that have been developed with marketing applications. The Stanford Research Institute (SRI) developed the VALS (Values, Attitudes, and Lifestyles) typology to assist in the explanation of our similarities and our differences. The latest version created by SRI Consulting, VALS2, identifies eight lifestyle segments based on two dimensions, "self"-orientation and resources. The original VALS typology segmented U. S. adults according to clusters of shared values and beliefs, with the view that an individual's inner values and attitudes engendered corresponding patterns of observable behavior. The VALS2 system classifies the population according to psychological drives that affect purchase behavior more directly than values. In the new system, psychological motivations rather than social values are the primary domain of interest. Resources include such factors as income, education, self-confidence, and health ranging from minimal to abundant. The self-orientation dimension captures psychological attributes that drive consumer choices. The three "self" or life orientations are principle, status, and action and these three orientations are further subdivided between higher and lower levels of resources creating six of the designations. The remaining two categories represent two groups at opposite ends of the resource spectrum: Strugglers and Actualizers.

The principle-oriented groups designated the Fulfilleds and the Believers are guided by their perspective as to how the world ought or should be. They are moved by ideas and beliefs, not by impulse. The Fulfilleds with more resources are mature, reflective, indifferent to status, and open-minded. The Believers with

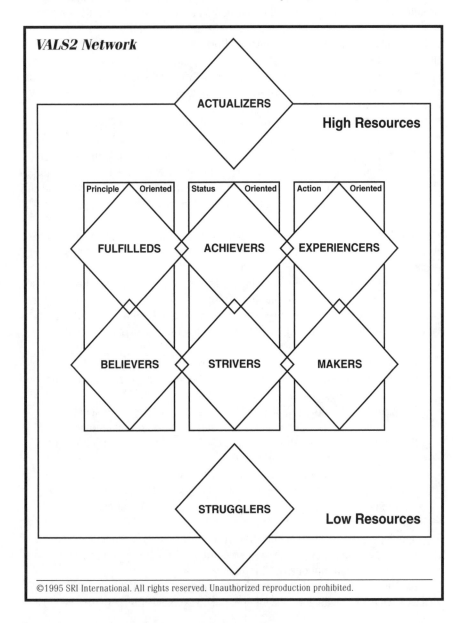

fewer resources tend to be more conservative, more literal, and more patriotic than the Fulfilleds with a focus on family (Piirto, 1991, p. 80–83).

Achievers and Strivers are the status-oriented segments of VALS2 and as the title implies these people are role-conscious and seek approval from a valued social group. Their self-image is largely defined by the opinions of others. Achievers generally seek this self-orientation through work and career while the lower resourced Strivers focus upon style and emulating others with greater resources (Piirto, 1991, pp. 80–83).

The action-oriented groups called the Experiencers and the Makers share a predilection for making things happen or being involved with events or people who are. These people seek adventure and exploration and tend to be more impulsive and resistant to social controls. Both groups tend to be younger than in the other categories. The younger of the two groups, the Experiencers, prefers sports, the outdoors, and things that are new while the Makers are a bit older, have fewer resources, and gravitate towards do-it-yourself projects and activities (Piirto, 1991, pp. 80–83).

The remaining two groups at opposite ends of the resource scale are termed Strugglers and Actualizers. Strugglers tend to be older, less skilled, and less educated than any of the other groups, and their "self"-orientation focuses on safety, security, and meeting basic life needs. The Actualizers have the highest income of the eight groups and are successful people interested in personal growth and the finer things in life (Piirto, 1991, pp. 80–83). They have a wide range of cultural and intellectual interests.

Another set of values groupings has been identified by American LIVES of San Francisco, California through numerous surveys and focus groups. It suggests that Americans can be divided into three different groups that reflect their values and the meaning they associate with life activities. These three distinct world-view groups have been labeled Traditionalism, Modernism, and Cultural Creatives with each of these three divisions having subgroups as well. An overview of these three groups includes the following (Ray, 1997b, pp. 29–33):

- Traditionalism (56 million adults—29 percent of Americans) defined by traditional and conservative values and beliefs; on average older and less-educated than the other two groups.
- Modernism (88 million adults—47 percent of Americans) places value on personal success, consumerism, materialism, and technological rationality; age, income, and education reflect national averages but tend to be slightly more male than female.
- Cultural Creatives (44 million adults—24 percent of Americans) believe in environmentalism, feminism, global issues, and spiritual searching; tend to be affluent, well-educated, and on the forefront of change.

This typology suggests that while the three world-views coexist, modernism is the most predominant currently with Traditionalism declining and the Cultural Creatives growing in numbers and influence.

Another psychographic approach that incorporates different value categories with widespread applications for specific target marketing activities is Claritas

Corporation's PRIZM (Potential Rating Index for Zip Markets). If you want to know where the softball players live or who rents the most videos or frequents gambling casinos, this system is your answer. The first version of PRIZM divided the 36,000 zip codes into 40 lifestyle clusters. The revised version features 12 subgroups with 62 groupings attesting to the increased diversity of lifestyle choices within society today.

The designations and descriptions often help to create a picture of these people. The 12 subgroups include such designations as inner suburbs, country families, and urban uptowns creating similarities of type by location and amount of resources. The 62 groups really begin to get at the heart of lifestyle differences. For instance, the cluster Upward Bound is described as going to aerobics, owning pagers or beepers, and reading science and technology magazines, while the cluster Single City Blues buys lottery tickets, drinks domestic beer, and listens to football on the radio (Reardon, 1995, p. 16–17).

People's values lead to the attitudes and opinions that they hold which in turn manifest themselves as choices people make about their behaviors, activities, experiences, and lives. Such choice parameters hold great potential for experience marketers.

The Change Coordinate

A loving and energetic child turns into a sullen, lethargic teen seemingly overnight. A career-oriented newspaper editor has her first child and takes a walk on her career. A longtime smoker turns away from his two-pack-a-day habits after 32 years. The daily discomfort of arthritis severely restricts the daily life patterns of an active 66-year-old retiree.

While these instances seldom take center stage in more traditional target marketing approaches, they form a critical piece for experience marketing. The elements included within the fourth coordinate called change include life stages, life events, health, stages of change, and seasonal and cyclical changes. These changes may be gradual, sudden, progressive, anticipated, or unexpected, but the impact of these changes generally has a significant impact on the needs of people and their seeking of experiences.

The types of changes within this coordinate may be biological, cultural, economic, demographic; or based on changes in health or attitudes; or just about any nuance influencing human behavior. Obviously, this coordinate is dependent on and interrelated to the other three. Perched between the core and choice coordinates, it maintains a precarious balance between the two as well as being heavily influenced by culture. It's an interesting and complex coordinate. While puberty is clearly biological and its onset predictable within a certain age range, the downturn of the economy and its subsequent flood of early retirements is not so easily anticipated. The rise and fall of the divorce rates can be traced to shifts in cultural traditions and values and attitudes as well as the economy and life stages. The interrelated nature of change with other coordinates within the people variable need to be closely monitored by experience marketers.

Life Stages and Events

Life stages is one such element within this change coordinate with variations and interactions with other factors. The transition from baby to toddler, the onset of puberty as well as midlife transitions are all developmental stages that alter the needs of people and the significant others in their lives. People have different needs as they move from one life stage to another and these life stages are ever evolving.

The biological changes of development are a significant factor. Puberty serves as a starting gun for a whole host of new needs and interests for adolescents. The shift from wanting to be with family to peer group and from same sex to mixed sex groupings has enormous ramifications for the experience industries. Adolescents aren't the only ones experiencing biologically-related changes. Psychologist Karl Jung believed that fairly significant changes occurred at midlife with people transitioning from adapting to their external world to adapting to their inner self. Wolfe writes of maturing personalities moving away from a materialistically based value system to a more introspective and altruistic nature (Wolfe, 1992, p. 42). Both of these biological-development patterns hold implications for experiences.

The "how" and "when" of life stages are changing as well. Puberty is occurring earlier in the United States while adolescence is being extended and stretched out to the mid-twenties in some cases. Menopause remained in the closet for years, but the large number of Baby Boomer women along with attitudinal changes will move it to center stage. The roots of life stages are most often biological, and the developmental needs created include not only physical but emotional, social, and spiritual ones as well.

Major life events can sometimes be related to these life stages and are also undergoing a great deal of change. Major life events such as graduation from high school or college, marriage, divorce, birth of first child, retirement, or death of a spouse are important happenings that create certain needs for products, services, and experiences. Mergenhagen points out in her book, *Targeting Transitions—Marketing to Consumers During Life Changes*, that two factors influencing this element of change include the repetition of these events and their unpredictability. The age at which it is common or deemed appropriate to graduate from college, get married, have a child, or retire has drastically changed. The number of times that people marry, divorce, or change jobs also has increased significantly over the years.

Opportunities generated by life transitions include the following: marriage and remarriage, parenthood, divorce, care giving and death, graduation, career change, retirement, and moving (Mergenhagen, 1995, pp. 16–18). The longstanding Social Readjustment Rating Scale developed by Holmes and Rahe provides an even more extensive list of life events ranging from the more serious such as death of a spouse, divorce, marital separation, or jail term to more minor life events including such things as changes in sleeping or eating habits as well as vacations and family get-togethers. There are 43 life events listed in this scale including positive events such as outstanding personal achievement or gain of a new family member

❖ The number of displaced homemakers, women whose principal activity has been homemaking and who lost their main source of income due to divorce, separation, widowhood, or spouse's disability or long-term unemployment, grew about 12 percent in the 1980s from 14 to 16 million (Stuck at Home, 1994, p. 6).

Fast Facts

❖ According to the National Center for Health Statistics about 20 million Americans have trouble with their hearing compared with 13 million in 1971.

❖ The U. S. Census Bureau reported that the percentage of elderly living in poverty declined from 24.6 percent in 1970 to 12.9 percent in 1992.

❖ A 1995 *USA Today*/Gallup poll found that 70 percent of Baby Boomers expect to work after they retire as compared to the 12 percent of the over 65 population currently working.

❖ The International Health, Racquet and Sports Club Association reported that January and September continue to be the months with the highest rates for new membership enrollment, citing an increased membership rate of 11.1 percent and 10.0 percent respectively (Outlook, 1996, p. 9).

and more negative events such as death of a close friend or foreclosure of a mortgage. An important thing to note about this social readjustment scale is that life events whether they be good or bad do give rise to needs that require addressing and, therefore, serve as a force within the change coordinate.

Health

"As long as you have your health" is an old adage but the implications for loss of health or change in health status is enormous for the experience industries. A variety of factors has heightened the importance of this element. Medical advances have extended life expectancy for Americans as well as saving the lives of premature infants and accident victims. Robotics and communication systems enable people with disabilities to function at higher and more independent levels. The growing emphasis being placed upon health by aging Baby Boomers, the wellness movement, and insurance companies adds to the importance of this element.

As the number of older Americans grows so does the importance of this factor. The aging process is accompanied by a variety of chronic diseases and disabilities that bring with it changes in physical, mental, and social needs. As age increases so do various types of limitations. Those limitations can affect mobility, sight, hearing or speech and language impairments. Of adults ages 15 to 34 years, only 7.5 percent of them report a functional limitation while that percentage soars to 49.8 percent for adults 65 to 74 years of age (Reedy, 1993, p. 16).

As the 76 million Baby Boomers approach maturity, the focus they will bring to the *life in one's years* rather than the *years in one's life* will augment the importance of this variable. The products being marketed for hair loss and wrinkles are just the tip of the iceberg as major focus upon both the cosmetic and physical signs of aging will take center stage. More serious shifts in attitudes and behaviors related to diet and exercise will surface as well.

Age, Stages, and Life Events

Age is related to and is a predictor for life stages. These life stages are patterns of life progressions related to the developmental stages of growing and living but are subject heavily to other influences such as life events. A study conducted for *Modern Maturity* by Roper Starch Worldwide divided Americans into seven life stage segments. They are as follows (Edmondson, 1996):

- *Nervous Novices:* 30.4 million people with a median age of 31 who are virtually novices as it relates to adult life experiences.
- *Clock Watchers:* the 28.5 million young adults with a median age of 32 who are pursuing a future while beset with stage-related transitions such as changing jobs, and getting married or divorced.
- *First Families:* the 57.1 million Americans with a median age of 37 who are fully employed, fully married, and newly but fully nested.
- *Second Chancers:* a median age of 45 represents the 19 million Americans who are on the brink between younger and older segments of life stages and are pursuing a second chance or new beginning after some kind of major life change usually resulting from external factors such as change in marital or family status, job or career.
- *Continuing Caregivers:* those 13.1 million Americans with a median age of 55 who still have dependents—possibly an aging parent, a maturing child, or a grandchild—for whom they provide care.
- *New Mes:* the 15.2 million people with a median age of 55 who have experienced an internal change such as midlife crisis, career shift, or major illness.
- *Free Birds:* 24.7 million strong with a median age of 69 who are often retired and free from work and/or family obligations.

When health problems or even death occur to significant others, the impact of life events comes into play. Deteriorating health can turn a spouse, parent, or friend into a caretaker, creating all kinds of needs for experiences. The death of a loved one can also lead to a number of different needs for experiences.

Health can significantly impact on the amount of discretionary time and income as well as accessibility and need for supportive services. Often overlooked as a target marketing factor, health can and will play an ever-growing role in creating opportunities for the experience industries.

Stages of Change

Recall someone you know who after 20-plus years of smoking quits or somebody who decides to up and change careers after a near lifetime doing the same thing. While these changes appear to happen out of the blue, that may not necessarily be the case. Prochaska and DiClemente (1983, pp. 51, 390–395) developed a model for behavior change that included the following five stages:

- *precontemplation:* people not really thinking about the behavior as being appropriate for them;

- *contemplation:* people actually thinking about and considering a certain behavior for themselves;
- *preparation:* people have made a decision to change behavior and are putting into place needed elements to carry out the new behavior;
- *action:* people are implementing the new behavior for the first several times; and
- *confirmation:* people are committed to the behavior change and don't intend to return to previous behavior.

While these concepts were originally developed for social marketing applications such as smoking cessation and family planning programs, the continuum can be used by experience marketers. Experiences can be marketed based on perceived stage of readiness and promotional strategies, and message can be tailored accordingly.

It's important to note that other elements with the change coordinate such as midlife crisis, death of a close friend, or the start of a new year can also facilitate an individual's move from stage to stage. The readiness stages when used in conjunction with other elements within this parameter hold great potential for experience marketing.

Time

We diet like crazy in January but then stock up on high-calorie munchies at the end of the month for the annual Super Bowl observance. We literally spring into action with the good weather of April. After spring comes a summer spent pursuing fun which is followed by retreating behind closed doors in the winter months.

Time is a factor within the change coordinate. There are different sources of these time changes. Time changes can spring from biological urges, cultural dictates, or personal preferences but regardless of their origin, time has an impact. The impact of time on change can be seasonal or cyclical and either natural or man made.

The first sign of spring, or the arrival of April, whichever comes first signals the start of the gardening and growing season. In the United States, we have several seasons or cycles for starting over again. We make resolutions in the new year, plant shrubs and flowers in the spring, and sign up for adult education in September. We head

Labor Day weekend marks a mental and cultural seasonal transition. There are a myriad of experiences to celebrate and mark the move from summer to the more serious fall season:

- the Chicago Jazz Festival,
- New York's Hampton Horse Show,
- Milbrae Arts & Wine Festival held outside of San Francisco,
- the Burning Man encampment in northwest Nevada, and
- Southern Decadence in New Orleans' French Quarter.

back inside during the winter months when we stock up on home videos and computer games. Some cyclical changes have been created by society and only appear seasonal. We use Memorial Day to kickoff the summer fun marathon and November as the starting gun for the race to happy holidays.

Seasons and annual cycles aren't the only timing considerations within this factor. Consider the impact of time of day, day of the week, and time of the year to cite just a few examples. People have internal clocks. Some cruisegoers are up at dawn for the early morning aerobics class while others are just barely returning to their cabins from the late night evening entertainment. Restaurants and golf courses experience slowdowns on Mondays and hit a peak on Friday afternoons, Saturdays, and Sundays. Time of year is another factor to watch. Who wants to visit Washing-

Slice of Life

The Bank-Boston Companies created an advertisement for a home equity line of credit that bears a heading proclaiming that "Life's expensive" and then depicts life changes in graphic and dollar form that may require people to need additional financing. The list of time-related changes includes life stages, life events, and seasons.

College:	$15,850 a year
Braces:	$3,580
Minivan:	$31,999
Wedding:	$21,300
Credit bills:	$3,212
Vacation:	$4,280
House addition:	$28,640
Midlife crisis:	$18,260

ton, DC, in February when they can wait and see the cherry blossoms in the spring? Who wants to endure the crowds at Disney World over spring vacation when they can have Main Street practically all to themselves the first week in December?

Some cycles reflect the human condition while others are created by the society. Modern life has created a year-round compass pointing us in the direction of experiences. Hollywood times its big movie releases for the winter holiday

Action Agenda

❖ Identify two or more current target markets for your experience and specify the most important factors that describe or explain their participation.

❖ Identify how your current target markets differ from one another based on the factors within the 4Cs.

❖ Develop a framework for explaining or better understanding the interaction or interrelationships between the core, cultural, choice, and change coordinates as it relates to peoples' experiences.

❖ Create a list of key coordinate factors related to participation in your experience and try to identify new target groups for your business on this basis.

```
┌─────────────────────────────────────────────────────────────────┐
│                        Transition                                 │
│                         Tracking                                  │
└─────────────────────────────────────────────────────────────────┘
```

From	To
• Geographic—place of residence, employment, travel time and distance predisposition	• Core—age or stage, race, gender, ethnicity
• Sociodemographics—age, gender, income, occupation, education, marital status, ethnicity, religious affiliation	• Culture—cohort, EIO, household, religion, geography
• Behavioral—usage, skill, specialization, benefits sought, loyalty status	• Choice—values and/or attitudes, preferences, behaviors, lifestyles
• Synchronographics—time of day, week, year; length of time, season	• Change—life stage, life event, health, readiness, seasons or cycle

season and the summer months. Drypers Corporation designs winter diapers with snowmen and hockey playing penguins to seasonalize purchasing patterns. And we can't forget Hallmark and the other greeting card companies who serve as consummate reminders of the seasonal and cyclical nature of life's celebrations and experiences.

Time is either an obvious or often overlooked element within the change coordinate depending upon the circumstances, the situation, and the experience. An impending change or the occurrence of such a change creates previously undiscovered needs that serve as the impetus for seeking out a particular experience.

Keep an eye on it.

Sources

Boutilier, Robert. (1993). *Targeting families: Marketing to and through the new family.* Ithaca, NY: American Demographic Books.

Dacey, John S., & Travers, John F. (1996). *Human development across the life span* (3rd ed.). Dubuque, IA: Brown & Benchmark.

Edmondson, Brad (Ed.). (1996, May). The future of recreation: No picnic. *The Number News,* Volume 16, Number 5.

Feather, Frank. (1994). *The future consumer.* Toronto, Canada: Warwick Publishing.

Grossfeld, Stan. (1996, October 6). Landmarks to Christ. *The Boston Globe Magazine.*

The 100 millionth household. (1996, March). *American Demographics.*

Hyde, J. S., Fennema, E., & Lamon, S. J. (1997). Gender differences in mathematics performance: A meta-analysis. *Psychological Bulletin, 107*(2), pp. 139–155.

Jolley, Janina M., & Mitchell, Mark L. (1996). *Life span development: A topical approach.* Dubuque, IA: Brown & Benchmark.

Meredith, Geoffrey, & Schewe, Charles. (1994, December). The power of generations. *American Demographics.*

Mergenhagen, P. (1995). *Targeting transitions—Marketing to consumers during life changes.* Ithaca, NY: American Demographics Books.

Mogelonsky, Marcia. (1996, May). The rocky road to adulthood. *American Demographics.*

Murdock, Steve M. (1995). *An America challenged: Population change and the future of the United States.* Boulder, CO: WestviewPress.

Outlook. (1996, June). *Club Industry.*

Piirto, Rebecca. (1991). *Beyond mind games: The marketing power of psychographics.* Ithaca, NY: American Demographic Books.

Prochaska, J. O., & DiClemente, C. C. (1983). Stages and processes of self-change of smoking: Toward an integrative model of change. *Journal of Consulting and Clinical Psychology, 51.*

Ray, Paul H. (1997a, February). Using values to study customers. *American Demographics.*

Ray, Paul H. (1997b, February). The emerging culture. *American Demographics.*

Reardon, Patrick T. (1995, November 5). How place defines us, or does it? *The Chicago Tribune Magazine.*

Reedy, Joel. (1993). *Marketing to consumers with disabilities.* Chicago, IL: Probus Publishing.

Sandor, Gabrielle. (1994, June). The other American. *American Demographics.*

Strauss, William, & Howe, Neil. (1991). *Generations: The history of America's future 1584 to 2069.* New York, NY: William Morrow and Company.

Stuck at home. (1994, February). *American Demographics.*

Weizel, Richard. (1996, April 21). Who is this guy, anyway? *The Boston Globe.*

Wolfe, David. (1992, September). Business's midlife crisis. *American Demographics.*

Women of the future: Alternative scenarios. (1996, May–June). *The Futurists.*

Traditional target marketing usually relied upon geographic, sociodemographic, behavioral, and synchronographic factors for identifying groups  of people for whom a product or service would be designed. Generally, marketers would begin this process by envisioning potential markets either on the basis of potential user groups or benefits being sought. For instance, if the New York State Division of Tourism was identifying potential target markets, it could either list potential user groups such as families, singles, or married couples without children or it could start the process by listing benefits being sought by potential tourists such as enjoying nature, exploring history, or attending cultural events.

The outcome of either approach results in the development of specific experiences or the refinement of offerings, facilities, or services for identified target markets. An approach that would appear to be more useful for the experience industries in their attempt to identify and address the inner needs of varying and fragmented population groups is to utilize a combined approach. Such an approach to target marketing where the knowledge about particular subsegments of the population are used in combination with insights into emerging needs would be more effective.

Chapter 4

Particle Markets

If you want to get into people's wallets, first you have to get
into their lives.

Bink Garrison

People Plus

Gather any group of individuals with something in common together whether
they be family members, neighbors, coworkers, or even close friends and ask
them to define their idea of a perfect weekend or explain how they'd spend a
winning lottery jackpot. Just wait to be amazed by the number of quite different
definitions and responses. People can be so very different from one another. Even
people we perceive as being alike can't be counted on to respond similarly when
it comes to experiences. The personal and inner nature of experiences leads to a
veritable explosion of different preferences, patterns, and needs. The proliferation of lifestyle choices and growth of opportunities only contributes to the escalation of these definitions.

Consider venturing to a motorcycle rally, an antique show, a wrestling match,
or an art exhibit; get ready to be amazed at the number of people who seem to
share a similar point of view when it comes to investing their discretionary time
or money or both. Some of these people may share commonalties of gender, education, or life stage while others seem quite different from one another with the
event serving as the common bond. How does an experience marketer determine
what brings them together? What factors serve as key determinants of participation? Are the characteristics or descriptors of the participants as important or
more important than the benefit being sought from the experience? Is it something inherent within the experience itself that serves as a target marketing consideration?

The intricate and involved nature of people as individuals compounded by the seismic shifts of social change exacerbates ever-emerging and -changing needs for experiences. Such changes also lead to increasingly diverse groups of markets. Experience marketers are best served by learning as much as they possibly can about people and by never taking an individual or a group of people at face value. Rather experience marketers will need to create a "people plus" situation. People plus results from studying the specific needs or examining certain demographic or behavior groups. It can occur by creating mental snapshots of people based on one's enhanced knowledge of the four people coordinates and one's selection of the key elements on which to focus.

Psychographic Shorthand

Pulling together people plus profiles sometimes results in the creation of acronyms that serve as a form of psychographic shorthand. The term "Yuppies," standing for young, urban, professionals with a pattern of big spending and good living, was one of the first to enter the American vernacular. In fact, from a historic point of view it appears as if we've gone from Yippies ('60s social activists) to Yuppies to Yiffies and Yeepies all within a few decades.

Check out some well-known and lesser known psychographic nicknames:

- *Yuppies:* the original meaning of young, urban professionals was followed by Buppies (black urban professionals), Huppies (Hispanic), Guppies (gay), and Puppies (pregnant).
- *Dinks:* double income, no kids followed by Minks (multiple income no kids) and Sinks (single income no kids).
- *Dwiks:* dual income with kids.
- *Sitcom:* single income, two kids, with outrageous mortgage.
- *Yeepies:* young, energetic, elderly people into everything.
- *Opals:* older people with active lifestyles.
- *Grumpies:* grown-up mature people (former Yuppies).
- *Lumpies:* laid-back, unmotivated, middle-aged professionals.
- *Moss:* middle-aged, overstressed, semiaffluent suburbanites.
- *Yiffies:* young, individualistic, freedom-minded, and few.
- *Cocoes:* children of contradictory experiences.
- *Flyers:* fun-loving youth en route to success.
- *Skippies:* school-aged kids with purchasing power.

Particle Markets

These psychographic shorthand designations are actually particle target markets. Particle markets have been around for quite a while but have not been afforded the recognition they warrant. Particle markets involve the close examination of people in such a way that the marketer can pinpoint very specific traits, characteristics, or needs of people and combine these factors with other pertinent qualities to identify a group that possesses certain similarities useful in designing and marketing experiences. Such factors include characteristics and

Camp Gone to the Dogs set against the rolling hills and endless green fields of Putney, Vermont, is the spot for people willing to pay hundreds of dollars for people-poochie quality time that is unavailable or unacceptable anyplace else. Doggie campers from 34 states, Canada, England, and the Bahamas come to this place. The camp had a 70 percent return rate in its seventh year. While the focus of the camp is on fun and games, there are two distinct groups in camp. One group is extremely active and competitive while the other newly formed group called the Bon-Bon Club is the exact opposite, vowing not to overstress either themselves or their dogs. Camp founder and director, Honey Loring, provides more than 50 daily activities including tracking for beginners, lectures by top dog trainers, agility and obedience classes, kissing and tail-wagging contests, and swimming lessons (Ubinas, 1996, pp. A1, A5).

traits inherent within the four coordinates of people discussed in the previous chapter. For instance, age can and is a factor as it is with Yeepies—young energetic elderly people into everything. However, age is not the only characteristic describing this group. There are obvious health and lifestyle components of this determination as well. It is the people plus approach of identifying and combining other important factors and qualities that make particle markets so powerful a tool for experience marketers.

How do we make particle markets work for the experience industry? Such strategies are critical to the overall success of experiences for a number of reasons. The need for experiences is based on specific, personal, and individualized needs so that creating those experiences requires an in-depth understanding of who these potential participants are and what lies beneath the surface of their persona.

A second critical factor is the grouping factor. Groups of different people are attracted to and participate in the experience simultaneously. People don't always show up to an experience alone. Often they bring friends and family members along with them either willingly or reluctantly. The needs and expectations of these people may not overlap with those of the person who initiated the experience.

There may also be multiple groups of people involved in an experience simultaneously. You can't assume they are drawn by the same needs or attracted by the same benefits to the experience. Think back to the people attending the motorcycle rally or the art exhibit. Think they're all there for the same reasons? Not

Spend some time observing people as they "experience" your experience. Make a note of key coordinates: core, cultural, choice, or change. See if you can subsegment two to four groups on the basis of those factors, and as you observe them, attempt to note differences in needs revealed  or benefits sought. Then flip through the pages of your people plus mental photo album and see what you can learn about your new particle markets.

Clos*e*eup

Picture an anxious group of would-be river rafters sitting on the bank of the river ready to embark upon a four-day raft trip. Take a people plus approach to creating particle target markets for this group. Such an approach that identifies the inner or psychic needs and combines those needs with critical people coordinates can work in conjunction with one another to create a variety of particle markets for this experience.

Need/Group	Accomplishment	Adventure	Affiliation
Demographic Characteristic	Teens, middle-aged adults	Young adults	Families, couples
Specific Benefit	Looking for sense of self	Testing limits	Quality time
Lifestyle Profiles	Thrivers	Rough 'n' Readys	Neotrads

The key to using these particle markets is to create specific benefits, activities, or outcomes within the experience both to attract and to meet the needs of the various groups within the particles. In the rafting example, an outfitter could accomplish this in one of two ways. The company could either offer a variety of rafting options with varying levels of activity and skill level required, or it could design its rafting trip to incorporate a variety of activities or range of choices within the same trip. A more leisurely float trip down the river featuring plenty of easy paddling for the couples or family groups along with downtime for short hikes and picnics would be perfect for the affiliation-seeking particles. A weekend venture consisting of opportunities both to paddle and to rock climb for the individuals seeking sense of self and accomplishment would be perfect for people with those needs. However, that approach is likely to bore the people who would choose to go when the water was higher and faster; the climbs were steeper and more challenging, presenting a real adventure for the participants.

Every experience consists of a number of parameters; some can be altered or manipulated by the provider and some not. But the real trick to experience marketing is to be able to identify the particle or particles so well that within the experience itself, each group can find a part of that experience that attracts and fulfills its needs.

necessarily so, as people occupying the same place at the same time for apparently similar reasons may bring with them vastly different reasons for participating.

How does one design an experience to meet the various needs and communicate those needs to customers? This is one of the major challenges of any marketing, but more particularly so with experience marketing. Particle target marketing with its people plus enhancement is a possible way to meet this challenge.

Join us as we flip over the pages of today's photo album taking a shot at "people plussing." In fact, today's scrapbooks are full of all kinds of unique pictures thanks to the recent baby boomlet, increased longevity, and fragmentation of markets which include everybody from Yippies to Yuppies to Yeepies and Yiffies. Can't get a clear picture of these people? Keep turning the pages, and you'll find more on the Yippies, Yuppies, Yiffies, and Yeepies. While you're at it be sure to

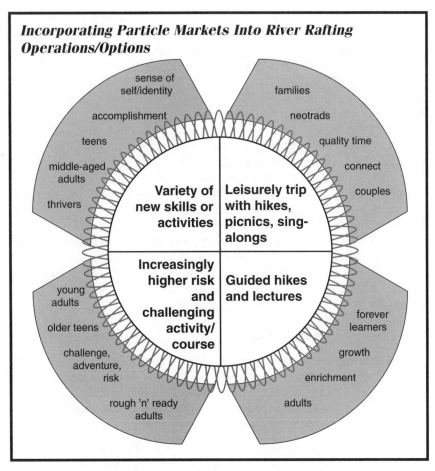

Incorporating Particle Markets Into River Rafting Operations/Options

sense of self/identity

accomplishment

teens

middle-aged adults

thrivers

Variety of new skills or activities

Leisurely trip with hikes, picnics, sing-alongs

families

neotrads

quality time

connect

couples

young adults

older teens

challenge, adventure, risk

rough 'n' ready adults

Increasingly higher risk and challenging activity/ course

Guided hikes and lectures

forever learners

growth

enrichment

adults

work on creating mental pictures of your own particle markets for your experience marketing scrapbook.

Age Plus Possibilities

Age is certainly and has traditionally been a natural starting point for beginning to understand people. While that holds true for today, adding new insights on aging certainly provides greater depth of understanding.

Older Adults

Older adults. What kind of term is that exactly? It's a term in need of a new definition and desperately in need of new terminology. Who is old today? By old do we mean over 50, over 65, over 85, or, as Willard Scott pronounces them, over 100? We've used terms such as senior citizens and goldenagers, but those terms just won't work anymore. They won't work because they lack definition; they just create a clear snapshot. Baby Boomers who coined the slogan "don't trust anyone over 30" are not going to take well to those kinds of labels as they mature.

The AARP reports that the number of people age 85 has tripled since 1960 and that people 100-plus are the fastest growing segment of our population. We need to subgroup old age in this country. Rather than lump everyone over age 50, or even 65, into one category and calling them mature consumers, categories such as mature adults (50–65), young-old (65–75), the old (75–85) and the old-old (over 85) need to be devised. This might serve as a springboard for additional insights into this rapidly growing group.

While subcategories based upon age may be a good start, it doesn't begin to develop a complete picture. What are some of the people plus factors that can be added to "old" to enhance our understanding of who these people are and what their inner or psychic needs might be. George Mochis at the Center for Mature Consumer Studies at Georgia State University uses gerontographics, segmentation based upon factors that make older consumers more or less receptive to marketing (Mochis, 1996, p. 46). He adds two additional components to his descriptors of the elderly and differentiates between people on the basis of personality type by designating people as either introverted or extroverted and by health status, good or poor. Using that as a basis, the Gerontographics Model results in the creation of four different types of older consumers as follows (Mochis, 1996, pp. 46–47):

	Extroverted	**Introverted**
Good Health	*Healthy Indulgers* (18 percent of older people) healthy, active, and interested in a variety of leisure, entertainment services.	*Healthy Hermits* (36 percent of older people) interested in home-centered entertainment and products.
Poor Health	*Ailing Outgoers* (29 percent of older people) interested in retirement housing options with health services.	*Frail Recluses* (17 percent of older people) interested in domestic assistance and home health services.

Mochis believes that the consumer outlook and preferences of older consumers is related to the multifaceted aging process as well as to the common experiences they've had and how they responded to those life changes.

Another people plus approach to older Americans is attributed to David Wolfe, author of the book *Marketing to the Ageless Market* (1990). Wolfe cites five key values helpful in explaining the behavior and subsequent behavior patterns of older individuals. These values are autonomy and self-sufficiency, social connectedness, altruism, personal growth, and personal revitalization (Wolfe, 1992, pp. 36–38). Additional suggestions when marketing to this group include the following:

- Don't target them specifically as "older" since research reveals people think of themselves as being younger than they actually are.

- Don't assume older people are all alike since their previous life experiences shape their values and preferences.
- Remember that the need for possessions for themselves is replaced by the need for experiences.
- Terms such as older, elderly, senior, or retiree may not be effective as labels.
- Integrate these people with other age groups to avoid isolation. (Who's In? 1992, pp. 4–5).

Wolfe reports on the LAVOVA (Lifestyles and Values of Older Americans) project that developed a framework of six possible ways to age. One aspect of LAVOVA was to analyze findings on the basis of four personality factors (Wolfe, 1990, p. 83):

- independent—dependent;
- extroverted—introverted;
- self-indulgent—self-denying; and
- open to change—resistant to change.

This analysis resulted in the creation of the following six categories of aging (Wolfe, 1990, pp. 82–83):

- Attainers:
    youngest, most autonomous;
    both healthy and wealthy;
    best educated and open to change;
    nine percent of population; median age of 60.
- Adapters:
    aware of needs and seeking ways to meet them;
    tend to be single, demanding, well-informed, and open to change;
    second highest income and home value;
    11 percent of population; median age of 74.
- Explorers:
    active individualists who forgo help from children;
    lived 20-plus years at same address;
    22 percent of populations; median age of 65.
- Martyrs:
    closed, uninformed, highly conservative;
    often divorced or single with low to moderate income;
    21 percent of population; median age of 63.
- Pragmatists:
    somewhat outgoing, middle of the road;
    cautious but open; living alone;
    moderate to lower income;
    21 percent of the population; median age of 76.
- Preservers:
    frail and frightened of change;

vulnerable, likely to be living alone;
one percent of the population; median age of 78.

Strauss and Howe in their predictions of behavior based on the four cycles of generations provide some insights into the two groups now making up older adults: the G. I. and Silent Generations. The G. I. refers to those people who were young adults during World War II while the Silent refers to people born during that time period. According to these authors, the elderly G. I. Generation are best represented as "super seniors" whose physical decline will impact them hard since they have always been accustomed to activity and accomplishment. It is suggested that they will stick together as a cohort group living out their lives in relative affluence in "senior-only" condos and planned care communities (Strauss and Howe, 1991, pp. 384–385). The members of the Silent Generation will not enjoy the comfort of their approaching retirement due to their feelings of guilt as to how the children they raised are doing and the uncertainty of today's world. These factors will cause them to reach out to other generations and the rest of the world. They will create a rise in volunteerism as a way to channel their talents and energies into helping society. They will discard the "senior" designation and both reside in intergenerational housing as well as pursue leisure options such as travel with other generations (Strauss and Howe, 1991, pp. 390–393).

In addition to health and personality factors, consider the generational differences included in an age span from 50 to possibly 100. That growing group of people over 85 years of age is actually the first generation in our history to live out a full human life span. Think of it. Back in the early years of the 1900s when many of the 85-plussers were born, the life expectancy was 47.3 years compared with 75.3 today. These folks are truly pioneers in living a full life, and they take to this trail with experiences unlike those shared by other generations of mature adults (Pappano, 1994, p. 27). They remember seeing Civil War veterans march in Memorial Day parades. They lived through both a flu epidemic and the polio scare. They grew up and lived in a time when people didn't talk about sex or go on diets.

The size and spending power of the maturing market is worth focusing on for all segments of commerce. Mark Zitter of Age Wave, Inc., a consulting company advising businesses and government on the implications of an aging society, calls the impact of American adults 50 and over the demographic discovery of the decade. Americans over 50 have combined incomes of more than $800 million, possess 51 percent of all the discretionary income, own half the luxury cars sold, and account for one-third of the spa and health club memberships (Doka, 1992, pp. 21–22). When we speak of goldenagers this group clearly spells gold for businesses who manage to provide the right kind of services in the right way for this affluent group. Households headed by the over 55 age group account for one of every four dollars spent by U. S. households with that percentage growing in the future (Underhill, 1996, p. 44–45). Underhill suggests that retailers in particular need to make a concerted effort to meet the needs of mature shoppers with changes such as comfortable chairs, waiting areas, rest rooms, and personalized, quality advice and service.

Other Adults

How do we define adulthood in twenty-first century society? Is one an adult when one is 18 and over and can vote? Does one become an adult on one's twenty-first birthday or does one have to wait until one reaches an adult-like milestone? Adulthood and the rites of passage associated with this life stage have become increasingly blurred. The Baby Boomers started this blurring as they began to delay or bypass previously traditional rites of passage such as marriage and parenthood. The cohort group who followed picked up this pattern and began stretching the time period from late adolescence to young adulthood into an entirely new way of life. Society hasn't helped with this demarcation either as laws have been passed that allow people to vote at 18 but not purchase alcohol until 21 years of age.

This is another instance of where adding a plus or an additional factor to a category of people may be helpful. Growing more mature at the end of the twentieth century and reaching the age of adulthood seem to differ from those of previous generations. Therefore, it is helpful to add the cohort factor and subdivide adults into their cohort groups such as the Baby Boomers and the so called Generation X who followed the Boomers.

Baby Boomers

The "never trust anyone over 30" cohort began turning 50 years of age in 1996. This is the group that significantly impacted every life stage they encountered. They caused school overcrowding and stopped a war. They married later, divorced more frequently, had fewer children or none at all, and it can be guaranteed they will influence this new life stage called maturing as they slide into it. They number 76 million and are half again as large as the generations that both precede and follow them. They are important players in the experience industry. After all, two of the ultimate marketers of all time, McDonald's and Disney, have catered to the maturing Boomer. Commercials featured Ronald McDonald as an aging hipster on the golf course and in a pool hall and even in a business suit all to push the Arch Deluxe, otherwise known as the "Boomer burger." Disney flooded the airwaves with commercials featuring the adventures of the over 40 crowd, showing Disney World as a virtual adult playground. The summer concert tours feature such names from yesteryear as the Moody Blues, the Allman Brothers, and Chicago. Movie production companies plunge into nostalgia with remakes of "Mission Impossible," "Sgt. Bilko," and "Leave It to Beaver."

How then do we deal with these aging adults? What will we call them and how will we envision their needs for experiences? Ken Dychtwald, founder of Age Wave, Inc., has spent the past decade spreading the word on the world of the elderly and strongly encourages marketers to find better terms than mature or seniors for targeting aging Boomers. Tentative labels include Empty Nesters, Primers, or Dychtwald's Middlessence (Guttman, 1996, p. 57). It is important to remember that not only are there a large number of these adults sitting out there but also that they are the most independent cohort group to date. They defy easy categorization. The only likely generalization to make about this group is that they have changed every life stage they've gone through, and it is relatively certain they will do the same with the maturing-aging process.

All the indicators seem to point to a barrage of products and services designed for this Middlessence. The members of this group have a tendency to delay many of the more traditional signs of aging, and they will continue to do so. They may retire early and start entirely new careers at 60. They may climb mountains and jump out of airplanes. They will increasingly look for ways to control their lives and the more visible and evident impacts of aging. They will pursue experiences rather than possessions as a way to live life fully.

All phases of life and business will change as the Boomers age. Industry experts predict that housing, healthcare, financial services, clothing manufacturers, and providers of health and beauty aids will be directing their products and advertising dollars towards reaching the aging Boomers. Home builders will switch from big houses to down-nested versions of homes and condominiums with separate sections and entrances for home offices, in-law suites, or returning children. Stores of all kinds will feature individualized products and services with a heavy emphasis on convenience. Clothing and cars will adapt to maintain a youthful but comfortable or relaxed fit.

It is important to note that this large group spans from 1946 to 1964, and all adults cannot be lumped into one maturing group of adults. This is particularly true of those people born at the end of the baby boom during the first years of the 1960s. These people are only statistically linked with their older brothers and sisters. They weren't around for Vietnam or Woodstock. In fact, their life has been one of continually facing the challenges of overcrowding. They came of age during the '80s not the '60s and their lives are shaped by the realities of Watergate, the oil crisis, and inflation. The more than 20 million people that make up this trailing edge of the boom are really more of a transition group sharing many of the values of the Generation Xers starting in 1965 (Stone, 1996, p. 1A).

Strauss and Howe, as you may recall, designate the Boomers as people born between 1943 and 1960 and having labeled this group as idealists predict that as the Boomers enter midlife they will focus less on the inner world of self and more towards the realm of social virtue with their politics becoming values-laden (Strauss and Howe, 1991, p. 396). They suggest that Boomers will apply this purposefulness to consumerism as well, looking for quality over quantity, uniqueness over comfort, inner satisfaction over outer popularity and will compel companies to focus on the bottom line of principles not just profits (Strauss and Howe, 1991, p. 398). It is further suggested that they will age in an independent mind-set and will not become either the busy senior citizen or loving grandparent but a new version of meditation and wisdom (Strauss and Howe, 1991, p. 404).

Younger Adults

Turn the pages of the scrapbook to look at the next group of adults, those individuals born between 1965 and 1976. They are called by a variety of names, Twentysomethings, the Boomerang Generation, the 13ers, and more often than not Generation X. The Twentysomethings originates from their predilection for not reaching decisive mileposts at predetermined times. They don't graduate from college at 22 within the traditional four years. The Boomerang term comes from the "start and stop" pattern of this cohort group. They go to school and return home. They get married and then come back. They get a job and return to their parents' home. In fact, more than one-fifth of 25-year-old Americans still live with their parents, and these include people who are married, living with a spouse, or employed full time (Mogelonsky, May 1996, p. 26). The 13er designation is due to Strauss and Howe and the Generation X label is left over from the Douglas Copland novel. The term Yiffies coined by a 1990 *Fortune* cover story might better describe this cohort group. Yiffie stands for young, individualistic, freedom-minded, and few (Dunn, 1993, p. 125).

This group is small in numbers. This baby recession was caused by the social changes of the '60s such as liberalized divorce laws, the birth control pill, the legalization of abortion, and the expansion of the economy particularly for women. All these factors conspired to produce the baby bust that followed the boom. This group of adults, like the cohort groups before them, are forging their own way and own sense of identity as to how life should be lived. They perceive work as having a different role in their lives and are more interested in seeking a balance between work and play. There are fewer of them to make up the new members of the work force so even though they are not faced with large numbers of competitors, the competition will seem stiff since the Yiffies live with competition on a global scale and, in addition, have clear ideas about just what they're looking for in the work world. They want work that is challenging, provides for freedom and flexibility, and allows them to enjoy their free time (Dunn, 1993, p. 126).

As the first latchkey group they were raised to be independent and fairly self-sufficient. Since there were fewer of them and parents felt guilty leaving them on their own, they have been lavished with toys and clothes rather than attention and time. This makes them particularly good consumers since they've been at it so long. A look inside their bedrooms, mostly in homes owned by Mom and Dad, gives credence to that consumerism. Get ready to find CDs, TVs, VCRs, credit cards, computers, sports equipment for all seasons, in-line skates and sneakers, keys to a fairly late model car, authentic looking fake IDs, and a variety of other amenities considered necessities in this cohort's world.

This is the group that was raised on Sesame Street and day care who now enjoy MTV and coffee bars. In fact MTV created a second channel, M2, to address the slightly older members of this group. They have been exposed to a myriad of external stimulation with a high-speed, excitement-filled, action-packed orientation that carries over into their preferences. They are more comfortable with computer games, cellular phones, and VCRs than they are with pick-up-sticks and nondigital clocks. This is a group that enjoys the 3Fs: food, fun, and friends. They go grazing, the act of wandering from place to place such as from one bar to a coffeehouse. They socialize in groups, and they are happiest with pals not partners. This emphasis upon groups draws them to sports bars, coffee salons, team sports, and special interest clubs.

Some marketers overlook this group because of its size and the fact the members are young and haven't yet reached higher levels of discretionary income. This would be a serious mistake for the experience industries. While the size of the group may be small in comparison to the Boomers, there are 44 million group members, and they would be the forty-fourth largest country in the world if we thought of them in that way (Dunn, 1993, p. 151). In addition, they have placed a heightened emphasis upon acquisitions as evidenced in their bedrooms, stereo systems, or cars. They also possess somewhat higher levels of discretionary income due to the lower cost of their living expenses and a preference for acquiring things.

Some marketers believe that this group could be better understood if people didn't continue to ignore the myriad of contradictions within their short lives and think the group would be better termed Cocoes: children of contradictory experiences. Think of the contradictions within their lives. They grew up during a long period of peace and economic prosperity only to face a major recession. They grew up living within the shadow of the cold war only to witness the demolition of the Berlin Wall and the fall of the USSR. They enjoyed unprecedented freedom and independence as latchkey children only to return home and become more dependent due to economic circumstances (Harrigan and Gilmartin, 1994, p. 24).

Another important factor and difference among this cohort group is the fact that the members are more tuned in through technology. They witnessed the Challenger disaster in 1986 when they were between the ages of 10 and 21. They watched the high-tech warfare of Desert Storm that played on prime time television, and they are networked to one another through the magic of E-mail and the Internet. This is the initial population of the global village and they have a great deal in common with other young adults throughout the world. This will surely have implications for marketing and experiences.

Strauss and Howe call this group the 13ers because they are the thirteenth American generation having been born between 1961 and 1981 and consider them members of the reactive generational cycle noted in chapter 3. They predict that the economic risk taking and cultural alienation facing this cohort group will cause them to seek stability in family life as well as to have significant impact on the growth of small, independent businesses and influence on products, style, and advertising (Strauss and Howe, 1991, p. 413).

Youth

Make way for the 1990s version of the baby boom. If you think you've been seeing strollers everywhere, it's not your imagination. The 1990 Census reports that there are 53 million children under the age of 14 (Guber and Berry, 1993, p. 8). Babies (and children) are back as their number portends, but the numbers tell us something else about this baby boom as well. This growing group is the most ethnically diverse group in the history of the United States. While the total non-white population of the United States is 28.4 percent, the percentage increases to 38 for children under five years of age according to the 1990 U. S. Census (Guber and Berry, 1993, p. 10). It is projected by the year 2005 that up to 60 percent of the population will be between the ages of 3 and 17 years (Sabir, 1996, p. 26). Make way for the first truly diverse population wave.

And that old adage about children being seen and not heard apparently doesn't apply to today's children whose voices and preferences influence where people eat and vacation as well as groceries purchased and videos rented. The impact of children on spending can be attributed to a number of factors including fewer children per household, single parents depending upon children within a household, older parents, and dual career couples (McNeal, 1992, p. 7). It's not just toys and candies either. Children are important as primary markets, influence markets, and future markets (McNeal, 1992, p. 15). They purchase or influence the purchase of goods and beverages, clothing, movies, vacations, groceries, computers, and even the family car.

They have unprecedented purchasing power. James McNeal, author of *Kids as Customers* and regarded as the country's leading expert on spending by children, originally estimated that children were spending or influencing approximately $150 billion annually (Horowitz, 1997a, p. 2A). However, according to the Toy Manufacturers of America, children aged 5 to 14 spent $27 billion in 1996, directly influenced $117 billion in purchases and indirectly influenced an additional $400 billion with personal spending for this age group projected at $67 billion by 2001 (Silverman, 1997, p. D3). No wonder business is targeting schools with an in-school television station and billboards plastered in hallways, bathrooms and on school buses. These kids have spending clout now and, of course, they are the market for the future.

They are a force to be reckoned with, and this is not overlooked by business. In 1996 McDonald's and Disney signed a 10-year deal where they agreed to serve as partners. Happy Meal trinkets will be based on Disney movie characters, and McDonald's will open outlets at the Florida and Paris theme parks as well as sponsoring the Dinoland attraction at Walt Disney World in Florida. This gives them a lock, or at least a lead, in the race for kids. Companies looking to attract the attention, influence, and spending power of children can borrow tips from Fox with their Kids Club and McDonald's with their Happy Meals. Sega has been particularly successful with sampling using its Sega Channel as a mechanism to let children sample new video games before they hit the retail stores. Mattel used meal tie-ins with both McDonald's and Burger King giving away miniature toy premiums of such brands as Hot Wheels cars and Barbie dolls. Even retailers not involved in the promotion reported increased sales (Fitzgerald, 1995, p. 21).

Even though marketers were all children once, marketing to children is not quite as easy as it seems. Children are sophisticated and experienced consumers and have some definite ideas about what they like. They are also avid TV viewers, making them accessible to the power of advertising messages. McNeal suggests that when developing promotional messages for children that marketers use the three P-tests: pro, parent, and pilot (McNeal, 1992, p. 178). The pro test refers to review by a person who understands how children think while the parent test focuses upon the appropriateness for children and parents alike. The pilot test is an opportunity to try out the message on children targeted. These three options could be employed when developing services or experiences for children as well.

Strauss and Howe call these children the Millennial Generation since they began appearing in 1982, and they will be the first generation of the new century. Following the four generation cycle, this group will be the civic type, meaning that they grew up increasingly protected as children and then rose to the occasion as adults making substantial contributions to society (Strauss and Howe,

---

 **Slice of Life**

Dan Acuff, coauthor of *What Kids Buy and Why*, groups children into the following advertising ages (Horowitz, 1997a, p. 2A):

- Birth to age 2: ads should be directed at parents whose goals for gifts rank in the order of safety, love, and stimulation.
- Ages 3 to 7: this is an age of fantasy when children seek power and control which explains the success of both Cabbage Patch kids and Power Rangers; influence of children upon their parents grows as evidenced by the "nag" factor.
- Ages 8 and 9: children get hooked on "causes" and desire toys and games that fulfill social or environmental well-being.
- Ages 10 to 12: high interest in games of challenge and rising importance of sports.
- Ages 13 to 15: double goals at this time to both "fit in" with friends while developing self-identity.
- Ages 16 to 19: end of childhood and toys and games as those items are replaced by CD players and pagers; this age group likes controversy in ads and products.

1991, p. 74). This prediction already seems to be coming true as the shift towards meeting the needs and protecting children is on. There's the huge increase in books and movies focused on the well-being of children and, of course, there was the March for Children on Washington, DC, in the spring of 1996. If this trend holds up, this group will be major players in the civic arena of their adulthood.

An important subsegment of this growing group is teens. Find SVP, a market research firm in New York, indicates that the teen population, people between the ages of 12 and 19, totaled nearly 30 million in 1996 with their numbers projected to grow to nearly 35 million by 2010, a more than 15 percent increase (Silverman, 1997, p. D1). They also found that the average teen has $70 a week to spend at his or her own discretion totaling $108 billion annually with personal expenditures for teens projected to reach $135.9 billion by 2001 (Silverman, 1997, p. D1).

While they may be substantive target market in their own right, they are also a group beset by a number of problems and challenges as well. According to child psychiatrist, George R. Holmes "adolescents are experiencing a wide variety of negative experiences that no previous generation has had to confront" (Holmes, 1995). Teen suicide, pregnancy, as well as smoking and drinking make them the focus of public, nonprofit, and social service agencies geared toward assisting this group through the troubled waters of today's adolescence.

Family-Household Plus Possibilities

Even a quick review of the section on youth begins to reinforce the notion that who you live with must make a difference in the marketing process. Robert Boutilier in his 1993 book, *Targeting Families: Marketing to and Through the New Family* has a number of insights and recommendations for marketers as they deal with the ever-evolving and complex family unit. He identifies five different types of household units (1993, pp. 10–11):

❖ Club Med has a Teen Club at Copper Mountain, Colorado, with teen-tempting programs such as mountain adventures, ski racing, snowboarding contests, and evening pizza parties.

❖ McDonald's brought back a whole host of kid promotions including Ty Teenie Beanie Babies, Disney CDs and cassette giveaways, and a copromotion effort with the Nickelodeon network.

❖ The Bloomington, Indiana, Parks and Recreation Department solves the "What is there to do around here?" perennial question with its Teen X-Treme Camp that offers team building, self-awareness, and physical and emotional challenges through canoeing, biking, hiking, and travel to sporting events, concerts, and amusement parks.

❖ Club Med, the former haven for swinging singles, set aside 10 percent of its $15 million advertising budget to encourage people to bring their kids along to the "antidote to civilization" (Guber and Berry, 1993, p. 131).

❖ Children are especially influential in shaping the family menus: 78 percent have a substantial say in where the family goes for fast food, and 55 percent get votes in the choice of full-service restaurants according to a *USA Weekend*/Roper Report on Consumer Decision Making in American Family.

❖ Fifty-seven percent of adults who travel with children say children are influential when it comes to choice of destinations for pleasure trips.

- the atomized (single roommates, singles, and childless couples),
- distanced (single mothers, blended families, and cohabitants with children),
- independent nuclear family (both parents and children living together),
- nondomiciled extended (extended family not living together but active participants in one another's lives), and
- domiciled extended (extended family living together).

Boutilier doesn't believe that the importance or value of family is diminishing, just changing over time, and he provides an overview of varying family structures on the basis of time periods (1993, pp. 10–14):

- traditional period: pre-1925, domiciled, extended families;
- modern period: 1925–1975, independent nuclear and nondomiciled extended;
- postmodern period: 1975–1990, atomized, distanced, independent nuclear, and nondomiciled extended; and
- neotraditional period: beyond 1990, distanced, independent nuclear, nondomiciled extended, and domiciled extended.

It is interesting to note the influence of economic factors on all of these household arrangements with the suggestion that reduced economic means in the twenty-first century will lead to larger and more interdependent households once again. Boutilier labels the post modern group, neotraditional, and cites commitment, care, community, equality, and diversity as characteristics of this new form (Boutilier, 1993, p. 13).

Boutilier believes that the household designations listed come into play in the family decision-making process and suggests that marketers ask the following questions related to this process (Boutilier, 1993, p. 84):

- for whom is the purchase being made;
- who are the principals in the decision-making process;
- what is the plot for purchasing;
- who wants what when; and
- assumptions about this process.

The Ps of the marketing mix take on a slightly different emphasis when placed in the family context as the product becomes "familized" in some of the obvious ways such as Camp Hyatt and McDonald's Play Places.

Households take on a different picture when factors such as age, cohort, and economic conditions are added to the mix. For instance, Grey researchers, feeling that the 1950s sitcom view of American life was wrong for today's world, sampled a representation of all U. S. households including single parents, childless career couples, and traditional families to identify four major attitudinal household segments that had varying perceptions of life and how life should be lived. They included the following (Piirto, 1991, p 101):

- *The Old Guard:* the oldest group of householders enjoying a peaceful and tranquil way of life almost totally unknown by the rest of the households.
- *Fledglings:* the youngest, smallest, and least affluent of the groups with a focus on getting started, whether the start focused upon career, school, or family.
- *America's New Grownup:* most householders fell into this group although they were subdivided into two distinct segments: the Vanguard and the Rear Guard; both groups want very much to have more time in their lives for having it all with the Vanguard group striving hard to reach this goal.

❖ The United Savings Bank in San Francisco took a slightly different approach and offered price breaks on financial services to families with a combined balance of more than $10,000 enabling extended families and several generations to pool their resources, and the bank was rewarded by increased deposits of 22 percent in that year (Boutilier, 1993, pp. 133, 141).
❖ MCI Friends & Families, which offered a 20 percent discount on long-distance calling, added 5 million new customers in the first 14 months of the offering (Boutilier, 1993, pp. 133, 141).

The Grey survey found that time was the most important commodity for this group known as America's New Grownups and they found that the more innovative Vanguard group devised five strategies to make the most of its most precious resource of time (Piirto, 1991, pp. 101–103):

- lightening up: doing less trivial and menial chores;
- sharing the load: having all family members pitch in to get chores done;
- getting and staying smart: using information to make consumer decisions;
- looking for shortcuts: gravitating to products and services that simplify and save time; and
- taking five: making room for five minutes of downtime or five days of vacation.

All aspects of variations within the family-household category including types of household units, changing time periods, and even attitudinal differences have impact on the marketing process. The identification of factors that appear to be important for a particular experience needs to be incorporated into the overall marketing approach.

Ethnic-Racial Plus Possibilities

The melting pot days of America are over, and there are a number of factors responsible for its demise. The Hispanic and African-American populations grew due to higher birth rates. Immigration continues to increase our population with the national origin of immigrants having changed over time with 40 percent of immigrants being Hispanic-Latino, 35 percent Asian, and only 12 percent European (Feather, 1994, p. 41). The melting pot is no longer made up of people sharing predominantly European roots and culture. Interracial marriages also contribute to this change as such unions have increased 78 percent between 1980 and 1992 according to the Bureau of the Census, Marital Status and Living Arrangements (Sandor, 1994, p. 38).

The shift of our society from the melting pot where all groups blended their ways and lived as one is giving way to a new way of interacting. This new approach is often referred to as a salad bowl. People exist within the same bowl touching one another but not losing their individual identity or distinct flavor. Evidence of the salad bowl approach as opposed to the melting pot are all around us. Salsa has replaced catsup as the number one condiment. Dining alternatives, particularly in metropolitan areas, reflect the spread of the emerging smorgasbord culture. This new wave of immigrants appear less eager to assimilate the dominant culture as those in the past have done. Acculturation is the term used to describe the way in which new immigrants merge their language and culture with that of their new country rather than abandoning their ways (Boutilier, 1993, 69).

Continuation of this trend could result in minorities comprising half of the total U. S. population by the year 2050 (Sandor, 1994, p. 38). Feather indicates that this sociocultural divergence is resulting in the global flow of people, customs, and information into local markets to form multiethnic *glocal* smorgasbords. Glocal refers to the current practice of combining global and local marketing strategies.

According to the U. S. Census Bureau reports and estimates:

Fast Facts

- the African-American population of about 33.8 million is expected to grow to 40 million by 2010;
- Asian-Americans make up the smallest minority group with fewer than 10 million, but that number should grow to more than 15 million by 2010;
- Latinos, the fastest-growing segment, with a current population of approximately 29 million is estimated to increase to 41 million by 2010, a rate five times faster than the general population; and
- the 33 million minorities are estimated to grow 50 percent faster than the nonminority population through the year 2050.

Experts in multicultural marketing point out that it is a mistake to assume that all nonwhite, non-European groups can or should be lumped together. Messages and experiences targeted for various groups must be culturally relevant. It is an error to assume all subgroups are the same. A Puerto Rican is not Mexican, and Mexicans are not Cubans. Koreans are not Vietnamese, and Vietnamese are not Filipino.

Working on making experiences and communication attempts culturally relevant is strongly recommended. Examples of language or cultural differences that didn't translate well are legendary embarrassments for the companies that committed those errors. Language can be a barrier in certain instances, but even when it isn't, people sometimes prefer the option of interacting and transacting with people who are like themselves. This same preference for presence carries over into advertisements and commercials. People are looking for people like themselves as being identified or associated with a product, service, or experience. Another suggestion made by ethnic marketers is to become associated with community events and concerns since these are often values of great importance to specific groups.

Examples of the impact of shifts in demographics include:

- the widespread and continued use of Bennetton's "United Colors of Bennetton" ad campaign directed at teens and young adults;
- the popularity of rap and hip-hop music among white as well as nonwhite teens;
- the increase in readership of such magazines as *Interrace* and *New People* as well as the introduction of new magazines such as *Moderna*, *Latino*, *Black Child*, *Today's Black Woman*, *Inside Asian America*, and *Vietnow*; and
- McDonald's created a commercial in which a Hispanic father and his daughter discuss her upcoming *quinceaniera*—fifteenth birthday social debut—while sharing an order of French fries.

Other People Plus Possibilities

Women

The traditional, mass marketing approach to both designing products and creating advertising messages generally reflected the white male as the definition of that mass market. Times have changed, and marketing for certain products, particularly big ticket items such as automobiles, life insurance, and home mortgages, has changed accordingly. As marketers have come to realize that women control or influence approximately $2 trillion of the $3 trillion in annual consumer spending in the United States, they have responded accordingly (Horowitz, 1995, B1).

Market research is beginning to make inroads into the critical differences between men and women as it relates to communication style, perceptions, attitudes and expectations, and, of course, shopping. Initial research indicates that men and women treat possessions differently. Women value possessions that enhance interpersonal relationships while men see products as a way to exert power over others or serve as status differentiations. "Compared to most men, most women seem to value caring over dominating" (Peter and Olson, 1994, p. 371).

Evidence that the marketplace is responding to these differences can be seen in the sneaker wars. Nike and Reebok have pushed male consumers and athletes, making them share center court as they reach out to the lucrative female sneaker market. The NPD research firm reported that for the first time women outspent men on athletic shoes by a margin of $5.4 billion to $5.2 billion in 1994. NPD also predicted that the men's market would become flat or decline with women's footwear expenditures increasing 19 percent to $6.2 billion (Enrico, 1995, p. B1).

The shift in advertising expenditures as well as content of the ads attest to the recognition of these gender differences. Nike has created empowerment ads

*Close***Seup**

National tracking of golf patterns reveals that female participation has increased from 4.5 million in 1986 to 5.2 million in 1996. Not all women play golf for the same reasons and in the same way as one another. A study indicating these differences created five different profiles of women golfers as follows (Ubinas, 1997, p. 1):

- Escape Artist—the 17 percent of women who play to get away from job or daily responsibilities.
- Traditionalists—the 23 percent of women who are primarily private club members who play to get outdoors and spend time with family.
- Hobnobbers—the 21 percent of female golfers who consider the game an image-raising or career-building activity.
- Golf Nuts—the 20 percent of the players who just love the challenge of the game itself.
- Party Putters—the 19 percent who play purely as a social activity.

that tie participation in sports by young women as a deterrent to domestic abuse and teen pregnancy. Reebok has countered with programs for young female athletes such as Girls' Sport Summit.

If these differences are apparent in attitudes and values related to products, just imagine the influence such gender differences must have upon experiences since they are undertaken specifically to address intrinsic needs.

Gays and Lesbians

Overlooked Opinions, a gay- and lesbian-oriented consumer research firm in Chicago, conducted a survey in 1990 that estimated the economic size of the gay and lesbian economy as $514 billion (Luckenbill, 1995, p. 65). While this estimate, as well as the number of Americans who are homosexual, often comes under controversy and is subject to conjecture, suffice it to say that, as the title of Lukenbill's book suggests, this market represents "untold millions." While there have been a variety of studies directed at this group, the most definitive is believed to be the Yankelovich MONITOR Gay and Lesbian Perspective conducted in 1994. According to the Yankelovich sample, approximately six percent of the population identified themselves as "gay/lesbian/homosexual" and that the sample was similar to the heterosexual population as it related to age, gender, ethnicity, occupation, employment, income, and political affiliation. However, homosexuals differ as they were more likely to have attended graduate school, be self-employed, and live in a large metropolitan area (Luckenbill, 1995, p. 92).

This study also uncovered five areas of differences between the homosexual and the heterosexual populations. They included the following (Luckenbill, 1995, p. 101):

- individuality and self-understanding,
- social interaction,
- diversity of life's experiences,
- independence, and
- skepticism and self-protection.

According to the findings, this group has a greater need to both understand and express themselves as well as an interest and predilection for socializing and experiencing new places, products, and things. It should also be noted that stress, lack of trust, and a psychology of disenfranchisement are a part of this picture.

This sense of disenfranchisement has important implications for experience providers. Since experiences must afford this group:

- the opportunity for recognition and respect;
- association with "people like me;"
- sense of emotional, social, and physical security;
- independence; and
- stress relief including self-indulgence and escapism. (Luckenbill, 1995, p. 106–107)

Fast Facts

- ❖ City comptroller Alan Hevis conservatively estimated that the Gay Games IV and Cultural Festival held in New York City in 1994 generated in excess of $400 million to the New York City economy (Luckenbill, 1995, p. 44).
- ❖ According to Voter Research and Surveys (VRS) in the 1992 Presidential election, 71 percent of gay men and 69 percent of lesbian women under the age of 45 voted compared to 56 percent for straight men and 58 percent for straight women (Luckenbill, 1995, p. 23).
- ❖ In 1996 two new travel books were introduced into the marketplace, *Fodor's Gay Guide to the USA* and *Gay USA.*

Companies or businesses interested in promoting products and services to gay and lesbian consumers must do so in a variety of ways. Corporations must have policies that are favorable to nondiscrimination practices on the basis of sexual orientation. There needs to be evidence of benefits which are sensitive to domestic partnerships and social diversity among employees (Luckenbill, 1995, pp. 113–114). Advertising is indeed a factor. The Apple computer ad that showed Martina Navratilova, a gay woman, standing next to Art Moon, a straight man, with both of them holding PowerBooks is the kind of ad that is well-received, and it appeared in both popular gay and lesbian publications as well as general interest magazines. Cause-related marketing and event sponsorships are other viable marketing options as well.

- ❖ Olivia Cruises and Resorts, an Oakland, California, company that is the nation's largest organizer of trips for women, arranged a trip for 659 lesbians through Club Med's Rent a Village program. In addition to the food and fun provided by a Club Med vacation, these women were afforded a vacation experience where they could be who they were and behave as they chose. Incidentally on this Club Med outing, 30–35 percent of the women had been on a previous trip with the company. Olivia boasts a return percentage as high as 50 percent on some trips (Adams, 1996, p. B15).
- ❖ American Airlines allows gay and lesbian customers to obtain bereavement fares in the event of the death of a domestic partner and allow frequent-flier miles to be used between domestic partners as well. They also employ a sales staff of five dedicated to the gay market.
- ❖ In 1993 Avis and in 1994 National car rental companies began to waive the additional driver fee for domestic partners.
- ❖ The Philadelphia, Pennsylvania, Convention and Visitors Bureau requested Gray Line Tours to offer packages to attract gay visitors resulting in Philadelphia Phrolic tour and Philadelphia Phantasy. The bureau also distributes *The Gay Guide to Center Philadelphia* and *Philadelphia Gay and Lesbian Travel Newsletter.*

It is of particular interest to note that many of the business opportunities cited by Luckenbill for this market include those within the experience industry such as food and drink, health and fitness, entertainment, and travel.

People With Disabilities

Take note of an opportunity to attract another significant and growing target market group. A report issued as part of the Americans with Disabilities Act found that 48.9 million Americans, nearly 19 percent of the population, have some kind of disability that interferes with normal functioning (Dicksinson, 1996, p. 15). This group, estimated to be one-fifth of the population or comparable to the population of Canada or the number of Spanish-speaking Americans, is not one to be overlooked. Targeting this group is a must for the experience industry.

The size of this market group is significant, but perhaps of even greater significance is the projected growth in this area due to the aging population and resultant limitations this will bring. The Baby Boomers are not going to stop experiencing life because their activity level has been impaired. They won't want to stop traveling or stop taking their grandchildren to fun places. Becoming

❖ The Total Workout in Petersburg, West Virginia, helps members with disabling conditions make the appropriate choices by designating in the program descriptions classes that are suitable for people with arthritis, people with heart conditions, or people using wheelchairs (Winters, 1995, p. 16).

❖ The Santa Barbara, California, Department of Parks and Recreation has a summer camp program for wheelchair-bound youngsters with wheelchair-bound counselors as role models.

❖ Sports stadiums and theaters are providing rail seating for attendees in wheelchairs as well as seating for their guests to afford them the opportunity to attend, participate, and experience.

❖ Sober Vacations International and Celebrate Life Tours offer a number of special vacation packages and trips for recovering alcoholics and substance abusers.

❖ Hospital Audiences Inc. (HAI), provider of cultural services for people with disabling conditions in New York City, publishes a guide for travelers and a hotline for information related to physical accessibility for cultural venues, hotels, and restaurants as well as adaptations for audio descriptions of performances, touch tours of museums, and sign language availability.

❖ Alamo Rent-A-Car offers personalized pick up and delivery of rental cars for physically challenged customers and National Car Rental will provide rental vehicles with hand controls with 24-hour notice and allows visually impaired customers to rent when accompanied by an able-bodied driver (Making Travel Accessible, 1996, p. A5).

❖ Hilton Hotels Corporations remodeled 2,700 rooms at a cost of $22,000 per room to make them fully accessible (Making Travel Accessible, 1996, p. A5).

cognizant of the potential of this group and making plans to have them become a part of an experience is not only the right thing to do, but the profitable one as well.

People Plus Geographic Location

What difference does place of residence make for experience marketers? Some of them are really quite obvious. People in the northeast United States are a big market for sunny resorts in Florida and the Caribbean during the inclement winter months. The resort areas of Palm Springs, California, and Puerto Vallarta, Mexico, would be more likely to target the weekend getaway crowds from Los Angeles and Orange County than people shivering in Manhattan.

Geographic locations translate into accessibility for certain types of experiences and are dependent upon terrain or climatic factors. It should come as no surprise that according to SRDS's Lifestyle Marketing Analysis for 1995 that geographic areas with the highest percentage of people involved in boating or sailing were Fort Myers, Florida, and Charleston, South Carolina, and that the places with the highest levels of snow skiing included locations in Alaska, Oregon, Montana, and Colorado where there is ready access to mountains and snow.

Geography does not always present a clear-cut picture of experience opportunities solely based upon physical location. For instance, the Pacific Northwest cities of Seattle, Spokane, and Portland buy the least amount of fast foods in the United States. Before you think that it's something in the Northwest's water, consider other cities with below average expenditures for fast food including Boston, Philadelphia, Baltimore, and Washington (Page, 1995, p. 179). What other plus factors are at work here?

Identifying geographic markets that are particularly good for specific experiences requires other things beyond just a good road map. In an attempt to identify good markets for a variety of different products and

❖ The National Health Interview identified a total of 231.5 million American adults aged 18 and over as having chronic activity limitations (Reedy, 1993, p. 75).

❖ Census Bureau estimates for 1992 found that 15.2 million Americans aged 15 and older were unable to see, hear, speak, lift and carry objects, climb stairs, or walk. Another 19 million have difficulty performing those activities and 14.7 million Americans have limited abilities to perform socially defined roles and tasks that involve such things as family, work, recreation, or self-care activities.

❖ The number of people reporting health problems is (Winters, 1995, p. 13):

    7.2 million with problems due to arthritis or rheumatism,

    5.7 million with back or spine problems,

    4.6 million have heart trouble, and

    13 million have diabetes mellitus.

❖ Americans with disabilities make up 9 percent of the population but account for 15 percent of all travelers (Making Travel Accessible, 1996, p. A5).

services, *American Demographics* combined data from two sources: national-level estimates of household expenditures by age and income in various product and service categories and metro-level household demographics by Strategic Mapping from Santa Clara, California (Mogelonsky, January 1996, p. 20). The results offered estimates of expenditures for such things as food away from home, alcohol, healthcare, personal care, and entertainment. Not surprisingly, the combination of geography with various demographic patterns produced results that made sense. Areas with higher income levels such as San Jose, California, and Middlesex-Somerset-Hunterdom, New Jersey, were identified as good locations for both eating out and buying clothes and, as could be expected, the areas with highest expenditures for healthcare included many locations in Florida with higher percentages of older Americans (Mogelonsky, January 1996, pp. 24–25).

Geography is terrific when combined with other plus factors that we know about people. For instance, a review of the parameters of an experience will help marketers understand the role and importance of location in their efforts. If an experience is a once in a lifetime pursuit as opposed to a weekly event, the impact of location varies. People may travel around the world to climb Mount Everest but won't venture more than two miles to go to a movie. Health and fitness clubs need to be located no more than 20 minutes away from home or work while it doesn't matter that the spa at LaCosta may require travel by plane for a weekend getaway trip.

Creating Particle Markets

True success for experience marketers is the creation of an experience that matches the participant's needs, wants, expectations, dreams, and aspirations. Such creation is both part art and part science. This chapter has provided information and suggestions for a number of people plus categories in an attempt to provide some of the science of this process. The art of this approach involves the marketer's selection of which specific plusses to select and how to intermingle these characteristics in such a way as to create a particle market.

Even large companies think small and construct consumer options and experiences based on geographic preferences. Some examples include the following (Horowitz, 1997b, pp. B1–B2):

- Friday's with its 345 restaurants nationwide allows its franchises to incorporate up to 30 regional items on menus alongside the 70 national items resulting in chicken-fried steaks being served in Texas but not in Michigan.
- McDonald's introduced its latest big burger nationally but with regional sauce variations such as mayonnaise in Iowa and pepper-mustard in Louisiana.
- Miller Brewing found that sales of Miller Lite increased when they added a Lone Star silhouette to each can distributed in Texas.
- *TV Guide* created 25 different regional covers for its NFL preview issue.

The art and science of particle market creation pays off in a number of ways. It enables an experience provider to design an experience that meets very specific needs and expectations. It allows for that same provider to communicate in a much more focused manner with this particle market. And last the effective creation of such a market ensures the satisfaction and delight of the participants who embody this particle market which means ongoing success for the experience provider. The travel industry can serve as a role model for experience providers desiring to create particle markets. The Closeup on the travel industry overviews the extent and success of this approach.

Review the approaches used by the travel industry and begin to practice on your own. Practice makes perfect when it comes to identifying, constructing, and creating particle markets. Reviewing the four components in chapter 3 and combining those components with additional information presented in this chapter provides a basis for constructing particle markets.

Create Your Own

A quick look at the three particles suggested in the Framework for Creating Particle Marketing reveals the Golden "Go For It" Girls, the Mild Ones, and the

Continued on page 102

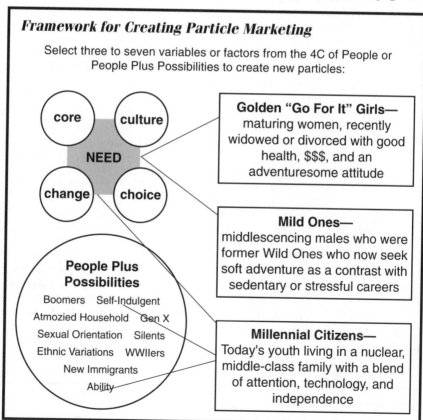

Framework for Creating Particle Marketing

Select three to seven variables or factors from the 4C of People or People Plus Possibilities to create new particles:

core culture

NEED

change choice

People Plus Possibilities

Boomers Self-Indulgent
Atmozied Household Gen X
Sexual Orientation Silents
Ethnic Variations WWIIers
New Immigrants
Ability

Golden "Go For It" Girls— maturing women, recently widowed or divorced with good health, $$$, and an adventuresome attitude

Mild Ones— middlescencing males who were former Wild Ones who now seek soft adventure as a contrast with sedentary or stressful careers

Millennial Citizens— Today's youth living in a nuclear, middle-class family with a blend of attention, technology, and independence

The Travel Industry

An industry that has taken people plus seriously and has applied psychographics to its target marketing is travel. The travel industry pulled it all together to create an understanding of who travels and what they need and want as well as how travelers differ from one another. Here is an overview of some of the information and suggestions pulled together using this process.

On one level it is easy to begin to develop a profile of important markets for the travel industry because there are two resources needed to travel: time and money. Those two factors have significantly changed the travel picture in this country. With the increase in the number of working women, there is more money to spend for discretionary activities such as travel, but decidedly less time and more difficulty coordinating travel plans between two jobs. As a result, there has been an increase in shorter vacations or weekend trips. Two-week family vacations are increasingly rare while one-week vacations are more the norm interspersed with a number of "weekend getaways" throughout the year. However, limiting a discussion of travel plans to just time and money wouldn't begin to create a complete picture of who's traveling or how, why, when, and where they're going. Review the following people plus factors shaping the particle markets of the travel industry.

Age and cohort groupings impact travel experiences in a variety of ways including the availability of time, availability of financial resources, and the willingness to use those resources as well as overall aim of traveling and benefits being sought. Cohort variations include the following:

- Depression Era: have time and money although careful about spending it; look for safety, comfort, and convenience; good market for group and off-season travel.
- World War IIers: beginning to have more time and interest in travel and are likely to cruise for convenience and travel for new experience and learning.
- Early Boomers: good prospects for soft adventure vacations as well as new age alternatives with a mix of sport and culture thrown in the mix.
- Late Boomers: good candidates for active, go-for-growth-oriented vacations as package with all encompassing prices so they bring the kids along.
- Busters: not willing or likely to let money, school, or career stand in the way of pursuing affordable but independent jaunts and activities.
- Boomlets: this group has been packed up and taken places almost since they were born and will continue to travel with parents, grandparents, and friends.

Make a quick mental review of travel options and see how the travel industry has responded to these different cohort groups. Grandtravel out of Maryland was developed specifically to create travel packages for grandparents and their grandchildren. The motor coach industry has expanded its base to incorporate off-season, reasonably priced tours to almost anywhere for the older traveler. Resorts including places like Canyon Ranch in Arizona where previously well-to-do, older matrons were pampered now invite families to come along for mountain biking and canyon hikes. Resorts in the Caribbean come complete with "nannies by the week" for families in need of such services.

Closeup continued

In addition to some generational differences in types of travel and the level of accommodations sought, there are some other people plus differentiations among travelers. Psychographics does indeed play a big part in the travel market. A 1989 Gallup survey focused the industry on some of these differences when it identified five different types of recreational travelers as follows:

- Dreamers—fascinated by travel and attach great importance to the meaning travel adds to their life;
- Adventurers—independent and confident, likely to seek new experiences valuing diversity in destinations and cultures;
- Worriers—lack confidence in their ability to manage the travel experience and this attitude causes them to travel the least of all groups;
- Economizers—seek travel as a break from routine and look for value rather than adventure or special attention; and
- Indulgers—look for travel to provide pampering and special attention.

Marriott Resorts in the Caribbean and Bermuda conducted a survey that found that almost half of respondents felt that their vacations fell short of their expectations. This led to the development of a vacation profile self-test designed to help travelers have the most satisfying vacation by ascertaining whether they are an Adventurer, Romantic, Athlete, or Indulger. As might be expected, these different categories of travelers look for different things while on vacation. The Adventurer looks to explore new places and cultures, the Romantic to enhance relationship with spouse or significant other, the Athlete to pursue new or favorite sporting activities, and the Indulger to be pampered. As a result of this exercise, Marriott was able to steer people towards various resorts that would best meet their needs and the needs of traveling companions.

The travel industry accommodates these different psychographic preferences in other ways as well. Road Scholar, a division of Saga International, mixes the pleasures of travel with the joys of learning. Splendid China, a new theme park in Orlando, Florida, provides the best of both worlds allowing more nervous travelers to visit China and experience the food, the culture, and the mysteries of the far East without leaving their native land and creature comforts. Global Fitness Adventures combines the luxury of a spa with the adventure of exotic locations. Motor coach tours have entered the new age by adding more amenities and incorporating opportunities for independent exploring while continuing to provide an economical and comfortable alternative for travel.

Think of the number of different cruise lines that exist. Each cruise line has a different personality destined to attract and suit different types of people. Carnival works well for families traveling with children who like to be casual and have fun. Holland America suits the tastes of a somewhat older more sophisticated crowd. The tall ships of Star Clipper and Windjammer Cruises attract the "let me kick back, relax, and be casual" crowd. Special Expeditions would be just the thing for the outdoor, adventure-oriented while Seabourn would be perfect for those people who enjoy exotic destinations but in a "tuxedo" kind of fashion.

The travel industry has done an incredible job of adopting a people plus approach to target marketing. They are able to combine the potential target groups with benefits sought in a most effective fashion.

Action Agenda

❖ Take a trip to your local drug store, venture into the toothpaste section, and spend some time practicing your ability to subsegment by demographics, benefits sought, and lifestyle preferences groups of people who chose a product.

❖ Conduct focus groups or intercept interviews before or after people participate in your experience to identify the benefit(s) being sought as well as needs that drew them to this particular experience.

❖ Review the people plus categories within this chapter—age, family-household status, health or ability level, ethnic-racial characteristics, geographic location—and attempt to pinpoint the characteristics, descriptors, or behavior most important for your experience.

❖ Select two to four subgroups of participants and create pictures of them for your experience photo album; be sure to incorporate as much information and detail as possible to get the clearest picture of these particle markets.

❖ Participate in an experience other than your own, observe the particle markets involved in this experience, and take what you've learned back to your place.

Millennial Citizens. The first group refers to maturing women, widowed or divorced, who have the resources (health, money, and attitude) to go forward and experience many aspects of life. Watch for them to pursue travel, learning opportunities, and some combination of pleasure and purpose. The second group identified, the Mild Ones, are mid-40s or so males who were probably once called the Wild Ones because they never missed an adventure. In this new life stage they will continue to be good markets for outdoor and soft adventure experience providers. The last group identified are the Millennial Citizens. These young people are likely to live in middle-class homes with two parents who both pursue careers.

Transition Tracking

From	To
Target Market Strategies	*Particle Markets*

Marketers traditionally envisioned target markets as being mass, segmented, or niche. Mass marketing strategies were undifferentiated and included everyone. Segmented strategies would develop specific approaches for various segments or groups of the market such as men or senior citizens. Niche markets were specific target marketing approaches for a small segment of the market such as women in the Midwest who were over 65 years of age and who lived alone. An additional target marketing approach that involved focusing on either the group of people or the benefit being sought was used as well.

Particle markets bring together the best of these approaches by creating strategies based on specific traits, characteristics, or needs of a group of people who share similar qualities. These people plus possibilities incorporate a strong psychographic component and can be used effectively to design and deliver experiences.

The support they received in the home coupled with their exposure to technology and sense of independence will thrust them into the prototype of tomorrow's high achievers and leaders. As a particle market they will both seek and have provided for them by supportive parents and adoring grandparents, great grandparents, and possibly even great-great grandparents all sorts of opportunities to grow and experience.

Every experience provider is different and as such is best suited to address certain types of needs and expectations. As the experience industry continues to bloom and grow and as people change, developing new and emerging needs, we invite you to create your own particle markets. Use the framework illustrated previously, make your own selections, and practice the art and science of creating particle markets.

Sources

Adams, Jane Meredith. (1996, March 24). "Free" week in Ixtapa. *Boston Sunday Globe.*

Boutilier, Robert. (1993). *Targeting families: Marketing to and through the new family.* Ithaca, NY: American Demographic Books.

Dicksinson, Rachel J. (1996, May). The power of the paralympics. *American Demographics.*

Doka, Kenneth, J. (1992, July–August). When gray is golden. *The Futurist.*

Dunn, William. (1993). *The baby bust—A generation comes of age.* Ithaca, NY: American Demographic Books.

Enrico, Dottie. (1995, October 11). Makers pick women as most valuable market. *USA Today.*

Feather, Frank. (1994). *The future consumer.* Toronto, Canada: Warwick Publishing.

Fitzgerald, Kate. (1995, March 20). Promotions gaining kid appeal. *Advertising Age.*

Guber, Selina S., & Berry, Jon. (1993). *Marketing to and through kids.* New York, NY: McGraw-Hill.

Guttman, Monika. (1996, April 22). Facing the facts of life. *U. S. News and World Report.*

Harrigan, Judy, & Gilmartin, J. J. (1994, June 24). Xers are misnamed: How about "cocoes"? *Advertising Age.*

Holmes, George R. (1995). *Helping teenagers into adulthood: A guide for the next generation.* Westport, CT: Praegers Publishing.

Horowitz, Bruce. (1997, December 18). Retailers in search of customers for life. *USA Today.*

Horowitz, Bruce. (1997, October 3). One taste doesn't fit all, shrewd sellers discover. *USA Today.*

Horowitz, Bruce. (1995, June 27). Big league advertisers line up to sponsor women's sports. *USA Today.*

Luckenbill, Grant. (1995). *Untold millions—Positioning your business for the gay and lesbian consumer revolution.* New York, NY: HarperBusiness.

Making travel accessible for all people. (1996, September 12). *USA Today.*

McNeal, James U. (1992). *Kids as customers: A handbook of marketing to children.* New York, NY: Lexington.

Mochis, George. (1996, September). Life stages of the mature market. *American Demographics.*

Mogelonsky, Marcia. (1996, May). The rocky road to adulthood. *American Demographics.*

Mogelonsky, Marcia. (1996, January). America's hottest markets. *American Demographics.*

Page, Heather. (1995, October). Fast-food facts. *Entrepreneur.*

Pappano, Laura. (1994, November 27). The new old generation. *The Boston Globe Magazine.*

Parents are listening to kids. (1990, January 24). *USA Today.*

Peter, J. Paul, & Olson, Jerry C. (1994). *Understanding consumer behavior.* Burr Ridge, IL: Irwin.

Piirto, Rebecca. (1991). *Beyond mind games: The marketing power of psychographics.* Ithaca, NY: American Demographic Books.

Reedy, Joel. (1993). *Marketing to consumers with disabilities.* Chicago, IL: Probus Publishing.

Sabir, Madirar Z. (1996, March). Ad execs to kids, "Buy this." *Black Enterprise.*

Sandor, Gabrielle. (1994, June). The "other" America. *American Demographics.*

Silverman, Fran. (1997, October 4). When spending is kids' stuff. *Hartford Courant.*

Stone, Andrea. (1996, March 22–24). Not boomers, not xers, they are tweeners. *USA Today.*

Strauss, William, & Howe, Neil. (1991). *Generations: The history of America's future 1584 to 2069.* New York, NY: William Morrow and Company.

Ubinas, Helen. (1997, July 31). When their way is the fairway. *Hartford Courant.*

Ubinas, Helen. (1996, July 8). Gone on dogs. *Hartford Courant.*

Underhill, Paco. (1996, April). Seniors as markets. *American Demographics.*

Who's in? Mature adults. (1992, October). *Programmers Information Network.*

Winters, Catherine. (1995, May). The Special Potential. *Club Industry.*

Wolfe, David, B. (1992, September). Business's midlife crisis. *American Demographics.*

Wolfe, David, B. (1990). *Serving the ageless market.* New York, NY: McGraw-Hill.

Flashback

Traditional marketing was based on the 4Ps of product, place, price, and promotion. The first P, product, consisted of a number of different levels reflecting the essential benefit of the product as well as add-ons such as features, style, and warranties. The second P, the place variable, originally referred to origin of manufacture and subsequent location of purchase. Price was the third variable and focused primarily on the actual amount of money required to purchase a product. The fourth P of traditional marketing was promotion. The experience marketing version of this P will be addressed in the next chapter.

Service marketing changed the role and meaning of the first three variables. In the service sector, the price variable merged with the place variable. As place became more than where something was manufactured, it evolved into where the customer would use the service. In a similar manner, the fact that the customer must be involved in the service, or make an effort to arrange for the service, influenced the definition of price to incorporate time and effort on the part of the customer. The role of the customer in the service process has substantially changed the traditional definition of product, place, and price.

Lovelock, Berry, and others included a number of elements within their frameworks of service marketing to replace or augment the existing traditional 4Ps of marketing. Factors such as nature of the service, involvement of the customer in the service, the absence of inventories, and the importance of time and distribution channels are examples. The advent of experience marketing builds on the factors established in the service marketing process and incorporates additional factors that relate directly to the inner needs addressed by experiences.

Chapter 5

The Third P: Peripherals

Is it just like Hertz? Not exactly!

repeated tag line from a Hertz commercial

Introduction to the Peripherals

The initial two Ps of experience marketing are parameters of the experience itself and people. The parameters of the experience serve as a substitute for the traditional first P of marketing, the product. The second P of experience marketing, people, reinforces an underlying fundamental of experience marketing that if people aren't present or involved then no experience actually takes place.

This third P of experience marketing, peripherals, refers to multiple factors and variables related to and involved in the entire process. Peripherals add to the substance of the experience. They provide meaning for the participant and can be used to differentiate experiences from one another. Many of the early peripheral factors entered the marketing realm with the introduction of service marketing and included such factors as physical evidence, participants, policies and procedures, public image, and political impact (O'Sullivan, 1991, p. 143).

This third P of experience marketing incorporates the place and price variables while also making room for the myriad of little things that make the experience the experience. The smaller Ps within peripherals include:

- place (including both time and location),
- price,
- packaging (physical evidence, perks, personalization),
- participants,
- policies and procedures,
- public image,

- patterns of demand, and
- popularity cycle.

Each of these eight smaller Ps encompasses a variety of factors shaping the experience and the impact of the experience upon the participant.

This sum total of peripherals reminds one of the tag line in the Hertz commercial in which the subordinate responsible for making the rental car arrangements repeatedly responds "not exactly" to his boss. While running through the rain, the boss, concerned with variations within the rental car experience, continues to ask about such things as location of the rental car office and availability of curbside drop-off.

The "not exactly" phrase repeated by the subordinate refers to the peripherals of their current rental car situation in comparison to the Hertz experience. The smaller Ps within peripherals, in conjunction with one another, make the experience exactly what it is for the participant. The number and range of smaller Ps within peripherals can vary substantially.

Place

Place can refer to and include any number of factors including the actual location where an experience occurs or the area or facility where the experience takes place. Place can also refer to timing or scheduling since people need to be "in place" to partake of the experience. The role and importance of place within experience marketing is substantial and incorporates the following:

- physical or geographic location;
- accessibility—convenience, number of locations, perception of accessibility;
- area or facility; and
- timing factors—time of day, week, month, season and frequency of event or participation.

Geographic location can and does make a difference. You can't downhill ski without mountains and sailing is nearly impossible without a body of water. Geographic location makes Florida and Arizona desirable in the cold, winter months while the cool breezes from the coastal waters off Nags Head, North Carolina, or the refreshing mountain air of the Grand Tetons are locations of choice for the summer months. Sometimes geographic location makes an unusual experience possible as in the case of Mount Hood in Oregon. Its location, elevation, and physical terrain make snowboarding a reality in July.

Geographic or physical location impacts the experience in other ways

Recall a memorable or favorite experience of your own. **TAG** Identify factors or elements that initially drew you to that particular experience as well as elements that either enhanced or detracted from that experience.

as well. Six Flags in New Jersey has a location that puts it within a day's journey of major Northeast population centers making it a winner in the proximity to target market category. Any experience provider that requires a substantial number of participants to make the business viable needs to select a location that is accessible to a sufficient number of people or is located in such a way as to make ease of access to the experience a reality.

Physical location also contributes to actual and perceived accessibility by participants. Ease of access or perceived ease of access is paramount. Convenience is key in today's world. A quick trip down any interstate highway with billboards extolling the "E-Z" on and off status of service providers reinforces this premise.

A highly visible or convenient location has promotional value as well. Miniature golf courses are often located adjacent to well-traveled roads featuring a large, attention-getting display of some kind to catch the eye of children trapped in the backseat of passing cars. Health and fitness clubs often locate next to busy commuter routes so prospective customers repeatedly see the location and begin to picture the club as convenient to both home and work.

The importance of location as it relates to convenience and proximity to people is a longstanding strategy of McDonald's. Its recent establishment of restaurants in Wal-Marts, gas stations, and public parks is just the latest entry as it closes the convenience gap for sizable numbers of people.

Accessibility and the perception of accessibility influence behavior. Michigan's Mackinac Island and Italy's Venice ban automotive transportation. This discourages some tourists who don't want to drag bag and baggage on and off the ferry or vaporetta and subsequently increases the number of day-trippers to both locations. This perceived inaccessibility can work in reverse as well as people flock to these two tourist spots knowing that they will have it almost to themselves at the end of the day. The same is true for more remote Caribbean islands or sections of

Physical Location and Accessibility

❖ Thousands of people take to the Appalachian Trail every year due in part to the trail's location from Maine to Georgia along the Eastern seaboard which is readily accessibly to 120 million Americans.

❖ The Radisson Empire Hotel in New York City took advantage of its location and created a Discover Central Park package that included a room for two nights, boat rental, picnic lunch, zoo passes, and tickets to a SummerStage concert.

❖ The residents in Unity Township, Pennsylvania, and Wichita, Kansas, find the latest bestsellers sandwiched between the meat and the produce sections of local grocery stores.

❖ The monastery of St. Michelle in northern France owes its immense popularity to its lofty location that is rendered both accessible and inaccessible due to tidal changes.

Area or Facility

❖ The Wilderness Lodge at Disney World with its three-story, double-sided stone fireplace captures the spirit of the great lodges found in the national parks at the turn of the century while being fully equipped with gourmet dining and outlets for hair dryers.

❖ Summerside at Mount Tom, Massachusetts, is really two facilities in one: an action-packed water park for children alongside a pool complete with an outdoor cafe for adults.

❖ The McDonald's in Freeport, Maine, is located in the historic Gore House, a traditional New England colonial, to conform with both zoning regulations and attention to local aesthetics.

Hawaii that are more difficult to reach for tourists. Inaccessibility, real or perceived, heightens the value of some experiences for certain people.

This parameter will undergo vast changes and possible redefinition as technology proceeds to make inroads into experiences. The development and availability of virtual experiences and Internet explorations are sure to alter the way place is perceived and used with experience marketing.

Place can be the actual area or facility itself, and the role it plays varies within the experience. Not all areas or facilities which provide the same or a similar service are the same from an experience perspective. Sleeping in a lean-to shelter in the National Forest is an outdoor facility, but it is not the same as the KOA campground complete with cable TV hookup and hot showers. Fun seekers who are in search of nostalgia rather than high-tech would go to Coney Island in Brooklyn, New York, or Cedar Point in Sandusky, Ohio, rather than the newer Six Flags Amusement Park operations. A mountain retreat in the Adirondacks of upstate New York means going to a camp. The only wrinkle is the accouterments can range from the simplicity of Timberlock on Indian Lake with no electricity or car access to the deluxe exclusivity of The Point with handsome beds, fine linens, and champagne for each of the eleven guest rooms (MacIsaac, June 1996, pp. 87, 139). The facility or the area sure makes a difference! In fact, it can even make for entirely different experiences.

The precise setting within a location is a factor as well. Where one sits or where one is located can and often does make a difference. The people sitting in the front rows at any of the Sea World whale or seal shows know that the prized front seats can make for a more "refreshing" experience as the antics of the killer whales and sea lions make a real splash. Being seated in a restaurant next to the kitchen, the entrance, or the service area alter the dining experience. Securing seats front row, center for a rock concert is a different experience from dragging one's blanket to the lawn seating area. What's even more interesting is that there are people who prefer experiences at both ends of the spectrum.

Location can relate to number of locations. If an area or facility is either one of a kind or only available in one location, it is considered exclusive. There's only one Grand Canyon and one Paris so these locations are considered exclusive.

Location

❖ The Grand Hotel on Mackinac Island in the upper peninsula of Michigan, the Balsams in New Hampshire, and the Otesega in Cooperstown, New York, are "one of a kind," grand, resort hotels located in out of the way retreat spots from yesteryear (exclusive strategy).

❖ The Ritz-Carlton Resorts, luxurious places to play and stay, are located in a small number of upscale beach locations such as Amelia Island, Naples, and Laguna Niguel (selective strategy).

❖ Hotel chains such as Days Inns and Holiday Inns operate establishment in many medium-sized cities as well as the off-ramps of most interstate highways (intensive strategy).

Since there are four or five different countries in which people can experience an African safari, the number of locations for this experience makes these locations selective.

Experiences that either seem to be available everywhere or are clustered together are neither exclusive nor selective. Hospitals and miniature golf courses are available nearly everywhere. This density requires a concerted effort to infuse unique elements of an experience to attract their share of participants. Hospitals often specialize in a particular kind of service while the miniature golf courses go with themes of some kind. The premise behind this intensive strategy is to offer as many experiences in one location as possible. This resembles what is being done in the greater Orlando, Florida, area. Large numbers of experience providers have located there hoping to attract some of the large numbers of visitors to that area as their customers. Large movie theater complexes are beginning to use a similar approach.

Time

The old adage that timing is everything is certainly true for experiences. Since one has to be there to experience it, the timing and scheduling considerations are critical for experience marketing. Timing can refer to time of day, day of the week, or season of the year. Timing can also include the length of time required for the experience, the number of times people want or need to avail themselves of the experience as well as a host of other "timely" considerations.

This synchronographics of an experience included anticipating and accommodating the onset of life stages and life events. The examples of such timing-related experiences are nearly endless and can include adolescence and midlife crisis as well as traditional rites of passage such as graduations and retirements. Those experiences that recur on a regular basis such as Memorial Day Weekend and New Year's Eve are yet other examples.

The frequency of an activity or event creates a situation similar to that of locations. The summer Olympic Games happen once every four years and the

Time and Frequency Factors

❖ Racquet clubs regularly offer variable pricing based on the time of day the tennis players prefer to play with peak and nonpeak hourly rates with early morning and early evening hours generally garnering a higher fee than midday play.

❖ Golf courses and restaurants are often closed on Mondays or offer reduced prices since interest in either or both of those activities appear to be reduced after the hectic pace of the weekend.

❖ Vacationers who travel during holidays or school vacations know firsthand about seasonal timing with the inevitable overcrowding that can color the experience.

❖ Restaurants who cater to business people over the lunch hours designate certain items on the menu that can be served within a 20-minute time period promising to expedite the dining experience.

Passion Play at Oberammergau every 10 years making the desirability (and price) for such experiences higher due to the more exclusive nature of the offering.

Some experiences and events operate on a more selective basis by occurring or happening on an annual basis such as the famous holiday show at Radio City Music Hall or the Art Festival in Laguna Beach, California. High-school graduation parties and weddings occur regularly, but only occasionally for individuals and their families.

Some experiences are much more commonplace. People frequently go out to eat or take in a movie. Restaurants and movie theaters are examples of experience providers who need to practice an intensive frequency strategy since these experiences are likely to happen often and on a recurring basis. This repeated participation is recognized as an important marketing component of experiences. Airlines, restaurants, coffee shops, and even grocery stores are designing reward programs as incentives to encourage people to come and spend their money repeatedly with a specific experience provider.

Timing can be a boon or a bust. If an experience is offered at a time that is impossible, inconvenient, or unappealing for people, they can't or won't show up for the experience. When Amtrak downsized by cutting back the daily service on certain routes and replaced it with unusual scheduling such as every third day, they lost customers. They subsequently ended up dropping those routes since the unusual schedule didn't meet a scheduling pattern that customers could identify easily.

Price

An additional P of the peripheral variable is price. Price used to mean one thing and one thing only, the cost of the product or service. Service marketing changed all that when marketers realized that some services involve the physical presence of the customer. The definition of pricing for experience marketing expands significantly because experiences require physical presence and generally the psychological involvement of the participant. If your body needs to be there and your psyche is involved, then the price goes up as well. The price variable includes:

- monetary—direct and indirect;
- nonmonetary—opportunity (time, association, effort) and intrinsic (association, social, sensory, psychological);
- intangibles—perception, elasticity of demand, impact on behavior;
- pricing objectives—surplus maximization, cost recovery, usage maximization, market disincentivization; and
- pricing strategies—interest, demand, competition.

Monetary Costs

Price is both monetary and nonmonetary. It takes more than money for an experience to take place. The monetary portion of price includes both direct and indirect costs. Direct cost is the fee or charge for the experience, and indirect costs are other expenditures associated with the experience. The direct cost of skiing is the fee plunked down for the lift ticket. As if the reality of paying $50 to hitch a ride up the mountain isn't enough, the indirect costs add up as well when you factor in the expenditures for equipment (purchase or rental), clothing, transportation to the ski area, and lodging and meals, if needed.

Monetary costs can escalate when both direct and indirect costs are considered. The cost of being treated at the Mayo Clinic in Rochester, Minnesota, is a direct cost which is possibly covered by medical insurance. But the costs of transportation or having a companion stay in a hotel during your treatment are indirect costs born by the individual not the insurance company. Sometimes, indirect costs are hidden, unexpected, or unanticipated which gives rise to the popularity of inclusive pricing packages for experiences.

Nonmonetary

The monetary expenditures are not the only price one pays for being part of an experience. Nonmonetary costs consist of opportunity and intrinsic prices paid for participating in an experience. Opportunity costs refer to time required by an experience that precludes time spent in other opportunities. There are a number of factors within this cost. Getting to and being a part of an experience may require the participant paying a price for time, energy, and effort. The investment of these personal resources may result in missed opportunities elsewhere. Some experiences have a higher nonmonetary price than others.

Golf and skiing come with a high time price tag. Most people can't downhill ski or golf in their backyard so there is some travel time required. Playing nine holes of golf doesn't fit within most lunch hours, and one rarely hears of people taking a 20-minute downhill ski break. An additional cost can be the time and effort required on the part of the would-be golfer or skier since these activities usually require lessons and practice time to fully enjoy the experience. Parents enrolling their child in a youth sports program may be more than willing to pay the registration fee and purchase the needed equipment, but they feel the strain of making time to transport the child to practices and games or helping out with coaching or fund-raising.

There are also intrinsic costs involved in some experiences. If one has ever bemoaned either duffers or hot-dog skiers in order to experience one's favorite outdoor sporting experience, then such costs are familiar. Intrinsic costs can include association, social, psychological, and sensory tolls of experiences. These nonmonetary elements can add to the price one ultimately pays.

How do people decide whether to tour Italy independently or with a motor coach tour? They check out the price(s). The group tour package may be less expensive because all costs are fixed prior to departure. But people debate the trade-offs of efficient, no surprise travel with getting stuck with a less than desirable seat mate or missing the little, out of the way, restaurant that doesn't cater to tour groups.

In addition to association prices that people are willing or unwilling to pay, there are also social costs involved in experiences. Getting physically inactive adults to don skimpy exercise clothes or join an aerobics group where they envision hordes of trim and toned people may be asking people to pay too big a price. Travel by small plane that requires each passenger to state his or her weight prior to boarding may be too high a price for some people to pay.

Ever get too cold skiing or too exhausted hiking? Sensory price is one that is often overlooked but is certainly critical to experience marketing. Travel to exotic or remote destinations often involves experiencing "less than customary" comfort levels for some basic necessities. People have varying levels of tolerance when it comes to smell, heat, taste, sights, sounds, and comfort, not to mention the feelings of fear or exhilaration that may indeed be a part of a culturally rich experience.

What about internal feelings about the experience? Sometimes the perceived fear or risk from participating in an experience may be too high a price for potential participants to pay. There are psychological costs associated with a number of experiences. Some people can't bring themselves to parasail because of it. Some people can't bring themselves to attend a large, social event because of it. These psychological feelings, choices, and barriers can create an additional layer of pricing within an experience.

These intrinsic prices of an experience present interesting challenges for the experience provider. The impetus to become involved in the experience often relates to a particular social or sensory need, but the actual involvement by the participant requires a balance between the perceived need and the reality of the experience. People may dream of sailing the high seas on a turn-of-the-century schooner, but they may also find the motion of the boat, the level of comfort, or the dish washing a higher price than they wish to pay. That explains why some people would rather experience the grand hotel era of the national parks in Disney's Wilderness Lodge where they experience a rustic setting without having to crawl under a bed in search of an electric outlet for the hair dryer.

Intangibles

Pricing isn't a cut-and-dried issue. There are variables and unknowns that surround pricing such as participant's perception of price, elasticity of demand, and the impact of price on behavior. For example, the burning question of elasticity of demand is just how sensitive participants are to price changes. If airlines raise their rates by 20 percent, how many customers will choose alternative modes of transportation? Experience marketers are often faced with trying to project how a change in price will impact the customer and the ultimate revenue picture. Such price changes are not easily predicted. A price is considered inelastic if people are not willing to pay more for the experience and elastic if they would be willing to pay a higher premium for a greater real or perceived value.

There are other nonrevenue aspects of pricing which are somewhat intangible. Perception is one of them. A steep price creates expectations on the part of people. People don't expect Motel 6 to do much more than "leave the light on" for them in a small, basic, clean room in which to spend the night. However, the higher rates of the Ritz-Carlton lead people to expect many things which are far different on the basis of that price. The reverse can work against experiences as well. If a Greek island cruise package seems like too good a deal, potential tourists may pass on it by thinking there must be something wrong with the ship, the airline being used, or some other aspect of the tour package. Remember, an experience involves the physical, mental, and emotional well-being of the participant. Going on a cut-rate cruise where one is in fear of one's safety is not comparable to shoving a pair of half-price shoes to the back of the closet.

The perception of the value of an experience is intertwined with price. As a society, Americans are programmed to relate money with value. One often hears people expressing whether or not an experience was worth it. A hot air balloon ride at dawn over the Serengeti during the wildebeest migration costs $350 per person, but it may very well be worth it. Conversely, not being charged a fee to sit on the riverbank watching fireworks while being attacked by mosquitoes and getting stuck in traffic for 45 minutes after the event may not have been a good deal.

Fees can be used to influence behavior. If a restaurant requests a credit card to hold a dinner reservation, the person making the reservation is more likely to either show up at the appointed day and time or call and cancel the reservation. Airlines offer substantial fare reductions to travelers who stay over a Saturday; not a particularly popular policy among business travelers. Governments often try to raise taxes on "sins" such as tobacco and alcohol under the guise of diminishing their use.

Pricing Objectives

Experience providers aren't left out of the pricing picture. They are involved in two ways. They identify the pricing objectives and establish the actual price for the experience. They are also able to influence the nonmonetary costs of the experience as well. The price established for the experience may relate to the objectives of the organization. The most obvious and common pricing objective is

Pricing Objectives

❖ Seasonal resorts from ski areas to tropical beaches charge higher rates during the peak season to generate profit to offset reduced revenues in the off-season (surplus maximization).

❖ Nonprofit organizations such as YMCAs charge fairly high rates for their adult fitness centers to generate funding to provide youth services (surplus maximization).

❖ Airlines sometimes offer a free companion ticket with a full fare purchase (usage maximization).

❖ Ski areas and resorts provide children's meals, day care, and kiddy camp programs at cost to make it easier for parents to enjoy their experience (cost recovery).

❖ Taxes on cigarettes are continually raised in an attempt to discourage people from smoking (market disincentivization).

generating a profit, and while this holds true for most cases, there are indeed other pricing objectives such as cost recovery, surplus maximization, usage maximization, or market disincentivization (Kotler, 1982, pp. 305–309).

These four objectives achieve different ends for the organization as well as influence price:

- surplus maximization: generate as much revenue as possible to create a surplus;
- cost recovery: generate revenue to meet the costs of providing the service or experience;
- usage maximization: establish a price that will attract as many people as possible to the experience; and
- market disincentivization: establish a price that will discourage people from participating or influence the nature of their participation.

Pricing Strategies

There are many factors that influence establishing a price, and they all don't occur in a vacuum. If the cost of providing the experience increases, the interest in the experience wanes, or competitors cut their prices, setting aside the pricing objectives of the organization. It is amazing that advance purchased, tourist class fare flights from New York to Los Angeles on all the major airlines are exactly the same price. Generally, the impact of competition works to lower prices. If a major airline announces a price reduction promotion, the other airlines tend to follow suit. If a new entry into the birthday party business comes on the scene with lower fees, the advent of this competition will certainly impact prices.

Interest and demand factor into the pricing equation also. Prices based on demand are market driven and based on the users' preferences, patterns, and perceptions. Peak and off-peak hours of the day as well as days of the week or time of the year are clearly identified with pricing reflective of these differentiations as well.

Rarely do experience providers use one pricing objective or strategy. They operate using a combination approach that they juggle over time and on the basis of circumstances. Experience marketers have to be cognizant and ever vigilant of asset revenue generating efficiency, the extent to which the organization's assets are being used to achieve full potential for generating revenue (Lovelock, 1991, p. 122). This presents an ongoing challenge. Airlines monitor load factors and hotels check occupancy rates. Fitness clubs track membership renewals and hospitals keep a close eye on their census. It's important to remember that pricing influences behavior. If two of the twelve flights from Chicago to Los Angeles are under booked, increasing the number of excursion seats available resulting in lower fares may influence leisure travelers to book one of those two flights.

While technology enhances the ability of an organization to undertake this balancing act, it is still challenging at best. Does a hotel want to advance register a conference group at a reduced rack rate of $138 per night versus attracting tourists to their hotel who would foot the bill for the regular rate of $225 per night. How can it be done?

Lovelock makes a series of suggestions to help in this process (1991, p. 126):

- clearly identify potential target markets;
- predict volume of business for each market;
- devise a revenue mix balance of revenue and usage;
- incorporate specifics for pricing and dates for each market;

Pricing Alternatives

❖ Delta airlines created Delta Express, a low-cost carrier, to ferry passengers between cities in the Northeast and Florida; other carriers lowered their fares on these routes in response to the price competition.

❖ Early bird dinner specials are notorious in areas such as Arizona or Florida where price sensitive retirees pack restaurants when other people are still at work, on the beach, or at the golf course.

❖ Resorts in Florida, southern California, and Arizona vary their prices based upon the demand for sun, fun, and warm weather resulting in a peak, off-peak, and shoulder season pricing; Canyon Ranch in Arizona offers 30 percent discounts in July and August while its counterpart in the Berkshires of Massachusetts maintains regular pricing during this time period.

❖ The long awaited concert tour by Fleetwood Mac came complete with ticket prices in excess of $75 while tickets for perennial favorites the Beach Boys, who appear every summer in multiple locations within a geographic area, were priced in the range of $30.

❖ Cruise lines provide substantial price discounts to people who book well in advance of the cruise and to people who wait to book at the last minute.

❖ Family restaurants have specials where children can eat free when accompanied by an adult purchasing a dinner.

- develop pricing guidelines for each group at various times; and
- monitor and evaluate performance over time.

One of the primary tenets of emerging management strategies is the premise that different customers are willing and able to pay different prices for essentially the same service. One function of pricing within the experience industry is to identify these target market subsegments and to devise prices accordingly. With the new millennium emerging, people booked everything including hotel suites at Times Square in New York, the Space Needle in Seattle, and group tours to the Pyramids to welcome the new century. The prices charged for those experiences reflected the differences between those people wanting to experience the unique and the unusual as opposed to those people looking to stay in Time Squares on a Wednesday night in April of 2003. There are a proliferation of differences among people as they relate to value of an experience and their willingness to pay significantly different prices.

Packaging

Packaging is an additional factor included in peripherals. There are a number of related factors within this category including:

- physical evidence,
- levels of service,
- perks,
- personalization, and
- unusual attributes of the experience.

These factors in connection with one another provide a sum of variations that add up to equal the total experience.

Physical evidence is one such factor. It's not the actual physical location of faculty but rather a collection of incrementals which change the environment creating a certain ambiance or enhancing existing parameters of the experience. While ambiance has become an overused term, it does speak to a variety of elements that make up each experience. Living, thriving, green plants seem to add so much to a setting. Chairs carefully arranged around a fireplace create a feeling of warmth and comfort. There are health and fitness clubs that have the feel of a visit to a doctor's office and others that create the feeling of being at a party. Many of these intangible feelings are created by physical evidence.

Mehrabian and Russell (Bateson, 1995, p. 221) created a model for environmental psychology that proposes that basic emotional states can be attributed to physical characteristics: pleasure-displeasure; arousal-nonarousal; and to a lesser extent distressing-relaxing and exciting-gloomy. They found that people react to places in two general but opposite ways: approach or avoidance.

Approach reactions suggest that positive features of a particular setting create a desire to stay while the exact opposite is true with avoidance when there are factors that create an urge to leave an environment. Hospitals have revamped to create a new look more welcoming and less threatening. Even little things such as appropriate background music is important and experience providers like health clubs whose membership spans several cohort groups struggle to find the right music to feature at the club. Outdoor and adventure tour providers walk a tight-rope helping participants find the right balance between basic amenities versus the thrill of the climb, hike, or expedition. While this model is conceptual in nature, it should remind experience marketers that even simple changes in the physical environment may pay off for them in big ways.

Another aspect of packaging relates to various levels of the service or the experience. Resorts offer rooms with an ocean view or a garden view (sometimes a euphemism for the parking lot) or poolside. Cruises provide cabin accommodations at varying deck levels. Airlines offer first-class, business, and tourist seats. Many hotels have created different levels of service for various levels of accommodations often in the same or adjacent buildings. Rental cars come in subcompact to luxury or specialty vehicles.

Imagine checking in to a roadside Holiday Inn and not finding that all-purpose coffee shop/restaurant that's always present. That's exactly the case if you booked a reservation at a Holiday Inn Express and failed to notice the "express" designation tacked onto the name. Most of the hotel chains including Hyatt, Marriott, Holiday Inn, and Days Inn have created a number of variations within their offerings resulting in full-service, business-oriented, long-term stay, and basic levels of service establishments all operating under different names. Marriott has Fairfield Inns, Courtyards, Marriott Hotels, and Marriott Resorts with different levels of experiences being afforded their guests.

The packaging can also include things referred to as perks and personalization. Perks are the little extra niceties that are included as part of the experience package. Levels of service often differentiate themselves through the use of perks. Personalization, on the other hand, doesn't always involve an additional extra but the willingness and ability of the experience provider to recognize participants as

Packaging

❖ All Nippon Airways features the Fullflat Seat for its first-class customers; this seat features 180 degree reclining capability along with pillows, blankets, and a line of cabin casual wear including cardigans and sweat pants.
❖ To contribute to the authenticity of ambiance for the out-of-doors experience, Rockusterics, Inc. sells speakers camouflaged as rocks for use by pools or patios or at zoos.
❖ Courtyard by Marriott features a living room–like arrangement in the lobby area complete with soft chairs and a fireplace to create a place where guests can sit, unwind, have coffee, meet other guests, or read the newspaper thus simulating being at home.
❖ The airport in Pittsburgh, Pennsylvania, includes street-like concourses complete with sidewalk cafes and small shops that make passenger waiting time seem to evaporate.

Personalization and Perks

❖ When a customer buys hot dogs and mouth-wash at the grocery store, the checkout coupon dispenser responds providing coupons for mustard and a competitor's mouthwash.

❖ Frequent travelers who are members of Hilton's HHonors system don't have to stand in line at the end of the day answering endless questions about their choices for room location or size of bed because such personal preferences are logged into Hilton's guest information system.

❖ Virgin Atlantic Airway's first-class passengers can brush up on their putting or soak in a hot tub while waiting for the plane at London's Heathrow Airport.

❖ At the retrokitsch Beauty Bar on 14th Street in New York City patrons can "rye and dry" as they sip cocktails while under the hair dryers.

❖ Holiday Inns at Busch Gardens in Tampa and International Drive in Orlando combined the best features of a fast-food restaurant, a convenience store, and a snack shop and created "convenience courts" so guests no longer have to leave the hotel to trek down unfamiliar streets in search of a snack or shaving cream.

individuals and accommodate their individual preferences within the realm of the experience.

Another aspect of packaging not to be overlooked relates to attributes or characteristics of the experience that are unique, unusual, or innovative. These factors range from outstanding characteristics of the experience to smaller, seemingly unimportant things which substantially enhance or even create an experience where there wasn't one. Experience marketers should be cognizant and ever vigilant of opportunities within this variable since the applications for the experience industry are endless. For instance, there are a number of different motor coach tours out of London to see the countryside. One such tour includes high tea and an overnight stay at actress Jane Seymour's country estate outside of Bath. The uniqueness of that tour differs substantially from a more traditional drive to Bath that includes dinner at a roadside restaurant followed by an overnight stay in a standard tourist-class hotel room in London. There is a myriad of options within this experience variable.

Participants

Another factor with the potential for significantly impacting the experience is participants. The impact and potential of other people involved in the experience was cited as a core part of the first P of experience marketing. Participants are once again mentioned here under peripherals to reinforce both the importance and the need to address this impact within the experience.

Participants include a wide range of people including behind-the-scenes, initial contact staff, and front-line staff as well as other people participating in the experience. It is the relationship and interaction with and among these participants that influence or alter the experience. The impact and influence can be enormous.

Unusual Attributes or Features

❖ The Hotel Triton in San Francisco features a guest suite designed by the late Jerry Garcia as well as one designed by Carlos Santana. The Santana suite features memorabilia from the rocker's career as well as a meditation area with candles, incense, and a prayer pillow.

❖ Taos, New Mexico, with its appeal to artists and art lovers, added a new hotel to its landscape called the Fechin Inn as a tribute to Russian born artist and woodcarver Nicolai Fechin, who lived in the area in the late 1920s. In addition to hand-carved woodwork throughout the hotel, the hotel helps to support the Fechin Institute.

❖ The new Mayo Clinic in northeast Arizona will be one of the most patient-friendly facilities. It will include guest quarters for patient's family members, soundproof walls in patient's rooms, as well as digitized x-rays that can be pulled up on computer and remote monitoring systems.

❖ Mike Veeck, son of Hall of Fame baseball executive Bill Veeck and co-owner and president of the minor league St. Paul Saints, adds innovative touches to the 6,329 seat Midway stadium such as making it possible for fans in the outfield to sit in a hot tub, get a haircut, or have a massage. The team also features a pig named Tobias who delivers game balls to the home plate umpire. It's rumored that the pig's trainer makes more than some of the Saints' ballplayers (Antonen, 1996, p. 1C).

❖ The Strasburg, Pennsylvania, Red Caboose Motel offers a rail car room from the Pennsylvania Railroad. The Heritage Inn in Evans, Colorado, has a Wild West Suite complete with tent and covered wagon, and the Cinderella Palace Suite located in the Ramada Inn Grand Court in Mundelew, Illinois, has a Plexiglas Cinderella coach.

The initial contact that people have with an experience provider is often at a distance via phone, mail, fax, or E-mail. The personnel on the other end of that communication can be critical. The decisions and judgment that potential participants make about the experience and the choice of a provider can relate to that exchange. A contact person who doesn't have a clue how to answer fairly standard questions probably won't get the customer. A contact person who responds with an attitude reflecting the nature of the experience as well as creating a genuine connection with the prospective participant is the absolute best representative. Contact people who have actually skied the mountain or taken the cruise to Alaska have a substantially better chance of getting a commitment from the potential participant than someone who simply reads the company brochure to the caller.

The front-line personnel who meet, greet, interact with and provide the experience must meet certain requirements. Even though people like to think that appearances aren't important, they must look the part as well as act and think the part. Do they look approachable and competent? Do they appear to be interested in each participant as an individual? Remember, experiences are not the same as going through the car wash. They are integral to the inner needs and desires of people who need to have a demonstration of an effort to meet their needs and expectations.

The importance and impact of front-line personnel vary based on the nature of the experience. If there is an element or perception of danger within the experience, the competence of these people must be clearly evident. If the experience involves interaction of a personal nature as would be the case with various spa treatments or healthcare services, competence must be augmented by a compatible, caring attitude on the part of the experience provider.

What about the other people involved in the experience? How important are they to the overall outcome of the experience? Some women refuse to join health clubs where the exercise rooms are open to both sexes. Others wouldn't think of joining a gender restricted establishment. Some older adults only travel with people of a similar age while others would not unless the experience afforded them the opportunity to interact with people of all ages.

The behavior or performance of those other participants becomes part of the experience as well. Many golfers bemoan being trapped behind a slow moving group of players. Some people are bothered by the pace of a trek slowed down by less experienced or less capable participants. Younger singles going to a Club Med that targets families are understandably disappointed.

People can make a difference in a variety of ways. Sometimes the involvement of people who are well-known or famous can make a difference in the experience. As celebrities have started to frequent places such as Montana and Idaho, the property values and vacation attractions of these places escalate. When Dr. Chopra, the new age health guru, agrees to hold seminars over a weekend at an upstate New York spa, the number of spa visitors over that weekend increases substantially. Sports memorabilia shows that feature personal appearances by sport legends drive the gate revenues up as well.

Experiences and the values of experiences can be significantly enhanced by the element of other participants. On the other hand, if the word gets out that the "wrong" kind of people frequent a experience with "wrong" being defined by the target market, the reverse is also a possibility.

Participants

❖ Disney World in Florida hosted a Soap Weekend at its Disney/MGM Studios theme park featuring Susan Lucci and other ABC soap opera stars.

❖ The Rosarito Beach Hotel located on the Baja peninsula in Mexico employs recreation staff who are the first ones to dance in the crowd or organize and participate in the special event contests to generate involvement among guests.

❖ Many hotels and resorts train all staff including maintenance and housekeeping personnel to greet guests when they encounter them on the property.

❖ Some resorts including Hilton Pointe in Phoenix and Kiawah Island in South Carolina set aside and designate pools for adults only and family groups.

❖ The Mall of America restricts access to teenagers unaccompanied by adults in the evening hours to counteract their potential negative impact among other shoppers.

Policies and Procedures

Few things can be as annoying or as enticing as the policies and procedures practiced by an experience provider. Everyone knows the types of things such as registration requirements, refund policies, payment options, and guest usage rules can work for or against a person jumping into an experience or selecting a particular experience provider.

Policies can change an experience. The recent policies established by insurance companies have dictated length of stay for certain procedures and in some cases eliminated hospital overnight stays for some types of surgery. This certainly changes the hospital or surgical experience significantly.

Policies can also influence or shape behavior. Some hotels and resorts mandate five-night stay policies during peak holiday periods. Some colleges and universities have significantly changed their policies related to alcohol consumption on campus. Such policy changes may influence the behavior and preferences of both potential students and their parents, but in different ways.

Public Image

Public image is sometimes difficult to quantify, but it is always there. Every experience provider has some kind of public image. Some images are carefully cultivated while others are haphazard. Some images are designed to reflect or incorporate the philosophy of the organization while others attempt to relay meaning for their participants. Disney with its stringent dress code and maintenance standards vigorously cultivates its wholesome family image. A long-term care facility with littered public areas and nonuniformly dressed staff may take a much less stringent approach.

Public image may or may not be within the complete control of the organization. Disney's trouble with Christian groups and Nike's problems with its foreign factories are both examples of this. Accidents involving the experience can happen as well. The ski resort with a lift mishap and the hospital with the surgical

- ❖ TWA altered a standard industry policy allowing leisure travelers three days to purchase flights with restricted fares as opposed to 24-hour limits imposed by most of the major airlines.
- ❖ Frequent fliers are finding it more difficult to take truly free trips as airlines have introduced policies requiring a $50 charge to redeposit miles into an account or USAir's charge of $50 to mail an award when reservations haven't been made 21 days in advance.
- ❖ Carnival Cruise Lines has instituted a policy restricting young people under the age of 21 from cruising with them unless accompanied by an adult.
- ❖ Nordstrom, the legendary department store known for its "no questions asked" return policy, lives with the legend that they allowed a dissatisfied customer to return tires when the store didn't even sell tires.

Public Image

❖ State tourism slogans attempt to create an image for would-be tourists. For example, Florida bills itself as the Sunshine State (naturally) or a place to Return to Your Senses. Some slogans are perfectly logical. Arizona is the Grand Canyon State, and Alaska goes with All Things Wild and Wonderful. Other attempts at creating public image try to connect with consumers' needs in some way such as Illinois' A Million Miles from Monday and New Jersey's What a Difference a State Makes.

❖ In an effort to be perceived as one of the country's premier marine facilities, the Virginia Marine Science Museum undertook a $35 million expansion to add a 300,000 gallon, open-ocean aquarium containing sharks and barracuda; an aquarium featuring endangered and giant sea turtles; a river otter habitat; interactive exhibits; and an IMAX 3D theater.

❖ Many members of the American Hotel and Motel Association including the Disney-owned properties in California and Florida and 360 franchisees of Holiday Inn worldwide participate in Good Earthkeeping, a program that provides in-room cards to offer guests the opportunity to conserve water by reusing sheets and towels.

❖ The Body Shop, a popular retail chain offering a variety of soaps, lotions, and personal products, has highly visible policies related to both community and the environment. It is committed to sustainable trading relationships with communities in need such as the Kayapo Indians in Brazil and the Native Americans of the Santa Ana Pueblo in New Mexico.

error are unable to control the reporting of such incidents. Public image can be a powerful, but double-edged sword.

Patterns of Demand

People start lining up the night before to get tickets for the Rolling Stones tour or whatever group happens to be hot at the moment. During holiday weeks people jam airports and create havoc in ski lift lines because everyone wants to have an experience during the same time period. One of the most difficult things for experience marketers to handle is demand. It can be predicted and anticipated in many instances. Everybody wants to fly the Wednesday before Thanksgiving, and many theatergoers want dessert and coffee after the performance.

Unfortunately, it just isn't possible to inventory experiences. One can't stockpile ski weekends or hot air balloon trips. It just can't be done, but there are alternatives for ameliorating this condition. Lovelock suggests either modifying capacity or demand (Lovelock, 1991, p. 128). Modifying capacity involves changes to the actual experience through alterations to the facility, equipment, or personnel. Managing demand is a bit trickier because, in this instance, the experience provider has to make changes that he or she hopes will alter the patterns of demand on the part of the participants. Changes in hours of operation may spread

Managing Capacity and Demand

❖ Hospitals open and close units just as ski resorts open and close ski lifts and lodges to address variations in demand.

❖ Airlines change equipment from 757s to 727s to accommodate fluctuations in demand for certain routes at specific times.

❖ Disney World sometimes exaggerates waiting time so guests will be pleased that it didn't take as long as they thought it would.

❖ The Saltwater Cafe in Nokomis, Florida, offers a special New Year's Eve late afternoon party complete with dinner, dancing, and a champagne toast. This event appeals to the somewhat older, nonevening driving crowd, and it doubles their New Year's Eve capacity.

❖ The Outback Steakhouse, a restaurant chain with a reputation for long waiting lines, doesn't take reservations, but it does provide diners with a beeper so they can wander around doing nearby errands or enjoy the large front porch area where diners can sit, sip, and be patient.

❖ Western Pacific Airlines offered mystery fares as a way of filling up seats. Passengers are told at the time of booking how to dress for the weather and on departing they receive a packet on their destination complete with package deals and discount coupons. Round trip cost is $99.

or restrict the demand within a range preferred by the experience provider. Offering fewer choices or options within the experience may enable the provider to modify the demand. Creating special price incentives for visiting the theme park on a Wednesday or traveling on a Tuesday may enable the experience provider to modify demand as well.

Lovelock points out that such changes always impact the quality of the service, and this is even more true for experiences. There is a difference between optimal capacity and maximum capacity. Dining by candlelight overlooking the bay in a relatively empty restaurant on a Wednesday night in April is quite different from dining on a Friday evening in July when it's standing room only. There is a difference between dining and dancing on New Year's Eve as opposed to any night in May.

Contrast the differences between demand and capacity among sports fans and concertgoers. People are often energized by the capacity crowd and remember the time they were at the ball park or a concert with a sold-out crowd. The nature of experiences is indeed related to demand and capacity but not always in the most obvious ways.

Popularity Life Cycle

A much broader perspective on demand for experiences incorporates the popularity life cycle. Just as clothing styles come and go, so do experiences. There was a time when in-line skates were a novelty, and now everybody including grandparents use them. There was a time when snowboards weren't allowed near a ski lift, and now ski areas court the boarders. Experiences come and go in

The Psychology of Waiting

Bateson cites a longstanding theory of queue psychology developed by Maister that consisted of an equation reflecting the relationship between perceptions and expectations and suggested that satisfaction equals perception minus expectation. This theory suggests that people are satisfied if service received surpassed their perception of the expectation. Maister suggests eight principles that can be used to influence customers' satisfaction with waiting as follows (Maister as cited in Bateson, 1995, p. 224):

• unoccupied time seems longer than occupied time;
• preprocess waiting seems longer than in-process waiting;
• anxiety enhances perception of length of wait;
• uncertain waits feel longer than defined waits;
• unexplained waits feel longer than explained ones;
• unfair waits feel longer than fair waits;
• the more valuable the service, the more palatable the wait; and
• waiting alone seems longer than waiting in a group.

Additional suggestions for altering both the process and the participant's perception of the process include (Bateson, 1995, p. 231–232):

• determine the acceptable or allowable amount of time people are willing to wait;
• distract, entertain, or physically involve the participant during the wait;
• remove people from lines if possible;
• modify arrival behavior by informing people about peak and nonpeak times;
• keep personnel not serving participants out of sight;
• create alternatives for the impatient types; and
• make use of the power of friendliness and empathy.

In today's time conscious society, the patterns of demands and the ways in which these impact and influence people's participation in experiences or the experiences themselves are substantial and are an important factor for the experience provider to address.

terms of their popularity. At one time it seemed as if there couldn't be enough indoor tennis courts, and now some indoor facilities have been recycled as soccer centers.

How can the experience marketer project the rise and fall of his or her experiences? Such predictions are both art and science. The product-program life cycle can be applied to this pursuit of prediction. Generally, every product, program, or service goes through a predictable pattern of popularity as evidenced by the number of people participating. By tracking the number of participants over time, the experience marketer can gauge the stage in the popularity life cycle and take appropriate action based upon each stage.

A look at the graph of the popularity life cycle reveals that there are five basic stages within the life cycle: introduction, takeoff, maturity, saturation, and decline. The decline stage has a number of variations. There are certain characteristics related to each stage based on numbers of participants. For instance,

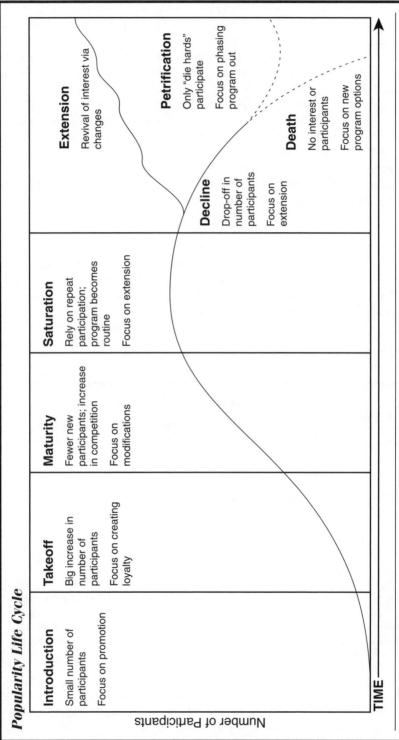

Popularity Life Cycle

Introduction

Small number of participants

Focus on promotion

Takeoff

Big increase in number of participants

Focus on creating loyalty

Maturity

Fewer new participants; increase in competition

Focus on modifications

Saturation

Rely on repeat participation; program becomes routine

Focus on extension

Extension

Revival of interest via changes

Petrification

Only "die hards" participate

Focus on phasing program out

Decline

Drop-off in number of participants

Focus on extension

Death

No interest or participants

Focus on new program options

Number of Participants

TIME

Source: O'Sullivan, 1991, p. 78. Copyright ©1991 Venture Publishing, Inc. Reprinted with permission of Venture Publishing, Inc.

introduction usually means a small number of participants while takeoff represents just that, a sizable increase in the number of people involved. Patterns of participation are included on the graphic.

The graphic also includes a marketing focus for each of the stages. Each stage suggests a different, appropriate marketing activity. During introduction, the marketer would focus on promoting the experience while during saturation, the emphasis would be upon changing the experience to maintain viability.

While it is difficult to explain or predict patterns of popularity, it is safe to assume that most experiences will go through this life cycle. Experiences destined to be fads just go through the stages more rapidly. The important thing for the experience marketer is the management of the life cycle. Participation numbers and revenue projections must be monitored over time to correctly pinpoint the stage of the experience so that appropriate marketing action can be taken.

There are variations and subtleties within all of these stages that impact on the art and science of these predictions. For instance, there are a number of factors that impact the length of time an experience will remain in the introductory stage. Such factors include ease of the experience, visibility of the experience, and cost of the experience. If the experience requires a skill that's hard to develop or is held in a remote location where it takes people longer to become exposed to it, the introduction stage is extended. Experiences that are easy to do, attract a great deal of attention, and don't break the bank naturally will move through the introductory stage more quickly.

Experience Life Cycle

There was a time when no one had ever heard of aerobic dance. Aerobic dance illustrates the stages of the life cycle. This experience started with a small group of adult females who chose to sweat and raise their target heart rates while dancing in place. Before long, aerobic dance was in the takeoff stage with women everywhere getting in step, creating overcrowding and waiting lists among providers.

After while these high-stepping, heart healthy women began to tire and lose interest in aerobic dance. This didn't spell the end of aerobic dance, not by a long shot. Before people could even put away their leotards, there were new versions of aerobic exercise programs with slight differences and modifications. Providers made small changes in aerobic dance initially. They changed the music used or changed the name of the classes. Exercise providers then went after people who had dropped out of classes as well as the nonaerobic people who had been sitting on the sidelines. As aerobics entered the saturation stage, providers extended the life cycle of aerobics with such things as low-impact aerobics, coed aerobics, water aerobics, and children's aerobics. Step and slide aerobics closely followed these market extensions.

Have we seen the end of aerobic dance? That's fairly unlikely as we now see an upsurge in nonchoreographed aerobic dance options for people who want to work at their own pace or explore their inner selves. While it may not continue to reach the unprecedented numbers of participants, aerobic dance has successfully reinvented itself as it moved through the popularity life cycle.

The takeoff stage is a mixed blessing. The happiness induced by maximum capacity or standing room is quickly surpassed by the demands of trying to balance capacity versus demand. There is a great deal of pressure upon the experience provider to perform this balancing act. A good job now secures a loyal customer base in light of the growing competition that comes with the next stage. The next stage, maturity, comes sometimes with competitors rather than hordes of participants.

Maturation and the stage that follows it, saturation, resemble one another. The increase in participation slows during these two stages and eventually begins to decline in saturation. During the maturation stage, competition is from other providers. During saturation the experience faces competition from other activities and experiences that seem more desirable to people. In both of these stages, the marketer needs to change peripherals within the experience. Peripheral changes can either differentiate one's organization from one's competitors or change the experience itself to appear new and attractive to participants.

As numbers of participants drop, the experience enters the decline stage. Still, the experience provider has alternatives. He or she can continue to change and modify the experience to extend the life of the experience. Such extension alternatives make the experience more attractive and desirable for participants. Electing to concentrate heavily on that smaller group of participants remaining interested in the experience is also an option. The provider can also discontinue this experience completely and pursue a new experience for people. This would be the case for entrepreneurs who continue to reinvent themselves.

Peripherals—
The Big and the Small

❖ The Pointe Hilton Resort in Phoenix, Arizona, uses a rooster crowing followed by a shortened version of reveille as the morning wake-up message.

❖ Europeds, a company specializing in walking and cycling tours of Europe, offers the Doggie Walk as an opportunity for dog lovers to walk in the French countryside with the four legged members of the family.

❖ If you're an opera lover and can't visit New Mexico several times a year to take in the opera season, don't worry. The Santa Fe Opera schedules its season so that performances of different operas are featured on consecutive nights of any given week. This enables visitors to partake of the entire season in a week's visit.

❖ The Palm Desert Hyatt Resort and Spa keeps spray bottles filled with water poolside so sunbathers can cool off without leaving their lounge chairs.

❖ The guides for the Ben and Jerry's factory tour let visitors know that a tour is about to get underway by the ringing of a cowbell.

❖ Tauck's Motor Coach Tours bills itself as the "Cadillac of Tour Services" and backs up the claim with overnight stays at four star inns and resorts, all-inclusive gourmet meals, no "Hello my name is" tags, and a focus on individualized, personal enrichment.

Action Agenda

❖ Examine your organization's experience from a peripherals' point of view, from prearrival to completion, and identify significant or obvious peripherals within this experience.

❖ For each of the significant peripherals identified, create a list of variations for those peripherals that would alter the experience either positively or negatively.

❖ Take a look at the peripheral elements within the experience that appear to be less central to the experience and brainstorm ways they can be changed to add delight for the participants.

❖ Interview participants to check their perceptions of peripheral factors that are significant to their involvement with the experience.

❖ Check perceptions of various user groups for your experience to better meet the needs of specific target markets.

❖ Run a tally of the monetary and nonmonetary costs of your experience and consider ways to rework the price.

Changing, Arranging, and Staging the Peripherals

There are a number of categories of peripherals, and each of those categories are filled with even smaller factors that can enhance or detract but most certainly make the experience what it is. What's an experience marketer to do? Something, everything, and anything is the answer. The myriad of Ps within this variable were meant to be changed, arranged, rearranged, and staged for the purpose of creating a desired experience for the participant.

Traditional marketing called for manipulation of the marketing mix variables: product, place, price, and promotion. This advice holds even greater weight and import for experience marketers who have the good fortune to have a host of variables ranging from big to small to play with.

Transition Tracking

From	To
• Traditional Ps of marketing: 　product 　place 　price	• Ps of experience marketing: 　place (time and location) 　price (monetary and nonmonetary) 　packaging
• Service Marketing Components: 　nature of service 　involvement of others 　absence of inventory	participants 　policies and procedures 　public image 　patterns of demand 　popularity life cycle

Sources

Antonen, Mel. (1996, June 21). Veeck carries on dad's creativity. *USA Today.*

Bateson, John E. G. (1995). *Managing services marketing* (3rd ed.). Fort Worth, TX: The Dryden Press.

Kotler, Philip. (1982). *Marketing for nonprofit organizations* (2nd ed.). Englewood Cliffs, NJ: Prentice-Hall.

Lovelock, Christopher H. (1991). *Services marketing* (2nd ed.). Englewood Cliffs, NJ: Prentice-Hall.

MacIsaac, Heather Smith. (1996, June). The best of the Adirondacks. *Travel & Leisure.*

O'Sullivan, Ellen L. (1991). *Marketing for parks, recreation, and leisure.* State College, PA: Venture Publishing, Inc.

Since experiences arise from within each person based upon his or her psychic or inner needs, it appears as if the more traditional marketing P, promotion, won't necessarily work for experiences. The fourth P of experience is PerInfoCom. This term incorporates the essential elements of *per*sonalization, *info*rmation, and *com*munication and reflects the specific needs of people as they seek experiences.

The traditional fourth P, promotion, involves creating awareness for a product and service and subsequently driving the purchase. The four major forms of promotion—advertising, personal contact or selling, sales promotion, and publicity—share the same overall goal but differ from one another. Advertising appears just about everywhere in all forms of paid media from billboards to television and is an impersonal form of communication. Publicity is also a nonpersonal form of communication designed to attract media attention or coverage, but it differs from advertising in that it is not purchased or necessarily controlled by the company. Organizations actively use grand openings, celebrity visits, and charitable donations as planned publicity events while misfortunes such as the Tylenol safety scare or Nike's Third World factory problems are examples of noncontrollable publicity. Sales promotion involves encouraging participation or purchase through an incentive of some kind and can include price discounts and giveaways. Personal contact or sales, the fourth type, involves direct communication with one or more potential purchasers or participants.

Many products and services rely heavily, although not exclusively, on advertising as a method to accomplish this goal. Believing that purchasing a service was different from purchasing a product, George and Berry (1991, pp. 407–411) suggested guidelines for improving the effectiveness of advertising and maintained that service advertising should:

- have a positive effect on contact personnel;
- capitalize on word-of-mouth;
- provide tangible clues;
- make service easily understood;
- contribute to continuity; and
- promise what is possible.

Suggestions such as these changes resulted in the appearance of such promotional options as the red Traveler's umbrella to add symbolism to insurance and tag lines such as "we're number two so we try harder" by Avis to better explain the service or reinforce promises.

Chapter 6

PerInfoCom, the Fourth P

In this age of smart TV set-top boxes and Web sites that
sort and store real-time video, where goes one-size-fits-
all advertising?

Don Pepper and Martha Rogers

PerInfoCom—What Is It?

Whether you're deciding to send your only child on a wilderness adventure or
helping your parents select a "forever" retirement center, it is necessary to review the promotional pieces provided by the organization. Experience providers,
like providers of products or services, produce materials designed to communicate with their potential customer. Promoting a particular kind of bread or dry-
cleaning establishment isn't the same as weighing the options for that only child
or an aging parent. While products, services, and experiences alike require promotional efforts on the part of the producer or provider, it is virtually impossible
that the type and approach to the promotion can or should be similar.

Experiences aren't sandwich bread. Experiences go way beyond dry-clean-
ing. Experiences involve not only the attention or physical presence of the individual, but also his or her involvement and participation in the experience itself.
Since the need for the experience often arises from an invisible inner need, promotion which has traditionally been an externally driven marketing mix variable
will not address the expanded needs of experience marketing.

PerInfoCom, a hybrid term born out of the specific objectives that need to be
addressed in experience marketing, replaces the more traditional P of promotion. PerInfoCom incorporates the need to communicate with people and to inform them about their needs as it relates to a particular experience while simultaneously doing so in such a personalized manner that will move them to take
action.

PerInfoCom	
necessity	Per (*per*sonalize and/or *per*mission)
integration of	Info (*info*rmation)
the basis	Com (*com*municate)

Role of Communication, Information, and Personalization

Communication as a Base

PerInfoCom depends on communication. Communication remains the lifeblood of the PerInfoCom variable. The AIDA model of the response hierarchy is as old as commerce itself having been created by Strong in 1925. Still in use today, this model indicates that buyers or potential consumers pass through the successive stages of awareness, interest, desire, and action en route to actual participation or purchase (Strong, 1925, p. 9). By using this concept the provider is aware of buyer readiness or response stage and can plan the message of the communication accordingly. Kotler identifies three consecutive but distinct stages in the prepurchase communication process as being cognitive, affective, and behavioral (Kotler, 1980, p. 475).

Incorporate Information

The rise of the experience industries that coincides with the onset of the information era greatly heightens the role and importance of information. The added emphasis placed on knowledge and information soars daily as we function in an increasingly more information-oriented society. You won't convince a health addict to buy a year's supply of antioxidant food supplements unless you provide the scientific evidence and documentation that goes along with the product.

Our increased dependence on (or obsession with) information continues to grow. One edition of the Sunday *New York Times* contains more information items than the typical adult in 1892 was exposed to in his or her entire lifetime (Davidson, 1991, p. 26). Even our language keeps expanding. Since 1966 more than 60,000 words have been added to the English language (Davidson, 1991, p. 24).

Make It Personal/Receive Permission

Personalization is part of today's marketplace. It is seen everywhere. Not only does *Time* magazine have East and West coast editions but also one for Canada (where *color* is spelled *colour*) and they can insert specific advertising directed at these different readers. Resorts and hotels create databases of their more frequent guests in order to ensure that their personal preferences are met. L. L. Bean has more than one catalog so that personal differences and preferences of certain customers can be incorporated into its mailings. Print ads as well as commercials for radio and television are currently being created so that the viewer or listener imagines that the message is just for him or her.

A double use of the "per" of PerInfoCom is permission. Internet marketing pioneer, Seth Godin of Yoyodyne Entertainment, believes that marketing is entering a new era where advertising will change from interrupting to inviting. Godin cites the commercial interruption during a favorite television show or the telemarketing call at dinner time as examples of the "interruption" model of advertising. He suggests that the emerging model for marketing will be built around permission where we persuade people to give their attention to a product or service (Taylor, 1998, p. 200). Such an approach creates a positive relationship with the potential consumer and works well for the experience industries.

Experience Marketing Communication Stages: ARIMA

Communication is the essential building block of any kind of promotion. There is no promotion if there is no communication. If a product has been developed and no one receives notice of its existence, it's as if the product doesn't even exist. A slick ad for a comprehensive retirement community can be created, but if it doesn't communicate with the target market by addressing its concerns and expectations for whatever reason, the facility won't survive for long.

The five stages within ARIMA, the experience communication process, include attention, recognition, inclination, meaning, and actuation.

Attention

This information about purchase preparation and stages of decision-making is helpful for understanding the process as it relates to experience marketing. The rise of the experience industry coincides with the rapid escalation of messages and the introduction of a plethora of new products, services, and experiences. Getting the attention of people remains the initial stage of communication in experience marketing.

There is just so much out there, and people are so busy with growing demands on their time and attention, that the initial stage of this communication process is breaking through and grabbing their attention. This is easier said than done. Now instead of three network television channels most homes have 50 or more channels coming into their living rooms with the projected 500 channels becoming more of a reality daily. Check out your local newsstand and marvel at the number of new entries for your reading pleasure. There are

ARIMA Stages

❖ Attention
❖ Recognition
❖ Inclination
❖ Meaning
❖ Actuate

❖ The average American receives 49,060 pieces of mail in a lifetime, one-third of it junk mail, according to the National Association of Professional Organizers; it is also estimated that executives lose one hour each day to disorganization. A 12-foot wall could be built from New York to Los Angeles with the amount of office and writing paper thrown away each year, and of the paper that is saved and filed away only 20 percent is ever read again (Associated Press, 1996, p. B7).

Fast Facts

❖ The average American is subjected to more than 3,500 advertising messages a day which represents double the rate from 30 years ago (Stern, 1993, p. 10).

❖ From 1963 to 1993, advertising expenditures across all media sources soared from $12 billion to $138 billion (McCann-Erickson Worldwide, 1993).

❖ According to Standard Rate and Data Service, Americans chose from 11,000 different magazines, 10,000 newsletters, and 1,600 newspapers in 1994.

❖ Advertising expenditures in 1997 exceeded the industry's expectations and increased 6.6 percent to $187 billion (Wells and Lieberman, 1997, p. 2B).

❖ The Worldwide Web didn't exist in 1990, but by 1996 there were 11.5 million Americans using the Web with more than 28 million having access to it. It is predicted that by 2000, 52 million people worldwide will be connected (Taylor and Wacker, 1997, p. 156).

even a variety of different magazines addressing how to live. You can live light, live right, live now and can receive hints for living in just about any interest or demographic category of interest. It is possible to break through. Think of what bullfrogs did for Budweiser and what Tiger Woods has done for Nike.

Recall, if you will, the stages of an experience. The initial stage is referred to as the preexperience, and subsegments of that stage include need recognition, alternative search, and preparation. The stages of the experience marketing communication process naturally need to reflect the stages people go through as they become involved with an experience.

Recognition and Inclination

Cracking the communication glut barrier is only a start. One's message needs to take on the next two closely related stages within experience marketing communication, recognition and inclination. How does one let a potential consumer know that he or she has a particular need, a need that matches the outcomes provided by a segment of the experience industry. One can shout to the entire world that it

When members of the Silent Generation were born between 1925 and the early 1940s, the average American, according to the Advertising Research Foundation, spent 4.4 hours on media of all types and was exposed to 76 ads daily. The members of Generation X, that cohort group born between the '60s and the '80s, is only halfway through their life span, and they spend approximately nine hours a day on the media and are exposed to almost 150 ads a day (Taylor and Wacker, 1997, pp. 71–72).

has a need to relax or for personal growth, but how does one frame that message in such a way that it strikes a chord within a person so he or she can recognize that he or she has such a need? A popular winter commercial that plays in the colder climates of the United States featuring pasty, frustrated, frozen office workers screaming "I need it bad" followed by a picture of the same folks soaking up the sun in a tropical setting is certainly a rather effective start.

Identify three of your more recurring communication challenges; they can be difficult target markets, lack of response to promotional efforts, or any situations or issues related to this area. Then as you review the PerInfoCom marketing techniques and strategies, brainstorm how some of the options can address those challenges.

One of the biggest challenges for marketers is to help people recognize what their needs are. So often feelings of unrest exist without a clear resolution at hand. One can't always count on need recognition to make experiences a reality for someone. There are thousands of people who realize that they need to lose weight or feel the need to interact more often or more positively with family, but how does one move the potential participant from recognition to inclination? Much easier said than done.

These two closely connected stages are interesting and challenging as well. Some people may move from recognition to inclination almost instantly while others may take a more extended period of time to become inclined to learn more about an experience or even involve themselves in the actual experience. Information that reminds, reinforces, and supports their beliefs and efforts and prompts people to do something about this need is required. This information may be about the need in general or related to specifics of an experience provider.

Meaning and Actuate

The third stage in this process is called meaning, and it articulates exactly that. How does one communicate with people in such a way that they realize that an experience has meaning and, therefore, importance and value in their lives. There are numerous examples of industrywide efforts to convince people that going on cruises, stopping smoking, or visiting the Bahamas are meaningful and valuable alternatives for them. This stage needs to help the would-be participant discover or recall why this experience would be important to him or her or how it might add value and meaning to his or her life.

The final stage is to actuate, and this stage, too, is a fluid and ongoing stage. We've somehow moved people through these other stages and have convinced them that a particular experience has meaning and value for them, but how do we get them up off the couch and onto the golf course? How do we get them actually to throw away the cigarettes or whatever else it is that we have in mind for them? To actuate means to put into motion or to cause someone to move to act. This is not the easiest of tasks, but one that needs to be tackled. If we can reduce the risk for the person or make it more convenient to do whatever it is we want him or her to do, we have greater chance for success.

Techniques and Strategies
for PerInfoCom

PerInfoCom incorporates a number of challenges for reaching people, sharing information, and creating interest and action on the part of experience participants. These multiple challenges can be categorized as follows: getting attention, creating relationships, influencing behavior, and making the most of resources. There are a host of promotional techniques and marketing strategies that address these challenges with some of them focusing upon more than one.

Raising Awareness or Getting Attention

Before would-be participants can even consider partaking of an experience, they need to know that such an experience exists and recognize they may have a need that can be addressed by such an experience. There are a number of marketing concepts and strategies that hold great promise for experience marketers as they tackle this dual challenge to gain the attention and raise awareness including positioning, lifestyle marketing, event marketing or sponsorship, and guerrilla marketing. Positioning and lifestyle marketing are two concepts that are uniquely directed towards the specific requirements of potential clientele. These two techniques attempt to pull people to the experience. Event marketing, sponsorship, and guerrilla marketing are clearly directed towards alternative approaches of breaking through and pushing the product, service, or experience into the mind of prospective customers.

Positioning

When Ries and Trout first introduced the concept of positioning to the marketing world in 1982 they suggested that the bombardment of society with media messages, new products, and advertising overload necessitated a focus to battle for the attention of consumers' minds. Positioning incorporates the actual design of the experience specifically to meet the needs of a particular group of people. The experience marketing message related to a specific experience must reach out and personally speak to those people for whom the message has been created.

There are three elements within positioning: creating an image, communicating benefits, and differentiating one's product or service from competing products or services. These same three elements are important considerations within the positioning process for experience marketing as well. Island resorts may project an image of a virtual oasis of relaxation and enjoyment to potential guests. The position each resort holds within the mind of its guests is further enhanced by the list of specific benefits or amenities it offers, such as private beach, saltwater or heated pool, or ocean view accommodations. Resorts may then begin to differentiate themselves from the competition by such things as all-inclusive pricing for meals, a focus on a particular type of recreational activity such as golf or water sports, or perhaps by restricting the presence of singles or children as some resorts like Couples or Eden II do. All of these elements add up to create a

Club Med started out life providing simple tenting vacations for French travelers. Shortly thereafter, it evolved into basic, but fun-filled adventure-oriented clubs located in out-of-the-way destinations designed to attract mostly singles. Club Med's prosperity was in large part due to the impact of the Baby Boomers who came of age and fueled the growth of the industry everywhere. The market position held by the club at that time allowed for casual dress, beads replacing wallets, and plenty of young people serving as GOs, or gentle organizers, to fuel the fun for their cohorts.

Suddenly everything started to change. Club Med, that one time haven for singles, suddenly started adding family plans and kiddy activities to regain the folks who had once frequented their establishments and now had spouses and children in tow. Through the years, Club Med has undergone other changes as well. The aging Boomers were also running out of steam so Club Med created a positioning campaign featuring swimmers just floating in inner tubes with the slogan, "the antidote to civilization" and a later slogan, "life the way you want it." Other changes have taken place as well. Sailing ships for Boomers who want the cruise experience and pampering without the pomp and circumstance is one of those changes. Club Med is now piloting a concept called Renew Yourself at its resorts in Mexico by adding yoga, tai chi, and classes on health and wellness to its lineup. A second tier line of clubs has been established to provide Club Med–like amenities and experiences at a reduced price.

The current challenges being faced by Club Med are a result of its past success with positioning. Club Med was so strongly perceived as being swinging singles, fun getaways that it became difficult to move away from that position and attract visitors whose needs have changed over time.

specific perception for the vacationer. An in-pool bar usually suggests partying singles while a tot pool and playground signals families.

Implementing Positioning Within the Experience Industry

Since positioning is so critical to the connection that the experience deliverer makes with a participant, it is not a process to be undertaken lightly or without regard for the myriad of steps to create a viable market position. There are a number of steps within this process of implementing positioning for the experience provider commonly referred to as the six Ds of experience positioning (Reposition '95, 1995):

- Detail the specific needs or range of needs that can be accommodated within your type of experience.
- Depict the specific groups of people who may well be seeking to fulfill the needs that are provided by your experience.
- Delineate the exact benefits target market groups seek to take away from the experience.
- Decide on the image or position you want to create in the participants' mind as it relates to your experience.

- Design the experience as well as the communication message accordingly.
- The final D: demonstrate, deliver, and delight by providing people with what you promised!

Lifestyle Marketing

Another strategy attempt to personalize the awareness process is lifestyle marketing. Americans have become very different from one another. Sure, they live in different geographic locations and hold different types of jobs from one another, but we're talking sizable individual differences in their approach to life. We're talking lifestyle; choices people make about how they live, work, and play and how those choices make individuals different from one another.

One example of the impact of lifestyle marketing on society is magazines. Remember when they were few in number with broad readerships such as *Life* with its memorable cover photos or *The Saturday Evening Post* with its Norman Rockwell portraits. All that has pretty much changed. A quick check at the newsstand reveals a plethora of reading options including such titles as *Tactical Bowhunting, Snowboard Life, American Cheerleader,* and *Modern Dad* just to cite a few. In fact, even in this day and age of media conglomerates, the growth in independent and narrowly focused magazines has soared with the number of new magazines introduced in 1995 reaching a record 838 (Pogrebin, 1997, p. C16).

There are a variety of different factors that can become viable components for lifestyle marketing as the titles of the latest magazines can attest. Some components that influence lifestyle marketing are related to the traditional demographics. Movies such as *The Bridges of Madison County* and *The First Wives Club* are tagged as women's movies. Some components can relate to generational

❖ A Prudential ad shows an older woman opening a ballet school which indicates that she is financially self-sufficient and could benefit from the advice of a financial planner. This ad had a strong response from working women who were drawn to her strong and independent nature while revealing her softer and funnier side with a humorous wink to the audience.

❖ A Sunday newspaper magazine insert called *React* published by Advance Magazine Publications is designed to draw teen and young adult readership and features articles such as zapping out unwanted tattoos, what's in from coast to coast, as well as sports news directed at teens.

❖ The Federal Housing Administration has a new bridal registry savings account where families and friends of newlyweds can deposit cash wedding gifts directly into an interest-bearing account to help newlyweds scrape together a down payment for a house.

❖ Database America maintains 250 databases enabling marketers particularly direct mail advertisers to identify people who have moved recently, "upscale" grandparents, or pet owners.

Being cool has always been an "in" lifestyle but grabbing the cool market has also been a tough target for marketers. Today the prime target of this coolness market are teens who spend $65 billion a year on everything from sneakers to speakers. (Horowitz, 1996, p. 1–2B)

Giants of the business world go to extraordinary lengths to reach (and keep) this ever-evolving yet profitable group—teens who define what's cool for themselves and others as well. Some of the "cool lifestyle" marketing activities include (Horowitz, 1996, pp. 1–2D):

- Nike's distribution of Air Max shoes to exclusive shops in small numbers creating a buying frenzy.
- Levi Strauss' modern version of research anthropologists interviewing teens in their homes while going through their closets to furrow out ideas about their lives and lifestyles.
- Airwalk, shoe provider for skateboarders and snowboarders, uses ambush marketers in trendsetting cities such as New York and Los Angeles to plaster ad posters around construction sites and abandoned buildings.
- Mountain Dew sponsors a mountain biking team that travels around the country drinking Mountain Dew and attracting teens to the races where they are interviewed about their views as to what is cool.
- Tommy Hilfiger provides rap singers with complimentary clothing hoping that stage appearances and promotional materials featuring its clothing line will speak to the teen market.
- Calvin Klein created a new fragrance for teens that's being promoted as scent strips located on Ticketmaster rock concert ticket envelopes.

influences or cohort groupings. Musical hits from the Baby Boomer era are turning up regularly in car commercials. Cars are being designed and touted as "not your father's" type of car. Other factors such as cultural or geographic location can be found in lifestyle marketing as well.

Some of the challenges to lifestyle marketing include strategies to attract more than one lifestyle group within the same message or experience. For example, many gay and lesbian couples have similar experience preferences as Dinks (double income, no kids). Another challenge is finding balance in the lifestyle message so that it is not overly obvious to the intended lifestyle group. Lifestyle marketing, while critical to attracting and meeting the needs of a specific group, must continually attempt to bridge the gap between the niche of the lifestyle group and the broader market.

Event Marketing & Sponsorship

This strategy of marketing and sponsorship seeks to get the attention of potential experience participants by reaching out and going to where they are. Event marketing consists of creating or supporting events in exchange for access to participants. Sponsorship, while often linked to event support, has launched an expanded life of its own by securing exclusive rights of products and services in specific venues. According to *IEG Sponsorship Report*, a Chicago-based newsletter that tracks sports, entertainment, and cause marketing worldwide, expenditures on this type of marketing totaled $9.6 billion in 1993, an increase from the $8.5 billion expended the previous year.

Events are big business as sponsors line up to link their name with everything and anything from art exhibits to zoos. Events enable companies to refine and reach their target markets in ways they would be otherwise unable to do by utilizing more mass marketing alternatives. There is a connection between events and activities to which people are attracted, and companies are able to get the attention of particular markets through event sponsorship. Companies desiring to reach an older, more upscale market may sponsor a cultural event such as a concert, theater production, or art exhibit. If the same company wanted to reach a high-income group with greater age diversity, it might choose to support a golf tournament. The real value of event marketing and sponsorship is the ability to zero in on exactly the people one is trying to reach through lifestyle pursuits and interests.

There are a variety of alternatives and options available to companies interested in this marketing strategy. A company can elect to seek sponsorship for an existing event or venue or decide to create an event of its own. Philip Morris is a regular sponsor of major art exhibits across the country. Some companies create their own event as did Seagrams when it created The Absolut Best of L. A., a four-day lifestyle event targeting upscale consumers on the back lot of Universal Studios. It invited other "best" brands such as Perrier, Starbucks, and Mondavi wines to participate in this event.

Corporate sponsorship is becoming more competitive today as the number and type of organizations vying for exclusive sponsorship rights grows. The competition extends beyond the dollar amount as corporations realize the importance of exclusivity. VISA is the only card one takes to the Olympics or certain restaurants. It gets complicated. Originally Coke had the rights to use the Dallas Cowboy name and logo, then Pepsi reciprocated by buying the pouring rights in Texas Stadium where the Cowboys play (Frank, 1996, pp. B1, B8).

❖ ESPN created the X Games for the sole purpose of attracting a growing Generation X audience for its newly developed channel, ESPN2.
❖ VISA now calls itself the "official" credit card of Atlanta and the "preferred" card of San Francisco.
❖ The After Shock's Virtual Reality Tour '96 was created by Jim Beam Brands Co. to promote its new hot-cool cinnamon liquor by taking eight custom-designed virtual reality games to 2,000 bars in 45 cities.
❖ St. Francis Hospital and Medical Center in Hartford, Connecticut, dedicated its new 10-story patient care center by throwing a full-day party and celebration for the community including free entertainment, food, and art exhibits.

A new twist of corporate sponsorship emerges as "municipal marketing" where soft drink, car, and credit card companies spend an estimated $20 million nationally linking their products and services to desirable locations (Wells, 1997, p. 4B). The beaches in Los Angeles County have made Ford Rangers the official vehicle and Speedo the official lifeguard bathing suit. The stakes in municipal marketing continue to climb. Boston Garden is now the Fleet Center. In San Francisco, Candlestick Park has been renamed 3Com Park, and Cincinnati's Riverfront Stadium is Cinergy Field, both named after corporate sponsors.

We've just seen the tip of the iceberg as it relates to event marketing and sponsorship. Its potential for zeroing in on very specific markets makes it fertile ground for marketers. The other added bonus of this approach that can't be overlooked is the experiential nature of this marketing strategy. This approach has a double bang for the buck because it provides the people a company wants to know and reach with an experience specifically designed for them.

Guerrilla Marketing

Another push-oriented marketing strategy devised to break through and get the attention of target markets is guerrilla marketing. This strategy recognizes the difficulty of capturing the people's attention due to the bombardment of information, especially advertising messages. The necessity for breaking through the myriad of messages and the blitz of different approaches leads to an increasing reliance on this approach where providers try to seize (hijack) the attention of the marketplace.

Some of the more shocking things done in the name of advertising are really an attempt to get the consumer's attention. Calvin Klein's controversial

> ❖ Use of look-alike priority mail in bright colors leads the recipient to believe it is urgent and important when it may well be just another solicitation.
>
> ❖ An aerobic, high-stepping Santa Claus from the Wellbridge, Massachusetts, Health and Fitness Club conducted a step aerobic class in a local supermarket near the holiday season.
>
> ❖ Tequila maker Jose Cuervo bought a Caribbean island and then applied for a seat in the United Nations.
>
> ❖ A solicitation letter from the Alzheimer's Association indicated that "latest research news" was enclosed.
>
> ❖ Taco Bell bought full-page ads in newspapers nationally declaring that it had secured exclusive corporate sponsorship of the Liberty Bell only later to scream "April Fool"; they spent $400,000 on ads that generated more that 400 stories and national TV coverage.

commercials selling jeans and unisex fragrances came under attack from a variety of sources on a regular basis. This eventually became part of the entire campaign, and Calvin Klein thrives on the controversy and attention. Delta Airlines grabbed its week in the spotlight when it created a living billboard with guests eating a complimentary lunch sitting aboard a replica of Delta transatlantic business class in the middle of Times Square.

Influencing Behavior

If an initial purpose of PerInfoCom is to raise awareness of experiences and needs related to those experiences, then an equally important component of the process is that of influencing behavior. Four techniques used for this purpose are incentives, loyalty marketing, cause marketing, and social marketing. The first three techniques cited are directed at influencing consumer purchasing behavior while the last approach, social marketing, addresses changing people's behavior in a more socially positive manner or altering their behavior related to a social issue.

Incentives and Loyalty Marketing

Use of incentives whether they were giveaways, coupons, or price discounts have long been a way to influence consumers' purchasing patterns prompting them to take action. Health clubs offer special incentive price packages if people purchase a membership prior to the official opening of the facility. Early bird dinner discounts serve as an incentive to convince some people to dine earlier than planned. Children eat free at some restaurants when accompanied by one or more adult diners. Sponsors of road races offer complimentary T-shirts or water bottles to the first 200 people who register for the event. Coupons, a longtime incentive, are still in use primarily to influence people to purchase a new product or try out the new driving range.

Many of these incentives moved into the big time and resurfaced as more extensive, sophisticated loyalty marketing programs as companies began to realize the cost and value of retaining customers rather than replacing them. One such option involves frequency programs. Market research indicates that it is five times more expensive to attract new customers than it is to retain current customers. Such research found that 20 percent of those customers account for 80 percent of the company's business, and such findings have reinforced this marketing approach.

American Airlines set this concept in motion when it created AAdvantage, its frequent-flier program, in 1981. Within about 18 months all major airlines had a similar program, and since that time just about everyone has gotten in the act as have small businesses which use simple, inexpensive, incentive programs such as frequent customer cards to cultivate customer loyalty (Fulkerson, 1996, p. 44).

The potential benefits of such an approach are underscored by two simple but powerful concepts, lifetime revenue and share of customer. Lifetime revenue refers to the total amount a single, loyal customer will spend on a product, service, or experience over the course of his or her lifetime. Using actual purchase patterns and past behavior as predictors of future action, one major pizza chain calculated the lifetime revenue from a single loyal customer as $8,000 (Lacek, 1995, p. 20). The second concept, share of customer, refers to the percentage of business received from a particular customer. If a business traveler takes 10 flights a year and only two of those flights are with a particular airline, that airline's share of that customer is 20 percent. This means that the other 80 percent of the customer's airline business with other companies is a big marketing opportunity from a loyalty approach (Lacek, 1995, p. 20).

Cause Marketing

Two other marketing alternatives that hold potential for experience marketing that take a slightly more altruistic approach are social and cause marketing. While the two approaches are often associated with one another, their goals and focus are really quite different.

Cause-related marketing is more business centered. It's a growth industry. *IEG Sponsorship Reports* indicates that spending in this area has increased from $78 million in 1988 to $485 million in 1996 (Kadlec, 1997, p. 63). This trend,

Slice of Life

The entire area of frequent-flier miles and subsequent affinity cards has expanded way beyond anyone's original expectations. People rush to pick up dinner checks. People acquiesce to root canal work or pay a five percent surcharge at a clearance sale. All in the name of frequent-flier miles. Randy Petersen, publisher of *Inside Flyer*, estimates that a determined, but infrequent flier could easily rack up about 100,000 miles in a year by charging everything such as eating out, making a lot of phone calls, refinancing his or her mortgage, making home improvements, buying music or magazines, taking vacations, or making donations (Alexander, 1996, p. 6E). Evidently when it comes to stacking up frequent-flier miles the sky is not the limit. Yes, loyalty incentives can and do influence behavior.

referred to as "strategic philanthropy," links products, services, and experiences with causes that count with consumers as a way to differentiate the organization from its competitors and to influence behavior. Companies may undertake cause-related marketing by donating money to a specific cause based on percentage of purchases, creating socially responsible programs, or allowing employees to take time off to volunteer for a cause or issue.

Cause marketing serves a dual purpose. The advertising related to the social cause generates attention and awareness for the organization. However, a big advantage is that research reveals that while cause-related marketing won't compel a consumer to make a purchase that he or she normally would not, it does influence his or her behavior to purchase the product or service whose cause is important to him or her. It can and does pay off. Sebastian International, a hair-care products company, built a marketing program around saving the rain forests and within five years doubled annual sales from $50 million to $100 million (Cross and Smith, 1995, p. 103).

Social Marketing

Social marketing differs from cause-related marketing. While they both have social responsibility as a basis, the purpose of social marketing is to benefit people and not primarily the bottom line of corporations. Once almost entirely dependent on public service announcements, social marketing now uses commercial marketing techniques to influence the voluntary behavior of target audiences to

❖ The Fashion Footwear Association of New York and QVC joined together during Breast Cancer Awareness Month to host a FFANY Shoes for Sale with about 70,000 pairs of designer shoes being sold at half the retail price on QVC with all proceeds benefiting breast cancer research and education.

❖ *Bon Appétit* and the Make-A-Wish Foundation teamed up with a gaggle of entertainers for the annual Wine & Spirits Focus, a fund-raising event featuring food sampling with cities' top chefs and restaurants as well as wine tastings and representatives from various international tourist offices.

❖ The '96 version of the famous Neiman Marcus holiday catalog featured a highest bidder mail auction offering a life-sized replica of an X-Wing Fighter from Star Wars (there were just a few of them made). Minimum bid was $35,000, and any amount over that went to Starbright Foundation to help children with serious medical challenges.

❖ Dirt Devil, Cross pens, McDonald's, Coca-Cola, and Proctor & Gamble are chasing aging Baby Boomers with their support of the Arthritis Foundation.

❖ General Motors and Ford are dueling over the top spot in the war on breast cancer. GM paid $4 million for a three-year fashion show sponsorship while Ford sponsors Race for the Cure, a road race for breast cancer research.

improve their personal welfare and that of society (Andreasen, 1995, p. 7). The similarity between the two lies with the intended outcome of improving society or the world as we know it.

Social marketing focuses its attention on the individual. The goal of social marketing is to change behavior that will eventually have a positive impact on the individual's life and possibly that of society as well. Social marketing campaigns to help people stop smoking or inform people of the dangers of drinking and driving fall into this category as do social marketers who attempt to change attitudes to related personal, social, and environmental issues.

AIDS Project Los Angeles and BBDO West unveiled a public service campaign themed: "There's life after sex" to tell young gay men not to throw away their lives with unsafe sex. Active Living Healthy Lifestyles, a joint social marketing program of the National Recreation and Park Association and the Centers for Disease Control, helped public park and recreation departments nationwide involve the public in physical activity pursuits that were good fun and were good for them. There is no limit to the numbers of "risk" behaviors that can be targeted through this approach. Campaigns such as the public awareness project launched by the Illinois Association of Park Districts are also a form of social marketing. In this instance the organization was not trying to change individual behavior but rather was attempting to create awareness and change attitudes about the importance of preserving and protecting open space.

Creating Relationships

Once the previously mentioned challenges have been overcome and the marketing techniques have led to attention, awareness, and behavior change on the part of the consumer, the next natural step is to create a relationship with that participant. If two of the purposes of PerInfoCom are to raise awareness and influence behavior, an equally important component is the creation of relationships. Three techniques used for this purpose are information, affiliation or associative, and interactive marketing. A commonality among these three strategies is the exchange between the participant and the organization. The differences among the strategies are the nature of what is being exchanged.

Information Marketing

One can't discount the rapidly escalating role that information plays in marketing today especially when it comes to experiences. If the prospective experience is going to involve one's physical presence and psyche, it's critical that people have information to help them make the choice that's right for them as well as to enable them to be comfortable enough with each choice.

Feather identifies an emerging concept of consumer spending that involves a shift from spending to "info-based value" (Feather, 1994, pp. 78–79). This concept maintains that value is created when information creates special meaning for the customers and enhances the purchase experience. While consumers fully

PHOTOGRAPHED BY JACK LANE

A kid can't run his toes through concrete.

Will you ever grow too old to remember the feel of grass on your bare feet?

It's a feeling every child should know, but we may run out of grass. The bulldozers are digging up the green like there's no tomorrow.

But there *is* a tomorrow. There are lots of tomorrows. Tomorrows beyond our lives. So let's think of our kids, and their kids, and generations to come.

Let's make sure there'll be some grass for them to run their toes through.

That's where your local park district and forest preserve come in. The people there are concerned. Support their programs. Become involved in their plans.

And your children won't have to run their toes through concrete.

Support Your Local Park Districts and Forest Preserves

ILLINOIS ASSOCIATION OF PARK DISTRICTS

Reprinted with permission of the Illinois Association of Park Districts, Springfield, Illinois.

expect to be informed about the personal and social benefits of a purchase, they are also looking for additional types of information. The exchange of information can form the basis of a relationship between the consumer and the organization.

The dissemination of information for marketing purposes is not entirely new, but its role in the PerInfoCom process has been heightened and has led to the introduction of some new approaches through information marketing. Informercials, advertorials, and personalized newsletters are a few of these techniques.

Informercials are especially effective formats for the experience industry as evidenced by

some of the high-profile efforts of Walt Disney Co., Club Med, and Busch Entertainment. The typical 30-minute formats offer a number of advantages for providers within the experience industry because they actually have the time to

❖ Inter-Continental Hotels, drawing on inside information from their worldwide network of concierges, publishes a pamphlet called "Concierge Confidential" filled with inside hints for having fun or doing the unusual in various locations. Activities such as renting a bike at the Spanish Steps in Rome to pedal through Borghese Park or going to the salt mines via a privately guided day trip to the Wieliczska Salt Mine in Warsaw are included in this booklet.

❖ A Williamsburg informercial features a four-day package for a family of four for $455 including lodging and unlimited visits to five attractions. It was shot in a spontaneous, "experienced" fashion relying on visitor testimonials from adults and children who painted a realistic, insightful view of such a trip.

❖ Macy's in-house advertising department created "Ten to Count On" print ads that give women information they can use by telling them 10 new items they can buy or trends they can follow to update their wardrobe.

❖ The City of Beverly Hills, California, has a video exhibiting the charms of this small city with the dynamics of a big city, and it comes complete with a welcoming letter from the mayor.

❖ NordicTrack finds success selling its aerobic exercise equipment by providing a free video and brochure for perspective customers who call their 800 number.

❖ Hotel guests don't have to search for phone books in nightstands or drag them around the room. On Command Video which provides movies in a third of the nation's hotel rooms has signed to provide Bell Atlantic's InfoTravel service of the Yellow Pages that gives traveler's information about rest, night life, and local services. An added feature is the automatic dial to a selected restaurant with a return call back to your room phone when connected. It can also create a map that has "turn by turn" directions to that restaurant as well as a discount coupon which can be retrieved at the front desk (Business Travel, 1996, p. 4D).

explain the experience. It's the kind of explanation that's difficult in a 30-second commercial or on a single print ad page. Participants are able to feel more comfortable with the experience and the experience provider because they feel as if they have established a basis for such involvement.

Not all information takes a video format; there are a host of printed options that are very popular. Newcomers include advertorials and magalogs. Advertorials are a cross between advertisements and editorials. These tend to be highly effective since people don't always recognize the overlap or blur between what seems to have been reported rather than promoted.

Infomags or magalogs, information infused catalogs, are making the scene where articles and lifestyle information are taking over the pages, and the merchandise almost appears to take second place. *Spa Finders News* is one such example. This glossy, seasonal publication intersperses articles on exercise, self-acceptance, sunscreen advice, and self-hypnosis with ads and special promotions from member spas. The cruise industry takes a similar approach with *World of Cruising* filled with plenty of inviting pictures, articles on kids' camps and new spa facilities as well as upcoming cruise schedules.

Newsletters are particularly popular because they can be easily personalized with today's technology and sometimes simulate or suggest common bonds. *Backroads Active Traveler* is filled with news, notes, and travel tips from this active travel company. Many segments of the retail industry such as jewelry stores and car dealers create and disseminate quarterly or monthly newsletters to exchange information and maintain relationships with their better customers.

Affiliation or Associative Marketing

Everybody wants to belong or at least feel as if he or she belongs. Everyone wants to feel as if he or she is a part of something bigger or more important than himself or herself. That's what's led to the implementation of affiliation or associative marketing. Due to the interconnected nature of their focus, the two terms are used in conjunction with one another, but they differ slightly from one another as well. Affiliation marketing plays on an individual's need to feel as if he or she belongs somewhere or someplace and that this membership or relationship comes with some kind of privileges. Associative marketing addresses a similar inner need while enabling people to associate themselves with something or someone of importance to them.

Commercial health clubs have *members* rather than mere customers who pay for a service. YMCAs differentiate themselves from commercial health clubs by advertising that at the Y you belong. American Express boasts that membership has its privileges in much of its advertising. The privileges of membership have extended to other experience providers. Zoos, aquariums, art museums, and theater companies all offer memberships to their clientele. For the cost of an annual membership, people are afforded certain privileges such as access to best seats, reduced pricing, and special members-only events. Added bonuses of membership sometimes include free parking and reduction of time waiting in long lines. Affiliation marketing has evolved to provide people not only with a sense of belonging but also with added benefits and privileges and as so is quite effective.

THIRTY DAYS OF FAMILY FUN

Any time of year is a good time of year to focus thirty days on family fun! Seasonal celebrations, holiday fetes, and being a tourist in your own time offer great family activities to promote.

GROUP PACK ACTIVITIES OF FAMILY FUN			
Project	Item #	Page	Project Price*
Magnetic Frames	SB6-GP1020	5	$ .58
Friendship Bracelets	SB6-GP599	14	.13
Silver Streak Streamers	SB6-GP631	18	.08
Ancient Culture Panels	SB6-GP735	46	1.60
Color-Me Calendars	SB6-GP568	41	.53
Terrific T-Shirts	SB6-GP409 S/M/L	41	2.33
Heart Light Lanterns	SB6-GP887	39	1.15
Family Trees	SB6-GP2	25	.27
Handprint Poem	SB6-GP445	25	.37

*Price per project. See 1996 S&S Full Line catalog for the price per kit.

ACTIVITY IDEAS!

Activity ideas for program leaders:

1. Publish a calendar of ideas for families to be "tourists in their own town." The list should include free and inexpensive activities available locally. Remember, most people will visit another community before they stop and think to look at what is available close to home.

2. Share a promotional effort with one of your local media outlets and have a contest for kids which challenges them to come up with the craziest ideas for family fun for under a designated dollar figure. The winning entry wins the experience for the whole family. Encourage them to write what makes their family so much fun to be with.

3. Have your group come up with activities and suggestions to send to Family Fun Magazine. What? You've not heard about Family Fun? It's available at the local magazine stores and offers wonderful activity suggestions for young children and their families. Maybe you can get them to do a story about your special program!

4. Create Homemade signs for the refrigerator, garden, bathroom, etc... to promote positive ideas for the whole family.

23

People pay large sums of money to join private clubs so that they can affiliate or associate with people like themselves or people whom they emulate. Not all people are either able or interested in such direct contact with a desirable individual or group of people. This leaves an opening for associative marketing where people are afforded various options of appearing to be associated with somebody famous or someone with good taste or a special interest of some kind. People shell out sizable sums of cash to be able to wear Michael Jordan's style of sneakers or to outfit themselves with a Notre Dame football jacket so they can vicariously feel associated with people or organizations that have value to them.

The use of names and labels whether they be on Martha Stewart's towels at Kmart or a Ducks Unlimited logo on a VISA card are all a part of this strategy.

Interactive Marketing

Interactive is one of those buzzwords in the new world of marketing as companies scramble to integrate technology options with their overall marketing plan. While everybody is talking about it and even more people are trying to get into it, it is difficult to get a handle on exactly what interactive marketing is or can be. Examples include such alternatives as home shopping, informercials, CD-ROMs, commercial on-line services, interactive 800 numbers, the Internet, kiosks, and virtual reality (Williamson, 1996, p. S-3).

While it may be hard to conceive that interactive marketing can change the world, it most certainly will and, in fact, already has. Interactive marketing really opens up the doors for the permission model of marketing that Godin has been promoting. Imagine never again feeling hunted or harassed in a car dealer's showroom. Cars are now being purchased via the Internet or television. Even the more traditional shopper venturing into a dealership will be afforded computer searches and virtual reality test rides. CD-ROMs will afford the home shopper guidance and information as he or she looks for the home exercise equipment right for his or her situation. Kiosks will pop up everywhere people roam providing on-the-spot information and assistance. Virtual reality will enable people to analyze and determine the suitability of a particular experience for them. The options for meeting, greeting, and interacting with people are nearly endless.

Such reliance on technology makes for equal opportunity marketing as big and small businesses have an equal footing in this arena. In fact, some smaller companies have displaced larger more prominent companies solely on the basis of their approach to the Internet. Early brand Web sites such as Ragu and Zims didn't just advertise on the Internet, but their ads included some fun and funky content, and their sites were highly trafficked because of it. Ragu started off by delivering Italian lessons on-line. Levi positioned itself as the place kids go to find the ultimate definition as to what's cool.

Web sites won't be the only engaging way to reach participants. Store displays include interactive point of purchase opportunities where either by screen or voice the customer can input information that will guide him or her to the right product choice. These particular types of interactivity will assist people in understanding why a product is better or different from the competition's (Beresford, 1995, p. 28). The "big boxes," those large warehouse-type stores, can provide suggestive sell directions by generating personal information through their individual customer card. The specialty stores, big and small, can avail themselves of such interactivity to assist customers who can't even begin to understand which of the 47 styles and types of sneakers are right for them.

Two aspects of interactive marketing are what Peppers and Rogers refer to as invitational and solicited advertising. Invitational ads will "invite" the user to hear or view the message perhaps in exchange for some incentive, a form of permission, and the solicited approach enables customers to seek out specifics of a product or service when ready to buy (Pepper and Rogers, 1997, p. 32).

❖ The Levi Strauss Web site lets people browse through the many Levi styles and products, and it also features interesting offers such as a Levi's 501 contest for the MTV Music Awards or an opportunity to enter one's old denim jacket in its search for the oldest Levi's jeans jacket contest (http://www.levi.com).

❖ The California Department of Tourism with an interactive 800 telephone number allows people to select travel preferences ranging from Fun and Family to Romantic Getaways and then faxes specifics to the caller.

❖ PepsiCo in an attempt to promote Mountain Dew soft drinks gave 500,000 teens beepers to create a network; they beeped them weekly with discount offers and prize drawings, and those who called back on a toll-free number heard recordings from sports and entertainment celebrities. Prizes included personal snowboarding lessons, a trip to MTV's Beach House, and recording sessions at SONY studios.

❖ Cover Girl introduced a Web site where teenage girls could get answers to questions about their skin tone, hair, and eye colors and then receive specific suggestions for colors of makeup.

Making the Most of Resources

We live in a new age of limits. There are limits to the resources available whether it be money to purchase advertising time or the time or energy it takes to seek out and to participate in experiences. These limits placed on resources create the impetus for experience providers to make the most of existing resources when they attempt to implement PerInfoCom.

The techniques and strategies incorporated in this section include real marketing, ambush marketing, and 3Cs marketing. These approaches differ substantially from one another, but the essential commonality is the focus on saving time, money, and energy in the experience marketing process.

Ambush Marketing

High-profile marketing efforts can result in substantial financial outlays for large corporations. Becoming the "official" card of Atlanta was a serious investment for VISA. Likewise, it takes substantial investment to either have a sports complex named for a specific corporation or even to assure pouring rights for a soft drink at the venue. Smaller enterprises are faced with a different challenge since they just can't pay for access to heighten visibility.

Enter ambush marketing. The necessity for breaking through the myriad of messages without expending a great deal of money, or any money in certain instances, is the prime objective of this approach. Nike is the king of ambush marketing as proved by its repeated success with Olympic "perceived" sponsorship. Choosing to not pay the $40 million for official Olympic sponsorship, it was often incorrectly identified as a sponsor of the 1996 Olympic Games in part because it opened Nike park, a $3 million retail center and sports museum in a parking garage near Centennial Olympic Park. Nike billboards in Atlanta featured the slogan "You don't win silver, you lose gold," and its ads during that time period featured a montage of athletes engaged in Olympic-like sports (Wells, 1996, B1).

Ambush marketing doesn't always involve such high-powered approaches. Some of the techniques are more subtle and certainly less costly. When Snapple faced growing competition from beverage imitators and wanted to regain its cool image particularly among the younger crowd, it implemented ambush marketing by parking a sampling truck near the television studio where "The Late Show with David Letterman" is taped. They handed out free drinks and T-shirts, and, sure enough, they showed up on camera.

Real Marketing

What is real marketing, anyway? Real marketing is about time, place, and the individual participant. Today, thanks to technology, the general pace of life, and growing expectations related to individualization and personalization, people have come to expect exactly what they want as well as when and where they want it. Companies waste resources when they ignore these "real" marketing issues.

Real time is the time that works for the consumer. Pizza delivery in 20 minutes, ATM machines, and 24-hour grocery stores make "on demand" the watchword for today. Real place refers not to where the store or factory is located but where the consumer is. Pay-per-view television, home fitness equipment, and

It can start with the Burger King logo on the side of the school bus in the morning. It can be Mountain Dew advertising banners in the high-school hallway. It can include "Enter the crunch zones" on Frito-Lay vending machines or branded refrigerators holding Pepsi or Coke products. Many school districts faced with declining tax dollars to support everything from basic equipment to extracurricular supplies are being funded by advertisers practicing real place marketing. Channel One, a weekday morning show, beamed directly into school buildings comes with commercial sponsorship. A local Dr. Pepper bottler paid three large suburban high schools in the Dallas area almost a $100,000 for a seven-year vending and signage contract. ATT will spend $150 million over five years in a more subtle way providing Internet access to schools. Taco Bell and Pizza Hut supply food to hundreds of cafeterias across the country who in turn sell their products to students. Nike supplies a girls' high-school basketball team in Beaverton, Oregon, with sneakers, warm-up gear, and equipment bags.

It's only the beginning. The Colorado Springs school district's marketing program rolled out an aggressive school bus ad program in 1994 to supplement its $146 million annual operating budget. The district now collects $113,000 annually from ads on school buses and in school hallways by Pepsi-Cola, Burger King, 7-Up, the American Cancer Society, and local retailers. The district hired a local advertising firm to boost the ad revenue to as much as $500,000 in the future. The New York City Board of Education hopes to raise $25 million over five years by selling ad space on 3,000 school buses (Glamser, 1997, p. 3A).

Such efforts capture real time and place variables.

home delivery of gourmet meals redefines place as Channel One goes to schools and CNN goes to airports.

We used to read a magazine called *Life,* then *People,* and now *Self.* People view themselves as individuals whose needs and preferences are the "real" object of marketing. We can circle the globe knowing that the hotel chain's computer system serves as a type of advance team relaying needs and preferences prior to arrival.

We are very much into real time, real place, and real self, and as a marketing strategy it is not a nicety but a necessity. Going to the places where potential participants live, work, and play will become the name of the game. Advertisers are rushing into schools where lucrative, impressionable, and growing markets exist. Brands of all kinds from beverages to pizza are moving into shopping centers, large stores, and public parks—anywhere they can reach large numbers of people. If people want to place catalog orders at 3 A.M. or eat dinner at 3 P.M., the mechanisms to make that happen have to be in place. The presence of Zines on the Internet will allow individuals to express their own preferences incredibly easily. Burger King didn't know the eventual ramifications of its slogan, "Have it your way." It will become the watchword for all of industry throughout the world.

❖ The two largest greeting card makers, American Greetings and Hallmark, entered the latest advance in the right time, right place, right people marketing option as they enable customers to personalize greetings cards by computer. Personalization isn't the only "real" thing about this option. Their choices along with names and addresses of those for whom the cards were designed are then forwarded to company headquarters where technicians print and mail them for the right dates and times throughout the year. As an added bonus they send you a reminder around the time they sent dear old Aunt Martha a birthday card so that you can respond appropriately when she thanks you for your thoughtfulness. Computer packages let the senders customize the image on the front, the verse inside, and even the logo on the back. Think about it—you can do all your shopping at once, at the time that's right for you (Nelson, 1996, B1).

❖ Vail, Colorado, the nation's most-visited resort, created an industry first by adding an in-flight concierge to some Vail-bound flights to help visitors plan their stays. The service which premiered in December 1996 on American Airlines flights from Newark was designed to help travelers make last-minute bookings for car rentals, ski school lessons, and other activities while still on the plane because in today's fast paced world families often don't have the time to sit down and discuss what they'd like to do on vacation and when.

❖ Cover Concepts Marketing Services tapped into a network of 22,000 day-care centers that pass along product samples and coupons to toddlers and their parents (Thomas, 1996, B1).

❖ Corporate recruiters head to Florida during spring break and accept resumes and interview college students right on the beaches as a way to reach Gen Xers as potential employees.

❖ The Philadelphia Museum of Art packaged the only North American exhibit of 180 works by Cézanne by arranging hotel packages that included tickets, transportation, and lodging as well as discounts from Amtrak or US Air.

❖ Six Flags over New Jersey entered into a coupon agreement with Burger King restaurants within a day's drive of the park featuring directions to the Six Flags as well as discount offers for park admission and add-on deals for Burger King purchases.

❖ Disney got help to hype its new acquisition of ABC through a working agreement with McDonald's and GM; McDonald's carried posters, tray liners, and TV guides touting ABC shows; and GM gave away a 1997 Pontiac Gran Am to one ABC viewer each night during premiere week in September 1996.

❖ Fast-food franchises are beginning to practice "dual-branding" by combining two or three restaurants in the same quarters, cutting costs, and building traffic as evidenced by the 40 Wendy's in Canada that operate with donut shops and PepsiCo's practice of putting KFC and Taco Bells together.

Real marketing is really about the bottom line by affording companies real access to target markets in the time, the place, and the way that works for them. Such an approach increases the return on marketing investment.

3Cs Marketing

In this day and age when identifying potential customers is a high priority and trying to break through the myriad of different promotional messages out there can be incredibly expensive, one viable opportunity for accomplishing both of these tasks is the options with 3Cs marketing. The 3Cs include the techniques of comarketing, cross promotion, and combination marketing. All three of these techniques focus on making the most of marketing resources.

Comarketing is a partnership relationship that is a definite win-win for all the parties involved whether there are two or twenty. Comarketing simply means that the business or brand doesn't go it alone, but, rather, it joins with other related, noncompeting companies or products to share customer base and to save money on a number of operation costs.

Cross promotional efforts can involve sharing the costs associated with marketing and promotion. A number of local tourism providers have created mechanisms for this approach. A group of experience providers who have some kind of common theme such as geographic location can band together and undertake cooperative advertising ventures sharing the expense of printing and distributing a brochure that promotes visits to their locale.

Another approach is for businesses to share customers with one another. Businesses whose products, services, or experiences support one another in some way such as rental cars, camping suppliers, and adventure outfitters could create a similar type of promotional tool. In this instance, not only would they be sharing the expense of the advertising, but also they would be sharing their

❖ Northwest Airlines created a Dream-Perks Auction in which frequent-flier miles could be used as currency to participate in an auction for some of the most incredible items. Hosted by Sotheby's out of New York, frequent fliers bid on such experiences as a tour date with B. B. King at which the lucky bidder would be presented with a Lucille guitar from Gibson; a stint as an honorary ringmaster with the Barnum & Bailey Circus in the city of the bidder's choice; a personalized San Francisco reunion for sixteen; or a Sotheby-hosted wine tasting excursion to Los Angeles, New York, or Europe. The sky was the limit with this contest.

❖ MCI's Holiday Entertaining Tipline, complete with an 800 number, brought together celebrity suggestions for decorating, dining, fashion, and etiquette for the season. Celebrities included were fashion designer Issac Mizrahi on how to look one's best when entertaining; wine expert Robert Mondavi on selecting special wines; and Joan Rivers with upbeat suggestions for intermingling family and friends at holiday gatherings. MCI made a donation to the March of Dimes Foundations on behalf of the participating celebrities.

❖ Never to be overlooked in the low-tech, high-touch wars for market share are giveaways such as the somewhat infamous "Drink Pepsi get stuff" campaign where Pepsi drinkers buying the product from specially marked packages collected points and got free stuff. "Stuff" included denim jackets, mini sports balls, CD cases, blue shades, beach chairs with can holders (for Pepsi products) as well as such enticing items as mountain bikes. PepsiCo ran into a bit of trouble when the commercial promoting this incentive featured a Harrier jet fighter plane redeemable at 7 million premium points, and one point collector tried to cash in on the offer. Neither Pepsi nor the Department of Defense was particularly amused.

❖ The Fox Network was one of the first to move into the membership aspect of this category with Kids Club. The Fox Network developed Kids Club as a way to grow its market by targeting the growing numbers of the Baby Boomlet and to have that market grow along with them since it will be a substantial market of the future. A basic communication tool of this membership is the seasonal magazine which includes a variety of discounts on what the network calls "cool spots" within the reader's area such as fast-food restaurants, miniature golf courses, and children's museums. Of course, also included in the magazine are a variety of incentives, or tie-ins, with television characters to encourage more viewing of, you guessed it, the Fox network. There are contests included in the magazine and they are fairly amazing especially in terms of the experiential nature of the prizes. The Autumn 1996 issue of *Totally Fox Kids* featured a number of contests for readers. An eight-year-old won a truckload of new Power Rangers Zeo toys, but he also got to keep the truck the toys came in even though he couldn't drive for another eight years. A preteen girl won an all-expense paid trip to New York City complete with a $1,000 shopping spree and lunch at Fashion Cafe.

customer base with a high likelihood of potential business with the others. In a manner similar to ambush marketing, they are making the most of their resources and communicating with people who may be predisposed to their product, service, or experience.

Action Agenda

❖ Identify three of your most frequent groups of participants and identify how the stages of communication might differ for the various groups.
❖ Select a challenging or difficult-to-reach target market for your organization and analyze the three stages of PerInfoCom for hints or suggestions as to how better to reach them.
❖ Brainstorm how lifestyle messages or approaches might vary for different groups of participants and give specific examples.
❖ Review the current promotional efforts for your organization and see how many of the PerInfoCom strategies are currently being used.
❖ Take a look at the various PerInfoCom strategies suggested in this chapter and create three new approaches that you could begin to use.

The last of the 3Cs approach, combination marketing, is a double or triple whammy of marketing and promotional techniques. This approach takes one or more marketing strategies and combines them to create an effort that gets attention, influences behavior, or creates a relationship. It is a true "making the most" strategy and often results in some of the more creative promotional approaches.

Transition Tracking

From	*To*
Traditional Marketing	Experience Marketing
• Promotion	• PerInfoCom
• Interruption	• Permission
• Advertising	• Positioning
Publicity	Lifestyle
Promotion	Event Marketing
Personal Selling	Sponsorship
	Guerrilla
	Loyalty
	Cause
	Social
	Info marketing
	Affiliation or associative
	Interactive
	Ambush
	Real marketing
	3Cs (comarketing, cross marketing, and combination marketing)

Sources

Alexander, Keith. (1996, September 17). Earning frequent-flier miles on the ground. *USA Today.*

Andreasen, Alan R. (1995). *Marketing social change.* San Francisco, CA: Jossey-Bass.

Associated Press. (1996, October 7). Tools of organization making life disorganized. *Hartford Courant Business Magazine.*

Beresford, Lynn. (1995, October). Marketing smarts. *Entrepreneur.*

Business travel. (1996, October 1). *USA Today.*

Cross, Richard, & Smith, Janet. (1995). *Customer bonding—Pathways to lasting customer loyalty.* Lincolnwood, IL: NTC Business Books.

Davidson, Jeff. (1991). *Breathing space—Living & working at a comfortable pace in a sped-up society.* New York, NY: MasterMedia Limited.

Feather, Frank. (1994). *The future consumer.* Toronto, Canada: Warwick Publishing.

Frank, Robert. (1996, September 4). Signing O'Neal costs the Lakers Coca-Cola deal. *The Wall Street Journal.*

Fulkerson, Jennifer. (1996, July). It's in the customer cards. *Advertising Age.*

George, W. R., & Berry, L. L. (1984). Guidelines for the advertising of services. In C. H. Lovelock (Ed.), *Services marketing: Texts, cases and readings,* (pp. 407–411). Englewood Cliffs, NJ: Prentice Hall

Glamser, Deeann. (1997, January 3). This class brought to you by. . . . *USA Today.*

Horowitz, Bruce. (1996, September 4). The quest for cool—Marketers want to seem like what teens want to be. *USA Today.*

Kadlec, Daniel. (1997, May 5). The new world of giving. *Time.*

Kotler, Philip. (1980). *Marketing management* (4th ed.). Englewood Cliffs, NJ: Prentice-Hall.

Lacek, Mark. (1995, October 23). Loyalty marketing no ad budget threat. *Advertising Age.*

McCann-Erickson Worldwide. (1993, December). *Worldwide insider's report.* New York, NY: Author.

Nelson, Emily. (1996, September 4). Dearest mom, greetings from my CD-ROM. *The Wall Street Journal.*

Pepper, Don, & Rogers, Martha. (1997, June 2). Marketer-customer dialogue comes to fore. *Advertising Age.*

Pogrebin, Robin. (1997, January 2). Magazines multiplying as their focuses narrow. *The New York Times.*

National Recreation and Park Association. (1995, January). Reposition '95: A future for parks and recreation. *PIN: Programmers Information Network,* Vol. 6, No. 1 Arlington, VA: Author.

Stern, Aimee L. (1993, January 19). Courting consumer loyalty with the feel good bond. *The New York Times.*

Strong, E. K. (1925). *The psychology of selling.* New York, NY: McGraw-Hill.

Taylor, Jim, & Wacker, Watts. (1997). *The 500 year delta—What happens after what comes next.* New York, NY: HarperBusiness.

Taylor, William C. (1998, April–May). Permission marketing. *Fast Company.*

Thomas, Paulette. (1996, October 28). Show and tell: Advertisers take pitches to preschool. *The Wall Street Journal.*

Wells, Melanie. (1997, May 28). Advertisers link up with cities. *USA Today.*

Wells, Melanie. (1996, July 18). Nike struts its Olympic look. *USA Today.*

Wells, Melanie, & Lieberman, David. (1997, December 9). Advertising spending beats expectations in '97. *USA Today.*

Williamson, Debra Aho. (1996, March 13). Building a new industry. *Advertising Age.*

When the postwar affluence fueled high-speed industrialization, there was little thought or attention given to the customer. There didn't need to  be. Factories with heavy production schedules hummed in faraway places while their customers were happily nestled in their homes satisfied with whatever the factory produced for them. And that's the way it was at the beginning of the acquisition era.

However, times changed, and built-in obsolescence and the onset of increased competition particularly by the Japanese auto industry led to a new era. This is the time period when Peters and Waterman, Drucker, and Juran focused attention on excellence in both production and service. The growth of the service sector requiring a greater level of consumer involvement also heightened the focus on the customer.

This age of the customer and its emphasis on doing the right things led to "smelling the customer," "searching for excellence" and into the TQM (total quality management) era when organizations spent a great deal of their time and resources measuring everything and anything that related to the product or service. The emphasis on excellence, and the thought that such excellence was defined by the customer, was the beginning of a reawakening for customer service in the United States.

Chapter 7

Customer-Centered Experiences

The customer-centered company has the willingness and ability to bring the customer to the very center of its organizational being.

Richard Whitely and Diane Hessan

The Customer Continuum

Since the customer is certainly at the center of every experience and most personal services, this attention to and emphasis on the participant are necessities within the experience industry. There is actually a continuum of strategy levels addressing the importance and the involvement of the customer. These four levels of the customer continuum are customer service, customer care, customer connection, and customer collaboration.

Product	Service	Experience
Service *Care*	*Connection*	*Collaboration*

While each designation places the customer first, each is significantly different in its focus and scope. As one moves from a product to a service to an experience focus, the levels of attention to the customer move along the continuum.

From Customer Service to Customer Care

Customer service is the initial designation on the customer continuum and can be simply defined as meeting the needs of the customer or participant. It refers to the ability of an organization to conduct business in a timely and competent manner. An early study that asked customers to define quality customer service identified the following four criteria: personal attention, dependability, promptness, and employee competence (Zemke and Schaaf, 1989, p. 8).

While this level in the continuum is an essential element of any marketing approach, merely treating people nicely and providing them with a prompt and dependable service or experience is only the tip of the iceberg. A customer service approach where experienced personnel smile in greeting, move the customer through the line promptly, and give the standard "have a good day" salutation is a start, but it's not an absolute strategy.

Keep the experience you provide for people in mind as you review these four levels of the continuum. Identify ways in which you currently meet each level or move along the continuum en route to becoming customer centered.

Customer service, even good customer service, is not really enough to ensure the type of experience one wants for people. Since the ultimate goal of any customer-centered strategy is both to attract and retain customers, organizations need to move beyond the basics of customer service.

Customer care differs from customer service. A shift in emphasis from providing a quality service to becoming more interested in the customer occurs at this stage. Experience personnel would begin to anticipate individual needs and preferences of participants. Calling people by name and creating special adaptations for them are just some of the small modifications that raise the customer continuum from service to care.

The components of customer care are closely aligned with the RATER dimensions of service quality developed at Texas A & M pinpointing the following five factors (Whitely and Hessan, 1996, p. 82):

- reliability—dependable, accurate service;
- assurance—knowledgeable, courteous, trust-inspiring employees;
- tangibles—facilities, equipment, and staff appearance;
- empathy—degree of caring and individual attention displayed by staff; and
- responsiveness—willingness to assist customers.

Customer care is another mile marker along the way toward moving the customer to the center of the experience. The mind-set that enables the experience provider to shine his or her light on the customer and to respond to the anticipated needs of each customer is what customer care represents.

Moving Along the Continuum

While most organizations either aspire, or allege to aspire, to customer service or customer care, there is a growing belief that merely serving or caring about one's customer is not quite enough. Peppers and Rogers in both of their books, *The One to One Future: Building Relationships One Customer at a Time* and *Enterprise One to One: Tools for Competing in the Interactive Age*, maintain that an organization can tell just how focused it is on its customers by evaluating its responses to the following questions (Webber and Row, 1997, p. 128):

❖ When the bridal couple brought their Great Dane along with them to their wedding reception, the catering establishment brought out a plate with a huge "doggy" bone rather than tossing the mutt out.

❖ Special delivery for moms as Price Mart in Oklahoma and Kroger Supermarket in Houston designate stork parking places up front for pregnant moms and new mothers, and at McCormick Field in Asheville, North Carolina, the local baseball team has added Expectant Mother Zones.

❖ A newlywed couple on a Saturday evening TWA flight were showered with attention and special treats including a bottle of champagne and a snapshot taken of the couple on board.

- Do you retain your customers?
- Do you treat different customers differently?
- Do you create a learning relationship with your customers? and
- Do you organize around your customers?

Such questions and concerns lead organizations to continue their journey along the customer continuum recognizing that customer service and care are important but should not be the end of their efforts.

Customer connection takes over where customer care ends and raises the customer continuum to a new level. Customer connection reflects a concerted action on the part of the experience provider to reach out and create a genuine connection between the provider and the participant. Why is customer connection important to organizations? John Naisbitt pinpointed the necessity for making a customer-centered approach a mainstay of organizations when he made the following case for retaining existing customers (Schaaf, 1995, p. 19):

- the population of the United States is relatively static and is estimated to grow at a rate of just over one percent per year for the next two decades; and
- income growth in this country is also relatively static and is growing at a rate of about two percent a year which translates into negative growth in light of inflation.

Even a cursory look at this data clearly points out to experience providers that the days of replacing dissatisfied or less than ecstatic customers with new ones is no longer a viable option if future vitality is to be maintained. That's where customer connection comes into play when moving up the customer continuum. Customer connection is exactly that. It's a link between the experience provider and the experience participant that goes beyond just knowing who the person is by reaching out to establish a two-way relationship.

Such a relationship begins to forge a bond of loyalty between the participant and the experience provider. Creating such loyalty is no easy task in today's

Some lifetime values of loyal customers have been calculated as follows:

Fast Facts

- Carl Sewell, the Dallas Cadillac dealer, calculates that each customer who ventures into his showroom is a potential lifetime value of $300,000.
- The average loyal grocery store shopper is worth nearly $4,000 a year.
- The moderate frequent flier who travels coast to coast on American Airlines once a month is worth $20,000 over a five-year period (Peppers and Rogers, 1993, pp. 37–38).

The payoff of even a five percent increase in loyalty lifts the lifetime profits of industries per customer as follows (Sellers, 1993, p. 57):

- 95 percent—advertising agencies;
- 85 percent—branch bank deposits;
- 85 percent—publishing;
- 84 percent—auto and/or home insurance;
- 81 percent—auto service; and
- 75 percent—credit cards.

marketplace. Six factors that impact on consumers on a daily basis to diminish customer loyalty include the overwhelming abundance of choice, ease of availability of information, individual feelings of entitlement, the trend towards commodization, personal sense of insecurity, and impact of time scarcity (Schriver, 1997, pp. 20–21). All of these factors cited reinforce the need to move one's organization along the customer continuum.

Loyalty marketing strategies play into this phase of the continuum because such approaches are essentially relationship marketing. Experience providers begin to rethink the way they relate to customers. Rather than tallying up the number of participants who come through the gate, they take up a new way of envisioning their customers. That new vision is lifetime value. Lifetime value

Close Seup

Saucony, an American manufacturer of athletic and exercise footwear, took a customer connection approach when it created a walking club targeted towards women. When women purchased a pair of walking shoes, they were offered a club membership that required them to complete a questionnaire. The information secured through the questionnaire enabled the company to place them in a club membership that focused upon one of the three benefit tracks: cardiovascular health, weight loss, or general fitness. Saucony could then provide each member with a walking kit and quarterly newsletter focused on her primary benefit area. A log book to track her progress was also included in the membership. When the member reached a new milestone, she sent in the logbook and received both an award and recognition for her progress from the company (Cross and Smith, 1995, p. 129).

❖ Most lifestyle magazines include a fax-back survey page in each issue to encourage the beginning of a relationship between the magazine and the reader while better determining what the readers need and want; Web sites for magazines even include surveys that can be completed on-line. The hope is that the person who sent the fax or completed the survey will buy the next issue of the magazine to see how his or her comments relate to other readers'.

❖ Local media outlets (both radio and television) create call-in opportunities, contests, and special events to facilitate more personal contact with their listeners or viewers.

❖ Virginia wineries have a newsletter for customers highlighting upcoming special events as well as special discount purchase programs. Menus and recipes, along with suggested wines to complement those meals, are also a part of the newsletter.

❖ Saturn Motors invited Saturn owners to attend a family-type reunion in Tennessee in the summer of 1995, and more than 44,000 of them turned out in a downpour to tour the factory and meet and greet the people who made their car.

❖ Harley Davidson has a membership club, HOG (Harley Owner's Group), that brings its owners from all around the world to meet, greet, and further ingrain Harley into their lifestyle.

calculates not only the one time revenue generated by a customer, but also the total value of that customer if his or her relationship with a business continues over his or her lifetime. Profitability begins to add up substantially when taking this approach.

The customer connection is invaluable to the experience provider. It enables organizations to establish an ongoing relationship with the participants by ensuring their continued patronage. It also leads to the creation of an information database. The database helps target the needs and expectations of customers while anticipating changes in future participation patterns. Both the relationship and the information serve as a springboard to the final level of the customer continuum, customer collaboration, the real competitive edge for experiences.

The relationship base, interaction, and information provided by customer connections solidifies the life span of the business relationship between the participant and provider. It can result in a relationship that goes beyond the framework of mutual respect and loyalty. It can lead to a partnership where both parties work together to create a mutually beneficial experience. The smallest example of such a customer partnership is the way many fast-food restaurants allow their customers to fix their own drinks. People are able to get their preferred amount of ice in glasses as well as cream and sugar combinations for coffee. While this approach was implemented to save time and money for the fast-food outlet, the unanticipated bonus was the customer's delight with it as well.

The customer continuum from service to collaboration also reflects a continuum from standardization to customization. From a customer service point of view, the participant expects to receive an experience that is safe and on time. However, as progress along the customer continuum is made, the expectations a

❖ MCI raised the level of customer collaboration in 1991 when it created Friends and Family that enabled every MCI user to receive a 20 percent discount for calling people in his or her circle. MCI then contacted members of the calling circle to invite them to join MCI at the request of a family member or friend offering them the 20 percent discount if they formed their own calling circle.

❖ At retail outlets Microsoft conducted a 10-city tour of its Explorasaurus Bus, a 45-foot tractor trailer decorated with dinosaurs and astronauts featuring hands-on interactive demonstrations. While involved primarily in product promotion, the Imagine the Magic contest in which students outlined ideas for "what the coolest computer could do" provided a basis for the beginnings of customer collaboration for new product ideas.

❖ Black and Decker, the tool manufacturer, began collaborating with its customers when it was losing market share to the Japanese and Sears and did so by creating living laboratories where its target market, male homeowners between the ages of 25 and 54, could actually engage in woodworking or home remodeling projects. Observation of and feedback from participants resulted in the creation of new tools or modification of existing ones (Caminiti, 1993, pp. 45–46).

customer has about being more closely involved in the design of the experience increases substantially.

It rises until customer collaboration, the ultimate of the customer continuum, is met. Sometimes customers behave as anticipated based upon group characteristics, but sometimes they break from the pack, so to speak, and want something unique and personal. This means collaboration on the part of both partners in the process. The collaboration process involves two phases: utilizing the customer information ascertained through the customer connection phase and the modification of the experience to meet these identified needs and desires. Both of these

❖ The Grand Wailea Resort Hotel & Spa in Maui, Hawaii, has created a unique customer collaboration program. This family resort boasts of a 50,000 square foot Spa Grande, a special haven for women; a 20,000 square foot Camp Grande and a 2,000 foot River Pool, a wonderland for children; and three 18 hole golf courses within the resort with four more nearby courses making it a golfing mecca. Billing itself as truly "The Best Family Resort," it has created a resort advisory program where for a fee of $1,000, advisory board members can enjoy a stay at a 50 percent discount from published rates on any type of room based on availability in exchange for providing the resort with advice and observations made during their stay.

❖ Raddison Hotels has created an advertising campaign featuring actual concierges from their hotels with the tag line of "By the end of their vacation, these kids will think 'concierge' is French for 'uncle'" to reinforce the way in which these folks go out of their way to find out what visiting youngsters want and then to make it happen for them.

- ❖ According to research done by Reichheld and Sasser, a mere 5 percent increase in customer loyalty can result in a 100 percent increase in profitability (King, 1996, pp. 6–7).
- ❖ Sixty to eighty percent of lost customers had reported being satisfied or very satisfied just prior to defection according to Reichheld and Teal (King, 1996, pp. 6–7).
- ❖ Research conducted by the Opinion Research Corp. of Princeton, New Jersey, shows that 90 percent of customers who love a company by rating it five on a scale of one to five will do business with that company again while only 30 percent of those who only like the company and rate it four on a scale of one to five will probably return (King, 1996, pp. 6–7).

Fast Facts

phases are conducted as a two-way relationship or partnership between the provider and the participant.

Customer collaboration is potentially powerful because it depends very little on mass media and merges the give and take of the exchange process until the bond is durable. In addition, this collaboration makes the participant a real partner in the operation, and he or she then takes on the task of spreading the word about this experience to friends, colleagues, and families. The ultimate outcome of customer collaboration is that the customer assumes the role of advocate where he or she actually does the marketing for the experience provider.

The interaction and interrelationship between the provider and the participant work in tandem continuing to create the experience needed and expected by the participant. Customer collaboration ultimately results in reduced costs for the experience provider. The traditional cost of advertising and promotion are lowered as these people become recruiters and promoters. Knowing the specific needs and wants of one's customers can result in lower costs since unimportant aspects of the experience can be altered or eliminated.

The old days of factories making things and people bringing those things into their home without question are over. The times when the business could say and people would obey in relation to specific needs and preferences are over as well. The customer continuum requires various levels of attention based on the actual type of experience being provided. The local miniature golf course may do quite well with a customer service approach that has competent, polite employees ensuring a dependable experience. However, the hospital or assisted-living center won't stand a chance of competing in a new world demanding highly individualized and need-based experiences if it doesn't travel farther down the customer continuum until achieving customer collaboration. The distance between doing things right and designing for the delight of the customer is a distance that can be measured by great success over the long run. Satisfaction is only the starting gate on the customer continuum, not the finish line.

Customer-Centered Experiences

Just knowing about the customer continuum and developing an awareness of the differences among the levels and added benefits of such differences to an organization is a good first step. But the even more important step is the action taken

Close-up

Matrixx Marketing, Inc., a fast-growing customer-collaboration operation out of Cincinnati with call centers scattered around the country, is an emerging model for experience marketing operations. This company doesn't manufacture anything. What it does is answer the phones and listen to the needs of customers for its growing client base. Among Matrixx's list of clients are Hitachi, DirectTV, Microsoft Network, Gatorade, and two of the three largest long-distance phone companies. Thirty-three out of the hundred largest public companies in the United States are among its clients. It attests to the growing importance that companies are placing on the needs of its customers.

Matrixx, a division of Cincinnati Bell, grew in 1996 from 9,000 to 15,000 employees with an accompanying revenue increase of nearly $100 million in that same year. What's its secret of success? It is not the number of people it has answering customer's phone calls but rather the skillful way in which those employees create relationships with those customers and collaborate with them to provide solutions.

They soothe the concerns of a worried, young mother whose baby is responding poorly to a formula change because they are knowledgeable of such behavior patterns. They even arrange to call the mother back in a few days just to see how things are going. The DirectTV subscriber who couldn't watch a basketball game that was locally blacked out was put on hold until the customer service representative found a station where he could find the game.

They establish relationships, create connections, and solve problems with and for customers. An added but important plus is the creation of databases. They learn so much about how and why people use particular products and services that they can pass that information along to their customers, the producers of those products and services (Fishman, 1997, pp. 108–112).

within an organization on the basis of one's knowledge and awareness of the levels of the continuum.

How far along the customer continuum does the experience provider need to travel? Which road map will providers need to follow as they proceed? There are no easy answers to these questions. There just isn't one definitive approach to moving one's part of the experience industry along the customer continuum. The nature of an experience brings into play people including the customer, providers, and other participants in the experience as well as the interaction with the experience itself. This creates a myriad of situations and scenarios where glitches can and do occur, and opportunities for better customer connections can present themselves.

"The smartest business is the one whose people and systems combine to produce the most effective action at the most opportune time" (Schaaf, 1995, p. 53). For the experience industry this means making the right thing happen for people in the right ways at the right time. After all, there's only one wedding day (or at least only one first wedding

Take out a sheet of paper and keep it handy while you're reading this section and be sure to jot down any ideas that occur to you for enhancing the customer-centered approach of your organization.

TAG

day), initial visit to a hospital, or only one vacation per calendar year. It has to be right. While there is no single method or approach that can be described for a specific experience provider or even an exacting approach for a subsegment of the experience industry, there is a framework for designing and developing a core approach for one's organization.

A customer-centered system can be developed that addresses the specific idiosyncrasies of the elements within the system:

- participants—the actual customers or users of the experience;
- personnel—the people behind the scenes and out front who influence the experience;
- process—the way in which various parameters of the experience are introduced, implemented, or coordinated; and
- provider—the experience organization itself and its role related to the other three elements as part of the system.

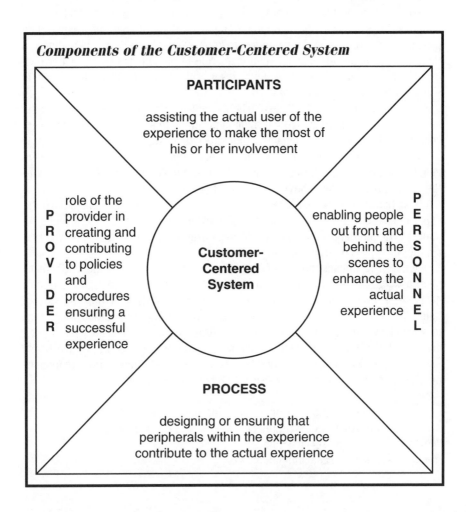

Components of the Customer-Centered System

PARTICIPANTS

assisting the actual user of the experience to make the most of his or her involvement

PROVIDER
role of the provider in creating and contributing to policies and procedures ensuring a successful experience

Customer-Centered System

PERSONNEL
enabling people out front and behind the scenes to enhance the actual experience

PROCESS

designing or ensuring that peripherals within the experience contribute to the actual experience

TARP (Technical Assistance Research Program) Institute research findings suggest that (Schaaf, 1995, p. 100):

Fast Facts

• 40 percent of the problems in a typical business are generally caused by the customer;
• an additional 40 percent of business problems are the result of system and design flaws; and
• the remaining 20 percent are caused by employees through acts of omission or commission.

The 4Ps of the Customer-Centered Experience

Can it actually be possible that 40 percent of all problems within a business are created by the customer? This seems incredibly ridiculous in a world where "the customer is always right" has become the watchword for doing business. This statistic was generated for all business types, not exclusively for the experience industry. Imagine what the percentage might be if we studied only experience providers who rely upon the customer to know what he or she wants and where the customer generally plays a significant role in the success of his or her own experience. It is likely that these numbers would skyrocket off the chart for personal services and experiences.

Experience providers will need to help people clarify their needs, goals, skills, and expectations in order to assist them in attaining this portion of the customer-centered experience. Attention to participants will need to become a high priority.

You can't have an experience without personnel of some kind. Never overlook or underestimate the importance of these people or automated servers to the entire process. The behavior on the part of your experience provider personnel is critical to the overall experience. In many instances these people are the experience. Their involvement or expertise forms the core of the experience. To many participants these people are the organization and serve as the only actual contact or representation for your company.

What is the impact and role of the experience process? Recall the TARP (Technical Assistance Research Program) Institute's findings cited in Fast Facts that 40 percent of customers' complaints are attributed to flaws within the system itself. Try to imagine that nearly half of the complaints result from things that may well be within the provider's control. Within the customer-centered system a great deal of attention needs to be focused on the experience delivery process itself. Leonard Barry heightens awareness for the importance of this component by suggesting that perceptions of service quality result from:

• customer expectations prior to receiving the service,
• the actual experience with the service,
• the quality of the service, and
• both service process and outcomes,

and that these components contribute to the overall evaluation (Schaaf, 1995, p. 128).

The final factor within the customer-centered system, and probably one of the most critical as it relates to truly putting the customer at the center of the experience universe, is the organization or provider itself. The reality of the situation is that it's the provider who actually has the most influence over the preceding aspects of the customer-centered system, participants, personnel, and process. Providers should direct their attention and effort toward the following: key aspects for customers, relationship with personnel, continuous everything, and the changing view of the customer.

There are a variety of alternatives available that can move an organization along the customer continuum en route to creating a customer-centered experience. Many of the techniques relate to the 4Ps of the customer-centered experience: people, personnel, process, and provider. Suggestions found in other chapters may prove useful as well.

Participant's Preparation and Assessment

The first category for implementing this approach relates to the participants themselves. Participants bring with them specific needs and idiosyncrasies that may influence or even significantly alter the experience. Three suggested techniques for addressing the people factors include the SNEP approach to experience outcomes, values framework, and scripting.

What's an experience provider to do? How can we assist participants in making the most of their experience? The SNEP (skills, needs, expectations, and preferences) approach to determining experience outcomes can be key. Mountain Travel-Sobek, a leading outdoor company, provides a Web site where clients can scroll through its many options, but it has decided against allowing bookings through its Web site. Since no two adventure trips or customers are alike, the company prefers to discuss the options with customers before they book. Consider the travel agent helping a client plan a six-week tour of Asia using such an approach:

SNEP Approach	Travel Agent Example
• *Skills:* talents, ability, attitude.	• Does the person need a certain physical stamina or knowledge of a second language?
• *Needs:* self, mental, social, spiritual, intellectual.	• Is the person traveling to meet people or develop an understanding of a new culture?
• *Expectations:* previous experiences or background.	• Has the person traveled extensively or is this the first foreign trip?
• *Preferences:* individual choices.	• Does the person prefer comfort over price or security over novelty?

Alternatives available for use with the SNEP approach include interviews or survey instruments that can range from the simple to the more in depth.

> People's happiness on tour depends quite a lot on their being on the right trip.
>
> Richard Weiss

A second technique to target what participants value and prefer is the construction of a preference framework. Such a framework enables an organization systematically but simply to assess what the participant values. In the case of some experiences, the two attributes plotted could be information and process. The varying levels of interest and the subsequent interplay with information and process result in the refinement of the four levels of the customer continuum. An example created to determine the participant's preference along the customer continuum for a health club is shown on this page.

A look at the framework for the health club example reveals participants with four different types of needs. The participants preferring customer service either have an existing knowledge of fitness or are not much interested in either the club's information or the care and expertise of its staff. Contrast that with individuals who are seeking more of a partnership with the health club as is the case with the collaboration designation where they are looking for a long-term, ongoing relationship. This type of framework could be developed for most experiences to provide the organization with recommendations regarding various participants and the levels and types of service required by each.

An additional technique that helps participants prepare for the experience is called scripting. Scripting is to experiences what rehearsals are to plays and can involve just the participant, the experience personnel, or a combination of both.

Preference Framework

more interest in individual		more use of information
Connection • knowledge of individual goals • personalized program • social exchange		**Collaboration** • long-term membership • in-depth and holistic program • ongoing monitoring
Service • fees, discounts or incentives • hours, location, equipment		**Care** • fitness assessment • appropriate programs and services
less interest in individual	INFORMATION	less use of information

(Left margin vertical label: P R O C E S S)

Source: Adapted from Value Orientation Framework by Whitely and Hessan (1996, p. 269).

❖ Prehospitalization visits for children undergoing surgery and programs such as childbirth classes are actually opportunities for the patient to become familiar with his or her role in the entire experience.

❖ In response to complaints by guests, Disney has been providing videotapes to travel agents in South American countries to help teen groups visiting the Florida resort to behave more appropriately.

❖ The Red Sox Fantasy Camp organizers sent participants explicit precamp training regimes six weeks prior to camp designed to build in participant success and reduce the risk of being sidelined with out-of-shape injuries.

❖ Adventure travel and outfitters designate various trips as they relate to level of skill and stamina required as well as recommended packing lists.

❖ Sea World locations clearly designate rows in their performance arenas that will incorporate the distinct possibility of being soaked, sprayed, or splashed by water during a performance.

❖ Especially at lunch time, some restaurants designate those entrees that can be prepared and served within a 20-minute time guarantee.

❖ Watercraft rental companies often provide an on-site paddling or operating practice area to get people ready before they head for "real" water, a "win" for risk-reduction as well.

When used with participants, it prepares them for anticipating what's to come and enabling them to perform appropriately within the context of the experience. When used for personnel, it's an attempt to ensure consistency, safety, or success within the experience.

Scripting activities can range from passive to active or from optional to mandatory. Scripting can take place in the preparation phase of an experience when the participant is still at home and getting ready for the experience, or it can take place on site prior to the experience. Some of these possibilities include packing lists, signage, instruction from personnel, and even some practice sessions.

In some instances where the participant has no previous experience with activities associated with the experience or the experience is relatively new or novel, the creation of a script where participants and personnel can work on and practice their parts would be most helpful.

Personnel

Personnel are an integral part of the customer-centered experience, and their role and behavior can make or break the experience for the participants. Getting the right kind of people to make the right kind of experience happen for participants takes some effort. Much of that effort takes place before staff is even hired or placed into service by the experience provider in the form of recruitment, selection, and training. Another aspect of customer-centered experience personnel is the ability to make things right for the participant. This aspect takes the form of empowerment and recovery.

There are a number of steps in the preemployment phase of personnel that can significantly contribute to successes within experiences. Activities within this phase include identification of needed skills, recruitment, screening, hiring, and training:

Steps in Preemployment Phase

- *Skill Identification:* technical skills, and interpersonal abilities needed.

- Analyze job duties and responsibilities to determine skills, attitudes critical to the experience.

- *Recruitment:* determine best places to find the type of skilled individuals needed.

- Aggressively go after the best candidates creating a large pool from which to choose.

- *Screening:* determine common duties and have this process screen for proficiency and promise in those areas.

- Take the time to fully complete this stage; use role-playing or problem-solving activities.

- *Training:* take the time to ensure personnel's preparation to go it on their own.

- Can include tours, orientations, modeling as well as ongoing activity.

Preemployment practices are a good start for ensuring a customer-centered experience, but there will always be instances in which the right thing just doesn't seem to happen when it should. In these cases, personnel need to be prepared for recovery. Recovery involves the resolution of customer's complaints and quick response to their needs. Recovery impacts solidly on the bottom line of a company.

How does the experience provider make recovery happen? The ultimate response to recovery would be to revise and revamp the process or system so all the little glitches are gone thus eliminating the need for recovery. But since so many of those glitches may be caused by the customers themselves or the vagaries of the situation, the provider needs to empower personnel to make it right for the participant. That's right. The employee must be allowed to do whatever he or

❖ Southwest Airlines has frequent fliers interview candidates for flight attendant positions.
❖ Hotels and resorts use videotaped participant-personnel encounters both to screen potential employees based upon their reactions and to train new staff as well.
❖ McDonald's and Avis provide newcomers with trainee badges and have them shadow experienced personnel.
❖ Disney goes with a four-day training for "cast members" at Disney University that includes traditions (history and mission), general information, and suggestions for interacting with guests.

Coca-Cola, in conjunction with TARP (Technical Assistance Research Programs) Institute, conducted a study tracking 1,717 people who had filed complaints with Coca-Cola. Results of the study showed that the ability of Coca-Cola to resolve or recover from these complaints had an impact on its ongoing success with customers:

Fast Facts

- the company was able to satisfy 85 percent of the complaints or comments;
- nearly 10 percent of those people whose problems had been resolved increased their subsequent purchases of Coca-Cola;
- the company's handling of the complaints led to an estimated 1.5 new customers based on the word-of-mouth factor; and
- if a customer's complaint was handled satisfactorily, there was a 90 percent chance that the customer would remain a customer. (Vavra, 1992, p. 112)

she thinks is proper to make it right for the unhappy or disgruntled participant. Reminding oneself of the bottom-line value of happy customers plus the detrimental impact of those who leave a place less than happy justifies this basic tenet of success.

While it's impossible to detail the specifics of the recovery operation that would work for an experience, take note of the approach used by Stew Leonard's Dairy Stores as they practice recovery. The STEW approach to recovery (Leonard, 1996):

S = Say you're sorry,
T = Thank them for complaining,
E = Explain what you're going to do about it, and
W = Win them back.

Process

The third P within the customer-centered experience is the process. Recall the TARP (Technical Assistance Research Program) Institute finding cited in Fast Facts that 40 percent of customers' complaints are attributed to flaws within the system itself. From an experience marketing point of view there are two different techniques that can address the challenges within the process or system: KAEs and MOTs. KAEs are key aspects of the experience from the participants' point of view and MOTs are moments of truth so labeled by Jan Carlson of Scandinavian Airlines who was the first to identify these small, repeated episodes of customer contact.

L. L. Bean, long considered one of the more customer-centered businesses, identifies seven KRAs (key result areas) in customer service: convenience, product guarantee, in-stock availability, fulfillment time, innovation, image, and retail service for its store in Freeport, Maine (Whitely, 1991, p. 136). McDonald's cites QSCV (quality, service, cleanliness, and value) as its standard and measures accordingly.

Listed below are some sample participant problem categories and exceptional examples of recovery compared with nonsatisfactory personnel responses:

Situation	Nonsatisfactory	Recovery
Unreasonably slow service	Staff continually gave customers incorrect information about the delay	No complaints but staff offered customers a free snack
Special need	Staff insisted customers keep the line moving or step out and let others by	Staff helped the ill person find nearest rest room
Response to customer error	When notified of loss staff explained it is not policy to track down lost items	Lost item returned to guest before guest noticed its loss
Attention to participant	Staff members could hardly interrupt their talking or reading to answer customers' questions	Staff made customers feel like they were the only ones in the place

Remember, it's not necessarily the problem or complaint that makes a participant walk away from the experience and an organization forever. It's the way in which the problem or complaint is handled.

The trick for each experience provider is to not measure everything or anything, but to do as L. L. Bean does and identify those factors or KRAs that are critical or important to the delivery of the experience. Knowing what's important to one's participants and measuring it will help to ensure success and future viability. Market research comes into play in this instance, and the importance-performance technique included in the next chapter will be a natural for helping experience providers identify their own KAEs.

A second strategy related to KRAs is MOTs or moments of truth. While some experiences are unique or customized, and some experiences are dependent on weather or the behavior of other participants, most experiences still go through such a predictable cycle or chain of events. These repetitive actions can be plotted in either a circular or linear fashion, and the expectations, preferences, or problems of customers can be tracked and altered accordingly.

An interesting aspect of many experiences is that the MOTs for experience personnel and participants are quite different. When examining the various stages of an experience, one notices the discrepancies between the two and can anticipate potential process problems. Since MOTs often consist of contacts between participant and provider personnel, it's important to note those differences.

An issue of *Fast Company* subtitled "The Ultimate Guide to Great Customer Service," provided a list of specific suggestions that focused on the role of individuals within organizations related to ensuring a good working and learning relationship with the customer. Those suggestions included the following (You Are the Company, 1997, special insert):

- customers talk to individuals not a "company;"
- great service relates to the attitudes of the individuals within a company;
- the customer is the only judge of great service;
- customers prefer to think of themselves as people rather than customers;
- there's no one "right" way to deal with a customer; every customer, conversation, and problem is different;
- individuals need to pass along customer's comments to the company;
- great service is not just about caring about customers, it's about creating a bond;
- individuals need not only to solve problems but also to create opportunities for the company;
- customer complaints should involve both listening and learning; and
- learn to anticipate problems by listening to people and looking for patterns.

If there was just one aspect of the customer-centered continuum that could be identified and implemented nearly immediately, MOTs would be the one. Seize that moment by making a graph of your own MOTs. This makes an excellent starting point for moving an organization along the continuum.

Provider Practices

It's the responsibility of the experience provider to attract the participants, staff the experience with competent and personable employees, and design and ensure that the experience process is customer centered. What else can the experience provider contribute to a customer-centered experience?

Stages of Experience	*MOT Differences*	
	Participant	*Provider Personnel*
Preexperience	We've been planning this rafting trip for months; it's going to be great fun.	The weather's good so it'll be busy today.
Preparation	We've never done this before; I hope we can figure out what to do.	Let's get underway and moving.
Anticipation	I'm so excited and nervous too.	These people ask the dumbest questions.
Postexperience	Wow! I can't believe we did it!	Let's move them out of here and get ready for the next group.

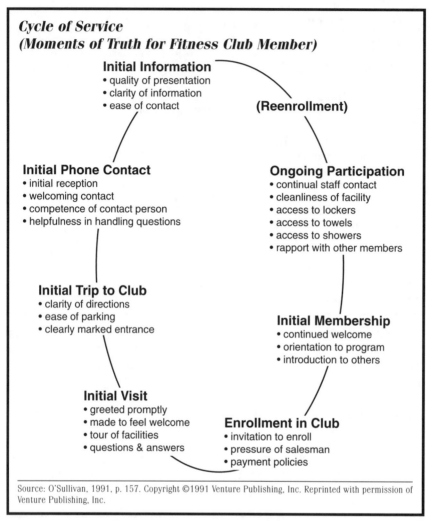

Cycle of Service
(Moments of Truth for Fitness Club Member)

Initial Information
• quality of presentation
• clarity of information
• ease of contact

(Reenrollment)

Initial Phone Contact
• initial reception
• welcoming contact
• competence of contact person
• helpfulness in handling questions

Ongoing Participation
• continual staff contact
• cleanliness of facility
• access to lockers
• access to towels
• access to showers
• rapport with other members

Initial Trip to Club
• clarity of directions
• ease of parking
• clearly marked entrance

Initial Membership
• continued welcome
• orientation to program
• introduction to others

Initial Visit
• greeted promptly
• made to feel welcome
• tour of facilities
• questions & answers

Enrollment in Club
• invitation to enroll
• pressure of salesman
• payment policies

Source: O'Sullivan, 1991, p. 157. Copyright ©1991 Venture Publishing, Inc. Reprinted with permission of Venture Publishing, Inc.

The most overriding demand placed on the provider to ensure a customer-centered experience relates to priorities. The provider must make participants, personnel, and process a high priority and not just in words but with actions. Exceptional experience providers realize that participants and personnel are both number one. Jan Carlson pointed out some time ago that in the service sector if you weren't directly serving the customer, you needed to be serving those who were (Bell, 1994, p. 181). Make personnel a number one priority.

One often overlooked aspect of staff support is the burn-out accrued by service or experience providers. Barbara Gutek, an Arizona psychologist, describes two different types of service transactions: relationship and encounter. A relationship transaction is one in which the participant comes to know the service or experience provider such as with a massage therapist or hair stylist while the encounter transaction refers to the quick, uniform, fairly anonymous service of the fast-food restaurants or flight attendants (Feeney, 1997, p. E2). In either instance, the experience provider is expected to display certain emotions in the context of the experience, and such emotional labor can lead to burn-out by experience personnel. The provider can support staff while improving the experience for the participant by devising alternatives both to avoid and to address such impact.

In addition to providers valuing and supporting staff, they also need to make sure personnel recognize that customers in turn are their number one priority. According to L. L. Bean, customers have unhappy experiences because employees (Whitely, 1991, p. 137):

- don't know they're supposed to create happy experiences for customers;
- don't get the resources they need to make happy experiences;
- lack the training to use the resources at hand; and
- have disincentives that don't encourage them to work for the customer.

Note that each of these reasons relates to things the provider can control. Factors such as providing the right kinds of resources, training for staff, and performance incentives all fall within the purview of the provider.

Experience providers further demonstrate the priorities of a customer-centered experience when they both empower and enfranchise personnel. Empowerment means giving personnel the discretion to make the right things happen for the customer and in turn the organization. Empowerment can involve routine discretion where staff members are given a list of alternatives which they can choose for making things right for the customer or creative discretion whereby employees both create and choose the alternatives (Bateson, 1995, p. 264).

Enfranchisement carries this concept further by empowering people to make decisions coupling this empowerment with compensation based on performance.

Close Seup

One stormy winter night while staying at a Marriott Courtyard, we encountered the following customer-centered experiences:

- When registering we were given a little smiley face circle cut out of simple construction paper and instructed to give it to a staff member who was particularly helpful to us during our short stay. We never got better service in our life. We had to go back to the front desk and request more construction paper cutouts. The stories we heard from employees who were hoarding their smiley faces rather than turning them in for the small, monetary reward were amazing.
- While awaiting a somewhat delayed dinner due to staff shortages caused by inclement weather, we were offered a complimentary glass of wine to make the wait more palatable. When we inquired as to why the pool was closed, the clerk at the front desk took a staff member off sidewalk duty to oversee a short swim in the pool.
- Upon returning home we noticed we had left a small personal item behind at the hotel. One phone call sent a staff member back to the room to recover and return the item to us promptly and pleasantly.

Customer service research conducted by the TARP (Technical Assistance Research Programs) Institute indicated that only four percent of "less than" satisfied customer complaints reached a person who could fix things and, in addition, found that customers:

Fast Facts

- would rather privately register their disapproval by going elsewhere than publicly delivering their disdain to front-line staff;
- don't know how to register complaints;
- believe complaining won't do any good; and
- fear the service provider might retaliate in some way. (Bell, 1994, p. 113)

While it has long been a part of the retail and sales industry, enfranchisement is a more recent addition to the personal service and entertainment arenas.

Both of these approaches have pluses for the experience industry. Such policies help to retain staff and to make better things happen for participants since staff becomes more customer-focused and quicker to respond to participants' needs. People who feel in control of their work life tend to feel better about themselves and their situation, and it shines through to participants with whom they come in contact. Enfranchisement also enables staff to implement a more systemwide response to increased demand for customization.

It is important to note that a full-blown integration of these two concepts in an organization does not come without a cost. Enfranchisement usually means higher labor costs. Empowerment generally translates into less consistency of service or the experience since it may be altered by the discretion of different personnel. A determination of the balance between the high costs of staff turnover and making things right for the customer is one that must be individually explored.

CloseUp

Northeast Alabama Regional Medical Center, a 1997 RIT/*USA Today* Quality Cup winner in healthcare, uses the continuous improvement process to identify what's important for its patients and ways to improve its practices, policies, and services. The area of customer concern that the center identified was the preadmission process for elective surgery. The preadmission process at the institution involved moving between six floors of the hospital for a total of four hours. A patient facing elective surgery stopped at admissions, anesthesiology, and then went on for a blood test, a chest x-ray, and an electrocardiogram. Bear in mind that this wandering around the hospital came complete with less than comforting sights, sounds, and smells.

An eight-person team studied the preadmission process from the eyes of the customer and recommended a one-stop shopping approach where all the services and tests came to a renovated, central location where the customer was. As a result the average preadmission time was cut by 30 percent (from 69 to 48 minutes) and elective surgery at this hospital jumped by 25 percent (Jones, 1997, p. 8B).

Continuous Continuous

In addition to supporting personnel in their pursuit of doing the right thing for the customer, experience providers also need to do their part to make things right for the customer. An overriding goal of the provider can be summed up in two words—continuous continuous—and that continual effort should be directed at complaints and improvements.

Experience providers must always make it easier for customers to complain, suggest, or impact the process. The experience becomes more customer centered if the provider encourages suggestions and makes the complaint process as easy as possible.

The customer service research related to complaints has even stronger implications for the experience industry. Since people must be physically present and involved in the experience, and the experience often addresses psychic or inner needs, the reluctance to complain and reveal one's shortcomings or disappointment is heightened. There are ways to get around this. Some hotel managers spend time in the lounge in the morning drinking coffee with departing guests to seek insight regarding ways the hotel could improve the experience. Disney

Action Agenda

❖ Visit to a local competitor or other experience provider and determine its level of the customer continuum. Make a list of customer-centered practices used for implementation at your organization.

❖ Conduct interviews with recent participants to identify their perception of your organization's level along the customer continuum. Be sure to note their suggestions for improvements at the same time.

❖ Make a list of cost-effective ways you could learn more about participants' needs prior to their actual involvement with your experience. Highlight ways to help them contribute to their own success or satisfaction with the experience.

❖ Review your recruitment and training process to see how you might make some small changes to better fulfill the needs and expectations of participants.

❖ Have staff create their own scripts for the STEW approach to recovery and have them role-play with one another.

❖ Bring staff together and see what kind of insight you can create related to the following categories:
  • participants' needs and wants,
  • participants' expectations of the experience, and
  • the components of actual experience.

❖ Develop a MOT model for all three phases of your experience. Decide what modifications can be made to enhance the experience for the participant.

❖ Don't try to take on the world. Identify three changes or modifications you can make to your system and implement them within the next two weeks.

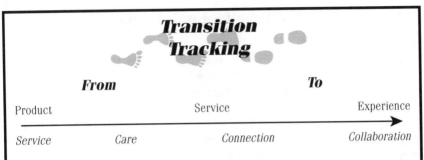

From			To
Product		Service	Experience

→

| *Service* | *Care* | *Connection* | *Collaboration* |

In the transition time from a product to a service to an experience economy, the public's perceptions and expectations in the area of what was traditionally referred to as customer service underwent a similar transition from service to care to connection and collaboration. The level of service increased incrementally as the actual presence and psychic needs of the participant became involved in the transaction.

To move along the continuum of customer-centered experiences, marketers need to incorporate the 4Ps into their approach which include participants' preparation and assessment, personnel, process, and provider practices.

has all its management staff spend a week on the front line to get a true feeling of what cast members and guests may be experiencing.

The provider is the link in the customer-centered system. He or she is ultimately responsible for and in charge of moving the customer to the center of that system by assuring the customer that every need, want, and expectation of the customer will be identified, monitored, and addressed on an ongoing, continuous basis. As people change so do their needs and preferences. The CQI (continuous quality improvement) process is a method to monitor what's important to the customer on an ongoing basis and to make the necessary changes or improvements.

Originally introduced in Japan by Deming, this approach, referred to as *kaizen* in Japanese, is more than just a management approach; it's a way of life where the focus is on continuing, gradual improvement of factors that are important to customers. CQI generally involves two steps: identifying one specific area of customer concern and working to improve that particular aspect of the experience.

Moving an experience along the customer-centered continuum is a strategy that works for the participant and the provider alike. It pays off for both of them. The 4Ps of a customer-centered organization—participants, personnel, process, and provider—are all aspects that lend themselves to continuous changes and improvements.

Sources

Bateson, John E. G. (1995). *Managing services marketing* (3rd ed.). Fort Worth, TX: The Dryden Press.

Bell, Chip R. (1994). *Customers as partners.* San Francisco, CA: Berrett-Koehler.

Caminiti, Susan. (1993, Autumn/Winter). A star is born. *Fortune.*

Cross, Richard, & Smith, Janet. (1995). *Customer bonding—Pathway to lasting customer loyalty.* Lincolnwood, IL: NTC Business Books.

Feeney, Mary K. (1997, June 16). In service industry, the "emotional labor" of showing you care. *Hartford Courant.*

Fishman, Charles. (1997, October–November). How can I help you? *Fast Company,* pp. 108–112.

Jones, Del. (1997, May 2). Winners triumph through teamwork. *USA Today,* p. 8B.

King, Elizabeth. (1996, December 31). Do right by the customer and you'll do well. *Sarasota Herald Tribune.*

Leonard, Stew, Jr. (1996, November 13). Speech presented at the Connecticut Recreation and Park Association Conference.

O'Sullivan, Ellen L. (1991). *Marketing for parks, recreation, and leisure,* p. 157. State College, PA: Venture Publishing, Inc.

Peppers, Don, & Rogers, Martha. (1993). *The one to one future: Building relationships one customer at a time.* New York, NY: Currency Doubleday.

Schaaf, Dick. (1995). *Keeping the edge—Giving customers the service they demand.* New York, NY: Dutton.

Sellers, Patricia. (1993, Autumn/Winter). Keeping the buyers you already have. *Fortune.*

Schriver, Steve. (1997, September). Customer loyalty: Going, going. . . . *American Demographics.*

Vavra, Terry G. (1992). *After-marketing—How to keep customers for life through relationship marketing.* Burr Ridge, IL: Business One Irwin.

Webber, Alan M., & Row, Heath. (1997, October–November). How can you help them? *Fast Company.*

Whitely, Richard C. (1991). *The customer driven company—Moving from talk to action.* Reading, MA: Addison-Wesley Publishing.

Whitely, Richard C., & Hessan, Diane. (1996). *Customer-centered growth.* Reading, MA: Addison-Wesley Publishing.

You are the company. (1997, October-November). *Fast Company,* special insert.

Zemke, Ron, & Schaaf, Dick. (1989). *The service edge—101 companies that profit from customer care.* New York, NY: New American Library.

Flashback

Thomas Dewey, then Governor of New York State, went to bed on election night in 1948 thinking he was to become the next President of the United States. All the polls indicated a landslide for Dewey. Imagine his surprise and the red faces of those publishers of newspapers across the country who on the basis of those polls, went to print with the news of Dewey's election. Harry Truman continued in office; the pollsters had been wrong. While the role and methods of market research have grown and become more sophisticated, the overall purpose of such research is to secure information which supports making better predictions for an organization. All elements of the marketing process including target market selection, manipulation of marketing mix variables, and strategic planning are dependent on such information.

The increasing dependence and importance of market research information led to the creation of MIS (marketing information systems) in the late 1970s and early '80s. MIS is a means to collect information and conduct research while creating a system to make better use of the information gathered.

Chapter 8

Infusing Information

Companies will have to gather as much information about
buyers as a personal dating service.

Fay Rice

Information Infusion: The What,
How, Why and Who

Market research and MIS (marketing information services) will continue to be a
vital and critical part of marketing. The knowledge and information explosion
together with the escalating need for everyone in the organization to service each
individual participant fuels the growing importance of projecting and predicting
future needs and preferences of participants. Increased profits and long-range
viability will go to experience providers who can collect and infuse information
throughout an organization as a natural and ongoing part of operations.

We are undergoing an information explosion. The sheer volume of information plus the myriad of information categories which are generated for probable
use in today's marketplace require a new world-view of how we interrelate with
information.

The infusion of information is no small undertaking. However, the following
process makes it realistic. The emphasis on sharing and integrating information
throughout the organization is superimposed upon the organization's standard
operating procedures:

- *What:* identifying the specific types of data and knowledge needed;
- *How:* collecting this data and information;
- *Why:* providing the information with meaning for the provider; and
- *Who:* sharing the information with others throughout the organization.

Take a quick look at a small portion of the statistics appearing on three pages of the November 1996 issue of *American Demographics:*

- The U. S. Department of Commerce's trend analysis of income sources between 1955 and 1995 indicates that there is less reliance on salaries and wages and an increasing dependency on transfer payments and other sources of income (Dortch, 1996, pp. 22–23).
- According to the Athletic Footwear Association, in 1995 men bought 33 percent of all sneakers sold while accounting for 44 percent of the money spent on such purchases; women bought 42 percent of the total number of sneakers to account for 41 percent of the expenditures; and children accounted for the remaining 24 percent of sneakers and 15 percent of expenditures (Dortch, 1996, pp. 22–23).
- Memberships in U. S. health clubs grew 25 percent between the seven-year period from 1988 to 1995 representing a membership of 19.2 million people (Dortch, 1996, pp. 22–23).

The provider needs to identify "what" he or she needs to know. He or she needs to develop a plan as to "how" to collect that information and to determine the impact such information can have for his or her organization. This will answer the question "why" to continue doing what is being done or if changes should be made. The "who," or the people involved with the information infusion, are also critical to its overall success.

Information: The What

If information is key to success in today's competitive marketplace and critical to decision-making for the future, how do we infuse it within our organizations? Marketers and trend analyzers everywhere struggle with answers and alternatives to this question. A natural starting point would be to designate very clearly the "what" of the information explosion. Organizations need to specifically and clearly identify exactly what information they need and what questions require answers.

Whether an organization is Club Med with properties strung out across the world or Club "Get-In-Shape," a relatively small fitness club in one geographic location, there is a certain amount of consistency in the "what" category as it relates to information. Information regarding any and all questions that are important to experience providers would fall into one of two categories: people and providers. In turn, there are three distinct levels into which both of these categories can be further subdivided: general, experience specific, and organizational specific.

The initial step to infusing information into and throughout a provider's system would be the development and identification of a concise but specific list of questions that are most meaningful to the operation.

Another aspect to the "what" stage of information infusion relates specifically to the information itself. To utilize information infusion effectively, it helps

Information Categories

(The "Whats")

People	Providers
General	

- What are people like?

- How are they changing?

- What are the implications for the provider?

- What's happening within the experience and personal service industry currently?

Experience Specific

- What people are most likely to avail themselves of the provider's type of experience?

- What changes are the provider's competitors making within their experience?

System Specific

- What does the provider know about his or her participants and their specific and individual needs, wants and preferences?

- What does the provider's system do to meet the needs and exceed the expectations of participants?

to know about some of the differences in data. Data and information come in quantitative and qualitative formats.

Quantitative data involves quantity or tangible figures and reports information percentages or statistical probabilities. Qualitative data involves less than tangible information and shares the customers' view of qualities that are important to them or to their perceptions of the quality of the actual experience. Qualitative data reports the participants' point of view by revealing a richer, more insightful type of information, but it lacks the sound research typically inherent with carefully constructed quantitative research.

Numbers and personal descriptions are not the only differences within information. Primary and secondary information also add to the differences in data collection and analysis. Primary data is collected specifically to find the answers to an organization's needs and may involve such things as surveys that may ask participants how they spend their leisure time. Secondary data is information which is not specifically gathered about the participants or to answer the organization's questions but which may have relevance for the organization.

Secondary data could be a survey that asks teenagers in America how they spend their discretionary money. While this information may not relate directly to the teens participating in an experience, there still may be implications the provider can draw from this secondary source on teen behavior.

Another difference between information to be shared is that it can be gathered internally or externally. Internal data is information secured through existing mechanisms established inside an organization such as telephone logs or

Information Branches

Type		Data/Information Sources		Specificity	
quantitative (numbers)	qualitative (qualities)	internal (within)	external (outside)	primary (direct)	secondary (indirect)
12 percent spend $40 or more per weekend	people find friendliness important	your monthly revenues	report in trade journal	specific for your company	info on another company

gate receipts. External data is information gathered from outside of an organization such as U. S. census data.

This quick overview of the differences in data and information is intended to assist in the infusion process by helping the reader to understand the range of possibilities and the ability to detect differences between the different classifications. Individuals interested in greater depth in this area should consult a market research source.

Tools and Techniques for the "How"

Recall that the title of this chapter is infusing information, not market research and not marketing information systems. This section provides an overview of the kinds of things that experience providers can undertake, either on their own or by contracting with an outside research firm, to better answer the questions identified in the TAG exercise.

Experience marketers can either get their own information or gather existing information. The "get" portion of information infusion usually involves primary data or information specifically about a provider's participants and operation. The

❖ The City of Raleigh, North Carolina, conducts a needs assessment of its population to determine the percentage of people interested in various recreation activities and facilities (quantitative, internal, primary).

❖ Leisure Research conducted phone surveys to ascertain motivational categories related to uses for leisure time (qualitative, external, secondary).

❖ The U. S. Census Bureau determines the number of households headed by single parents (quantitative, external, secondary).

❖ The gate attendant at a water park routinely asks departing customers whether they enjoyed their visit (qualitative, internal, primary).

Tag. You're it! You're the only one who can decide what you need to know. Take a minute to do just that before proceeding with the rest of this process.

Ask yourself, if there were three things you wish you knew about participants, what would they be? List them:

1.
2.
3.

If there were three pieces of information that would help you plan for the next three to five years, what would they be? List them:

1.
2.
3.

Keep these six pieces of information in mind as you read on!

"gather" portion of this section generally refers to collecting and bringing together information existing within or outside of a provider's organization.

Consider the ways a provider can "get" information about his or her participants and their reaction and interaction with his or her organization. The get section overviews surveys, observation, focus groups, and other ways to secure needed information. Check the resource section at the end of this chapter designed to direct the reader to other types of information that will be of help in further understanding people and trends.

People

Whenever we need information about people, surveys seem invariably to surface as the only choice. While surveys are a good choice in many instances, there are other "people" tools that work well for the experience industry. Observation and focus groups are two such tools.

There are many different ways to conduct the ever-popular survey. One can use the mail, the telephone, or face-to-face methods. One can incorporate open or closed questions or both. One can survey everybody, a random sample of a specific market, users, or nonusers. The possibilities are extensive. One must be sensitive to changes in behavior as it relates to surveys. People overrun with junk mail may inadvertently toss out a mail survey. People beleaguered with nightly telemarketing calls during the dinner hour may be reluctant or even unwilling to take the time to answer questions. People involved in face-to-face surveys often hate to take the time or to share information with another person.

There are a number of newer techniques that take advantage of some of these changes in behavior such as intercept surveys and computerized options. When using the intercept, the interviewer stands at a location and selects people to respond to a short survey. If used in high-traffic areas, the interviewer is able to gather information from nonparticipants as well as participants. An additional advantage is the ability to single out the type of people an interviewer is interested in surveying such as women or teens. A shorter, more focused set of questions is usually required with this approach. However, it does overcome the challenges and expense of phone or mail.

Surveys placed in computerized consoles (stationary or hand-held) or computerized touch screens are now available to serve as an interviewing tool. The placement of the computers and the selection of questions can meet a variety of needs for the experience provider. Computer survey instruments can be stationed at places where would-be participants stop to inquire about specifics of the experience itself. Imagine the wealth of information to be gathered at a tourist information center adjacent to a major highway. Instruments can also be placed to secure information from the participant prior to the actual experience or immediately after the experience. Three different locations and three different types of information can be secured. The impersonal nature of this interview technique also contributes to the honesty of responses. Another plus of this approach is that the data can be computerized which contributes to a fast turnaround with results.

While organizations almost automatically turn to surveys for people information, there is another choice literally right in front of them, observation. Consider the possibility of watching how people behave as opposed to what they say. It's similar to the "do as I say and not as I do" approach, and the information garnered is often revealing. In order for observation to be fruitful, it must include information from which the behavior can be observed or inferred and be repetitive, frequent, and predictable in some way (McDaniel and Gates, 1993, p. 275).

There are a variety of scenarios that observation can undertake (McDaniel and Gates, 1993, pp. 275–277):

- Natural versus contrived—observing actual behavior while participants wait versus asking people to try out a new activity.
- Open versus hidden—no attempt to hide the observer versus the "mystery" guest who comes unannounced and incognito or the use of one-way mirrors.
- Structured versus nonstructured—the observer makes tallies on a specific form versus general notes based on observer's perceptions.
- Human versus machine—people watching people as opposed to video camera monitoring.
- Direct versus indirect—observing people directly in current behavior rather than exploring past behavior.

There are limitless applications for observation as a method to collect information in the experience industry. Mystery guests posing as actual participants are good sources of information for hotels, airlines, amusement parks, and almost all experience providers. United Airlines uses frequent fliers out of Chicago to rate the full-service system on various routes. Open observation, or one-way mirrors, are often used by toy or playground equipment manufacturers to learn how children interact with a product under development. Another observational option is called freeze frame. Observers or video cameras capture images of an experience that is

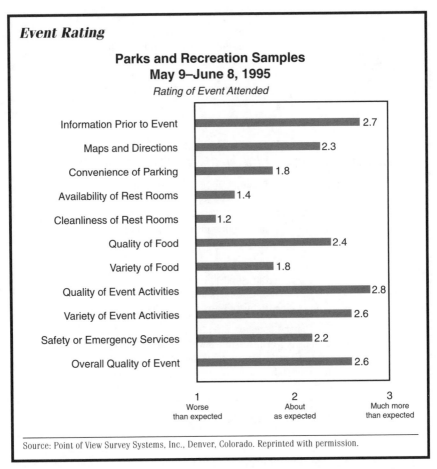

Event Rating

Parks and Recreation Samples
May 9–June 8, 1995
Rating of Event Attended

Category	Rating
Information Prior to Event	2.7
Maps and Directions	2.3
Convenience of Parking	1.8
Availability of Rest Rooms	1.4
Cleanliness of Rest Rooms	1.2
Quality of Food	2.4
Variety of Food	1.8
Quality of Event Activities	2.8
Variety of Event Activities	2.6
Safety or Emergency Services	2.2
Overall Quality of Event	2.6

1	2	3
Worse than expected	About as expected	Much more than expected

Source: Point of View Survey Systems, Inc., Denver, Colorado. Reprinted with permission.

going really well or is creating problems for either the participant or the provider. The freeze frame can then be analyzed to pinpoint positive aspects of the experience process or to identify and correct problem areas. Stationing observers at entrances and exits of amusement parks, zoos, and museums helps the experience provider determine exactly how people use the facility.

When attempting to gather greater insight or perceptions from people, focus groups are often used. Focus groups are a qualitative form of market research so they are not designed to provide the experience provider with either scientific or hard numbers but rather serve the purpose of uncovering interesting or useful information that could not have been secured through a survey or observation. Focus groups can be used to identify barriers to participation, find ways to add value to an experience, enhance customer service, determine participants' perceptions of an experience in relationship to competitors', or uncover effective advertising messages.

Focus groups generally involve 6 to 15 people and, as the name suggests, they generally focus on one experience or one aspect of the experience. People invited to participate in the focus groups can be either homogenous or heterogeneous, users or nonusers, depending on the information being sought.

The Centers for Disease Control in Atlanta commissioned focus groups to help determine potential barriers faced by adults when attempting to begin a physical activity or exercise program. The following is a brief report of the findings:

Healthy Eating and Physical Activity: Focus Group

Research with Contemplators and Preparers prepared for the
Centers for Disease Control

Summary of Themes and Implications for Marketing Campaign

Primary Themes: • Family is a priority
• Life is busy and stressful
• Life stages influence behavior
• Spiritual, mental, and physical health are connected
• Being healthy is desirable

Sega of America and the company's ad agency, Goodby, Berlin & Silversteen, conduct teen focus groups two or three times weekly and also hang out with 150 kids to look at their bedrooms or to observe their shopping habits at the mall. They've discovered that when teens shop for video games they are as price conscious as adults buying a new car (20 Companies On A Roll, 1993, pp. 29–30).

The People-Provider Relationship

Experience providers are often interested in securing information about people to better understand the relationship they have with the organization. There are a variety of mechanisms to use which include measures of both satisfaction and attribute identification.

A common approach is the customer or participant satisfaction technique. This is found everywhere—on the nightstand in hotels, tables in restaurants, and at the exits of many experience providers—and it seeks to answer the question, "Just how satisfied are you, anyway?"

While user satisfaction instruments may take a variety of forms, it is important that they account for the criteria of customer satisfaction devised as part of the Malcolm Baldridge National Quality Award. Two of the criteria necessary for this type of measurement is the understanding that satisfaction is defined by the customer or the user and not by the organization. It is also understood that management decisions need to be made on the basis of facts and data. Measurements of satisfaction generally include questions to collect certain kinds of information (McDaniel and Gates, 1993, pp. 745–746):

• screening questions—to determine if the respondents are people the interviewer has targeted such as current or recent users;

 Major companies and marketing and advertising firms are going to great lengths to secure market research information related to the needs, preferences, and consumer behavior of children and teens. Some projects include (Horowitz, 1997, 2A):

- Mattel underwrote a global study in a number of countries including the United States and China to examine what children had hanging on their bedroom walls.
- Levi Strauss & Co. provided children with throwaway cameras and video cameras and had them record accounts of how they and their friends spend their time.
- PepsiCo had its ad agency spend a weekend with 30 teenagers at a deluxe New Jersey hotel to talk to them about new Pepsi ads.
- Everyready's Energizer battery hired Kid2Kid, a research firm that used children to moderate focus groups of their peers.

- overall ratings—a rating of the respondent's feeling of the entire experience;
- performance ratings—measuring perceptions on a variety of specific aspects;
- intent to use or participate in the experience in the future;
- category usage information—in what other types of experiences are people involved; and
- demographic and lifestyle information.

The studies cited in the previous chapter on the customer continuum indicated that satisfaction does not necessarily mean that people will return to an organization or choose to do business with it again. This serves as a caveat to customer satisfaction. Sometimes satisfaction doesn't translate into bottom-line impact.

Another form of customer satisfaction that has as an added benefit while securing more information for the organization is those instruments that incorporate attribute identification into the process. One such form is the customer report card as introduced by Albrecht and Bradford. Recall the profound impact that the school report card could have on one's life. Albrecht and Bradford incorporate the use of important attributes or key elements of the service or experience into this monitoring tool. An amusement park would list possible key elements of a visit to its area on the customer comment card and ask customers to indicate two things: how important the attribute is to the experience and how well the park performed on that attribute.

Albrecht and Bradford also introduced the various levels of customers into this satisfaction scale. They cited the example of a hospital that may have had as many as four levels of customers: the actual patients, the admitting physicians, third parties such as ambulance companies and insurance providers, and noncustomers such as members of clergy, family members, and florists (Albrecht and Bradford, 1990, pp. 88–89). There are interesting applications here for experience providers to identify various levels of participants, some present and

NAME OF PARK

For the following statements, please check the appropriate box if you: [4] Strongly Agree; [3] Agree; [2] Disagree; [1] Strongly Disagree; [0] Have NO opinion.

[4] [3] [2] [1] [0]

The park was clean

Park facilities were well-maintained

Staff was friendly, professional and competent

I felt safe in the park

I don't mind paying fees to support parks

The park entrance was attractive and inviting

The staff was available to answer my questions

Concession staff was polite and service oriented

Park concession was well-stocked with appropriate items at fair prices

Rest rooms were clean

Signs in the park were adequate and understandable

Wildlife observation is important

Natural scenery appreciation is important

Brochures or literature on the park were available and adequate

Please list any additional facilities (such as cabins, campsites, swimming areas, etc.) that you would like to see in the state parks:

Date:

3/94

I have these comments concerning the park:

I am interested in being a volunteer or a member of a support group for this park. Yes___ No___

I am interested in being added to a mailing list for Florida Park Service literature. Yes___ No___

NAME:

ADDRESS:

PHONE:

Other Comments:

Moisten here, fold, seal and mail

Thanks for supporting
YOUR
FLORIDA STATE PARKS

Source: Florida Department of Environmental Protection, Tallahassee, Florida.

involved in the experience and others not directly involved but serving as important bearers of information.

An additional information tool for understanding how people perceive and rate an experience provider is the importance-performance analysis. This technique serves double duty as it allows an experience provider to identify those attributes of the experience that are most important to the participant while ascertaining the participants' perceptions regarding how well the provider is performing on those attributes.

Consumers today are overwhelmed by the number of choices for personal services or experiences, but they do respond when such providers take the time to track down what's important to them and what isn't. Complete customer satisfaction starts with the provider knowing and understanding what the customer wants. It is estimated that currently there's only about a 40 percent overlap between what management feels is important to the customer and what customers say is important to them (King, 1996, p. 6). A classic example of this is the research conducted by Marriott when designing a hotel for business travelers. Marriott learned that business travelers wanted a comfortable room with a large work space area and that they weren't interested in lounge acts and bellhops. The result was Courtyard by Marriott.

This is a particularly effective tool for experience marketers because participants are asked to respond to the attributes in a concise and easy manner. They rank the same set of attributes twice, once for importance and again for performance. In addition to being fairly simple to administer, the combined relationship of the attributes are presented in one of four quadrants with each quadrant representing a specific directive. These directives instruct the experience provider to concentrate on certain attributes, maintain high standards in certain areas, and to disregard attributes in the two remaining quadrants which consist of attributes that are not important to participants. The fitness class example listed in the Closeup shows four quadrants with specific action steps to be taken by the organization.

Techniques for securing information can also be termed opportunity marketing. There are a number of options that experience providers have for encouraging participants to share their perceptions and levels of satisfaction. Each interface with the participant or piece of information gleaned can become an opportunity for the experience provider to better meet the needs and expectations of his or her customers. Organizations need to make it easy for participants to share both the good and the bad since complaints are often very revealing and helpful.

Techniques for gathering suggestions and complaints should be made as easy as possible for people to use. One such example is British Airways' use of video cameras at Heathrow and Kennedy Airports. Arriving and departing customers can step up to the camera and leave their comments. Some people prefer this alternative to spilling their tale of woe to airport personnel. One must be creative and devise fast and friendly ways for customers to complain.

Make the complaints count. Personnel have been trained to turn complaints into opportunities which win the customer back, but the complaints should include the most possible information from the situation. Whiteley suggests that the experience provider has staff analyze customer's complaints and track such things as the emotions expressed by the customer, the expectations cited by the customer, the customer's perception of the service or experience, and any suggestions for improvement (Whitely, 1991, pp. 46–47). One should make the most of the complaint-suggestion situation as a way to uncover hidden opportunities to please and satisfy participants.

This is a graphic depiction of the results of an importance-performance survey conducted among members of a fitness class. The results of this survey reveal that the organization should continue its performance in the areas of activity level, location, variety of classes, and time schedule, just to name a few, while directing its attention to the registration system, parking, and the role and impact of other participants.

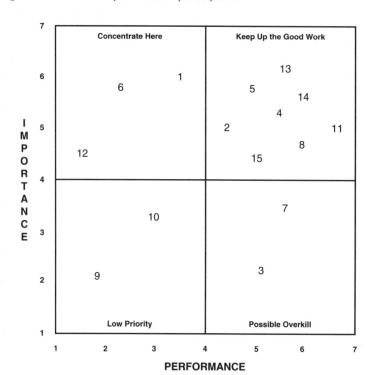

Attribute List

1. Registration	6. Parking	11. Music
2. Activity level	7. Child care	12 Other participants
3. Cost of class	8. Shower room	13. Instructor
4. Time schedule	9. Rest room	14. Variety of classes
5. Location	10. Temperature	15. Pace of class

Source: O'Sullivan, 1991, p. 211. Copyright ©1991 Venture Publishing, Inc. Reprinted with permission of Venture Publishing, Inc.

Suggestion boxes for both participants and personnel should be visible and accessible along with forms and pens to complete and register concerns or ideas as to how the experience or process of the experience can be improved. Experience providers desperately need this information. It is an incredibly valuable way to identify undiscovered needs or expectations of participants as well as a way to conduct an ongoing systems check. Not only does the provider need to provide options for this kind of information but he or she must also reinforce and encourage such feedback.

Suggestion boxes must be accompanied by a current update of suggestions received and action taken. People will spend the time to give information if they believe something will happen because of their effort. In addition, one needs to track the suggestions and feedback. Is there a pattern to the comments and suggestions, and what does that tell the provider about his or her operation? The Pareto principle applies to screwups in the system as well. It is likely that if the service provider monitors and tallies complaints, he or she will find that 80 percent of them are caused by 20 percent of the service-experience cycle.

Here are a few words of caution related to satisfaction surveys or measures. Spend time exploring the validity of the questions being asked as well as identifying methods for analysis of data and the availability of computer packages for such analysis. In addition, it is important that user satisfaction be tracked on a regular basis over time so that the provider has the ability to compare his or her progress or lack of it. It is important that the results of the findings are turned into action. If the provider doesn't intend to make changes on the basis of the findings, the questions shouldn't be asked.

One such example is the survey created by Presnell Gage and used annually by the organizers of the Boise River Festival. This survey tracked participants' opinions over time and requested preference information that could be used to change events and entertainment.

People Plus: Customer Databases

A tool that both hastens progress along the customer continuum and goes a long way toward infusing information into a system is the creation of customer databases. Customer databases are a new take on an old marketing custom. In the old days of doing business, the local butcher, baker, grocer, and even the candlestick maker knew the customer and the customer's family as well as individual needs and personal preferences. The baker might put aside that last loaf of rye bread knowing that a loyal customer always comes in Tuesday afternoons for such a loaf. The butcher would know when the family breadwinner was laid up with an injury and would extend credit during that time period. The candlestick maker didn't just make large numbers of one type of candle; he designed and produced his products based on his personal knowledge of his customers.

A "back to the future" marketing style is the latest strategy. The widespread use of computers and the development of easy-to-use software has brought us forward to old-fashioned information-based knowledge of people and their preferences. The inroads into database marketing are remarkable. Ford Motor Company has a database of 50 million while Kimberly Clark, manufacturers of Huggies knows the names of 10 million new mothers and American Express is in the enviable position of being able to identify people who made purchases from golf pro shops in the last year, attended a symphony concert, visited Europe, or did all three (McDaniel and Gates, 1993, p. 135).

Continued on page 202

♦ ♦ ♦ *The 1994 Boise River Festival*
♦ ♦ ♦ *Your Opinions Are Important*

| Please Follow Along on this Laminated SURVEY CARD |

① *How many years have you attended the BOISE RIVER FESTIVAL?* → | 1st | 2–3 | 4th |

② *Do you live in the Boise area? Live in Idaho? Live Out of State?* → [ ] – Boise

[ ] – Idaho

If NOT Boise: Vacation → | Yes | No | *Miles Away* → [   ] [ ] – ____

③ *Of the main events scheduled this year, which are your TWO or THREE favorites?*

The Hot Air Balloon Rallies → [ ]	Niteglow Balloon Show → [ ]
Children Events & Activities → [ ]	Nite Lite Parade & Floats → [ ]
Sporting Events & Activities → [ ]	The River Giants Parade → [ ]
Various Food & Beverages → [ ]	World Showcase Netherlands → [ ]
Music and Entertainment → [ ]	The Fireworks Grand Finale → [ ]

④ *What type of ENTERTAINMENT would you like to see added or expanded upon?*

JAZZ → [ ]	COUNTRY → [ ]	CONTEMPORARY → [ ]
OLDIES → [ ]	R & B – SOUL → [ ]	COMEDY ACTS → [ ]
ROCK → [ ]	MUSICALS → [ ]	_____ → [ ]

⑤ *On a scale of 1 (Poor) to 10 (Excellent), how would you rate the Festival on these:*

Amount & Quality of Media Coverage → [ ] (1–10)	Availability of Clean Rest Rooms → [ ] (1–10)
Usefulness of Maps and Schedules → [ ]	Cleanliness of Parks & Show Areas → [ ]
Usefulness of Signs & Reader Boards → [ ]	Off Stage Children's Events/Activities → [ ]
Suitable Parking or Shuttle Services → [ ]	The Recognition Given the Sponsors → [ ]
Security & Health Emergency Services → [ ]	Variety & Quality of Food & Beverage → [ ]

Your Overall Rating of 1994 FESTIVAL Activities, Shows and Services → [ ] (1–10)

Source: Presnell Gage Accounting and Consulting, Boise, Idaho.

⑥ *Estimate how you, or your group, might spend your MONEY during this FESTIVAL:*

♦ *Money for your lodging, such as any hotels or motels* → $

♦ *Money for your travel, such as gasoline or air fares* → $

♦ *Money for your meals, food, snacks and beverages* → $

♦ *Money for any FESTIVAL items, such as B–Shirts, etc.* → $

♦ *Money for some "just for fun" shopping at area stores* → $

♦ *Other money you intend to spend during the FESTIVAL* → $

⑦ *Would you please name some of the MAIN SPONSORS for this year's FESTIVAL?*

♦ _____ ♦ _____ ♦ _____

♦ _____ ♦ _____ ♦ _____

⑧ *How likely are you, or your group, to patronize the SPONSORS of this year's BOISE RIVER FESTIVAL in terms of using their products and services?*

Definitely Patronize → [ ]   Might Patronize → [ ]

Probably Patronize → [ ]   Not Important → [ ]

♦ ♦ ♦ The Boise River Festival Planners
♦ ♦ ♦ Want to Get to Know Our Festival Goers Better

NUMBER in GROUP ⇨ # of MALES → [ ]   # of FEMALES → [ ]

AGES of PERSONS ⇨ *Please give us the number of persons by category below:*

Persons Under 18 Years → [ ]		Persons 35 – 49 Years → [ ]
Persons 18 – 24 Years → [ ]		Persons 50 – 65 Years → [ ]
Persons 25 – 34 Years → [ ]		Persons Over 65 Years → [ ]

HOUSEHOLD INCOME ⇨ *Please estimate an annual income for your household:*

Under $ 10,000 annually → 1		$ 35,000 to $ 49,999 → 4
$ 10,000 to $ 19,999 → 2		$ 50,000 to $ 79,999 → 5
$ 20,000 to $ 34,999 → 3		Over $ 80,000 annually → 6

♥ ♥ ♥ THANK YOU for YOUR TIME! ♥ ♥ ♥

A first step in the customer database development is the identification and definition of best participants. The longstanding 80-20 rule of marketing applies here with 80 percent of revenues generally being generated by 20 percent of customers. Revenue projections, coupled with the evidence that it's less expensive to retain current customers, all point towards the value of identifying those customers. Hughes maintains that the principles of RFM (recency, frequency, and monetary) will serve the providers well in this phase of the development (Hughes, 1996, p. 156). The provider would want to answer the questions: who are the most recent participants, who participates most often, or who spends the most money on the offered experience?

It is important to identify the right people to include in a database. A secret to success is to collect information from participants in ways that are ethical and collaborative. It helps to devise strategies with which customers are willing and happy to share information with the experience provider. Hughes identifies a number of ways to accomplish this including issuing a special card, creating a club, or awarding frequency points (Hughes, 1996, pp. 180–181). Kraft Foods did this by developing a customer club for children called the Cheese and Macaroni Club. The Fox Network went with the Fox Kids Club. American Airlines led the way for adults with the creation of its frequent-flier program, and now airlines, hotels, and even mom 'n' pop operations have created similar kinds of programs that both reward good customers and generate information for their databases.

A second approach is to build a database through transactional means. Every time a participant comes in contact with an organization, the organization is able to track some new or additional information and enter that information in a growing data bank. This requires that the experience provider know exactly what pieces or types of information are most valuable when differentiating one customer from another. Do some participants visit every day, week, month, or year, and is this an important dimension of difference? Are there some people who always come alone or usually bring young children with them? Are there some participants who prefer to stretch out the time they are involved in the experience as opposed to those who like to zip right through it? Once the provider is able to pinpoint the specific status of differentiations, he or she can better target and serve participants. These important pieces of information can be incorporated into ongoing transactions with the participants.

The increasing availability of phone and software packages create ever-growing opportunities for database marketing that is individualized and personalized. Such packages will allow a provider to identify frequent customers instantly so that he or she can call them by name and reference their last experience with the organization. This is the way of the future. Database marketing can become the mainstay of customer collaboration.

Research Projects

Sometimes, there is no other way to get the information needed to make informed decisions about customers or an organization unless one undertakes a research project. Just securing or gathering information may not provide an experience provider with an understanding of how changes within his or her marketing mix or market strategies may impact on participants and their participation in the experience. That is where research plays a role.

Using the research approach, the experience provider changes or manipulates one or more variables or factors within the marketing approach and attempts to discover its effect on other key factors or variables. In experience marketing instances, the dependent variable that is being examined is often some measure of sales or participation rates or patterns. The independent variable, the factor that is being changed or altered to see if there is a change or relationship, can include elements of the marketing mix variables such as location, price, promotion, or some change in the experience parameters.

Research that seeks a causal relationship between these factors is subject to a host of research concerns including internal and external validity. These factors help determine if there are competing factors explaining the changes or whether the results of this study can be generalized to an entire population. The purpose of this chapter is not to make market researchers out of every reader but to provide a framework for options and concerns. Check out appropriate sources for further specifics. A starting place might be to review advertisements in *American Demographics* featuring a number of different firms available to conduct research studies. There are also a host of market research firms with specializations in various demographic groups or industries who specialize in undertaking research projects.

Techniques for the "How" to "Gather" Information

Experience marketers have two choices when it comes to the "how" of infusing information. They can either "get" the data or "gather" the data. While it may seem critical to collecting or "getting" the information that specifically relates to

❖ Houlihans Restaurants did a test market of an adult-oriented, upscale, steak restaurant in Kansas City, Missouri, called J. Gilberts to determine viability of concept as part of its expanded product line. The test was followed by a demographic study to identify potential locations with comparable demographics.

❖ Wyndham Hotels & Resorts annually sponsors Female Frequent Business Traveler contests where contestants must respond as if they were a CEO of a travel company suggesting changes they would make to improve business travel for women. As a way to identify the needs of this fast-growing segment of the market which makes up one-third of its guests, this contest comes complete with prizes such as vacation time, frequent-flier miles, and a business wardrobe. Information from a past survey resulted in extra-long phone cords, free in-room coffee and tea, shower massagers, bright reading lights, voice mail and data ports as standard amenities.

one's participants and one's organization, one should never overlook the wealth of information available externally as part of the knowledge explosion. While this secondary data hasn't been collected specifically to provide information about one's customer or system, it does stand ready to provide an understanding life-style of behavior patterns as well as insights into the world of marketing and commerce. The "gathering" portion of the data collection step can be internal, bringing together information collected by an organization on an ongoing basis, or it can be external information collected and published by an ever-growing number of outside sources.

Secondary information is available on a wide variety of topics and is easier, more convenient, and often less costly to obtain than primary data. The value lies in its ability to alert the experience marketer to potential changes or challenges within the industry, provide background information or support for marketing changes, serve to affirm need for primary data, or actually provide a solution to a specific problem or question. Drawbacks to secondary data can be that the infor-mation is unavailable or costly to purchase, as well as its lack of relevance to a specific population or situation or the lack of clarity about how the information was gathered.

Internal Gathering Approaches

Internal data is a starting point for this section since it involves data or informa-tion an experience provider routinely collects as part of the operation of an orga-nization and is readily available. Existing operations could include participant registration forms, usage pattern tallies, revenue reports, rental or occupancy rates, phone questions and inquiries, sales receipts, refund forms, suggestions or complaint reports.

There are two areas that need one's attention related to internal data collec-tion. First take a look at the wide variety of reporting mechanisms currently used in an organization and see how these transactions "add value" by enhancing one's knowledge of participants and their use of an experience. Be sure such mecha-nisms are organized or modified to augment the type and amount of information being generated. Take a look at the paper or computerized records churned out. Make this recordkeeping work to add value and information for one's organization.

Internal Data Collection Possibilities

Internal data collection possibilities include:

- Customer feedback forms—demographics (age, gender, etc.), geographic location (zip code).
- Telephone bills—geographic target market information, convenient time of day for customers to call, length of call and amount of information required.
- Sales receipts—participation patterns, waiting times, preferred benefit packages, zip codes.

- Loyalty programs—demographics, lifestyle characteristics, participation patterns, frequency and expenditure information (refer back to customer database).
- Telephone calls—demographic categories; types of inquiries; repeated questions; patterns of complaints, suggestions, concerns.
- Information requests—geographic locations, response from various advertising sources.

This list is by no means exhaustive, and it would vary based on the needs and practices of individual experience providers. The emphasis should be on making the most of internal operations as a means for securing information about one's customers and operation.

The recent advances in technology and cost reductions within technology make the comprehensiveness of data collection and analysis much more extensive and feasible for all providers. Supermarket chains have led the charge with their preferred customer cards. Such cards reward shoppers and the company simultaneously. The shoppers get special, unadvertised discounts and the store receives in-depth shopping and lifestyle information from the preferred customer. One advantage of using technology to collect internally generated customer data is that it can enhance the experience for the customer as well.

❖ Restaurants are providing waiters with hand-held terminals for order taking. Such devices eliminate needless trips to the kitchen, errors due to illegible handwriting, and calculation errors since the bill total is computed and printed automatically. In addition, the orders, when forwarded to the kitchen, are divided into separate cooking tasks with suggested sequence, minimizing delays and ensuring that the entire table's order is ready at the same time. Having these sales data on computer makes for quick and easy sales statistics, customer database, and inventory control.

❖ Computerized software programs used in hospital settings reduce administrative costs while allowing nurses and direct-care staff to spend more time with patients. Since anything that happens concerning the patient is entered in the computer program, the information is appropriately reflected in patient billing, hospital inventory, insurance reports, and case reviews.

❖ Hotels, car rental companies, and airlines make use of software to track reservation patterns. Such software can predict certain times, destinations, or days of the week when customer demand is either particularly high or low. Prices can be adjusted to maximize company profits and to provide information for future scheduling and load practices.

❖ Both Nickelodeon and Sega of America hold weekly on-line chats with kids capturing thousands of names to become part of their databases.

❖ AT&T has placed kiosks in drugstores that allow their card holders to swipe their cards and choose from a variety of coupons with coupon selections forming a profile of individual customer's purchasing patterns.

Gathering From Outside

The large number of sources for additional information and the volume of data generated by these sources reinforces the premise that information drives the twenty-first century. This information takes different forms as the more traditional printed format gives way to electronic and computerized databases and information. There are a variety of different sources for this information including government documents and publications, newspapers and periodicals, market research firms, and professional and trade associations.

The overriding suggestion for data gathering is to divide and conquer. Remember the "who" of sharing information. One can't possibly read or scan everything that's out there so one should involve others in the scanning activity to expand one's scope of sources. Another suggestion is to be simultaneously specific and broad by reading a variety of publications. Identify those sources that supply the most appropriate, useful, and specific information for one's organization. At the same time include a few offbeat or unrelated sources to provide a different perspective on what's happening.

Some Suggested Sources

Government Documents and Sources

Government documents and sources include:

- U. S. Census Bureau,
- Department of Commerce,
- Department of Education,
- Department of Health and Human Resources,
- Department of the Treasury,
- *Bureau of the Census Catalog of Publications,*
- *Guide to U. S. Government Publications,*
- *American Statistical Index,*
- *Census of Population Data,*
- *Census of Retail Trade,*
- *Census of Selected Services,*
- *Digest of Education Statistics,*
- *Economic Indicators,*
- *Measuring Markets: A Guide to Federal and State Statistical Data,*
- *Social Security Bulletin,*
- *Statistical Abstract of the United States,* and
- *Vital and Health Statistics.*

Newspapers and Periodicals

There is no limit to the titles that can be included under this category. First, identify those publications that one would place on one's personal list of favorites or "must reads." Some of our favorites (as is obvious by how often they're cited) are *American Demographics, Advertising Age, Futurist, USA Today, The Wall Street Journal, Fitness Management, Working Women,* and *Family Fun.*

Another technique is to make a list of those publications that rotate in and out of the scanning horizon by reading some of them once a week, once a month, or even three times a year. By identifying general interest categories such as major city newspapers, general news magazines such as *Time* or *Newsweek,* or such publications as *Atlantic Monthly,* one creates such a list. It's of interest and value to see what these publications are featuring.

Another recommendation is to identify general topic areas that one monitors. Sample subject areas that we keep an eye on include health, lifestyle, food, entertainment, travel, leisure, and business. Since there are numerous publications within these areas, consider alternating selections. For instance, one month we might scan *Men's Health* and the next month *Self* followed by *Prevention* the following month. We would do the same for business publications and alternate *Fortune, Inc.,* and *Business Week.*

There is no established plan. One has to assess what topics are most critical to one's target market and organization and read accordingly. Included in this rotating schedule could also be publications that are read by one's target markets or prospective target markets. A quick review of topics, types of products and services being advertised can provide a wide range of insights. Consider reading magazines published specifically for men or women, teens or mature adults, families, sailors or "techie" types.

The last category of things to read and scan is the offbeat or the "not really you" category. Check the magazine racks for the fringe or newly emerging publications. One will be amazed at the ideas and interests that exist. Include topics in which one lacks interest or background whether it be finance, science, or whatever isn't one's taste. Read just enough to gain an exposure and perspective in these categories.

Specialty Marketing and Trends Information

There are a number of marketing firms who conduct research, disseminate information on specific target markets or specific types of marketing activities. There are a number of them who have universal databases with vast amounts of information about purchasing, behavior, and media preferences. *Research Service Directory* is a good source of companies that provide information about companies that conduct market research or provide market research information. Marketing-oriented publications such as *American Demographics* and *Advertising Age* also include articles by such companies or advertisements for services and are good sources.

To provide an overview of the range and types of companies providing marketing information, the following is included:

- Specific target markets: Asian Marketing Communication Research, Hispanic Markets, Teenage Research Unlimited, Healthdemographics, Primelife, About Women, Inc., Kidfacts, and Roper CollegeTrack.

- Psychographic and/or lifestyle information: Claritas, Roper Starch, Langer Associates, SRI International, Donnelly, and SRDS' Lifestyle Marketing Analysis.

This list is by no means exhaustive. It is intended to raise the reader's level of awareness of what exists out there to meet marketing research and information needs.

There are also a number of trend newsletters published by marketing groups or business consultants available by subscription that provide a wealth of information for the experience industry. Some of those include the following:

- *Naisbitt's Trend Newsletter,*
- *Experience Industry Update* (ours),
- *The Numbers News,*
- *Public Pulse,*
- *Future Survey,* and
- *TrendScan.*

Professional Associations and Trade Groups

There are hundreds of trade and professional associations that focus on or represent members of the various experience industries. The quickest way to locate them is through the *National Trade and Professional Associations of the U. S. and Canada and Labor Unions.* These organizations provide a variety of services including data collection, trend projections, and service and experience overviews. Membership may include a number of publications, monthly journals, quarterly newsletters, annual surveys or they are often available for purchase. Information compiled by an association that targets a similar demographic, lifestyle group, or is in a related industry is a good source of information.

On-Line

Put on your surfing duds and take to the information highway. The Internet and Web sites are a combination of a market researcher's dream and an information scanner's definition of a gold mine. Any attempt at a listing is impossible. We encourage the reader to regularly surf and scan for information with direct impact for his or her organization.

Make It Have Meaning

The first step in the information infusion process was the clear identification of the specific questions and information needed. It is a natural and necessary starting point. The second step, the accumulation of that information, leads to a veritable mountain of paper and stats. What does one do with it? Unless one wants to drown in data and eventually give up the entire scanning and gathering process,

SRDS' Lifestyle Marketing Analysis—Golf

Lifestyles **Golf**
Base Index US = 100

The Top Ten Lifestyles Ranked by Index

Snow Skiing Frequently	186	Travel for Business	152
Tennis Frequently	178	Watching Sports on TV	150
Stock/Bond Investments	154	Real Estate Investments	147
Frequent Flyer	153	Own a Vacation Home/Property	143
Wines	153	Boating/Sailing	143

Home Life	Households	%	Index	Sports, Fitness & Health	Households	%	Index
Avid Book Reading	7,598,227	38.4	104	Bicycling Frequently	4,551,021	23.0	127
Bible/Devotional Reading	3,027,418	15.3	81	Dieting/Weight Control	4,570,808	23.1	103
Flower Gardening	7,004,615	35.4	104	Health/Natural Foods	2,968,057	15.0	89
Grandchildren	4,392,725	22.2	94	Improving Your Health	4,867,614	24.6	104
Home Furnishing/Decorating	4,986,336	25.2	113	Physical Fitness/Exercise	8,884,385	44.9	124
House Plants	5,856,967	29.6	93	Running/Jogging	2,987,844	15.1	129
Own a Cat	4,808,253	24.3	92	Snow Skiing Frequently	2,829,548	14.3	186
Own a Dog	6,984,828	35.3	103	Tennis Frequently	2,077,640	10.5	178
Shop by Catalog/Mail	6,133,985	31.0	105	Walking for Health	6,806,745	34.4	103
Subscribe to Cable TV	14,662,203	74.1	114	Watching Sports on TV	11,318,192	57.2	150
Vegetable Gardening	4,214,641	21.3	94				

Good Life				Hobbies & Interests			
				Automotive Work	2,552,529	12.9	88
Attend Cultural/Arts Events	3,442,947	17.4	111	Buy Pre-Recorded Videos	3,442,947	17.4	94
Fashion Clothing	2,928,483	14.8	107	Career-Oriented Activities	2,077,640	10.5	113
Fine Art/Antiques	2,414,020	12.2	110	Coin/Stamp Collecting	1,385,093	7.0	103
Foreign Travel	3,522,095	17.8	124	Collectibles/Collections	2,473,381	12.5	100
Frequent Flyer	6,608,874	33.4	153	Community/Civic Activities	2,176,575	11.0	121
Gourmet Cooking/Fine Foods	4,194,854	21.2	118	Crafts	5,105,059	25.8	95
Own a Vacation Home/Property	2,968,057	15.0	143	Current Affairs/Politics	3,878,262	19.6	117
Travel for Business	6,153,772	31.1	152	Home Workshop	5,678,883	28.7	110
Travel for Pleasure/Vacation	9,200,978	46.5	123	Military Veteran in Household	5,144,633	26.0	111
Travel in USA	9,082,255	45.9	126	Needlework/Knitting	2,691,039	13.6	88
Wines	4,076,132	20.6	153	Our Nation's Heritage	1,068,501	5.4	108
				Self-Improvement	3,779,326	19.1	104
Investing & Money				Sewing	2,770,187	14.0	83
Casino Gambling	3,601,243	18.2	136	Supports Health Charities	4,709,318	23.8	124
Entering Sweepstakes	2,829,548	14.3	94	High Tech Activities			
Moneymaking Opportunities	2,869,122	14.5	122				
Real Estate Investments	1,919,344	9.7	147	Electronics	2,394,233	12.1	104
Stock/Bond Investments	5,777,818	29.2	154	Home Video Games	2,631,678	13.3	108
				Listen to Records/Tapes/CDs	10,526,710	53.2	105
Great Outdoors				Own a CD Player	13,672,851	69.1	116
Boating/Sailing	2,968,057	15.0	143	Photography	3,719,965	18.8	106
Camping/Hiking	4,986,336	25.2	103	Science Fiction	1,582,964	8.0	89
Fishing Frequently	5,540,374	28.0	113	Science/New Technology	1,859,983	9.4	103
Hunting/Shooting	3,660,604	18.5	119	Use a Personal Computer	10,586,071	53.5	125
Motorcycles	1,622,538	8.2	108	Use an Apple/Macintosh	2,077,640	10.5	114
Recreational Vehicles	1,978,705	10.0	115	Use an IBM Compatible	9,398,848	47.5	127
Wildlife/Environmental	3,165,928	16.0	97	VCR Recording	3,799,113	19.2	99

The Lifestyle Market Analyst 1997	**Lifestyle Profiles**	**773**

Reprinted from the 1997 edition of *The Lifestyle Market Analyst*, published by SRDS with data supplied by The Polk Company.

one needs to devise a system. It does not have to be complicated. It needs to work for the provider. There are any number of approaches that can be used and additional techniques will be cited in the information infusion section to follow. Some suggested techniques to organize this ever-growing pile in a way that creates meaning for one includes:

- reading with a highlighter to zero in on the important part of article;
- toss all the interesting data and clippings into a folder that one sorts on a monthly basis;
- keep a small notebook just for jotting down interesting stats or information that one reads or hears about;
- create a scanning folder in one's computer and put the data under subheadings such as demographics, lifestyle, travel trends; and
- develop a filing system for one's data on an alphabetical or categorical basis.

One should experiment with different approaches until one finds something that works. The important thing is to create some mechanism for capturing what is scanned.

Now that the data is organized, one has to bring the data to life so it has meaning and purpose. There is an information hierarchy at work here. Not all information is created equal. Some is more critical or has greater applications than others. Some of the information gathered is not in a form where it lends itself to being used by one's organization. One needs to take steps to move the accumulated data up the infusion hierarchy as follows:

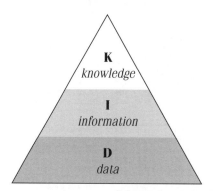

Think of it as kid's play with serious ramifications. This approach helps people move the vast amounts of miscellaneous data and facts that they've accumulated and helps them turn it into information and knowledge. This may involve sorting through the data and creating categories or detecting patterns of data that then provides information. The information may or may not apply specifically to one's organization, systems, or participants, and it may not immediately suggest options and alternatives to be pursued. It is at the top of this infusion hierarchy where the piles of data becomes information that can be transformed into knowledge that is useful for the specific experience provider.

Another approach to making meaning out of data is to analyze information using charts and graphs. These tools represent the data in a form that reflects its impact on one's organization. Bell and Zemke in *Managing Knock Your Socks Off Service* refer to the "magnificent seven" tools for this purpose including flow chart, cause-and-effect diagrams, Pareto diagrams, run charts, control charts, scattergrams, and histograms (Bell and Zemke, 1992, pp. 117–122). While the

An example of a newspaper article that may not seem to apply to providers of experiences is the article outlining Mount St. Mary's College's success in offering burial plots to alumni. Older alumni of the Emmitsburg, Maryland, campus saw it as a homecoming, and younger alumni constantly on the move saw it as a place to put down roots. University of Virginia tried a similar program and sold out quickly (Ashley, 1996, p. 10D).

How does the experience marketer turn this seemingly unrelated data into information and knowledge. This data can be moved along the hierarchy to become information and to eventually capture meaning for the experience industry:

Data
Universities are offering alumni the chance to be buried on campus and plots are being sold out at University of Virginia and others as an increasingly transient population looks for a final resting spot where it had roots and connections.

Information
Apparently, people of all ages feel "disconnected" from society and others; people need more opportunities for socialization and sense of belonging.

Knowledge
Let's create "belonging" types of options for our participants; maybe a Friday Night Group or single parents' social event.

plotting and applications of each of these seven tools vary from one another, one commonality is their approach to transforming data into useful information for an organization. Knowledge is created by identifying specific applications based on the information.

Infusing Information

Information infusion has three phases: the what, the how, and the why and all three phases require the involvement of the "who," the other people within the organization. How does one make sure the information permeates throughout the place? It's like the old adage, "if a tree falls in the forest and there's no one there to hear it. . . ." Knowledge and information don't really become useful unless people come into contact with it and do something with it. During the 1980s MISs (management information systems) were established in large companies to organize the information function and report findings to management. That effort was appropriate at the time, but it just isn't enough for today's experience industry. Such an approach won't do in the information-explosive environment of the twenty-first century. Data, information, and knowledge about one's customers, one's industry, related industries, and one's world are critical parts of an operation. Information must be shared and literally infused into every pore and part of the experience operation.

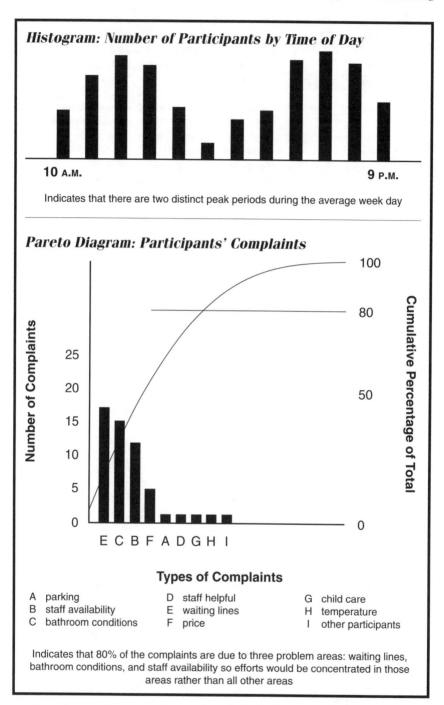

Histogram: Number of Participants by Time of Day

10 A.M.   9 P.M.

Indicates that there are two distinct peak periods during the average week day

Pareto Diagram: Participants' Complaints

Number of Complaints

Cumulative Percentage of Total

E C B F A D G H I

Types of Complaints

A	parking	D	staff helpful	G	child care
B	staff availability	E	waiting lines	H	temperature
C	bathroom conditions	F	price	I	other participants

Indicates that 80% of the complaints are due to three problem areas: waiting lines, bathroom conditions, and staff availability so efforts would be concentrated in those areas rather than all other areas

How do experience providers accomplish this? It can be done by implementing (not infiltrating) the CIA approach. A CIA approach represents a concerted effort to involve people at all levels throughout all aspects of the organization with information:

- *C*—collaborative collecting of data;
- *I*—identification of useful information;
- *A*—action or adaptation made on basis of C and I.

Think *C* for collaboration. It is essential that this task be a collaborative effort that includes and encourages involvement and input from each and every member of the organization. It was cleaning personnel who told hotel operators that they were throwing out lots of empty pizza boxes when cleaning rooms which eventually led to pizza being included as part of the room service menu in many properties. Experiences are common to everyone, and all personnel, whether support staff or senior administration, have observations and insights into what people are doing and how they prefer to do it.

Once people have accumulated facts, statistics, and assorted data, it's time for the next stage, identification of useful information. Information becomes useful when someone in the organization can make a connection between the data and some aspect of the experience. The infusing of information can occur when the experience provider takes the time and makes the effort to help personnel become skillful at making such connections. It is important to create ways in which one's organization identifies and makes sense out of information.

The last portion of this CIA process of infusion is to take action to change what one does or to make adaptations to part of one's marketing process. That is the purpose of creating knowledge out of the data collected. Knowledge makes it possible to apply what is known to make the experience and the process of the experience better for one's participants.

Look at some of the strategies suggested for the "CIA"ing of an organization. Use them as a starting point to create the techniques and mechanisms that are successful. What follows is a number of strategies incorporated under the heading, McSeek, designed to help a group infuse information into an experience.

- ❖ The Morale Welfare and Recreation Division at Naval Air Station in Brunswick, Maine, solicits information from staff including such things as newspaper articles, recently received junk mail, and enticing print ads. All material is placed in a folder in the conference room which staff frequent. The folder is packed up and routed to other facilities and offices on the base to make sure everybody has a chance to examine contents. Staff generate new program and promotion ideas based on gathered information.
- ❖ At Stew Leonard's Dairy Stores, the suggestion box is emptied every day, and the suggestions are typed up under various department headings and placed in the employee cafeteria where everybody can read the suggestions and respond accordingly.
- ❖ Campus food service operations at Southern Connecticut State University type up suggestions received from students and post them along with responses or actions taken.

Action Agenda

❖ Review the categories of information related to both people and experience providers and develop a list of specific pieces of information that would help your organization.

❖ In the next few weeks make an effort to respond to any surveys, interviews, or questionnaires that come your way. Make a mental note of your reaction to both the questions and the process.

❖ Try to think of three things you could learn about your participants or your experience through observation. Conduct an observation period and see what information you secure.

❖ Make a habit of picking up customer satisfaction or comment cards from places that you frequent, i.e., restaurants, hotels, other entertainment providers.

❖ Immediately install two suggestion boxes—one for participants and one for staff. Act on two suggestions from each source.

❖ Imagine that you wanted to create a customer database by determining who your "best" customers are, what kind of information would be helpful, and how to go about gathering that data.

❖ Review the forms and records currently being used in your organization and decide how to make the most of them as sources of information.

❖ Make a trip to your local library or tap into the Internet and look at census data and directories that provide statistical information.

❖ Identify a minimum of three (new to you) trade or professional organizations that might be of interest to you and request information about their services.

❖ Set aside an hour of your time to surf the Net and make new discoveries.

❖ Maintain phone logs for three weeks. If many of your calls are either complaints or questions about your offerings, use that as a sign to make some changes.

❖ Wander around your organization and ask any three participants and employees if they can identify three other programs, activities, or services being offered by your organization.

❖ Select one of the McSeek strategies and infuse that into your organization by next week.

McSeek

- Friends & Family: Ask staff to zero in on recent changes in behavior and preferences by giving each staff member three index cards and asking him or her to record a recent behavior change among friends or family members that he or she has observed. Cards can then be sorted into piles of similar changes to identify trends and serve as a discussion point at an upcoming meeting.

- Water Cooler: Place at the water cooler (or wherever people in your organization are sure to gather or pass by), a statistic, an article, or a cartoon, and ask staff to react to the information by writing applications or suggestions on a nearby white board.

- Trends Tune-Up: Once a month or quarter hold a gathering of staff members with the sole focus of making a series of minor modifications to your experience.

Transition Tracking

From	**To**

There was a time when market research was considered to be a nice thing to do within an organization. There was also a time when market information was considered the job of one separate department within an organization. Those days are over as the gathering of information about one's customer and one's industry is considered a necessity. There have been some additional shifts in thinking and approaches to this area including:

• Market research	• Infusing information
• MIS department	• Everybody's job
• Statistics	• Statistics and observations
• Research sitting on a shelf	• Information used continually for change and improvement.

- Party Power: Hold voluntary brainstorming sessions to review internal data; role play participants' actions and staff responses.
- MBPA (management by playing around): Recall "management by wandering around"? Now consider one for the experience industry, management by playing around. Take a group of staff members to an outing of your service or experience or to a nearby experience that may be unrelated to yours. Have them identify both the positive and the negative things that happened to them during the outing and plan ways to infuse those findings into your operation.

Sources

Albrecht, Karl, & Bradford, Lawrence, J. (1990). *The service advantage: How to identify and fulfill customer needs.* Homewood, IL: Dow Jones-Irwin.

Ashley, Beth. (1996, October 15). That eternal school spirit. *USA Today.*

Bell, Chip R., & Zemke, Ron. (1992). *Managing knock your socks off service.* New York, NY: AMACOM.

Dortch, Shannon. (1996, November). ka.lei.do.scope n. *American Demographics.*

Horowitz, Bruce. (1997, December 18). Retailers in search of customers for life. *USA Today.*

Hughes, Arthur M. (1996). *The complete database marketer* (rev. ed.). Burr Ridge, IL: Irwin Professional Publishing.

King, Elizabeth. (1996, December 30). Do right by the customer and you'll do well. *Sarasota Herald Tribune.*

McDaniel, Carl, Jr., & Gates, Roger. (1993). *Contemporary marketing research* (2nd ed.). Minneapolis-St. Paul, MN: Western Publishing Company.

O'Sullivan, Ellen L. (1991). *Marketing for parks, recreation, and leisure,* p. 157. State College, PA: Venture Publishing, Inc.

SRDS. (1995). *The lifestyle market analysis.* Des Plaines, IL: Author.

20 companies on a roll. (1993, Autumn/Winter). *Fortune.*

Whitely, Richard C. (1991). *The customer driven company.* Reading, MA: Addison-Wesley.

During the agricultural era, people lived on farms and were fairly certain about how they would spend their days and what their lives would be like in
the future. Life was predictable. Then came the industrial era. Large numbers of people relocated to urban areas and traded farm for factory but still life remained fairly predictable and structured. There weren't many surprises.

Life was simpler in other ways as well during the agricultural and industrial eras. There were fewer choices. There was a limited range of options related to schooling, working, or raising a family. This limited range of choice led people to live in ways that were quite similar to one another. During these eras those similarities led to the creation of one large mass market with fairly uniform needs, interests, and preferences.

Fewer choices characterized the marketplace as well. The Sears & Roebuck catalog held the shopping choices for much of the rural countryside; shopping was a simple matter. The limited number of choices available made life seem less complicated. When going out for ice cream the biggest decision to be made was vanilla, chocolate, or strawberry. Baskin & Robbins started us down this road of choices with their nearly limitless ice cream flavors, but that was only the beginning. Today's ice cream purchaser can choose between low-fat, no-fat, sugar-free, frozen yogurt, and sorbet.

One can pick any product category from automobiles to sneakers, and the expansion of choices within each category defies imagination. The days of the mass marketing approach to production and advertising were far simpler. The onset of the information era brought vast numbers of choices in how people live, work, consume, and play. It is not an easy time for marketing.

The changes wrought by the information era have led to substantial demographic, social, economic, and technological change. These changes have created a myriad of personal and lifestyle variations. The days when target markets could be constructed on the basis of age, geographical location, or some other demographic variable are long gone. The marketing challenges created by this era of differences among people is heightened by the changing expectations among those different groups of people as well. Not only are people different, but their expectations related to having their individual needs and preferences met have skyrocketed as well. They naturally expect that product, service, and experience providers will automatically anticipate and meet their ever-changing patterns and priorities.

Continued on page 220

Chapter 9

Meeting the Ever-Changing Needs and Preferences of People Through Marketing

Products have to fit the situational needs of consumers; transactions must be tailored to the particular situation at hand.

Jim Taylor and Watts Wacker

Change Necessitates Change

We are caught up in change. The world, nations, society, institutions, corporations, families, and individuals are scrambling to deal with the changes created by the transition from the industrial to the information era. Land and Jarman refer to this transition as a break-point between the two economies and suggest that this break-point has created a new set of circumstances that companies must now address. Companies must (Land and Jarman, 1992, p. 66):

- respond rapidly to customer changes;
- innovate to meet competition;
- add new and different value to products and services;
- develop partnering relationships with customers; and
- manufacture and sell to new, different, and smaller segments around the world.

The new demands created by customers, competition, and technology mean that organizations need to become much more agile. The definition of quality as it relates to products, services, and experiences takes on an expanded definition. If people's lives and lifestyles keep changing, and if their needs, preferences, and expectations change right along with them, organizations must change at that same pace. Experts are suggesting that it is indeed time for the agile organization. An agile organization is one that operates with a flexibility that embraces broader product range, shorter life span of products, and individualized production of orders.

An agile organization has the ability to provide its customers with products, services, or experiences customized to personal specifications. Such agility is characterized by (Goldman, Nagel and Preiss, 1995, pp. xvi, xvii):

- marketing that provides for customer-enriching, individualized combinations;
- production that results in service/experiences created for individuals or small groups; and
- design that involves everyone with a stake in the process including suppliers and customers.

> **Flashback continued**
>
> The rise of micromarkets and the expectations for customization necessitate new ways for organizations to conduct their marketing activities. If experience providers want to thrive in the future, they must embrace a new worldview of envisioning people and marketing. The watchword for today and the future is change—change among people, their preferences and expectations and change within organizations to meet those ever-evolving needs of people.

The emergence of this new way of life will cause marketing and management to stretch their boundaries to reshape their more traditional role significantly and to redefine the intent and focus of much of their activity.

The Swatchmobile is a perfect example of the direction in which marketing is headed. The Swatchmobile is a car that is a cross between a Mercedes-Benz and a Swatch. That's right. The high-end, German car manufacturer partnered with a Swiss watch company noted for its cute but inexpensive watches. The result is expected to be a car that gets 60 miles to the gallon, squeezes into tiny parking spaces, and with user-replaceable body parts, essentially changes colors based on the whim of the owner. Imagine being able to buy a mode of transportation that meets the current space and energy requirements while simultaneously giving the owner a double dose of grand status and fun simultaneously.

The Swatchmobile defines the bridge between the demands of the breakpoint for agility meeting the ever-changing needs of people. It responds rapidly to changing preferences. It's innovative. It adds new and different values to new, different, and smaller groups of customers around the world, and it is certainly a new way to look at partnering with customers.

As you read this chapter, imagine your experience as a Swatchmobile and try to conjure up ways in which you can use agility to put into place innovations that will meet the ever-changing needs and preferences of your participants in a way that adds value for them.

The Direction of Change

Change can take many forms; it can be incremental, systemic, or even dysfunctional. It is somewhat easier to recognize and deal with change if such changes can be viewed on a continuum. By viewing change as part of a continuum, it becomes easier to recognize some of the shifts that are taking place

Signs of a Shift

People Changes

Agile organizations will begin to change the ways in which they perceive their customers. These changes will incorporate changes in the way they view people and perceive their needs and preferences as follows:

From	To
• Customers	• Collaborators
• Demanding	• Expectant
• People's patterns	• Individual's priorities
• Customer satisfaction	• Personalized benefits

Marketing Changes

Agile organizations that have embraced the mandate of change will revise the way in which their organizations view and carry out marketing functions as follows:

From	To
• Mass marketing	• Mass customization
• Accuracy	• Agility
• Quality, value added	• Value enhanced and enriched
• Commodity	• Specialty
• Lifestyle	• Mind-set
• Persuading purchase	• Creating conversations and connections
• Creators of products and services	• Collaborators in experiences

and to identify the direction in which these changes are headed. One only need look at the current signs of a shift among the behavior and preferences of people as well as the end result anticipated from the continuation of such changes. These shifts and proposed changes address both the needs and preferences of people as customer and participants as well as the role of marketing and subsequent techniques and approaches.

People's needs, interests, and desires are constantly evolving, and they expect that organizations will make these new priorities and preferences a priority. People are no longer content to be just customers. It's their wedding, vacation, or hospital stay, and they insist on being a collaborator in that process. The recent customer service revolution has led people to revise their demands upward creating higher expectations. This emerging pattern leads to a move beyond satisfaction. Satisfaction becomes the baseline as people reach for the benefits that they personally seek.

The usual insights that marketers were able to draw from information about people based upon where they lived, how much they earned, and other more traditional target marketing descriptors no longer provides a complete picture. More valuable information related to people's lifestyles has become a much more important part of the process. However, even those lifestyle variations need to be augmented today. Today, it is not all that unusual for people "to live rural, work suburban, and have the mind-set of a city dweller" (Taylor and Wacker, 1997, p. 129). Consumers don't go to an organization to buy a product or receive a service; they go for the experiences the organization can provide them as they address their inner needs. These inner needs are based on lifestyle choices and are driven by the mind-sets of participants.

The shifts are substantive from the marketing point of view also. The lack of sameness among people requires that organizations make a major shift from mass marketing to mass customization. The definitions of the perfect college, the vacation of a lifetime, or the dream house defy easy answers. People will gravitate towards the organization and experience provider that can fulfill their individual priorities and to do so in a way that they can afford, think they can afford, or are willing to afford. Health clubs that offer a variety of levels of membership, each with varying types of services or benefits to customers, while advertising those memberships based on the monthly rather than the annual rates, cover all the bases.

Mass customization also relates to something else these new customers-collaborators want. Customers want things done right, and they reserve the right to determine what is right. If they change their minds about what is right, they expect providers to rise to the redefined vision and make those changes. The value-added technique of the late twentieth century is being supplanted by value defined individuality that serves to enhance or enrich an experience. Part of the ratio of enrichment-enhancement relates to the redefinition of experiences from a commodity to a specialty aspect of people's lives.

The relationship between the organization and the participant changes as well. The marketing activities engaged in by the provider will still include some aspects of influence and persuasion in the process. However, the central focus of marketing shifts to allow the participant to define the experience. This definition of the experience will be significantly shaped by ever-changing aspects of people's situations. Individuals will find their worlds continually bombarded by outside forces that compel them to make changes in how they live, work, and play. These ongoing changes in their personal circumstances and mind-sets will necessitate organizations that can recognize these changes, if not anticipate them, and respond appropriately.

Welcome to a new world where people are part of the process and marketing techniques are evolving as a means to create new and desirable opportunities for both participants and providers.

Marketing Responses

How then do organizations respond (rather than react) to these substantial and significant changes among people and marketing? While the range and scope of responses and reactions can be quite extensive, the following are just a few suggested options for experience providers:

- Agile operation—customizing experiences with an emphasis on both efficiency and effectiveness.
- Repositioning—recreating and revising experiences to meet changing and emerging needs and desires.
- Share of experience—capturing for your organization more of the time, money, and resources people expend on experiences.
- Glocal (Feather, 1994)—integrating the best of local and global marketing strategies.
- Value enriched—infusing the experience with whatever it takes to escalate and reposition its value to participants.
- Specialty experiences—shaping participants' perceptions of the experience, raising its level of value.
- Differentiation—finding an attribute that people value but can't find in other experiences or with other experience providers.
- PerInfoCom-Conn—heightening and refining PerInfoCom efforts so they become opportunities for connections with the customer: good conversations and meaningful encounters (the next version of PerInfoCom).

Agile Operations: Have It Your Way

Burger King may have been onto something all those years ago when it chose a slogan promoting personal preference. As society becomes more and more "me" and less and less "we," individualization drives the need for people to have it their way. The advances in technology fuel these expectations. The accent is on agility to respond.

The dressmaker of yesteryear designed "the right" dress for each individual customer by selecting preferred fabrics and adornments while tailoring it to the exact specifications of the customer's physical features. The difference between today's agile organization and the local dressmaker, however, lies in the agile company's ability to maintain high volumes of productivity while attaining specific customization. Consumers of the future want customized experiences, but not everyone is willing or able to pay the higher prices.

How do factories produce customized products in record time? How do service organizations rework their process to provide nearly instantaneous responses? How can experience providers do the same? The response lies somewhere in between streamlining an experience process to ensure prompt and reasonably priced opportunities while infusing one's organization with a flexibility to adapt, or accommodate, personal preferences of each participant.

Management consultants Gilmore and Pine identify four approaches to mass customization: adaptive, cosmetic, transparent, and collaboration (Gilmore and Pine, 1997, pp. 91–101). The adaptive alternative involves the creation of one standard product, service, or experience that the customer can adapt or alter on his or her own. Pier I Imports has an extensive selection of products designed to uplift the spirit. Aroma therapy products include soaps, bath salts, candles, incense, and music. Each of these products come with a designation for creating a mood that is sensual, relaxing, or energizing. But it's the customer who identifies which mood he or she is seeking as well as the product mix that he or she prefers.

The second approach referred to as cosmetic relates to the development of a standard product or experience, but the presentation to different customers varies. In this case, the packaging or promotion of the product or experience is what is being customized to meet the needs of specific groups of customers. Colleges and universities are experiencing substantial variations among characteristics of students. The traditional college students who attend college right out of high school find themselves sitting in classes next to more nontraditional students who tend to be older with more life experience. The images and benefits listed in advertising for these institutions can be quite different ranging from places that resemble a combination health club and coffeehouse to those that boast of a fast-track program of study leading to new career options.

The third customization technique is labeled transparent. In this case, the organization is able to identify easily the specific and fairly predictable needs of a group of participants and to develop its product or experience accordingly. This approach works well for airlines or hotels providing different services for two different groups: business and leisure travelers.

The fourth approach, collaboration, involves a dialogue with individual customers for the purpose of helping them to identify their specific needs. Once the specific needs are identified, the organization can replicate the customized product, service, or experience. The computer databases used by some hotels see to it that guest's preferences for nonsmoking rooms with a feather pillow are replicated worldwide.

Experience providers may find that the need to utilize more than one of these customization strategies depends on the experience, the competitive environment, and the needs of their participants.

- ❖ Levi Strauss has been offering "personal pair," custom-tailored jeans for women since 1994. Measurements are taken in one of its 55 Original Levi stores and then relayed by computer to the factory where the customer's unique dimensions are matched to one of the more than 10,000 patterns in its database. The "personal pair" is then mailed to the customer within three weeks.
- ❖ Guests don't just show up at the Disney Institute. They complete a planning and preference packet prior to their stay so the design and nature of their vacation can address their needs and interests.
- ❖ If one goes on-line to make travel arrangements, Biz.travel.com requires an in-depth personal profile at the beginning and then creates itineraries (flights, hotels, rental cars) that maximize frequent-flier miles and promotional awards.

Repositioning

Times change and along with it public perceptions and preferences. Recall the time when hospitals were just for the sick, and amusement parks were just for kids. Behaviors along with values and attitudes evolve and change over time. Such changes drive the need for organizations to reposition themselves and their products. The current pace of consumer change and escalating competition actually results in continuous repositioning. Local hospitals and bookstores have repositioned themselves as community centers where a customer may stop by for support group meetings, discussion groups, or coffee.

Such continual repositioning is not as easy as it looks. McDonald's, an experienced marketer, could attest to the challenges inherent within such an approach. It launched Arch Deluxe in an attempt to reposition itself to attract maturing Baby Boomers. Even the "Boomer burger's" kickoff at Radio City Music Hall didn't make McDonald's fans out of most adults. McDonald's soon returned to its original market position focusing on children as evidenced by the appearance of all those Teenie Beanies.

Repositioning has emerged as a priority approach as part of an overall marketing strategy. This strategy involves the two aspects already central to experience marketing: participants and the experience itself. Repositioning may involve an image change to update the look and feel of an experience or to make the experience more appealing to the prime target markets of such an experience. Pepsi may position itself as the cola drink for the "Pepsi Generation," but changes in how this younger cohort group defines and perceives itself over time will necessitate changing the image and message of the drink accordingly.

Generally, repositioning efforts include more than advertising or image changes. The emphasis upon the two factors (current and potential participants and their current and emerging needs) leads to at least six different tactics that an organization can employ—revive, retain, reach, reinvent, retrench, and redefine.

The repositioning options fall along a continuum from minor tinkering to major overhaul, but all are critical to the ongoing viability of an experience provider since people and their needs are ever changing. A low effort–low impact repositioning option is to revive. While current participants may seem happy with an experience and don't demonstrate any noticeable or significant need changes, the experience provider still ought to make changes in small portions of the experience to keep the experience interesting and enticing to the target group. That's why museums, regardless of how extensive their permanent collection, regularly schedule special exhibits as a way to maintain continued interest on the part of their patrons.

A second tactic, retention, is a bit more aggressive because it focuses on the need to keep current participants coming back. When a provider implements this strategy, he or she makes more substantive changes in the experience to address the evolving or emerging changes within his or her targeted group of participants. When Club Med made changes to accommodate small children and families, it was practicing the retention strategy by trying to keep former guests whose lifestyles had changed over time.

Repositioning Options

People's Needs	Participants	
	Current	*Potential*
Current	**Revive** (change small pieces of the experience to keep it exciting or interesting)	**Reach** (change the parameters to attract a new group or create a new use)
Emerging	**Retain** (alter the experience to address emerging needs of current participants)	**Reinvent** (change the core of experience to reach new participants)
Other Options	**Retrench** (alter parameters of the experience to discourage continued participation in an experience that is outdated, not profitable, or unacceptable)	**Redefine** (alter parameters of the experience to set an experience apart from competitors catering to a similar need or providing a similar experience)

Two of the other strategies, reach and reinvent, are more aggressive repositioning options. Reach involves substantive changes to the experience to tap into the needs of a participant group who is new to the experience. A novel but successful example of this strategy is Disney's schedule for release of the childhood classics such as *Bambi, Snow White,* and a host of others. These films are only available every seven years enabling them to capture an entirely new group of children with each rerelease. Another example is ski resorts. As participation levels at many ski areas declined, they revised their policies on snowboarding to reach this new group of outdoor sport enthusiasts.

Reinvent is the most aggressive of the category options and involves essentially changing the core focus of the experience to reach either a vastly different target market group or to address a previously unrecognized need. Walt Disney was essentially a cartoonist when he achieved even greater success by creating a wholesome, family-oriented theme park which recognized a previously untapped need. Ski resorts that add golf courses or water parks are practicing reinvention by bringing uniquely different target markets to their area in what was formerly referred to as the "off-season." This strategy may ultimately mean abandoning one business for another as was the case with St. Joe's Paper, a longtime paper manufacturing company, that decided to divest itself of paper production and refocus its real estate holdings on the resort and entertainment business.

Two other repositioning strategies with very different goals are retrench and redefine. Retrench attempts to discourage participation while redefine hopes to heighten overall participation.

Retrench involves altering parameters of the experience to discourage continued participation in an experience or behavior once the experience becomes outdated, unprofitable, or unacceptable. Airlines, hotels and restaurants are examples of providers that moved to restrict smoking as the behavior became more unacceptable to more of their customers. Disneyland turned out the lights on the 24-year-old, 500,000 light, Main Street on Electrical Parade, but not before it provided ample opportunity for the longtime fans of this event to reexperience the parade. In both instances, retrenchment was being practiced.

Activities designed to heighten participation in either a type of experience or a specific provider is the goal of the last tactic, redefine. When an experience provider practices this approach he or she tries to differentiate in the mind of potential consumers how a particular experience or experience provider differs from other competitors. Cruise lines are attempting to "re"define people's perceptions of cruises in an attempt to attract people who generally take land-based vacations. The additions of fitness facilities, spas, and more active, land-based activities are featured as ways to help the resorters decide to hit the high seas. Caribbean islands highlight the differences among themselves and carve out enticements to bring people to Jamaica rather than to Aruba or Martinique.

Share of Experience

There was a time when the tracking and reporting of market share was a mainstay for corporate America. Sales would fluctuate, but loss of market share was cause for real concern. While business may never outgrow its need for market share, it is, however, being replaced by a somewhat different perception of market referred to as "share of the experience." If a working couple with children goes out for dinner every Friday night of the year, does the restaurant want their business three times a year or three times a month? If the four-generation family

Mountain bikes were the "must have" toys of the early '90s hitting sales of $13 million in 1993. Mountain bikes accounted for 65 percent of the 10 million bicycles sold in 1996, but such purchases represented a two-year decline for these specialty use cycles. Everybody who wanted a mountain bike already had one, and this led the industry to a new dilemma. It needed to create either renewed interest or new markets for mountain bikes. To reverse the trend in this maturing market, manufacturers have created new forms of bikes to encourage trade-ins and upgrades. Funky-frame models, full-suspension bikes, city sporty bikes, and bikes with spokeless wheels are examples of this repositioning approach.

Another approach especially designed for the maturing Baby Boomer market is the comfort bike with cushy seats, strong suspensions systems, and upright handlebars. Battery-assisted cycles are still another strategy designed to attract new markets who might be looking for hassle-free alternatives to getting around town or exercising.

Since avid riders are moving on to other high-energy sports such as rock climbing, sea kayaking, and in-line skating, attempts are being made to rekindle excitement in the sport. Kodak, Bud Light, and Surf detergent are sponsoring major competitions. Sanctioned bike races have gone from 280 in 1990 to 950 in 1996 with TV exposure for those same years soaring from only three hours to 50 plus (Reilly, 1996, p. 21; Hardesty, 1997, p. D19).

Ski resorts eventually discovered that they couldn't remain profitable if they were solely dependent on the winter season so many of them gave themselves a lift by becoming summer resorts as well. Here are a few examples of such approaches:

- Sunday River in Maine offers guided canoe trips, fly-fishing expeditions, and Camp Sunday River for kids.
- Mount Snow in Vermont has made itself into one of the hottest mountain-biking centers in the northeast. Other summer options include its golf school, kids camp, and Friday Cabana night specials.
- New Hampshire's Loon Mountain features a Wildlife Theater starring snakes and cougars as well as Lumberjack Shows explaining the region's logging heritage. Other activities include an equestrian center and a mountain playground.
- Smuggler's Notch of Vermont has long positioned itself as the "family first" ski resort and goes big time in the summer as well with a Wishing Well, Watering Hole, and Raven's Roost Climbing Tower.

takes an annual holiday vacation, does the resort want every single one of those holiday ventures, or would it be satisfied to see the family just once or twice?

Experience providers need to change the way in which they view customers. Key concepts involved in this attitudinal shift are lifetime value and share of the customer. Businesses practicing traditional marketing measured their success by market share. They tried to sell as much of their product or service to as many people as possible and used that as the measure of their success. The new world thinking related to market share focuses on share of the experience.

While it's still important to have as many people as possible participate in an experience, it is even more critical to long-term viability that these people repeatedly take part in a provider's experience. Think of it as lifetime value. Does a community-based hospital want to treat all of a person's medical problems over his or her lifetime, or is it satisfied to deal with just his or her emergency appendectomy? Consider the impact on the bottom line between the health club that tries to bring in as many new members as possible within a year and the club that focuses on keeping each new member it attracts and securing as much of his or her fitness dollars as possible from sales of clothing, equipment, or specialized services.

This shift in emphasis takes into account both the value of a participant as well as the myriad of experience options available for people. There is only so much time, energy, and money that people have to expend upon experiences. Experience providers need marketing strategies that ensure they receive as large a share of those resources as possible.

Local + Global = Glocal

Feather, in his book *The Future Consumer* (1994), coins the term *glocal* to refer to an organization's ability to compete in the rapidly expanding world marketplace.

❖ The PGA National Resort and Spa in Palm Beach Gardens, Florida, is a golfer's dream with five 18-hole golf courses including the "champion" course designed by Jack Nicklaus and the "general" course designed by Arnold Palmer. The inclusion of a spa with the high-powered golf school represents an attempt to expand the resort's share of the experience. Expanding its service means it now attracts a golfer's companion as well as bringing to the resort people looking to recharge their batteries with plenty of pampering as well as to learn golf.

❖ Cruise lines offer significant discounts, room selection preferences, and special on-board opportunities to repeat sailors to maintain the relationship they have with their cruise line.

❖ A rent-free cellular phone is just part of the service provided by the Naples, Florida, Chamber of Commerce. Visitors to the area can stop by the chamber office, pick up a phone, and call local restaurants, attractions, and businesses participating in the plan without cost. Why take the chance that tourists leave the area to eat, spend, or play when they can capture the largest share of the tourism dollar for their community?

He defines glocal marketing as "offering tailored products for unique customers scattered across the global village marketplace" (Feather, 1994, p. 157). Taking a product, service, or experience from one country to another often presents some challenges as when KFC introduced its chicken in China, and "finger-lickin' good" was translated as "eat your fingers off." McDonald's, which sets a steady pace of global expansion, opened a restaurant in its hundredth country, Belarus, in December 1996, followed a few days later with its hundred-first country, Tahiti. Because McDonald's' hamburgers are served in France and China, certainly doesn't mean that carbonated beverages or prepackaged salads will be served in all locations. Just as a number of companies learned when translating advertising copy into other languages, there are certain things that simply don't translate well, and the same will be true of experiences as it was for ad copy.

Teenage girls in New Zealand may be interested in Michael Jackson and Madonna, and young Masai warriors in Kenya may wear Reeboks and Swatch watches. However, these examples of shared commonality do not entirely leap frog over the cultural and societal differences. In order to go glocal, experience providers must sift through shared needs and interests while paying close attention to the often subtle but significant differences between individual cultures. It's more than just language; it's the life patterns and mind-sets.

Visitors from the United States to other countries are often drawn by these differences in lifestyle and culture, but they sometimes have difficulty adjusting to the slower pace of life and the later dining patterns. In a similar manner, people from other countries and cultures may be drawn to products, services, and experiences that typify the American way of life but are puzzled or put off by some of the parameters of those experiences. Glocal strives to combine the best of both global and local approaches.

❖ When McDonald's opened its first restaurants in India in the fall of 1996, the Big Mac was replaced by the Maharaja Mac, two all mutton patties, special sauce, etc. Since 80 percent of Indians are Hindu and don't eat beef because cows are a sacred symbol, this was a glocal action. However, converting Brazilians with their predisposition towards leisurely dining was much more challenging. In Brazil, they may like beef but can't understand why anyone would value the fast-food approach.

❖ While Coca-Cola is tempting American teens with a new caffeine-rich drink called Surge, it has created something different for teens in Taiwan called Fei Uang which when translated means "flying high." This new brand of fruit and tea drink is specifically designed for Taiwan where such substances are an important sector of the soft drink market.

❖ When creating luxury overnight seats for its business class passengers, United Airlines found that cultural differences even involved seats. British passengers desired more privacy than others so United developed a side panel that can be raised from the armrest. In addition, they learned that people from some Eastern cultures didn't place a high priority on such privacy. They would rather they maintained greater visibility with the flight attendants to secure ongoing service.

Experiences do indeed vary by culture. Starbucks was created when its founder took a European trip and was so taken by cafes on the continent where Europeans lingered over a cup of coffee that he rushed home and started his own version. The rest is history. Still, the Starbucks' version of cafe society takes on the culture of its surroundings. Most Americans would expect service that was faster, don't take to the sharing of space with strangers quite as well, and define good coffee a bit differently.

Value Enriched

A key component of modern day marketing management has been the quality movement. In the last decade, quality became the byword for defining success in all areas of enterprise. Quick, responsive, error-free products and service have become the norm, the minimum that consumers have come to expect. They are no longer surprised by having things their way in the right time framework and at the right price. The quality race has driven most consumers to expect quality as standard performance.

It becomes more difficult to compete or differentiate products, services, or experiences solely on the basis of quality in today's marketplace. Experience providers must go to new lengths to ensure their viability in this newly defined world of quality experiences. In both small and big ways, organizations need to explore and identify ways to enrich aspects of the exchange with their customers, not always an easy task.

How do you enhance the value of everyday, garden variety fruits and vegetables? You do what they did at Stew Leonard's Dairy Stores where snow peas

Slice of Life

Disney's experience with cultural differences reflects the glocal principle. When Disney created Disneyland in Tokyo, it did not retain a financial interest in the project. This project went on to be quite profitable. So when it created Euro Disney in France, it retained a substantial financial interest in it. Both of these decisions resulted in financial losses for the company for two different but culturally related reasons.

The Japanese rebuilt their country using America as a model. They speak English, travel to the United States, and like American music, sports, and lifestyles. This appreciation for things American when coupled with the Japanese's preference for cleanliness made Disneyland a winner in that part of the world. The same can't be said for Euro Disney. The French prefer their culture and their language and go to great lengths to keep anything non-French out of their country. The French also live in a world where they have real castles as well as a preference for less sterile environments. Euro Disney did not experience the same financial success as the Tokyo version and required some adjustments to survive in Europe. It redesigned its restaurant service to reflect the pace at which Europeans prefer to dine at as well as their preference for beer and wine with meals. The company also had to modify the appearance code for their employees as well. Cultural practices and preferences related to hair, makeup, and hygiene vary from one continent to the other.

Two different countries with two vastly different cultures produced quite different results for Disney (James, 1996, p. 88).

and strawberries are unpacked and placed loose on the display counter where people pick their own. At the time this practice was first brought to light by Peters and Waterman in their book, *In Search of Excellence,* this practice was largely unheard of among grocery purveyors. Such practices are now standard as grocery chains enhance the value of the produce by allowing people to use their own judgment and discretion to choose.

How do you make grocery shopping a more enticing and less tedious task? Again, Stew Leonard's, the veritable Disney of dairies, finds ways to enhance and enrich these weekly treks to the grocery store. They have a bovine mascot that wanders the store to greet children. They sell tops of muffins only, not bottoms. Customers get to see real vegetable plants growing adjacent to the parking lot.

In some ways these small, and often unassuming modifications seem kind of strange. In this world where people are pressed for time, why would they want to take additional time to sift through and pick out just the right strawberries to take home with them? In a world where value and price are often interpreted to mean the same, why would people want to pay the same price and only receive the top half of the muffin.

It's because value is defined by the customer. "Customer value is the sum of benefits received minus the costs incurred by the customer in acquiring a product or service" (Treacy and Wiersema, 1995, p. 19–20). Valued added was a natural extension of the quality and value movement and is most appropriate for the majority of products and services used by customers. Producers are always adding new and improved features to their goods. Laundry detergent seems to improve endlessly with previously undiscovered new ingredients or features.

The service industry is continually trying to add value to its service by making the service more convenient or less time consuming for its customers. Tom Monahan of Domino's Pizza started us down this road with a money back guarantee if ordered pizza didn't arrive at the door within 30 minutes. Local park and recreation departments guarantee participation satisfaction by offering refunds to any patron who is dissatisfied with a program or service. Rental car companies that primarily competed on the basis of price now add a number of options to their service that add value or enhance the experience of their customers. There is a vast range of these options including such things as complimentary car phones, bonus frequent-flier miles, and even direct door pickup.

What parameters of the experience can be altered to add value or increase the convenience or pleasure of the experience participant? While adding value is important, it is only the first step along the continuum to reaching the real things that *are* important to experience participants. Day-care centers that have added technology to permit nervous parents to "pop in and peek at" the kids during the day are a prime example of value enrichment. Public park and recreation departments that provide before and after care for students right at the school are another such example.

The success in this area can be enhanced by adopting a form of what could be called components marketing. Initiated by Gateway Computers, this approach to marketing empowers the customer to dictate exactly which components of the computer or the experience he or she wishes to have. The provider can enrich the value an experience has for the participant by allowing him or her easily and almost seamlessly to select the components of the experience that are most important.

Specialty Experiences

Some of the more innovative products and services of the modern world have become so imitated, so much a part of one's daily life, that they are no longer perceived as being special. They join the ranks of commodities. Once upon a time, Kleenex and Scotch tape were incredibly special. These two products have become so imitated that they are now perceived as commodities with consumers generally referring to any facial tissue or paper adhesive as Kleenex or Scotch tape. The same thing has happened to services. Fast-food and quick-lube places now dot the consumer map. There's a bookstore and fitness club almost on every corner.

These products and services became commodities in the minds of consumers not only because they became commonplace, but they also reached commodity status because eventually they focused on price. While consumers have come to expect lower and more value-oriented pricing, competing solely on price is not the race marketers of experience should choose to run. Creating a competitive strategy based on price often leads down the road to the commodization of the experience.

The fitness club industry is an area of experience providers currently facing just this challenge. An overreliance on competitive pricing in the hotly contested health club market has led in many cases to devaluing the cost and benefits of

 **Slice of Life** The highly polished baby grand piano atop an oriental rug located in the atrium is flooded by sunlight and is one of the first things the visitor sees on entering. The myriad of amenities, the fitness room, the whirlpool, the library, and the small boutiques act in concert to meet the consumer's every need. Of course, the dining choices, the deli, the ice cream parlor, and the elegant dining room go a long way to convincing people that this establishment has just the right number of options for their dining pleasure.

Welcome to the world of upscale lodging; no, not exactly. Those particular amenities likely to be found in a host of luxury hotels and resorts around the world are not the case in this instance. The aforementioned appointments and amenities have become standard equipment in many of the newly established long-term care facilities operated by various corporations throughout the country. While these little touches of luxury may have little or no relationship to the quality of care or the experiences of the patients, they go a long way in shaping the perceptions and relieving the anxiety of the family members of the patients.

such experiences to the consumer. According to the 1996 International Health, Racquet, and Sportsclub Association's success survey, clubs charging higher prices actually had a slightly higher membership growth rate and experienced lower attrition rates than clubs discounting their services (Morgan, 1996, p. 1). A more effective alternative to attaining or retaining the consumer's perception of the special nature of an experience is to differentiate the experience in a way that's important to the participant. Some of these alternatives in the health club industry include the nurturing atmosphere of an all women's club; opportunities for camaraderie or socialization; or the holistic health orientation of services.

People can buy generic brand ice cream or Ben and Jerry's. Wal-Mart and Neiman Marcus both sell clothing and giftware. Long-term viability and success as an experience provider is related to the "specialness" the provider is able to maintain in the mind and spirit of his or her participants.

Discovering Differentiation

There is no doubt that markets will continue to fragment as people become more different from one another through age or cultural differences as well as life choices. The marketing strategies of agility, repositioning, glocal strategies, as well as value enriched, specialty experiences are just some alternatives for addressing this continued evolution among people and preferences.

One such approach that is related to the techniques preceding it is the discovery of differentiation. If organizations can discover areas for potential differentiation by offering participants something they value but competitors don't provide or by creating for the participant a desire or preference they have yet to identify for themselves, they will be successful. MacMillan and McGrath (1997) suggest a two part approach for

> We do have to fight against the "commodization" of the industry, and I think we're seeing that happen.
>
> John McCarthy

❖ The customer's lament that he or she didn't have leftovers to nibble on following Thanksgiving dinner at a restaurant was remedied by the Boston Park Plaza Hotel. It created a new holiday tradition by sending dining patrons home with half a turkey, an apple or pumpkin pie, and a quart of cider.

❖ The Peninsula Beverly Hills gives some guests all day to check out. Rather than requiring a late morning or noon check out, the Los Angeles–based hotel now allows guests to remain in their rooms 24 hours from the time they check in. This enriches the value for early morning arrivals, many of them international travelers.

❖ The Reuben H. Fleet Space Theater and Science Center in San Diego, California, as well as other science museums around the country is offering "camp-ins" where parents and children can spread out the sleeping bag, have some snacks, and solve a crime mystery by analyzing air samples and fingerprints with a cost for each parent-child team of $35.

❖ Western Pacific Airlines offers "mystery fares" allowing travelers to book a $99 round-trip flight to one of 23 cities the airline serves. The passengers choose the departure date for any day of the week subject to availability. The airline advises fliers about weather conditions to facilitate packing lists. Once they arrive at the airport, the passengers receive an information packet for the city where they are headed including coupons for restaurants and local attractions. Such fares allow the airline to fill empty seats. It's not just about making money since it could simply offer $99 round trips and let people pick where they want to go. It's about enriching the value of the experience with added adventure.

❖ Arrivals by United at London's Heathrow, Chicago's O'Hare, and Miami International provide premium-paying passengers with showers, a 6-by-12-foot suite with a heated floor, heated towel bar and terry cloth robes plus valet service while they are on an extended layover.

❖ People can now own a piece of the Four Seasons hotels as the company becomes the first luxury hotel chain to get into the time-share business. The first club opened 35 miles north of San Diego with 240 units, a fitness center, and pools, and shared an Arnold Palmer–designed golf course with the Four Seasons Resort next door. Since now people don't have the hassle of owning a vacation home, just enjoying one, this is truly value enriched.

the discovery of differentiation: mapping the consumption chain and analyzing the customer's experience.

The first approach, mapping the consumption chain, includes identifying and focusing on every step the customer has with a product, service, or experience. This approach includes initial awareness of customer need, the search process, criteria for final selection, methods of purchase, delivery, installation, and method of payment, as well as how the customer actually uses the product, service, or experience (MacMillan and McGrath, 1997, pp. 133–145). A thorough review of the consumption chain has led to such value enriched experiences as Car Max and AutoNation revolutionizing the ordeal of car shopping. The discovery differentiation has created food courts in hotels as well as the creation of a variety of dining experiences.

The other approach involves analyzing the customer's experience with one's product, service, or experience. In this phase of differentiation, brainstorming is used to create a list of possible areas, big or small, where the product, service, or experience can be differentiated. It is suggested that the standard five questions, what, where, who, when, and how be applied to each stage of the consumer experience. The authors use the example of candle makers exploring the vast possibilities of uses for candles as well as the related elements of a complete "candlelight experience" (MacMillan and McGrath, 1997). Candles can be used for celebration, aroma therapy, romance, religious observances, or even their original intent, illumination.

Such an approach can result in a much more intimate and comprehensive understanding of the customer as well as the ability to turn that newly found understanding into ways to demonstrate to the customer the provider's awareness of his or her needs, preferences, and desires. Such demonstrations lead to specialty experiences that are value enriched as defined by the individual participant. When Disney discovered that adults wanted to learn and grow while on vacation, it responded by creating first Epcot and then the Disney Institute. When cruise lines recognized that people wanted experiences within the cruise experience, they developed specialty restaurants on board the ship.

PerInfoCom-Conn

Every concept or theory is shaped and influenced by the elements and changes within its midst. When there are changes in the environment, there are changes within the approach. PerInfoCom, a newly created term featured in chapter 6, reflects today's requirements for personalization, information, and communication on the part of consumers. PerInfoCom stands at the ready to incorporate an additional element into its approach: *conn*ection. PerInfoCom-Conn will result from the need on the part of both consumers and providers to create a two-way connection.

Webster suggests that one thinks of every product, service, or experience as information that brings with it promised benefits and customer-defined value (Webster, 1996, p. 156.) He maintains that people don't view the traditional 4Ps of marketing—product, price, place, and promotion—as individual variables and that they no longer want to be persuaded to purchase or try an experience. They perceive persuasion as being one-sided communication.

All these suppositions suggest that PerInfoCom will expand from its original base as developed in chapter 6 to actively court and encourage connections between the experience provider and the participant. Such an approach reinforces the importance of creating customer databases and then using the information gathered. It also suggests that interactive marketing will involve both low- and high-tech techniques. The Web site that remembers the individual's last question or request will need to be offset by a more interpersonal opportunity for human contact and connection.

The beginnings of the "Conn" are already surfacing. The gatherings of Saturn owners and Harley owners are about connection. New technologies have led to

❖ The National Football League sponsors Football 101 classes around the country to help students of the game, primarily women, come to understand and enjoy this game more fully.

❖ The eighteenth James Bond movie, *Tomorrow Never Dies,* seems more like a commercial message than entertainment as clips from the film are used to advertise the 750iL sedan, a R 1200C motorcycle, Heineken beer, and Smirnoff vodka for Bond's shaken-not-stirred martini.

❖ Swatch watches sponsors the World Break-Dancing Championship in New York City, the Freestyle World Cup in Colorado, the Alternative Miss World Show in London as well as links new watches to carefully selected milestones such as Halley's Comet, the Earth Summit, and *perestroika* (Joachimsthaler and Aaker, 1997, p. 45).

❖ Cadbury's Chocolate in Bournville, England, turned a simple chocolate factory tour into a theme park chronicling the history of chocolate and Cadbury as well as a museum, restaurant, partial tour of the packaging plant, and a "chocolate event" store (Joachimsthaler and Aaker, 1997, pp. 45–46).

❖ Matrixx Inc. is a division of Cincinnati Bell providing customer service phone response systems for many leading corporations. These phone response systems provide manpower and expertise for a company's 800 numbers or customer service centers. When Matrixx's employees worried that there might be gaps in advice over the weekend, they volunteered to wear beepers so they could be available for customers (Fishman, 1997, p. 112).

❖ American Express calls cardholders to inquire as to why they don't use their card more frequently and attempts to identify ways in which to encourage greater usage.

Action Agenda

❖ Select two specific target market groups which are current participants in your experiences. Observe and identify changes in their needs, patterns, and preferences. Develop marketing strategies or changes that would address these changes.

❖ Assemble a group of staff and brainstorm ways in which your organization could become more agile and address the projected "people" and "marketing" changes.

❖ Develop a list of products, programs, activities, services, and experiences currently being provided by your organization. Identify those that might benefit from repositioning strategies.

❖ Select two or three organizations which you perceive as being innovative and successful in gaining and retaining participants and identify their strategies and techniques.

❖ Look over the list of potential new marketing strategies such as agile operations, share of the experience, and value enriched and identify those strategies with potential for your experience.

the creation of "virtual communities" such as the one created by on-line book-seller Amazon.com. A prominent feature of its Web site is the book review section where other customers share their reviews of books which can be quickly retrieved and read by potential customers. Such approaches to building community and connection through Web sites has been referred to as clique marketing.

Much of this transition can be traced to Web activities where consumers can attain immediate access to information that they have personally selected in a way and at a time they find appropriate. The next logical and highly valued approach will be a two-way connection. It is almost as if the communication and customer-centered approaches will converge.

Yes, the world is changing. As people become increasingly different from one another in their needs and preferences and as their expectations related to how organizations will address these needs and preferences, the role, scope, and techniques within marketing will need to change as well. The overall marketing strategy will shift as organizations strive to become collaborators with their participants rather than simply creators of products, services, and experiences. The

Transition Tracking

From	To
• People's patterns	• Individual's priorities

Creating databases and conducting lifestyle research remain important but will give way to an emphasis on meeting the individual needs and whims of consumers.

From	To
• Mass marketing	• Mass customization

The need on the part of experience providers to create an experience that is personal and individualized is critical but so is the need to do so in a cost-efficient manner. These two requirements give rise to mass customization.

From	To
• Persuading purchases	• Creating connections

Today's consumers will reject the notion that communication with them is directed at influencing purchasing and behavior patterns. New communication opportunities that reflect the balance between high-tech and high-touch will result in both virtual and real connections between consumers and organizations.

From	To
• Creators of products and services	• Collaborators in experiences

Car manufacturers will no longer just make cars. Hospitals will no longer solely treat patients. A relationship of collaboration between the producer and the participant will emerge that focuses upon the parameters of the experience rather than the product or service.

emphasis upon creating experiences that have value as defined by the participant is a requirement in today's marketplace. The ability to enrich and differentiate those experiences in ways that lead to a collaborative relationship between the consumer and the organization is the next challenge.

Sources

Feather, Frank. (1994). *The future consumer.* Toronto, Canada: Warwick Publishing.

Fishman, Charles. (1997, October–November). How can I help you? *Fast Company.*

Gilmore, James H., & Pine, B. Joseph, II. (1997, January–February). The four faces of customization. *Harvard Business Review.*

Goldman, Steven L., Nagel, Roger, N., & Preiss, Kenneth. (1995). *Agile competitors and virtual organizations—Strategies for enriching the customer.* New York, NY: Van Nostrand Reinhold.

Hardesty, Greg. (1997, September 29). Bicycle industry hoping for boost from boomers. *Hartford Courant.*

James, Jennifer. (1996). *Thinking in the future tense.* New York, NY: Simon & Schuster.

Joachimsthaler, Erich, & Aaker, David A. (1997, January–February). Building brands without mass media. *Harvard Business Review.*

Land, George, & Jarman, Beth. (1992). *Break-point and beyond: Mastering the future today.* New York, NY: HarperBusiness.

MacMillan, Ian C., & McGrath, Rita Gunther. (1997, July–August). Discovering new points of differentiation. *Harvard Business Review.*

Morgan, Thomas J. (1996, February). Letter from the publisher. *Club Industry.*

Reilly, Patrick M. (1996, October). Mountain bikes try for the top again. *The Wall Street Journal Classroom Edition.*

Taylor, Jim, & Wacker, Watts. (1997). *The 500-year delta.* New York, NY: HarperBusiness.

Treacy, Michael, & Wiersema, Fred. (1995). *Disciplines of market leaders.* Reading, MA: Addison-Wesley Publishing.

Webster, Frederick E., Jr. (1996, November–December). The future of interactive marketing. *Harvard Business Review.*

Flashback

Many large corporations, small businesses, or public and nonprofit entities have historically conducted their business in very similar ways. They aligned themselves in a hierarchy that focused on production efficiency. This same hierarchy directed the people in leadership positions to focus on the bottom line while separating themselves from the front-line work force delivering services or creating experiences. This led to organizations steeped in methods for tracking costs and market share and a work force more concerned with following the rules than pleasing the customer. The emphasis within this approach to running organizations was on management.

This management approach generally included a tactical planning emphasis directed toward doing things correctly. Eventually the pace of change and onset of increased competition turned the emphasis to strategic planning. Strategic planning incorporated environmental scanning, market projections, and internal assessment in order to accommodate the ever-changing needs of target markets and outside influences such as technological innovations or social upheavals. This resulted in an emphasis upon "doing the right thing" rather than "doing things right."

While strategic planning is one alternative for planning, the rapid rate and unprecedented impact of change on organizations requires a different approach. Future viability for organizations as we shift from the industrial to the knowledge era will require that organizations function much differently from the way they have in the past.

These differences will involve significant changes in the ways in which companies organize themselves, perceive and interact with employees, and deal with the issue of change itself. The transition to the information era will require the leadership of organizations rather than just the management.

Chapter 10

From Surviving to Thriving—The Shift From Management to Leadership

To survive—and succeed—today's companies must
DISCOVER new opportunities, INSPIRE their people to think
differently, EXPLORE ways to grow. The alternative is
extinction.

wording from an Innovative Thinking Conference brochure

Parameters of Organizational Change

We've downsized, rightsized, reengineered, and transformed, all in the name of change. The world has certainly evolved, and subsequent changes have impacted the way in which the world of organizations functions as well.

Within a relatively brief span of time, the economy has moved through the agricultural first wave to the industrial second wave and now, depending on which experts are consulted, is either well into an information third wave economy or possibly in the early stages of a fourth wave. One very significant impact that such economic shifts have on organizations is the nature of the relationship with resources. For farmers, the number of livestock or the available acres to be tilled was important as a resource but of little interest to the factory owner operating in the industrial era. That same indifference is seen today as factories sit vacant and abandoned in many places. The shift from the industrial to a knowledge-based economy moves the emphasis away from physical plant and production capacity to the importance of ideas, information, creativity, and vision (Maynard and Mehrtens, 1993, pp. 5–6).

There are other changes being created by this knowledge economy as well. The speed and versatility of technology has changed the game. Customers expect to have their every need, preference, and whim met in record time and at a good price as cited in the previous chapter. Information technology has changed the functioning of organizations also. Information is now available not only to upper levels of management but also to a variety of audiences both internal and external.

The changes brought about by the shift to the knowledge economy act together to create circumstances that impact on every organization. Goldman, Nagel, and Preiss in their book *Agile Competitors and Virtual Organizations* (1995) established the groundwork for making agility not just a watchword but a way of life within organizations. They define agility "as the ability to thrive in a competitive environment of continually and unpredictably changing marketing opportunities" (Goldman, Nagel and Preiss, 1995, p. 8). The forces they cite as serving as signs of this shift include (Goldman, Nagel and Preiss, 1995, p. 9):

1. marketplace fragmentation;
2. production to order in arbitrary lot sizes;
3. information capacity to treat masses of customers as individuals;
4. shrinking product lifetimes;
5. convergence of physical products and services;
6. global production networks;
7. simultaneous intercompany cooperation and competition;
8. distribution infrastructure for mass customization;
9. corporate reorganization frenzy; and
10. pressure to internalize prevailing social values.

Note how this list of forces cited reinforces the need to change marketing techniques and strategies as cited in the previous chapter and how those same forces require organizations to change their basic approaches to functioning as well.

This break-point between the two economies, a term designated by Land and Jarman in their book *Break-Point and Beyond: Mastering the Future Today* (1992) has led to those forces cited by Goldman, Nagel, and Preiss. The presence of such forces means that organizations need to change. Land and Jarman suggest a list of tasks that need to be undertaken as part of that change. These include (Land and Jarman, 1992, p. 66):

- unleashing the creativity of employees;
- planning geared to anticipate emerging problems and opportunities;
- understanding and working with outside pressure groups;
- producing quality within a work environment where managers and workers trust and value one another;
- integrating new technologies; and
- integrating diverse cultures in the organization.

To deal with all the market forces and external demands being placed on organizations at this time, it has been suggested that organizations, in order to thrive in the new economy, must be able to do the following (Goldman, Nagel and Preiss, 1995, xvi and xvii):

- organize to regenerate new capabilities from existing resources and
- shift from a management philosophy of command and control to a leadership approach where motivation, support and trust in people

complement the emergence of a knowledgeable, skilled, and innovative work force.

Change is not a choice; it's a new commandment. Disney, the longtime king of the experience industry, fell victim to reliance upon traditional approaches in management and a long-term view of success. The birth of the Mouse in 1928 led to the lengthy reign of Disney as the pinnacle of entertainment in this country. Even the death of its genius founder Walt Disney in 1966 did little to erode its stature. However, by 1983 corporate profits slid from a high of $135 million in 1980 to $93 million in 1983 with attendance at its own revered theme park, Disneyland, falling to its lowest level since 1974 (Grover, 1991, p. 3). This led to a hostile takeover attempt which eventually resulted in a regeneration of the organization by CEO Michael Eisner.

The emphasis on moving from a management to a leadership philosophy where the organization is allowed to continually renew and regenerate itself is not only a challenge, but also a mandate for survival into the new millennium.

Shifting Priorities and Practices

The continual onset of change places organizations in situations where they feel compelled to regroup and rearrange themselves in order to sustain or even possibly survive. The sheer number of changes impacting organizations is almost overwhelming, but one should attempt to envision them addressing and encompassing the major thrusts of change within the following areas:

- *Leadership:* a general shift in emphasis from management to leadership as well as a renewed focus on change;
- *Vision:* a subtle but steady shift from viewing profits as the entire purpose to including a realization of the organization's role in a bigger world;
- *Resource utilization:* changing importance placed on various resources as well as a significant alteration in how the organization perceives and interacts with those resources;
- *Competition:* movement from isolation to collaboration which changes the way in which organizations conduct business; and
- *Change:* the recognition that change is not only inevitable but also a desirable part of organizational activity.

From Management to Leadership

By far the most critical step for success in moving to the knowledge economy is the shift from management to leadership. Experiences must leave behind the more traditional approaches of the industrial-service era and embrace a new

As you consider ways in which your organization can move from surviving to thriving in the new economy, create a list of possible techniques and specific applications of those techniques that could be tried in your organization.

Organizational Changes

Overall Changes in Approach

From	*To*
• Management	• Leadership
• Mission	• Mission plus vision
• Predicting change	• Precipitating change
• Vigilant	• Versatile and virtual
• Orderly	• Chaod (chaos + order)
• Bottom line	• Circle costs

Changes Related to Resources

From	*To*
• Tangible assets	• Intangible assets (people, knowledge, information)
• Rules and regulations	• Creative culture and comfortable climate
• Big brother	• Nurturing coach or mentor
• Compliance	• Creativity
• Enforce	• Empower
• Technology as cost reduction	• Technology as experience enhancer

Changing Nature of Competition

From	*To*
• Corporate profiteer	• Community collaborator
• Just us	• Just all of us
• Isolation	• Collaboration
• Animosity	• Appreciation
• Hiding trade secrets	• Comparing industry standards

approach for how organizations can make experiences happen for their participants.

Management and leadership are common terms that are often used interchangeably. However, the two terms are indeed different from one another. "Management involves control, efficiency, and rules; leadership involves vision, direction and purpose" (Sattler and Mullen, 1997, p. 17). The demands of the changing marketplace in conjunction with the nonstop pace of change will result in a mandate that successful organizations either replace or strongly supplement a management approach to leadership.

The more traditional management role needs to give way to leadership. Management emphasizes the short-term and the status quo with a close eye on the bottom line. Leadership takes a more long-term view looking to inspire people and support change. Many people agree that things are managed and people are led. Leadership generally brings a dimension of interplay with people, that increasingly valuable organizational resource. The ability to communicate, inspire, and empower will make up a large part of that leadership role.

Kouzes and Posner (1987) developed a set of 10 commandments of leadership in their book, *The Leadership Challenge.* These rules include:

- Challenging the process
    1. Search for opportunities
    2. Experiment and take risks
- Inspiring a shared vision
    3. Envision the future
    4. Enlist others
- Enabling others to act
    5. Foster collaboration
    6. Strengthen others
- Modeling the way
    7. Set the example
    8. Plan small wins
- Encouraging the heart
    9. Recognize individual contributions
    10. Celebrate accomplishments

Many of these suggestions can be incorporated into experience organizations.

While leadership can incorporate a number of tenets, essentially it can be defined as the ability to mobilize an organization and its people to change in order to thrive in new and emerging environments. Such a definition of leadership requires four essential components: creation of vision, efficient and effective use of resources, redefinition of cooperation, and facilitation of change.

The mission of organizations states its purpose with a strong focus on the bottom line. Mission will now be supplemented by vision, a future orientation that incorporates the values of the organization as well as its purpose and profit. The resources of the organization, people, and technology rather than products and physical plant, will be supported in such a manner as to enhance organizational and customer enrichment. Cooperation will take on an expanded role and new definition that will seek the involvement and input from a variety of stakeholders. The final role of leadership will be to enable change to occur within the organization.

Vision

The most essential and basic element of leadership is vision. An organization requires leadership that both grounds

> Management is doing things right and leadership is doing the right thing.
>
> Peter Drucker and Warren Bennis

the organization and provides a guiding light for forward motion. That ability both to hold an organization together while moving it into the future is generally based on its vision. Collins and Porras discovered in the research that led to their book, *Built to Last: Successful Habits of Visionary Companies,* that companies experiencing lasting success were those that were able to manage simultaneously both continuity and change. They linked this ability to vision, a term they believe consists of two major components: core ideology and envisioned future (Collins and Porras, 1996, p. 66).

Core ideology consists of core values and core purpose which act as the glue to hold the organization together, especially throughout periods of change. Disney still holds as its core values imagination and wholesomeness as determined by its founder. Nordstrom holds fast to its long held belief in customer service. Collins and Porras point out that core values are internally derived and are not always reflective of the marketplace.

Core purpose, the other part of ideology, relates to the organization's reason for existing. Collins and Porras maintain that this purpose needs to go beyond the organization's product or output by capturing the soul of the organization in such a way as to reflect people's motivations for working within that organization (Collins and Porras, 1996, p. 68).

This core ideology needs to join with a second essential ingredient of vision, the envisioned future. The envisioned future needs to be a far-reaching projection of where the organization wants to be 20 years from now and what it wants to be doing. This is not an easy task. Collins and Porras outline some requirements of a well-defined envisioned future. They indicate that such a statement must be clear and compelling, tangible, energizing, and highly focused so that it will unify the organization to head towards its future (Collins and Porras, 1996, p. 73).

Core ideology and envisioned future work together to provide a vision for an organization. It is this vision that enables the organization to survive as an entity

Examples of core purposes that relate to the organization's reason for existence that also incorporates the soul and spirit of the operation include (Collins and Porras, 1996, p. 69):

- Fannie Mae: to strengthen the social fabric by continually democratizing home ownership;
- Lost Arrow Corporation: to be a role model and a tool for social change;
- Pacific Theaters: to provide a place for people to flourish and to enhance the community;
- Mary Kay Cosmetics: to give unlimited opportunity to women;
- Nike: to experience the emotion of competition and winning and of crushing competitors;
- Wal-Mart: to give ordinary folk the chance to buy the same things as rich people; and
- Walt Disney: to make people happy.

Jack Welch, CEO of General Electric, in his sixteenth annual letter to shareholders spoke of corporate culture, and also surprised readers with his assertion that GE's growth would come from areas such as financial services for aging Baby Boomers rather than in making things such as electric light bulbs and jet engines. One portion of Welch's letter includes these descriptors of a model GE executive (Henry, 1997, p. 7B):

The Culture . . . Finding a Better Way Every Day
GE Leaders—

- have a passion for excellence and hate bureaucracy;
- are open to ideas from anywhere;
- live quality . . . and drive cost and speed from competitive advantage;
- have the self-confidence to involve everyone and behave in a boundaryless fashion;
- create a clear, simple, reality-based vision;
- have enormous energy and the ability to energize others;
- stretch . . . set aggressive goals . . . reward progress yet understand accountability and commitment;
- see change as opportunity . . . not threat; and
- have global brains . . . and build diverse and global teams.

as well as to thrive in a new and changing world. Creating and maintaining a vision is the most critical role of leadership.

The vision an organization holds for itself provides the foundation for the development and maintenance of the organizational culture. Culture is the shared values and beliefs of an organization that influence the direction and priorities of the organization. Its overriding importance is its ultimate impact on the behavior of everyone within the organization.

Organizations with a culture that immerses the individualized needs of each participant along with an emphasis on agility and versatility are on the road to success in the twenty-first century.

Use of Resources

The knowledge era dictates that both technology and people are the important resources in this economy. However, it's not the physical presence of people and technology but the results of their interaction that are the resources. This interaction leads to highly valued, intangible outcomes for participants of experiences.

It's the intangibles—people, knowledge, information, reputation, and the interplay among these intangibles—that make the difference. It's not the quality of the food or the attractiveness of the tableware that makes dining at a restaurant on a Disney property different from a non-Disney eating establishment. It's the imagination of the Disney employee whose access to information and unleashed creativity led him or her to include animated fireflies for evening, outdoor dining authenticity that makes the difference. It's the interaction of these resources that

 **Slice of Life** Chrysler CEO Robert Eaton and Vice Chairman Robert Lutz have been getting a great deal of attention lately. The attention is due to their reputations as some of the world's best executives since *Forbes* named Chrysler its Company of the Year in 1997. Some of the attention is due to their antics to launch Chrysler's new products which found them cavorting in yellow rain slickers and smiling out from cereal boxes in stunts to launch new products. Their shared approach to management is really part of the new world-view.

Tips From Both Bobs

Six management tips from the Bobs:

1. Have fun. Encourage creative wackiness.
2. Set clear goals and make sure everybody understands them.
3. Take an active interest in parts of the business besides your own.
4. Give senior executives hands-on jobs so they don't just hold meetings.
5. Push responsibility down, don't interfere at lower levels.
6. Encourage managers to be leaders. Discourage personal competition for promotions or power. (Maynard, 1997, p. 4B)

can lead to the creation of those value enriching extras that make for specialty experiences for participants.

One way to fuel the journey to the future that Hamel and Prahaad allude to is through vision. That's why vision is considered the very basis for success in the future. However, there are a number of other approaches to resources that will help organizations thrive in the future. These approaches include an emphasis upon diversity, the effective use of technology, and strategies for attracting and retaining the best people.

Diversity

When organizations used to talk about diversifying, they were referring to managing assets. Such an approach to asset management holds true today. However, today's assets are not real estate or patents, but real people. If organizations expect to be a part of the global marketplace, they need to pursue actively a diversity within the workplace.

This case for diversity includes changing demographics and a global market that has provided huge incentives for organizations to make this a way of life within their workplace. Minorities, women, and older people, each having substantial money to spend, make up increasingly larger parts of the marketplace. Non-Hispanic blacks, Hispanic Americans, and Asian Americans have a combined spending power of over $600 million per year with increases projected due to the rapid growth of these groups (Myers, 1997, p. 20).

> It's not cash that fuels the journey to the future, but the emotional and intellectual energy of every employee.
>
> Gary Hamel and C. K. Prahaad

Companies that were the first to embrace diverse work forces a decade or more ago say diversity pays off. In addition to being responsive to emerging opportunities within a diverse marketplace, such approaches have other payoffs as well. Recent surveys indicate that diversity helps to attract and retain the best and the brightest employees and contributes to feelings of happiness and productivity among women and minorities (Jones, 1996, p. 4B). Companies need winning ideas that wouldn't have been made by a team of all white males to give them a head start in the global economy.

Tech It Up

The flip side of the resource equation is technology. The advances in software and cost reductions in hardware have made customer monitoring systems for experience providers affordable, accessible, and a necessity. Such "cybersystems" run the gamut from one or two pieces of "smart" equipment to full-blown systems linking a full contingent of information and people together.

Technology can perform routine functions more efficiently. The creation of customer databases can track trends, highlight problem areas, and clarify decision parameters. The impact on customer satisfaction and individualization of services or experiences is significant.

The networking capabilities of technology serve as a boon for substantially enhancing communication between and among employees and customers. In some instances, telephone and computer technology can actually provide the service for customers. Physicians and healthcare providers are utilizing healthcare surveillance systems whereby an interactive voice response system used through an

Within the highly competitive health and fitness club industry there are a variety of tech-type options. Data collection systems are being used to provide members with specific feedback to suggest that adjustments can be made in their workouts that lead to higher goal attainment which in turn leads to higher retention and profitability:

- FitLinxx System consisting of a Workout Information Center has small computer consoles called "training partners" that can be attached to each piece of workout equipment and after an initial session can recommend weight and repetition suggestions to the member with data transferred to the Workout Information Center so that members and trainers can review the progress.
- Aphelion's Workout Partner uses a touch screen to update individual programs and to print each day's workout, replacing workout cards; club trainers can then design workouts or customize fitness programs for members.
- Sportrak's new customizable club scheduling module uses a grid system to define time increments for staffing needs, membership fees, and club capacity.
- Innovateck Software's MemberTrack system provides front desk registration complete with photo, facility utilization, exercise logs, incentive tracking, class scheduling, risk screening, contact management, and goals and outcomes monitoring.

Rosenbluth International, a longtime leader and innovator in the travel industry, has harnessed the power of technology as a way to better meet the needs of its customers. By enlisting the financial support of suppliers such as AT&T, British Airways, Hertz, and Wyndham Hotels, it created an innovative and interactive technology called the Continuum. The Continuum is designed to replicate a business trip with customers going step-by-step through the process of planning and making a trip. Each stop along the way is sponsored by a different company and lets the traveler see options and make choices about his or her trip.

800 telephone number enables patients to report daily information about prescription drugs and Glucometer readings. The computer monitors who did or didn't call in as well as alerting healthcare providers to potential problems with certain patients. Workcare Group is customizing health promotion newsletters to meet the unique needs of each subscriber based on predetermined health risks.

Technology and its interplay with employees has vast potential for the mass customization mentioned in the previous chapter while providing other desirable attributes of experiences as defined by the participant. Since new applications of this interplay spring up every day, this aspect of the organization bears close monitoring.

Attracting, Retaining, and Growing the Best

Probably the ultimate leadership challenge in the knowledge economy will be an organization's ability to attract and retain the best employees and to create an

A classified ad by Sanders, a Lockheed Martin Company, looking for knowledge workers had the traditional listing of positions available but devoted substantial space with colored pictures of the "other reasons to join Sanders" that included a 9-day, 80-hour work schedule resulting in 26 long weekends a year. The ad then went on to list the kinds of activities and experiences that were possible during those 26 long weekends by listing the following: play golf, climb Mount Monadnock, play tennis, ski Pat's Peak, photograph covered bridges, try ice fishing, read a book, go to Canaan Speedway, eat Finnish bread in New Ipswich, relax at Hampton Beach, hike the Boulder Loop trail, take a nap, sample fresh bottled milk, shop for antiques, canoe the Merrimack River, pick apples, photograph a moose, watch the Moran tugboats, sail on Lake Sunapee, eat at Muriel's Doughnuts, pick wild blueberries, enjoy brilliant fall foliage, watch the fireworks at Riverfest, bike the White Mountains, talk to a professional logger, or go bird-watching.

In fact, this ad depicted how working for this company in this location would allow the employee to experience and enjoy life. The ad more closely resembled a promotional piece for a travel program than a job.

❖ Playing together is becoming an option for corporate America. Hollywood studio executives run the rapids down the Colorado River. The National Bank of Wilmington, Delaware, sent senior managers to a one-day cooking program in Manhattan. Estee Lauders' sales promotion department participated in a team-building day in a park setting. Outward Bound reports that corporate outings have developed into a $100 million a year industry (Glanton, 1997, p. F1).

❖ Employee sabbaticals are becoming more commonplace. American Express allows employees with 10 years of service to take community service leave for up to one year. At Hallmark Cards, employees can avail themselves of a six-month creative rotation taking a paid break from daily tasks to focus on a special topic of interest. McDonald's lets full-time employees take eight weeks of paid leave for every 10 years of service (Armour, September 1997, p. B3).

❖ Rainmaker, a consulting firm of New Haven, Connecticut, suggests specific techniques to retain the Generation X members of the work force. Suggestions include numerous training opportunities in the workplace, six-month (rather than annual) reviews, and rewards for stellar performance that incorporate nonfinancial incentives (Armour, October 1997, p. 5B).

❖ Companies are infusing R&R (relaxation and recreation) into the work environment by including quiet rooms for meditation and break rooms with Ping-Pong tables and foosball.

❖ Training is shifting to an emphasis on creativity and collaboration such as collaborating coaching sessions conducted by Celemi, Inc. of Avon, Connecticut, and the SFA (scan, focus, act) program provided by DesignWorks of Hilton Head, South Carolina. Design Works has an approach where employee groups practice what they have dubbed as "cerebral collaboration."

❖ Interim Services, a staffing and consulting firm out of Fort Lauderdale, Florida, conducted a study that revealed that nearly 75 percent of employees surveyed felt that promoting fun and closer workplace relationships made jobs more attractive and reduced turnover (Armour, December 1997, p. 5B).

❖ Sprint Business in Dallas holds ice cream socials and karaoke contests for employees and has an employee committee that plans activities for Sprint's National Fun Day at Work (Armour, December 1997, p. 5B).

environment where these people can bloom and grow. Being able to get and keep the best will become a competitive edge for companies.

This is not an easy challenge and defies just one set of guidelines or techniques to be implemented. An organization's success will be closely tied to its ability to create a work environment in which people can balance the demands of personal or family responsibilities as well as enabling employees to work and interact in such ways that the synergy leads to creative, effective, and innovative outcomes for the organization.

Organizations are incorporating a number of employee practices and policies to enable people to balance the demands of all phases of their lives. In addition, organizations are focusing on training alternatives that provide for connection, cooperation, and collaboration among their employees.

Cooperation

Management watches the bottom line and showers time and attention on its shareholders. Leadership doesn't ignore shareholders but redefines the more traditional interpretations of terms such as shareholders and competition. Organizations will reassess their attitudes and relationships with customers, competitors, suppliers, the government, the natural environment, and society as a whole. Organizations will begin to practice what the Japanese call *kyosei*, a spirit of cooperation where individuals, organizations, and society live and work together for the common good (Kaku, 1997, p. 55).

This approach does not discount the importance of generating profits, but rather it takes the approach that a rising tide lifts all ships and that by finding ways to collaborate with customer, suppliers, competitors, and community groups all parties benefit (Kaku, 1997, p. 56). Such collaboration stemming from the demands being placed on the world and its economy will give rise to a sense of social stewardship and a redefinition of competition.

Social Stewardship

There are those who believe that the business of business is no longer just business. When Maynard and Mehrtens cited differences between the industrial second wave and the emerging third wave of information, they also stated differences in how organizations within those waves function. Second wave companies focused on their need to be separate and to compete with one another. Third wave organizations recognized the need to become connected and to cooperate.

These same authors predict that the fourth wave following closely on the heels of the third wave will lead to co-creation among organizations and elements of society (Maynard and Mehrtens, 1993, p. 6). Such beliefs are based on the observation that many of societal institutions operating within the arenas of politics, education, religion, and social services are becoming increasingly less effective in their ability both to lead and to provide a foundation for society.

The fourth wave corporation will feel the need to shift its approach from providing services and experiences for a particular group of people to serving as a steward for a much bigger definition of future customers. This social stewardship may include some of the following (Maynard and Mehrtens, 1993, p. 9):

- universalization of capital ownership;
- internalization of social and environmental costs of doing business; and
- capitalization of natural resources.

Ben and Jerry's of Vermont, headed by the happy duo of premium ice cream makers, is just one example of a corporation that places values and purpose ahead of profits. This company and the growing group of approximately 2,000 companies with combined annual sales of nearly $2 billion are operating under the premise that business is no longer just profitable as corporations become dominant players in a world facing escalating social and environmental problems

(Hawken, 1993, pp. 54–61). Goals of a system of sustainable business would include the following objectives (Hawken, 1993, pp. 54–61):

- reduction in consumption of energy and natural resources;
- provision of secure, stable, and meaningful work for people;
- perceived as more desirable than current way of living and doing business; and
- should be fun, engaging, and strive for aesthetic outcomes.

Long before Congress started the "welfare to work" idea, the Marriott Corporation had launched a unique training program for just this purpose called Pathways to Independence. This program is over six years old and operates in five cities. This six-week program takes people sometimes on welfare, homeless, illiterate, having criminal records, or recovering from alcohol or drug addictions and helps them learn not just how to perform needed tasks with the hotel but how to show up on time, open a bank account, and other life skills. This program has been most worthwhile for Marriott. It costs about $900 to replace employees so the $2,200 cost of the training program is covered as these graduates stay a little over twice as long as other employees (Phillips, 1997, p. A20).

❖ There are a number of advertising firms who have banded together in an attempt to make cigarettes and other tobacco products "uncool" and not attractive for children.
❖ AT&T Corporation granted all of its 127,000 employees worldwide a day off with pay to perform volunteer work. It is predicted that it will result in a million hours of community service in a one-year period (AT&T to Grant Day Off, 1996, p. B8).
❖ 24 Fitness of Pleasanton, California, created a new apparel line called Hard Times to sell in its chain of facilities. The garments are produced by Incarcerated Industries, a privately owned company that hires and trains San Quentin prison inmates. The club chain is donating the funds generated from this new product line to the National Association of Midnight Basketball Leagues (Outlook, 1996, p. 21).
❖ Private firms that profit from providing services to public schools have formed a trade association to pool resources and to provide money-saving public-private partnerships with schools. The Education Services Council brings together private contractors who profit from the estimated $30 billion spent on outside services for such things as transportation, food services, and after-school care.
❖ Title Nine Sports, a catalog company selling sporting attire for women, teams its employees, a bunch of would-be camp counselors who spend most of their nonworking hours playing and coaching, with an organization called SportsBridge. Employees spend a week at camp encouraging inner-city adolescent girls to get involved and stay involved with sports.

Co-Opetition

This newly defined sense of purpose for organizations will not be limited to customers, suppliers, and other stakeholders. Organizations that will thrive in the future will redefine competition as well. This new definition of competition is sometimes difficult to comprehend and accept, especially since competition is so ingrained into the American psyche. We know who the other team is, and we want to beat them at practically any cost.

Competition is a time honored practice that is giving way to a win-win approach that will significantly change strategy and practice within organizations. Such a shift will substantially change the playing field as we move from isolation to collaboration, from animosity to appreciation, and from hiding trade secrets to highlighting best practices of industry standards.

A new mind-set for competition called "co-opetition" is on the horizon. The term "co-opetition," credited to Ray Noorda, founder of Novell, Inc., a network software company, suggests that companies within an industry explore methods both to compete and to cooperate simultaneously (Henricks, 1996, p. 76). Adam Brandenburger, professor at Harvard Business School and author of *Co-opetition: A Revolution Mind-Set That Combines Competition and Cooperation,* believes that this new approach is a way to avoid destruction among competitors by fostering ways to work together to discover new markets or grow existing ones for all participants including competitors, suppliers, and customers (Henricks, 1996, p. 76).

While it may go against traditional business instincts, competition resulting in price wars doesn't necessarily help anyone in the long run. When airlines gang up on a new low-cost carrier in the market and run it out of business with low fares on competing routes, everyone loses. The airlines lose money. The upstart company folds and passengers have fewer options which results in their staying at home or taking the car.

❖ Three of Orlando's largest theme parks, Universal Studios Florida, Sea World of Florida, and Wet 'n' Wild, have created an alliance which permits visitors to their area to buy one ticket good for admission to all three parks. This attempt at co-opetition is designed to lure vacationers away from Disney World that now offers three theme parks and three water parks and has become a one-stop vacation center for a growing number of visitors.

❖ City government, a private foundation, and a Catholic school are joining forces in Baltimore's southeast neighborhood near Patterson Park to offer people nine years of free tuition at St. Elizabeth of Hungary school with the purchase of a renovated row house.

❖ LSG Lufthansa Service/Sky Chefs is spending $1 million to team up with United Airlines in a research project to increase substantially the amount of food served to passengers, monitor feedback, and persuade United to spend more money on catering.

In the twenty-first century we may entirely redefine what is meant by competition. Mollner believes that there are two basic world-views, one for the material age and one for the relationship age. The material age world-view operates under the assumption that the "universe is somewhere between two and an immense number of separate parts each of which competes for its own self-interest in relation to all things." This reflects a kind of survival of the fittest approach. The second world-view of the relationship age assumes that the "universe is an immense number of connected parts, each of which cooperates with all other parts in the interest of the universe first and only secondly cooperates or competes in the interest of itself or any subgroup of parts" (Mollner, 1991).

The whole premise behind cooperating to compete is to harness the resources of all those involved in the process including the participants, suppliers, and would-be competitors to create added value, meaning, and success for the participant. Such cooperation needs to start within an organization because it refers to internal cooperation as well. The keeping of secrets or hoarding of resources is clearly a part of the old hierarchical framework of how an organization functions. It just won't work for survival in tomorrow land.

The number and type of partners involved in co-opetition needs to be expanded. We need to share information with participants, suppliers, and partners. Goldman, Nagel, and Preiss suggest that such cooperation results in the reductions of cycle time, development and operating costs as well as the acceleration of technology transfer (1995, p. 118).

When the Legendary Ghan, a train in Australia, wanted to improve the quality of its experience for customers, it didn't compare itself to other rail systems but rather to hotels and restaurants that were recognized as the best performers in the hospitality industry. The subsequent improvements restored the popularity of this travel experience.

Close **Seup**

Another concept typically not part of the old mindset of competition is benchmarking. Benchmarking had its origins in the total quality movement and involves the process of comparing an organization's performance either to an industry standard of excellence or to the best performance by competitors.

Steps in the process include the following (Certo, 1997, pp. 555–557):

- identify an area of service or experience that you would like to examine or improve;
- measure level of performance in that area;
- compare measurement to either existing industry standards *or* identify an outstanding industry performer in that area and compare your standard to its performance;
- decide how your performance can be improved or surpass the benchmark;
- implement a pilot study for improvement; and
- implement the improvement.

 A recent study for benchmarking best practices in workplace health promotion was conducted with cosponsors Eli Lilly & Company, CITGO Petroleum, 3M Corporation, Kaiser Aluminum and Chemical, the Mead Corporation, Nortel, and UAW/Chrysler Corporation. They commissioned the American Productivity and Quality Center (APQC) to study benchmarking on workplace health promotion programs and practices.

The following were some of the findings related to this study (O'Donnell, Bishop and Kaplan, 1997, pp. 1, 6):

- best practice health promotion programs had existed from 2 to 65 years with the mean of 11.5 years;
- programs averaged 10 internal full-time equivalents of staff and 4.8 additional full-time equivalents composed of external vendors;
- 1995 annual budgets averaged $56.60 per employee;
- 73 percent of the programs had special programs for employees designated at high risk; and
- 92 percent of the programs offered fitness, smoking cessation, and stress management programs.

Facilitating Change

At the start of this chapter, leadership was defined as the ability to mobilize an organization and its people to change in order to thrive in new and changing environments. In the long run, the leadership of any organization will be assessed on exactly that outcome. Has the organization changed in ways that enabled it not only to survive but also to thrive in the new economy?

It's all about change. The ongoing challenge of creating change within organizations is the ultimate leadership task, especially since such change needs to be integrated within all activities and areas of the organization.

The Challenge of Change

Organizations don't survive without change. Today's climate requires real change rather than the incremental change that worked so well in the past. Real change is a double-edged sword. Organizations become successful because they've made changes, but in order to continue to thrive, they need to leave behind some of those former changes to make room for new ones.

Tushman and O'Reilly (1997) in their book, *Winning Through Innovation: A Practical Guide to Leading Organizational Change and Renewal* indicate that there are two different games to be played within the framework of innovation and change. The first change is internal and is essentially defensive using the old tried and true approaches that focus on being more efficient and productive. The second innovation game takes a more external focus and involves playing to be effective and competitive in the forefront of change and the future (Pitts,

> You have to embrace change, not just to succeed but to survive.
>
> Ken Chenault

1997, p. 6). The first, more traditional game of change is about surviving while the second game of innovation relates to thriving.

Three Types of Change

It's almost as if there are three types of change organizations need to target: anticipated, unpredicted, and precipitated. Most organizations have adjusted well to anticipating change. The emphasis on strategic focus leads to an expectation that people will change and the popularity of particular experiences will grow and go. Organizations now know that such strategic planning is a necessity, not a nicety, and act accordingly.

However, the other two types of change require a heightened awareness of change and a significantly expanded approach to such change. The second type of change focuses on the unexpected; change that cannot be predicted. Organizations need to be ready for the wild card, those changes that seem to come out of nowhere and immediately shake up the entire industry. For example, the travel industry had to deal with this unpredictable change after a Paris-bound TWA plane went down amid rumors of terrorism.

Companies organized to master unpredicted change create scenario exercises in which they can explore the impact and prepare for almost anything. What if tobacco products were declared illegal? The tobacco industry has been preparing for such a possibility, but what about other related industries. How would this impact on coffee and chocolate consumption? What impact would it have on healthcare companies, sporting events, billboards, and the local convenience store? Practice exercising your creativity related to "what if" scenarios.

The third type of change is equally important and challenging to address. How does an organization not predict change or deal with change, but how is it able to actually precipitate change? Nike had been trying to break into the lucrative golf footwear and apparel market for a number of years. Nike, a company with great appeal and knowledge of emerging, younger target markets, realized that the old game of golf would not be the same as the new game of golf. It was just waiting in the wings for Tiger Woods, or someone like him, who represented the new world and way of golf.

Organizations that are ever alert to rumblings subtle and otherwise can be ahead in the precipitating change sweepstakes. The recent flurry of "how to" books and books dealing with spirituality and simplicity are examples of such

Reductions in product life cycles reveal the following (Tappscott as cited in Pritchett, 1996, p. 32):

- In 1990, it took six years for a car to go from concept to production; today it takes only two years.
- Most of Hewlett-Packard's revenues come from products that didn't exist a year ago.
- Ninety percent of Miller Brewing Company's revenue comes from beers that didn't exist 24 months ago.

Fast Facts

❖ A slogan from the Stew Leonard's Dairy Stores, a relatively small operator in the world of giant supermarkets chains, has a saying . . . "The BIG don't eat the small. The FAST eat the slow!" When a customer focus group revealed that people felt the fish wasn't fresh because it was prepackaged in cardboard and plastic wrap rather than displayed on ice, the stores didn't wait the 10 weeks to order the custom fish counter. They wrapped plastic around plywood, piled chipped ice on top of it and were in business.

❖ The Swatchmobile, a joint manufacturing effort by Mercedes-Benz and Swatch watchmakers, provides owners with a kit that enables them to alter the color and design of much of the body as often as they like.

rumblings. Some resorts and vacation travel providers discerned those rumblings and created or re-created vacation options around those preferences. Did Americans feel the need to simplify their lives or bloom and grow, or did resorts and travel companies somehow help to create that need for them?

Speed Counts

Another aspect of change is an organization's ability to respond quickly to desired or needed changes. Customers get impatient. Customers regularly change their preferences and priorities on their schedule, not the schedule of the provider. There are always new fads, changing priorities, and replacement technologies. It can appear as if everything is conspiring to do you in, but not if you practice what Meyer (1993) refers to as "fast cycle time."

Fast cycle time is based on a philosophy that organizations need to provide the highest quality product, service, or experience in the least amount of time to satisfy the participant's need. This concept was originally used in manufacturing, but today it has many applications for personal services and experiences. Fast cycle time has both external and internal benefits. External benefits of fast cycle time include:

- being first which yields higher profits;
- being positioned as an innovator;
- establishing industry standards;
- enhancing customer satisfaction and fulfillment; and
- making the provider a tough to copy, tough to keep up with organization.

Internal benefits of fast cycle time include (Sattler and Mullen, 1996, p. 56):

> We really have to start thinking about reinventing Disney— again. The last two companies I worked for, ABC and Paramount, had become number one in their respective industries, only to begin to stagnate after a decade of success.
>
> Michael D. Eisner

- reductions in overhead through restructuring of policies, procedures to maximize efficiency;
- empowers the work force to make decisions and deliver quality to customers;
- increases sense of accomplishment as progress moves forward and doesn't drag; and
- enhances staff retention due to the challenging nature of the process.

Southwest Airlines would be a prime example of both internal and external fast cycle time. The policies and employee empowerment practices of Southwest has enabled it to slash costs and provide air transportation that competes with

Clos*e*eup

During the 1990s Disney grew over 610 percent with almost half of that growth emerging from businesses that didn't exist in 1985. New business ventures brought into the Disney family between 1984 and 1996 include:

- international film distribution,
- television station ownership,
- radio and radio network broadcasting,
- radio station ownership,
- the Disney Stores,
- the convention business,
- live theatrical entertainment,
- home video production,
- interactive computer programs and games,
- World Wide Web sites,
- professional sports team ownership,
- telephone company partnership,
- Disney Regional Entertainment, and
- Disney Cruise Lines.

When the Magic Kingdom opened in Disney World in 1971, there was one theme park and 1,808 hotel rooms. By the time of Michael Eisner's tenure, there were two theme parks, 6,373 rooms on property, one small water park, and 26,000 square feet of convention space. In 1996, there were three theme parks, 23,421 rooms, two very large water parks, two nighttime entertainment centers, and two vacation club complexes plus 234,000 square feet of convention space, six championship golf courses, and an Indy Car race track.

But the growth doesn't stop there. Plans for 1997 included 2,000 more hotel rooms, a 95,000 square foot convention center, a giant sports complex which would be home to the U. S. Amateur Athletic Union, the training site for the Atlanta Braves and the Harlem Globetrotters. Further expansion in 1998 includes their largest theme park ever, Disney's Animal Kingdom, two new Disney cruise ships, a second theme park for California called Disney's California Adventure, and a second theme park adjacent to Tokyo Disneyland called Tokyo DisneySea (*The Walt Disney Company 1996 Annual Report*, 1996).

ground transportation. These practices and approaches have naturally led to the external benefits of fast cycle time.

Reinvention

Reinvention is the ultimate outcome of change. Consistently attention has been focused on the need of all organizations to reinvent themselves periodically. Reinvention is a culmination of most of the aforementioned strategies with a healthy dose of innovation tossed into the mix. Innovation doesn't necessarily mean sizable dollars in research and development but rather the cultivation of a corporate culture embracing change, new ideas, and risk that permeates into the farthest corners and lowest levels of an organization.

Few things could be more critical to the experience industry than the ability to continually reinvent itself. The needs, preferences, desires, and whims of people will not remain stagnant. People will seek resolution to their needs with organizations who keep track of their changing requirements as well as deliver the experience that best meets those needs. Such reinvention will be an ongoing activity for successful experience providers.

Mirage Resorts, a collection of gambling casinos, was ranked number two for innovation in *Fortune's* poll of most admired companies. Mirage Resorts CEO, Steve Wynn, goes with a fairly basic but industrywide creative idea: "Give people great service, good food, and entertainment they can't get in Kokomo, and they will pay for it" (O'Reilly, 1997, p. 62). The Wynn-operated Treasure Island casino

Action Agenda

❖ Review your organization's mission and vision statements to see how well they will work for the future.

❖ Make a list of specific behaviors and practices of your organization to determine if the operational philosophy takes more of a management or leadership approach.

❖ Talk to employees of the organization to identify ways to make better use of their time and talents.

❖ Identify ways in which your organization practices the new definition of cooperation.

❖ Select two or three organizations which you perceive as being innovative and successful; identify areas with potential benchmarking opportunities.

❖ Create a change and innovation report card for your organization and consult with others in the organization as to your future plans for change.

❖ Hold a "what if" brainstorming session and see how well you can conjure up factors with potential change and impact on your experience. Be sure to suggest ways in which you might precipitate such changes rather than just react.

❖ Review the section on shifting priorities and practices that spotlight changes in management and leadership, mission and vision, resource utilization, competition, and change and suggest modifications within your organization.

Transition Tracking

From	To
• Management	• Leadership

To shift from the control and cost containment focus of management to incorporate the communication and empowerment characteristic of leadership.

From	To
• Mission	• Vision

To augment the core purpose of a mission statement with the values and forward motion that vision brings to an organization.

From	To
• Physical assets	• Resources (human and technological)

To move away from the emphasis on tangible assets such as machinery and real estate and focus on developing and empowering the interplay between technology and employees.

From	To
• Competition	• Collaboration

To shift an organization's emphasis from winning at any cost to an attitude where the involvement of the many stakeholders in the process leads to a win-win situation for all.

From	To
• Change as inevitable	• Change as desirable

To create an attitude whereby people within the organization view change as vital, necessary, and as a means for thriving rather than just surviving.

in Las Vegas features white tigers off the lobby, a tropical rain forest eating area, and an authentic pirate ship battle on the hour in the evening. It is also the first casino to generate more revenue from nongambling sources than from gambling.

Whether it be the *R* words involved in repositioning strategies including revive, reach, retain, reinvent, retrench, or refine, or others such as revitalize, there is a necessity for all organizations, public, nonprofit, private, or corporate, to incorporate as many thriving strategies as possible into the ongoing, everyday way of doing business.

Sources

Armour, Stephanie. (1997, September 8). Workers view sabbaticals as two-edged swords. *USA Today.*

Armour, Stephanie. (1997, October 13). Xers market the workplace. *USA Today.*

Armour, Stephanie. (1997, December 29). Recruiters work hard to showcase fun side of jobs. *USA Today.*

AT&T to grant day off to promote volunteerism. (1996, November 18). *The Wall Street Journal.*

Certo, Samuel C. (1997). *Modern management* (7th ed.). Upper Saddle River, NJ: Prentice-Hall.

Collins, James C., & Porras, Jerry I. (1996, September–October). Building your company's vision. *Harvard Business Review.*

Glanton, Eileen. (1997, September 13). Corporations see payoff in having employees play together. *Hartford Courant.*

Goldman, Steven L., Nagel, Roger, N., & Preiss, Kenneth. (1995). *Agile competitors and virtual organizations—Strategies for enriching the customer.* New York, NY: Van Nostrand Reinhold.

Grover, Ron. (1991). *The Disney touch.* Homewood, IL: Business One Irwin.

Hawken, Paul. (1993, October). A declaration of sustainability. *Utne Reader.*

Henricks, Mark. (1996, December). Joining Forces. *Entrepreneur.*

Henry, David. (1997, February 21). GE chief takes well-read look into future. *USA Today.*

Jones, Del. (1996, October 15). Setting diversity's foundation in the bottom line. *USA Today.*

Kaku, Ryuzaburo. (1997, July–August). The path of *kyosei. Harvard Business Review.*

Kouzes, James M., & Posner, Barry Z. (1987). *The leadership challenge—How to get extraordinary things done in organizations.* San Francisco, CA: Jossey-Bass.

Land, George, & Jarman, Beth. (1992). *Break-point and beyond: Mastering the future today.* New York, NY: HarperBusiness.

Maynard, Herman Bryand, Jr., & Mehrtens, Susan, E. (1993). *The fourth wave: Business in the 21st century.* San Francisco, CA: Berrett-Kuehler Publishers.

Maynard, Micheline. (1997, January 13). At Chrysler: The Bobs' management style spells success. *USA Today.*

Meyer, Christopher. (1993). *Fast cycle time—How to align purpose, strategy, and structure for speed.* New York, NY: Free Press.

Mollner, Terry. (1991). The 21st century corporation: The tribe of the relationship age. In John Renesch (Ed.), *Traditions in business.* San Francisco, CA: Sterling and Stone.

Myers, Gerry. (1997, April). Mutual respect. *American Demographics.*

O'Donnell, Michael P., Bishop, Carol A., & Kaplan, Karen L. (1997, March/April). Benchmarking best practices in workplace health promotion. *The Art of Health Promotion.*

O'Reilly, Brian. (1997, March 3). The secrets of America's most admired corporations: New ideas new products. *Fortune.*

Outlook. (1996, October). *Club Industry.*

Phillips, Frank. (1997, February 21). Hotel chain's push produces workers. *The Boston Globe.*

Pitts, Edward. (1997, January). Playing to win both games. *Fitness Management.*

Pritchett, Price. (1996). *Mindshift.* Dallas, TX: Pritchett & Associates.

Sattler, Thomas P., & Mullen, Julie E. (1997, January). Topping the leadership pyramid. *Fitness Management.*

Sattler, Thomas P., & Mullen, Julie E. (1996, November). The benefits of fast cycle time. *Fitness Management.*

Tushman, Michael L., & O'Reilly, Charles A. III. (1997). *Winning through innovation—A practical guide to leading organizational change and renewal.* Boston, MA: Harvard Business School Press.

The Walt Disney Company 1996 Annual Report. (1996). Buena Vista, FL: The Walt Disney Company.

Signs

of a **Shift**

Shopping malls are no longer merely convenient locations for a broad selection of goods and services. They have become entertainment centers for the entire family offering rain forest restaurants, amusement parks, and learning centers. Retail stores are also different. Pet supply stores offer themed events, training classes, holiday parties, and veterinary services. Bookstores have become the latest social spot across the nation for hanging out, having coffee, and meeting friends.

And it's not just where we shop that's changed. The how of shopping is evolving. Our mailbox is filled with catalogs that provide tips, hints, suggestions, recipes, and other recommendations for creating our own uniquely pleasurable experience. And what does it take to sell a car today? It's certainly the cubic square foot of the engine but the high-powered salesperson waiting to spring on the customer as he or she enters the dealership has now been replaced by an entirely new experience. Much of this change is attributed to Saturn and the way it revolutionized the car-shopping experience.

Retail is not the only industry that has been impacted by experiences. The infusion of experiences has spread to other products and nonpersonal services as well. Why just sign up for any old credit card when some cards provide opportunities for customers to get a chance to play golf with their favorite pro or go on safari? Why just watch television or listen to the radio when there are some stations that actually let the viewer and listener become part of the experience? Home Depot is more than a place to buy plumbing supplies just as Kinko's is more than a place to make copies.

People now make choices about where they live, work, and play on the basis of the type of experience infused within a physical location. Times Square in New York City was once a "stay away" zone, but it has now become a newly fashioned, urban renewal destination suitable for all. Wineries that were once limited to tasting programs now offer festivals, volksmarches, children's fairs, cooking classes, and retail stores to attract day-trippers or vacation sojourners. The local farm is now just as likely to have been transformed into an office park, golf course, petting zoo, or cooking school.

The shift to infusing experiences into products, places, and nonpersonal services is well underway. The signs of the shift are practically everywhere.

Chapter 11

Experience Infusers

Consumers today are in the market for "experience facilita-
tors," equipment or services that help them pursue novel
pastimes that set them apart from the crowd.

Carol Farmer

Experience Infusers: Who Are They?

What do shopping malls, mail order catalogs, pet stores, wineries, banks, television stations, car dealerships, bookstores, supermarkets, farms, cities, and credit
card companies have in common? At first glance, they may each stand alone as
an industry which simply creates products, supplies or services in a unique manner to satisfy either basic needs or desires. However, this particular list of industries reflects the cadre of what can be referred to as experience infusers who
have established new performance standards for incorporating parameters of
the experience and experience marketing strategies into their product, place, or
nonpersonal services.

The battle to capture the attention, interest, and purchasing power of the
discerning consumer has created a new playing field of competition at the brink
of the twenty-first century. Having the lowest price or the most convenient location can be short lived if the experience provider is unable to create strategies
that provide consumers with opportunities to experience a product or service in
ways which are stimulating, meaningful, enriching, and personally pleasurable
for them.

The applications of experience marketing techniques transcend organizations such as amusement parks or cruises which exist specifically to provide
experiences. The applications of such marketing techniques and strategies surface in industries that infuse an "experience edge" into their marketing mix to
meet consumers' demands and expectations for more. This experience edge allows

for direct participation, engages consumers, provides an opportunity to develop a skill or perspective, and may satisfy a psychic or inner need.

Experience Infusers: What's Happening?

When Michelin introduced travel guides in 1898 as a way to entice people to drive to desirable destinations as a means to increase sales of automobile tires, it laid the groundwork for experience infusions. Infusing experiences into the marketing strategy and the corporate culture are more noticeable each year. Often, the applications create a destination; require a physical presence and/or participation; have an emphasis on fun, entertainment, or socialization; embark upon nostalgia for parents and children; can add value to a purchase; or may feature connections to a cause which has meaning in the mind of the consumer.

Many of the various industries within the category of experience infusers are making experiences a part of their overall marketing strategy, and manufacturers of products would be one good example. Toothpaste cleans teeth. A car moves people from place to place. A sneaker protects the foot and provides a surface for motion. At a quick glance, these and other products may seem to be purely functional, but products today are about far more than just function.

Some time ago, a number of manufacturers, particularly of automobiles and athletic footwear, shifted their marketing focus to incorporate elements of experience marketing. All but the most essential or basic products are now being infused with some aspect of an experience. Kids select sneakers based on who wears and endorses them just as their parents select their cars based on status or lifestyle messages infused in the automobile advertising. Wearing Michael Jordan's sneakers and driving a Cadillac, BMW, or a Lexus signifies something well beyond just function.

In addition to products, the entire retail industry has infused experiences in nearly every aspect of its varying operations. The Mall of America located outside of Minneapolis, Minnesota, is an experience destination complete with movie theaters, miniature golf, ice-skating, and amusement-like rides. Even individual stores are becoming less store-like and more experiential. FAO Schwartz now adds an individual, enticing touch to each new store. There's a giant toy box with a five-story high Raggedy Ann inside its Orlando store and a four-story tall Trojan horse in the Las Vegas store that rears its head and blows smoke.

How we shop is changing as well. Catalogs aren't just for country folk as they become the preferred shopping method for time-crunched consumers who enjoy the new experiences being provided by catalogs. Catalogs are segmented and targeted to various lifestyle groups so that the right kind of products will find their way to the consumer's house. The lifestyle connections of catalogs are incredibly strong.

Such lifestyle changes have led to other changes in the retail experience, most notably with how we need or want to shop. Grocery stores are now one-stop shopping destinations where one can take care of dry cleaning, banking, prescriptions, videos, and photo developments on a 24-hour basis. Some stores now include branch libraries, day-care centers, fitness clubs, and food courts where retirees meet for an early dinner or business people have a quick lunch. Saturn took the hassle, pressure, and discomfort out of purchasing a car. Its fixed price, family-oriented process nearly revolutionized the industry.

Experience infusions are not limited to products or retail, and they are effective for nonpersonal service providers as well. Nonpersonal service providers are now that large and growing category that can include housecleaning, car repairs, banking, credit cards, and the many subsegments of the communications industry. All of these areas have become more impersonal and commoditized over the years which make them prime candidates for experience infusions.

We hire people to cut our lawns, clean our houses, launder our clothing, compute our taxes, and install our computers. The dry cleaner that started a singles introduction service in a New York City neighborhood found that it now has more business than it can handle. The computer consultant who never sighs, rolls his eyes, or becomes impatient answering basic questions forges a lifetime bond with customers.

Competition does strange things to industries, and nowhere is that truer than in the communications industry. Television didn't eliminate the radio, and the Internet hasn't hurt magazine readership. Turn your radio dial and begin to list the different types of listening experiences. Do the same with your television. Cable stations are creating smaller and smaller niches for all interest areas and going to great lengths to connect with their viewers.

By infusing experiences into the core marketing strategy, industries continue to chart new courses for improving the way in which they attract new business and retain customers in an effort to remain competitive and differentiate themselves from other products or providers.

Parameters of the Experience

The first P in the experience marketing mix is the parameter of the experience which incorporates the actual dimensions and attributes of an experience. Components within parameters include stages of the experience, the actual experience, need(s) being addressed through the experience, the other people involved in the experience, and the role and relationship with the provider of the experience. Experience infusers have incorporated a number of these components into their overall marketing strategies. Particular emphasis has been on the dimensions of the experience itself. They have found ways to create, alter, or combine elements within the experience to infuse their product, store, company, or destination with an experience that becomes the center of the attraction for the consumer.

Donna Karan's Scents and Sensuality collection is based on aroma therapy and nature. Her thick hand-poured candles come in two scents, invigorating and calming, allowing people to make the stay-at-home experience either more exciting or relaxing. The Ontario Mills megamall, an outlet center located about an hour outside of Los Angeles, houses the American Wilderness Experience. This experience turns a shopping destination into a family outing. The high-tech minizoo that houses rare animals from land and sea is just steps away from the stores.

❖ Media Play, a book, music, video, and computer store, features books displayed on end tables, comfortable window seats for listening, director's chairs with popcorn for video pre- viewing, and plenty of computers for play and practice throughout the store. It's like spend- ing a relaxing day at home.

❖ Pier I Imports launched its own line of music CDs for various moods including romance or relaxation as a way to sell related aroma therapy products.

❖ The original NikeTown in Chicago provides a maze of alcoves with shoes and cloth- ing for specific sporting activities alongside an aquarium and basketball court.

❖ CBS Masterworks Dinner Classics consist of themed experiences such as Dinner in Spain or Sunday Morning Brunch by including appropriate music and recipes in one package.

❖ White Flint Mall in Maryland offers rock climbing; golf putting, driving, and swing analysis machines; downhill ski machines; and other tantalizing activities wrapped around a dining and social club atmosphere.

Visitors (as opposed to shoppers) can wander through the display space divided into separate sections for desert, forest, and ocean, and then exit to retail floors and restaurants.

Border's Books, whose boundaries expanded to include music as well, isn't content to be merely a bookstore. It brings books and other good things to life. It holds video slumber parties where children are invited to bring a pillow and wear their favorite pajamas while watching a free video. It sponsors an alternative to the Super Bowl extravaganza with activities for parents and children including high tea in the espresso bar, classical music, and face painting in the children's department.

These are all examples of experience infusion. Products are utilizing tech- niques to create or alter the experience for consumers. Auto manufacturers held focus groups with women to determine ways to make cars easier for them to drive. Changes in athletic equipment have improved the performance of participants.

Slice of Life

There are many sporting goods stores that would like to at- tract the volume of shoppers and visitors that Bass Pro Shop does. Customers enter this sporting goods store through a large lobby with a stone fireplace. They can watch fly-fish- ing demonstrations, gaze at the 32,000 gallon game fish aquarium, and test their skills at the pistol and archery ranges. Younger visitors can go to the laser arcade while adults visit the 200-seat Lunker Lounge that serves microbrews and buffalo burgers. This store, based in an outlet mall halfway between Chicago and Milwaukee, is a serious sportsman's store that has augmented its sales by creating experiences such as having Santa arrive in a red bass boat. The store plans to build on its success by adding a collectors' gun shop, outdoor fishing stream, golf driving range and hiking trails in the wetlands area across from the parking lot (Woodyard, 1997, pp. B1–B2).

The basketball was modified for women in the early 1980s to a circumference that was suitable to a smaller hand size. The hitting surface of tennis rackets has gone from 72 square inches in 1976 to 137 square inches in 1996 to afford the player more control and contact space. Skis have become shorter, lighter, and wider. The use of space-age materials and design improvements has led to the creation of all types of new golf clubs.

These changes and improvements have had a significant impact upon experiences. Whether it's better handling or longer drives, these changes allow people to experience greater success at sport activities. Such opportunities for positive reinforcement will likely lead to renewed participation and benefit the bottom line with additional sales of equipment.

Products and nonpersonal services are also being created or changed to meet emerging psychic or inner needs of consumers. Sales of gas fireplaces have soared as people seek the warmth, serenity, and relaxation of a fire without the need to drag in the wood and clean out the ashes. The old-fashioned recliners that dads across the country used to fall asleep in while they watched TV have been updated to create a more contemporary experience for couch potatoes including trays for food and beverages as well as double versions for family togetherness. Housecleaning services are being repositioned as providing a way to spend more quality time with family.

Some products, particularly technology, are impacting on experiences in ways that they were not originally intended. Computers and the subsequent on-line

Close**Seup**

Jerome Duncan Ford, a 40-year-old dealership in suburban Detroit, underwent a $9 million renovation that included a sky-high atrium and spiral staircase. Automobile prices are fixed with no negotiation, naturally. But there are a number of other changes as part of the new ways cars will be sold that go beyond fixed prices and spectacular physical features. It modeled its changes on the Ritz-Carlton concierge service poised to listen and respond to the needs of its customers. It decided to make its dealership a people business, not a car business, and it does so in the following ways (Eldridge, 1997, p. 3B):

- There are themed display rooms where truck showrooms have hay, shovels, and hard hats while Escort sedans feature Little Mermaid book bags and Saks Fifth Avenue shopping bags in the opened trunk. The sales people stay out of the showrooms until summoned by a customer.
- Sales people are equipped with laptops that contain videos and complete pricing and financial information for specific vehicles. This enables the sales staff to make house or office calls.
- Customers pick up their vehicle in a bright and attractive area next to the showroom where both the customer and a technician in a lab coat inspect the car.
- The company features a consignment lot where customers can sell their used car by paying Duncan Ford a fixed fee of $100 which includes processing tags and registration.
- Future plans call for the addition of a Midas Muffler, Jiffy Lube, Goodyear Tire shop, car washes, and a 24-hour ATM.

services allow family members around the world to say good night to one another. Teenagers hiding away in their rooms may feel more a part of life in Australia via their chat room experiences. Fantasy sports conducted on-line allow participants to function as owners of baseball franchises where they get to pick their players building a dream team while using real-life statistics of these players. They go on to compete in virtual leagues scattered across the country and around the world. Beepers signal parents when children have arrived home and let people know when their glasses are ready to be picked up at the mall. There's just no end to the ways in which technology can and will impact upon our daily lives and subsequent experiences.

In addition, experience infusers have taken an incredibly successful marketing strategy by using experiences or the suggestion of an experience as a way to create a connection with customers. People are drawn to the novel, the unusual, the hard to get, and the one of a kind experiences that not everybody on the block or at the office can have, and experience infusers are rising to meet this challenge of personalized fun.

Often the parameters of an experience so perfectly mesh with the needs of certain groups of people that success seems inevitable. However, sometimes the impact of people upon the experience can significantly change, alter, or even endanger the experience itself. The city of Santa Fe's economic viability is sustained by an unending flow of tourists who crave a steady diet of traditional Hispanic and Native-American art, food, architecture, and ceremonies. Downtown Santa Fe, New Mexico, looks much like it did centuries ago with its low skyline and adobe buildings. The streets are narrow and winding and devoid of automobiles. Santa Fe was settled by the Spanish and remained part of Mexico until 1848 giving this place a distinctively foreign flavor.

However, this nonstop flow of tourists often results in a tourism culture rather than cultural tourism. This same sort of tourism dilemma has occurred in other Western destinations such as Aspen, Telluride, and Jackson Hole. Tourists and visitors decide to relocate to these areas, driving up the prices of real estate and displacing local residents. The newcomers bring with them all the amenities of their past lives—swimming pools, golf courses, and gated communities. The natural resources, forests, rivers, and mountains which originally made the area desirable become playgrounds, displacing agriculture as a source of income for the local people. This loss to the local people further detracts from the cultural motif of the area. The success of Santa Fe as a desirable destination is being eroded because of that same desirability that contributed to its success in the first place (Clifford, 1997, p. C2).

People

The second P of experience marketing is people because of the integral role that their patterns and preferences play within the experience industries. Without people, there would be no experiences. The 4Cs of this second P are core factors that include age, gender, and other demographics; culture which refers to cohort grouping, household, and religion to cite just a few; choice which incorporates

People looking for the unusual, the hard to get, or the out of the ordinary, need look no farther than:

- The Discover card created a sweepstakes where the grand prize was being a part of a National Geographic Explorer filming expedition; talk about an experience edge.
- Southwest Airlines and VISA joined forces in the Personal Party Sweepstakes where the lucky winner got to invite 100 friends and family members to fly with him or her to a Sea World Park; not an experience available to the average person.
- WXRT FM with listeners throughout the Midwest joined with Miller High Life in offering a unique, mystery trip. Contest winners were flown to Chicago to an undisclosed destination where they were to experience a big name performer in a small club setting. The members of this mystery party tour ended up at the Club Vic to hear David Bowie in a much more intimate setting than is possible normally.
- The Discovery Channel's flagship store in Washington, DC, comes complete with a high-definition television theater, 15 interactive computer stations for a virtual dinosaur dig or an aircraft identification game. That's in addition to the forward section of a B-25 and the 40-foot skeleton of a *Tyrannosaurus rex*.
- The nation's No. 3 long-distance phone company apparently managed to get tens of thousands of customers to switch to Sprint in order to take advantage of the company's early access to Rolling Stones concert tickets. For a reported $4 million, Sprint got to do a little body piercing by sticking its trademark "dropping pin" through the Stones' tongue logo. The real bonus was the access to a large block of tickets, as many as half the seats at some of the 32 venues. The deal allowed Sprint to make these tickets available to new or existing customers before ticket sales opened to the general public. A new customer would sign up by phone with Sprint and then be directly transferred to Ticketmaster to buy Stones tickets. Who says you can't always get what you want (Mohl and Wen, 1997, B2)?

values, attitudes, and preferences; and change which addresses elements such as life stages and events, health, readiness, and seasons and cycles.

The vastness and variety inherent in this P of the experience marketing mix makes it a significant component within the overall marketing strategies for most industries infusing experiences. The most effective of such strategies is the ability of various industries to create particle markets on the basis of some combination of the four factors.

Radio stations survived the onslaught of television by focusing on niche markets that later evolved to particle markets. Turn your radio dial and just begin to make a list of the different types of listening pleasures—rock, hard rock, lite rock, country, oldies, jazz, classical, easy listening, all talk, all news—and you can begin to see the basis for targeted marketing efforts. What then needs to be done is to combine elements of the 4Cs to devise experience infusions that work well.

Radio stations create different sweepstakes, contests, and giveaways that incorporate the needs and wants of each group. Many of these contests feature an experience that specifically targets the needs and desires of their target audiences. For instance, a Mother's Day contest that provides lucky callers with tickets to the ballet for a mother and her daughter with the grand prize a day at a local spa including limo transportation, works well on the easy-listening station but would be totally inappropriate for the rap station. An "oldies" station in Madison, Wisconsin, created a summer giveaway that provided one happy winner with a new deck addition for his or her home and a fully catered party featuring a local oldies band. The deck barbecue would not have been a winner in an urban market with a greater number of apartments than houses or with the non-Boomer age group.

There are a number of product manufacturers and service providers that strive to meet the inner needs of their customers. Credit card companies position themselves to create an emotional or personal connection with their particular card. MasterCard's "Priceless" campaign tries to connect this theme to intangible rewards such as intimacy, romance, and love. One ad shows a woman waiting for her husband at the opera while another ad shows five generations of a family waiting to have their picture taken. One ad shows a scenic road in Tuscany and the shadow of a man biking in that area. The ad cites the cost of the 18-speed bike ($1,225) and the cost of shipping it to Italy ($235). While it doesn't cite the other obvious costs such as airfare and hotel accommodations, it does make the point that there are some things in the middle-aged lifestyle that are indeed priceless.

Financial services, investment companies, and drug companies have infused experiences into people's lifestyles and life changes as well. Their ads say very little about taking a prescription or saving money. Instead they feature grandfathers dancing with grandchildren at their weddings or a divorced, older woman starting her own business and a new life.

As consumers' needs change, so do the products and experiences they seek. Changes in consumers' preferences for different kinds of experiences have furthered product line extensions. There are now cars for family outings and car pools, off-road adventure, or the thrill of speed. There are now shoes for walking,

---

It was thought that television and computers would play havoc with the publishing industry, but magazines that have successfully identified a demographic group with lifestyle or life stage changes have been rewarded with success. Two such examples:

Spotlight on Success

- One such magazine reflecting the experiences of a new lifestyle is *The Source,* a gritty, urban-oriented magazine that speaks to young black males. The magazine celebrates the hip-hop culture while straddling the line between readership and mainstream advertisers. Vans cosponsored by the magazine and one of its sponsors, Mountain Dew, went into city playgrounds and local hangouts in New York and Los Angeles trying to connect with trendsetting urban youth.
- One of the more successful magazine launches in recent years was *Men's Health.* Named as one of the 10 hottest magazines in 1995 and 1996 by *Adweek,* this magazine provides "solace and support for aging Boomer men" (Peterson, 1996, p. 4D). Such rapid success was accomplished by addressing a previously unmet need. This reinforces the value of zeroing in on a niche market and meeting its specific expectations.

running, aerobics, basketball, or cross-training that were soon followed by sneakers that would make the wearer feel like a Michael Jordan, ready to overcome personal challenge. The use of new technology resulted in sneakers that enabled the wearer to jump higher or run longer. Similar types of extension occurred in the car industry.

Products have also been designed, modified, and positioned to reflect individual lifestyles as well as inner needs. Industry marketers use a variety of mechanisms to speak to those needs. The selling of cars to Americans has accelerated the approach to infusing an experience edge with information, activities, and by building core market identity. Nissan spent over $200 million on the "Life is journey . . . enjoy the ride" campaign. These ads were intent on emphasizing entertainment and fun, not features and price. Athletic shoes led the way directing advertising messages toward the lifestyle or psychological needs of their potential consumers. Nike's "Just do it" and "I can" messages struck a resounding chord with consumers. These two industries demonstrated the ways in which products can be infused with lifestyle and inner needs resulting in profits for their respective industries.

There is virtually an unlimited array of options that can reach particular groups of people through experience infusion:

- Publix Supermarkets delivers in a big way for parents and their newborns with the Publix Baby Club that comes with free gifts, valuable coupons, plus advice for baby's first two years.
- The birth of Lipton Tea Shops was a result of the company trying to make a connection with a younger audience through a fresher image for its product.
- Targeting the pattern of overspending on the part of Americans during the holiday season, the PNC Bank of Pennsylvania ran a January How to Get Out of Debt Faster contest in which potential customers who completed an application for a home equity loan or line of credit would automatically be entered in its $10,000 Debt Relief Giveaway. This giveaway contest was held every week for the first seven weeks of the new year with the bank providing the lucky debtor with $10,000 to be applied towards reducing his or her burdensome bills.
- Credit cards join with local and national associations and special interest groups to offer cards that feature pictures of ducks for the Ducks Unlimited group or school colors or organization logos for still other groups.
- The Cedar Springs Christian Lifestyle Store in Knoxville, Tennessee, sells boutique and specialty items ranging from the divine to the decorative in its 20,000 square feet of retail space in its main store. It also has an additional branch store and an outlet center.
- MasterCard joined with Mattel in creating Cool Shoppin' Barbie, a Barbie doll that is prepared to go on a shopping spree with all the equipment including a Barbie-sized credit card with a MasterCard logo on it.

The athletic footwear battle is one of the most heated in contemporary business, and the lifelong payoffs of capturing loyal consumers is immense. The two biggest players in this arena, Reebok and Nike, used technological advances and celebrity endorsements as strategies in this battle. Reversals in their fortunes have caused them to place greater emphasis on advertising campaigns reflecting an experiential focus on psychic or inner needs.

Reebok has used the "athlete like me" strategy with its "This is my planet" promotional campaign. The "mental housecleaning" in its print advertisement imbues: "There are dust bunnies in my head with names like fear and doubt. They hide, mocking me. And when the pounding of my heart becomes deafening, they just disappear. This is my planet." Selling the shoe appears to be an afterthought to making the emotional and psychological connection with the customer. By hinting that it knows who you are and understands your challenges, the ad campaigns suggest that Reebok has designed its product to meet those needs.

A quick overview of the variety of messages used by Nike reveals its intent to connect with people's self-talk. Some of those messages are:

- Athletic achievement is not the end of one challenge but the beginning of the next.
- Victory = Balance + Discipline + Attitude + Guts = Nike.
- NO ONE ever works out and REGRETS it. You never go for a RUN, and then when you're FINISHED, WISH you would have just stayed home. You NEVER climb a mountain, get to the TOP, and say, "I should have been CONTENT to STAY where I WAS." [and of course, the ubiquitous]
- Just do it.

Due to a variety of factors including changing public perception related to exercise and the antics of professional athletes has led Nike to create a new slogan for its company, "I can." The "I can" commercials feature children and amateur athletes. These images include a series of quick pictures of athletes such as swimmers, weightlifters, and youth football players in the throes of competition.

But more important, they connect with the changing inner needs of growing consumer groups. That large group of consumers, the Baby Boomers, has moved to a new life stage, and that new life stage exchanges achievement and competition for a more meaningful experience.

Peripherals

The third P of experience marketing, peripherals, refers to these many factors and variables related to and involved in the entire process. Peripherals add substance and definition to the experience by incorporating factors such as place, price, packaging, policies, public image, patterns of demand, and popularity cycle into the entire experience itself.

When is a grocery store not a grocery store? When is a service station not a service station? How can we tell our local branch bank from the convenience store? We can't and the reason we can't is that the variety of ways these industries have altered and manipulated the peripherals. The branch bank is located next to the

❖ Land Rover has gone so far as to create Land Rover Centres for the sale of its vehicles. These centers resemble Adirondack cabins with rustic beamed ceilings. The sales staff look more ready to go on safari than sell a vehicle. They have an off-road track so a Range Rover or Discovery can be put through its paces on something more challenging than pavement. The Centre also features a whole array of exclusive Land Rover clothing, gear, and vehicle kits, items including trek caps at $14 or folding field stools for $180.

❖ L. L. Bean, the catalog turned retail store in Freeport, Maine, decided years ago to remain open around the clock. Since employees were working anyway, it thought it might as well be open for customers if they were driving through town. More recent additions to its retail environment include a front porch where the customer can sit and try out Adirondack chairs, trophy wildlife winking in the stairways, and a new L. L. Kids store with high-tech interactive exhibits and a Trail of Discovery which includes a bike trek, hiking trail, and climbing wall.

❖ Land's End has taken notice of ways in which catalog competitors are reaching out to customers and has implemented experience marketing in its own. Land's End, a competitor of L. L. Bean, opened a Travelers Inlet shop in the Minneapolis–St. Paul International Airport. This shop features travel products, a concierge service, and free activities for the children.

❖ Some home decorating stores are incorporating feng shui, the Chinese belief that placement of objects, colors of rooms, and the overall design of buildings and homes influence health and well-being, into their services.

❖ Kmart has altered the look and the consumer's perception of its sheets and towels by using Martha Stewart designs.

flower stand which is really part of the supermarket except that since it is incredibly time consuming to find the food, more people are stopping at the gas station where there is bread and milk but no service. How's that for peripherals!

There are a host of options within peripherals. You can change your location and move to a more nontraditional place. The same is true of time, and there are nearly endless possibilities when it comes to ambiance and changes within the product or service venue. Some nonpersonal service providers alter the experience usually by making the service more convenient or the process more pleasant for the customer. Check out car repair service. Auto repair venues, historically bastions of cracked plastic chairs and throwaway coffee cups that double as ashtrays, have cleaned up their act. They've change the "waiting" experience by creating clean, comfortable lounges with refreshments, television and magazines to pass the time.

Policies and public image are peripherals on which experience infusers have increasingly started to rely. A major challenge confronting large retail chains is their perceived lack of being part of the local landscape. Chains such as Wal-Mart and Home Depot are not always greeted with open arms by communities who feel that they will change the personalization of the shopping experience and potentially drive local, family-owned and -operated stores out of business. Many

❖ CVS Pharmacy opened its first health center located in a store in New Bedford, Massachusetts. The CVS Health Connection Center staffed by a nurse and a pharmacist is a joint venture with health insurance and drug companies as a means to differentiate themselves from the competition and to connect with issues important to their customers. Other chain drug stores now hold high blood pressure screenings or serve as centers for flu shots as a way of becoming part of the community.

❖ At the holiday season, Barnes & Noble offers a free gift-wrapping service that is staffed by local charitable or nonprofit groups with donations for wrapping going to the local causes supported by the group who has volunteered to wrap on that particular day.

❖ Home Depot makes a concerted effort to become a contributing part of the community and has what it calls an "unwavering commitment to community." It transforms this slogan into action by forging partnerships with local affiliates of Habitat for Humanity and supporting local community initiatives. Such local initiatives have included sponsoring three-on-three basketball tourneys in Charlotte, North Carolina; working with Boys and Girls Clubs in Mobile, Alabama; and youth mentoring programs in Harrisburg, Pennsylvania.

❖ Consignments for a Small Planet with several resale stores in Connecticut helps customers feel good about their purchases by educating them about the hidden values and benefits of recycling.

❖ American Express joins with local restaurants during the winter holiday season to donate a portion of sales for feeding the needy.

of these chains have attempted to create a community connection as a way to overcome these objections or to become associated with a worthy societal cause. Smaller or more locally owned stores take whatever opportunity comes their way to help customers understand that they are good neighbors as well and often do so by contributing funds or merchandise to local causes or events.

PerInfoCom

The experience marketing version for the traditional P, promotion, is PerInfoCom which incorporates the essential elements for informing and attracting participants to experiences in the twenty-first-century marketplace. These elements are personalization, information, and communication. There are a wide variety of options within this experience marketing variable, and this category of the experience industries has made good use of them.

If ever there were a segment that made good use of the options within PerInfoCom, it's this one. The celebrity endorsements and logos are found on products everywhere to target lifestyle-based connections. Catalogs contain more information than most books, and Home Depot holds almost as many classes as local adult education providers. Nike is notorious for its ambush marketing successes most notably at big events such as the Olympic Games. Credit cards have

❖ Wheaties, the cereal synonymous with sports celebrities, launched the celebrity endorsement approach back in the '50s and over the years has featured 25 people drawn from 12 different traditional sports. It put a fresh face on this approach when it elected to put the face of the Wal-Mart bass fisherman of the year on a new box.

❖ McDonald's Happy Meals are consistently popular because of their tie-in with movie characters or popular toys such as when people were buying burgers and tossing them away to get the Ty Teenie Beanie Babies.

❖ The After Shock's Virtual Reality Tour was created by Jim Beam Brands Co. as an interactive event to promote their new hot-cool cinnamon liquor. Eight custom-designed virtual reality games were taken to 2,000 bars in 45 cities to launch this new brand.

❖ Nike is involved in hundreds of summer camps with specific sports designations including junior golf, tennis, girls basketball, soccer, lacrosse, softball, volleyball, swimming, as well as Camp Nike, multisports camps for kids of all abilities, and Nike Mountain Air Sports camps where campers participate in mountain biking, ropes courses, hiking, and jet skiing. One of Nike's latest ventures is the Nike World Masters Games, a 14-day multisport event for athletes 30 years of age and over cohosted by the City of Portland, Oregon.

❖ Vintage Books, a division of Random House, turned to experiences as a way to generate additional books sales. It provides bookstores with guidelines for starting book discussion groups as well as support kits for specific titles.

❖ Local, family-owned hardware stores such as Katz Hardware in Glastonbury, Connecticut, not only stop by the customer's house to check out his or her latest lawn problem, but also holds an old-fashioned ice cream social every spring with hot dogs, ice cream, and banjo music.

❖ Dillard's Department Stores offer social etiquette classes for young ladies ages 5 to 16 to help them acquire style, poise, and social graces.

❖ L. L. Bean created shooting and fishing schools to offer enthusiasts of all skill levels expert training which improved their experiences.

❖ The Grapevine-Colleyville Independent School District in Texas with 13,000 students signed a 10-year exclusive contract with Dr. Pepper and 7-Up for $3.45 million. This deal resulted in Dr. Pepper logos painted across the rooftop of two of the district's schools which lie in the flight path for Dallas–Fort Worth International Airport (Hays, 1998, p. D4).

❖ VISA joined with experience providers in seven different city locations to create travel books filled with shopping, eating, and entertainment information and coupons. These books were titled *South Beach—America's Riveria* for the south Miami beach area and *Sunny Money* for San Diego, California.

❖ Philip Morris took over three ranches in Montana and Arizona to promote Marlboro cigarettes in its Party at the Marlboro Ranch promotion where the winner gets a five-day trip and cash to spend as he or she river rafts, fly fishes, and mountain bikes around the ranch that also features bonfires, cookouts, and bands.

❖ The Wine Rave Tour is reggae music, hip-hop DJs, and grunge fun. This tour was dreamed up by the Wine Brats, a group of Gen Xers who grew up in some of the Sonoma, California, wine families, to show younger people how to mix wine with their lifestyle, breaking the wine generation gap.

tie-ins with frequent-flier programs and special interest groups incorporating both loyalty and cause marketing approaches.

And this group is certainly no stranger to event marketing which it has entered in full force. Saturn held a family reunion. Jeep created Camp Jeep. This approach can include either joining an existing event as a sponsor or creating one of its own. Either way, such events and activities enable product manufacturers to connect potential consumers to their product or connect people to others like themselves. Heublein created the beach volleyball tour and literally brought the sport into the mainstream while garnering significant publicity and name-brand recognition.

Some companies don't elect to create their own events, but rather choose to sponsor existing events. This is an effective way to reach particular target market

*Close***eup**

The automobile industry has successfully implemented a variety of PerInfoCom approaches:

- Volkswagen and Trek created a dynamic duo by infusing a copromotional effort that offered a mountain bike as a premium with every Jetta purchase. Capitalizing on the activity of mountain biking and emphasizing the space-age technology used by both products, Volkswagen managed to reinforce the quality aspect in the eyes of the consumer. It became more than a fad advertising strategy and influenced an entire industry to get real with experiences (Rubin, 1996, p. B1).
- General Motors' People in Motion campaign recognized the priority people placed on family and incorporated that preference into its promotional efforts. GM included seats treated with Scotchgard, affordable vehicles, and "pregnant crash dummies" research. The People in Motion campaign spoke to the values that consumers cared about most.
- The New Dodge Hidden America series offered regionalized listings of activities for family pleasure. Published once a month in a weekend edition of *USA Today,* it included traditional events as well as offbeat happenings within driving distance of the region.
- Jeep promoted visits to national parks in sizable, special advertising sections promoting seasonal sporting activities such as snowboarding, snowmobiling, and ice climbing. This is a further attempt to engage consumers in quality experiences that link the car image with active and pleasurable pursuits.
- Ford linked its Explorer to the nostalgia of scouting badges by creating a visually attractive print ad that displayed a range of badges promoting the various uses of its vehicles. The scout-like badges included such things as cloud counting, canyon cruising, trendsetting, bird-watching, paradise finding, fish finding, finding one-self, rainbow racing, and extreme vegging just to name a few.
- Volvo, long the equivalent of the sensible shoe, shifted its advertising messages for its all wheel vehicles to "Life. Liberty. And the pursuit of just about anything you please."
- The Toyota advertising campaign with Sly and the Family Stone's 1970s hit "Everyday People" playing in the background features people, not cars, and focuses on common life activities and wishes such as "I'll never take my wife for granted" or "I'll spend more time with my kids."

groups and to connect with them when they are out enjoying themselves. Almost every international or local event has become dependent on sponsorship. VISA is the official card of the Olympic games. Dodge is the official truck of the rodeo circuit. Local newspapers support summer community concert series in their market area. Corporations infuse their products with a special excitement or advantage by such practices.

One effective component of PerInfoCom is positioning. Positioning a declining product can often revitalize it. The death knell for cigars almost tolled a few decades ago when industry sales dropped an average of five percent a year since

Spotlight on Success

Event marketing can go a long way to reach challenging target markets and impact the bottom line as well. A newer entry into the PerInfoCom world, permission marketing, seems to be able to accomplish similar results.

Companies interested in reaching the 15 million teenage boys who annually spend more than $50 billion had to look no further than the X Games. This event was created by ESPN as a way to expand its market and reach young adults who weren't interested in traditional football, basketball, tennis, and golf. Some people refer to this event as an Olympic-like version of a street brawl. It has over-the-edge events such as freestyle skateboarding and combination activity endurance races and has attracted such big time sponsors as Proctor & Gamble, AT&T, and VISA (Horowitz, 1997, p. 10B).

Interactive marketing is probably one of the most promising strategies for PerInfoCom because it can take either a high-tech or a high-touch approach, but, most important, it facilitates a give and take between the provider and the participant. One innovative approach to such interactivity was used recently by H & R Block when it wanted to introduce a new service called Premium Tax that was designed for people in the upper-income bracket. This approach was developed by Internet marketing pioneer Seth Godin who believes in practicing what he calls "permission" marketing. He defines this approach as persuading consumers to volunteer their attention.

Godin is president of Yoyodyne, a company that builds all of its campaigns around creating relationships using the Web, E-mail, and other on-line media in conjunction with games, contests, or sweepstakes. In the marketing of Premium Tax, it started with banners on various Web sites announcing that H & R Block had a "we'll pay your taxes" sweepstakes. More than 50,000 people who both knew H & R Block and paid taxes responded by providing Yoyodyne with their E-mail address. These people became players in the contest and gave H & R Block permission to tell them about its new service in exchange for the chance of having their taxes paid.

They received three E-mail messages per week for a period of 10 weeks that required them to answer trivia questions about taxes, H & R Block, and other related topics. Naturally, each of these E-mail messages included information about Premium Tax. Over the 10-week period, 97 percent of the people who entered the sweepstakes stayed with the game. An analysis conducted at the end of the promotion found that for the people who participated in the activity, 34 percent of them understood Premium Tax, and the percentage increased to 54 percent for those people who participated actively in the contest (Taylor, 1998, pp. 200–208).

their peak in 1964, but any rumor of the death of cigars was premature due to a concerted public relations effort by the Cigar Association of America. This campaign eradicated the cigar's connection with gangsters, grandfathers, and smoke-filled back rooms and replaced it with one filled with celebrities, status, and a desirable lifestyle. It planted cigars in movies and played up the habit as practiced by Rush Limbaugh, Madonna, Wayne Gretsky, Demi Moore, Arnold Schwarzengger, and Bill Clinton. It tried to connect cigar smoking to more youthful celebrities while simultaneously reminding people of the place cigars hold as part of ritual celebrations.

The industry's effort coupled with a seemingly grass-roots backlash against political correctness has led to positive results. Sales of cigars over the past five years rose 26 percent to $4.39 billion with sales of the expensive, premium cigars playing a big role in that increase. All due to lifestyle repositioning cigar bars, cigar stores, cigar dinners, and cigar clubs are springing up everywhere (Klein, 1998, pp. A1, A4).

Recognizing and Responding to Customer's Needs

Due to the growing preference on the part of consumers for highly individualized and personalized products and services, it is critical that experience providers are able to use market information to recognize current and emerging needs of their customers as well as to match those needs to customer's preferences for experiences. Organizations need to incorporate target market and trend information directly into the design and delivery of the experience. The combination of these customer-centered strategies with the infusion of information creates the right kinds of experiences to retain existing participants and to reach emerging markets.

Experience infusers need to find out what customers want. Direct Tire Sales in Watertown, Massachusetts, prides itself as being there for its customers by finding out what they want and giving it to them. The waiting room is spotless and includes a high-tech coffee pot, an aquarium, and magazine racks filled with Newsweek, Discover, and Cosmopolitan. Employees wear ties and are incredibly polite. The bottom line is that their customers pay a 10–15 percent premium price for the service that includes free rides, loaner cars, and an 800 telephone number because they receive an experience that matches their needs and preferences (Jacob, 1993, pp. 23–24). After conducting consumer research, Hallmark opened its own stores, Hallmark Creations. These stores include just the types of experience that customers described including quiet space for selecting cards, comfortable surfaces for writing or choosing wedding invitations, and added amenities such as the child-friendly touches of crayons and papers and coffee for shoppers (Green, 1997, P. 29).

Some experience infusers, most notably grocery stores, have elevated collecting data about the preferences and patterns of customers to an art form. The preferred customer cards that are scanned at the checkout counter not only serve as a reward to good customers in the form of discounts but also simultaneously

Kinko's might have gotten its start back in 1970 in a converted hamburger stand, and it might have grown 10 years later to be a funky, medium-sized, antiestablishment company that primarily provided low-cost copies for college students. However, a great deal has changed since then. Kinko's has grown to become a large venture with 865 locations in six countries with annual revenues estimated at $800 million. These changes are due to the experience Kinko's creates for its customers. What Starbucks is to coffee connoisseurs, and what Home Depot is to the do-it-yourselfer, Kinko's is to the growing group of self-employed professionals and their home offices.

One operation in Chicago in 1985 decided to stay open 24 hours a day, 7 days a week because of customer preference, and the idea just caught on at other Kinko's locations. Kinko's success and growth is not due simply to its reasonable prices and 7-days-a-week 24-hours-a-day policy; it's about great service, access to technology, advise and assistance, as well as a place to hang out. It truly has become "your branch office" as it indicates in its advertisements. The staff at Kinko's serve as pseudo coworkers for the free agents they support and as consultants for the "digital-on-demand" era in which these independent contractors function. They don't just print resumes, they provide advice and make suggestions. They don't just provide technology, they help the customer make use of it.

Kinko's also plays an additional important role for that growing group of self-employed, the telecommuters. It is the new millennium version of the virtual water cooler or break room where people can get together, interact, and learn from one another (Roberts, 1998, pp. 164–179).

become a veritable gold mine of consumer information. There's plenty of room for other experience infusers to follow their lead gathering important customer data. Such information is key to the eventual design and delivery of customer-centered experiences.

An example of a retail environment where information leads to the infusion of customer-centered experiences is Recreational Equipment, Inc. [REI]. Before REI built a new store it surveyed its customers who happen to be members of this cooperative venture. All four elements of the experience edge as defined by its customers—entertainment, environment, education, and engagement—are incorporated into one place, REI's flagship store in Seattle, Washington. This $30 million complex is 100,000 square feet housing 60,000 different items and features a glass-enclosed, 65-foot climbing pinnacle, a 470-foot long biking trail, a rain room, and an illumination station. The purpose of this facility is to start with entertainment and move beyond actually to educate and engage the customer with its products. People can try out the Gore-Tex jackets in the rain room, practice purifying water in the brackish water pool, as well as wander through aisles that resemble hiking trails.

Creating outdoor adventure for unique audiences, the store also has an outdoor trail for wheelchairs, and to top off the purchasing experience, an Outdoor Recreation Information Center is located on site to assist with planning trips. REI has not simply sold the products necessary for a personal outdoor adventure; it has embarked upon a commitment to support the entire experience its products represent for the people who frequent its stores (Ransdell, 1998, pp. 182, 191.)

❖ NBC's "Today Show" returned to its 1950s studio window where people visiting New York City show up with signs and waves for friends and families watching back home. They augment this connection by creating opportunities for on-site viewers to exchange pleasantries with Matt, Katie, and Al and create experiences such as the Friday morning live concert featuring well-known musicians visiting the Big Apple.

❖ The America's Health Network's show "Ask the Doctor," replicates the old-fashioned family physician providing sensible advice.

❖ "People's Court" creates connection with both high-tech and high-touch formats as it allows viewers to E-mail their verdict for each case and then takes to the street to interview street viewers for their take on the case.

❖ "Dinner and a Movie" provides viewers with a rerun of an old movie favorite along with an evening at home with friends. During the commercial breaks real people talk about the movie and share cooking duties for preparing dinner. They even include recipes for "what's cooking" on that particular evening and the menu usually has a tie-in to the movie.

❖ To kick off the ninth season of the Emmy-winning "The Simpsons," the Fox network gave away a 2,200 square foot house located in Henderson, Nevada, an exact replica of the Simpson house.

❖ Each day "Live With Regis and Kathie Lee" contacts a viewer who not only wins a prize but also gets a chance to chat personally with Regis and Kathie Lee.

❖ The Romance Classics cable network's program "The Dress to Di For" gave women across the country a chance to see one of the three gowns previously owned by Princess Diana that the network owned as the 18-wheeler show mobile traversed the country letting people try on the glass slipper of a princess and enter a drawing to win one of the gowns.

It is critical that experience infusers make a connection with their customers. It is always challenging for manufacturing, retail, and nonpersonal service operations to reach out and to create some kind of relationship with their consumers. The communication industry especially radio and television have been most effective in their efforts.

Marketing Changes

People's needs, interests, and desires are continually changing, and customers have now come to expect that organizations will automatically incorporate these new priorities and preferences into their experiences. Such an expectation on the part of the consumer requires organizations to recognize and act on emerging marketing strategies. New marketing strategies include such techniques as mass customization, agility, value enhancements, creating conversations and connections with customers, and collaboration within experiences.

Options within this area can be high-tech or high-touch and can include major changes or little differences that mean a great deal to customers. Amway, the granddaddy of relationship retailing, is now coupling those relationships with technology to enhance value for the customer. Its computer programs create

Local television stations are especially prolific at infusing experiences into their marketing and programming as a way to create connections with their viewers and hold on to ratings. Take a look at the variety of options put into place by WFSB, Channel 9 in Washington, DC:

- the consumer news show not only offers information and warnings about products but also teams up with local car dealerships to offer child safety seat checks for parents;
- the health segment features "Buddy Check 9" where the station reminds women on the ninth of every month to do their buddy check for early breast cancer detection;
- pets from local area animal shelters appear weekly in an attempt to find them new homes;
- the morning weather segments include temperatures as submitted by area elementary schools, and the early evening segments feature temperature and rainfall amounts submitted by individuals in the viewing area;
- the channel's lead weatherman is the "official meteorologist" for the D. C. United soccer team, the Kennedy Center for the Performing Arts, the Kings Dominion Amusement Park, and the MCI Center; and
- the station's slogan, "Whatever it takes," reflects its mission to serve the community; a recent example of the slogan in action is the coordination of a program to distribute free carbon monoxide detectors to needy families after a local tragedy.

profiles of each customer resulting in the automatic shipment of a variety of household needs on a weekly, monthly, or quarterly basis. A household need never run out of paper towels or vitamins again. It's like having a personal housekeeper, and working mothers never need to feel guilty again about failing in their role to keep the kids in toothpaste.

Saturn took a relatively low-tech, high-touch approach to selling cars. Customers are treated as if they are new friends soon to become valued family members. They arrive to pick up their new car and are presented with roses and balloons and receive a standing ovation from the employees at the dealership. People like to feel as if they are special and treasured individuals and that they have made the right decision on such a large purchase. The Saturn process helps people meet these important, psychic needs.

Rockport, a division of Reebok, took a high-tech, high-touch approach when it created a retail environment in San Francisco to continue to build on its heritage as a good walking shoe while attempting to engage and motivate customers. The company claims that the store is "not a new shoe store, but a new state of mind." It uses high-speed scanners to analyze customer's feet for customized shoes. It also provides licensed massage therapists offering complimentary reflexology, free bottled water, and plenty of information on foot health, walking, travel, and an overall concern for health and well-being (Green, 1997, p. 32).

Ken Miller of St. Louis who owns two garden stores and a mail-order catalog business took a relatively low-tech approach. To increase sales during the off-season winter months, Miller packages his $32–$42 "bag o' bugs" as birthday presents, gag gifts, and holiday treats! To make the bugs more appealing, he often

❖ Interactive Custom Jeans offers a wilder and wider alternative to custom jeans over the Internet.

❖ *The Boston Globe* newspaper invited readers to compile a list of books that should be read by every well-informed citizen and then created an on-line book club among its readers.

❖ Soap operas have taken to cyberspace where sites with interactive features enable fans to become part of the story, even selecting possible outcomes for a particular plot or character.

❖ The Custom Foot Stores uses infrared scanners to measure each foot precisely so that a pair of shoes can be made with the one shoe bigger or smaller than the other since most people have different size feet.

❖ A store for preteen girls located in suburban Boston, Massachusetts, specializes in preteen clothing and also provides anxiety-free shopping for sport and party wear by taking the stress and strife out of the preteen and mother shopping trip.

❖ General Nutrition Centers (GNC) has put machines in several of its Live Well stores that custom mix daily vitamins, shampoos, and lotions for people based on personal issues such as age, sex, exercise routine, or other health needs.

includes companion items such as T-shirts, books, and even holiday tree ornaments. The success of the "bag o' bugs" catalog has resulted in the even more popular Bug-of-the-Month Club. Subscribers receive a new insect each month during spring and summer. It arrives discreetly boxed or in the form of eggs stuck to cards. Miller's Bug Your Mother promotion for Mother's Day was such a hit that more celebration events continue to be planned (Fletcher, 1996, p. B1).

Slice of Life

Capturing an increasing share of an experience should be an overall goal of any experience provider, and some of them have proceeded with such an attempt.

A small seaside restaurant on Martha's Vineyard turned its staff shirts into collectible items. The famous Black Dog Restaurant T-shirts that feature different colors representing which summer the customer visited the island eventually led to the creation of an entire line of clothing, a thriving catalog business, several retail outlets, and other experiences. Between the boat neck sweaters, minitotes, and field bags, customers will find a variety of experience marketing techniques. Pictures of people wearing their famous Black Dog mascot apparel in various locations such as on the equator and in Venice, Italy, are sprinkled throughout the catalog. Special recipes from the restaurant for grilled marinated shrimp and blueberry apple bread pudding are detailed. Taking experience marketing one step further, this company bought a boat and now offers seagoing schooner trips.

Is it selling T-shirts, tote bags, food, or sailing trips? It is offering a complete experience package to reinforce where customers eat, vacation, and clothe themselves. Catalogs go way beyond just products and serve as an effective way to educate and engage consumers resulting in a big payoff for this industry.

Organizational Change

Change is the keyword in this aspect of experience marketing, and the biggest change is the shift from management to leadership. Organizational changes inherent within this shift include an overall approach such as identification of vision, precipitation of change, and becoming versatile and virtual. Other aspects of needed change within organizations relate to use of resources and the changing nature of competition.

The successful companies within this industry segment recognize that they can't stand still. They need to embrace change. They need to think outside the box and create innovative approaches to infusing experiences into their products and

Continued on page 289

❖ After 50 years of decline, the Inner Harbor in Baltimore underwent its first renaissance in the early '80s with the construction of a convention center, shopping pavilions, and aquarium. During the celebration of its two-hundredth birthday, an additional $500 million was infused to expand a second rebirth to include Port Discovery, a Disney-designed children's museum; a $20 million Power Plant project designed as an "adult-oriented entertainment complex" that includes a Barnes & Noble, a blues and comedy club; and an eight-screen film center (Goodfriend, 1997, p. 7D).

❖ Gateway Computers has reconfigured the way computers are manufactured and sold by allowing the individual customer to specify his or her needs and preferences without having to show up at a store.

❖ In late August and early September, Home Depot heads back to college. It packs up popular student items such as carpeting, cork boards, hand vacuum cleaners, and designer lamps in a campus caravan. It arrives not just with products but with Dorm Decorating 101 classes that answer those important questions about maximizing room space and security.

❖ Myrtle Beach, South Carolina, building upon the draw of its beaches added golf and country music to become a full-service destination.

❖ The producers of pork got together in the face of declining meat consumption in the United States and developed a campaign that repositioned pork as "the other white meat" and created a link between pork and the perceived healthier meat, chicken.

❖ U-Scan Express is a self-checkout system for grocery stores where customers scan and bag their groceries, pay with cash or credit card through an automated teller machine with transactions monitored on video.

❖ Midway Atoll, the Pacific launch pad of the famed World War II naval assault, was essentially left dormant until 1988 when the island became a wildlife refuge. The island is now known as a haven for green sea turtles, endangered Hawaiian monk seals, over two million sea and shore birds, and has become a mecca for military buffs and ecotourists alike.

*Clos**eup***

The Entertainment and Sports Network started life in 1979 as a small, shoestring venture, out of central Connecticut. There was little about its initial broadcast of local college soccer games and women's collegiate bowling that indicated its full potential. Who could imagine that there was an audience for nonstop sports viewing and that such activity would become so valuable? Apparently there was and is an audience since ESPN reaches into more than 73 million homes and the company was purchased by Disney and Hearst for an estimated $8 billion (Jurkowitz, 1998, p. 18).

Well, the rest is history, but what is even more interesting is the way in which ESPN has employed savvy experience marketing techniques in recent years to generate even greater success. An awareness that the more traditional sporting events such as football, baseball, golf, and tennis were of less interest to the younger viewing audience, it created ESPN2. ESPN2 is a second sports channel that targets primarily the Gen X niche and features more adventure and offbeat sporting coverage such as beach volleyball, motorcycle racing, cheerleading competitions, cyberfitness, and karate. This fast-growing new cable network surpassed the 54 million mark for viewers in 1997, and ESPNEWS, launched in the fall of 1996, reached five million homes as of 1997 (Keedle, 1998, p. 19).

The company recognized the viability of expanding its services beyond the scope of home viewing. It created the X Games. The *X* stands for extreme, and this annual event includes competition in in-line skating, skateboarding, and marathon-like endurance races. Initially conceived as programming for the ESPN2 network, it has evolved into a sponsorship opportunity similar to the Olympic Games as major companies seek a novel but effective way to connect with young males in particular.

There is little end in sight for growth as this network expands to cover all the bases. ESPN is reaching out to create other experiences for its viewers. There's the ESPN Store, ESPNZone, ESPN Radio, *ESPN Magazine*, and ESPN Grill on Disney's Boardwalk complete with television monitors in the rest rooms.

The Times Square section of New York City had fallen upon hard times and had become synonymous with seediness. The 42nd Street Development Project, started in 1992, transformed the mecca for the homeless, crime, and smut into an entertainment district that draws millions of people from around the world (Davidson, 1998, p. 13). The historic theater district is now home to three theaters including the New Amsterdam Theater restored by the Walt Disney Company.

Spotlight

on

Success

Just some of the facts and figures related to the restoration of Time Squares as an entertainment district include (Davidson, 1998, p. 13):

* on one night alone, 5,000 people walked past the Virgin Megastore between midnight and 1 A.M.;
* the project generated $2 billion in new investments that will generate $328 million a year in additional tax revenue; and
* street crime in the area dropped 50 percent between 1993 and 1997.

Bottom Line

- ❖ Home fragrance sales have grown 10 percent per year to become a billion dollar industry (Washington Post News Service, 1996, p. A4).
- ❖ It is estimated that the 1998 Nike World Masters Game will pump $113 million into the Oregon economy (Wells, 1997, B1).
- ❖ Outdoor World, a sporting goods store in Springfield, Missouri, is billed as the state's top tourist destination drawing 4 million visitors a year (Woodyard, 1997, p B2).
- ❖ Since Bass Pro Shop opened in the Gurnee Mills mall, business at the mall has increased by almost 40 percent (Woodyard, 1997, pp. B1–B2).
- ❖ REI which opened its first store in 1975 now has 49 stores in 21 sites and annual sales of approximately $500 million. Five-year sales projections for the flagship store in Seattle were nearly reached in the first year (Ransdell, 1998, pp. 182, 191).
- ❖ According to Stanley Eichelbaum, president of Marketing Developments of Cincinnati, the well-conceived store with an entertainment format typically sells 60 percent more merchandise per square foot than traditional stores of the same size (Woodyard, 1997, pp. B1–B2).
- ❖ Jerome Duncan Ford relies on referrals for new customers and not advertising saving it $700,000 per year (Eldridge, 1997, p. 3B).
- ❖ The transformation of historic canal systems into hiking and biking trails has resulted in the creation of 1,107 miles of trails along 35 historic canals that draw 8.1 million hikers and bikers a year (*USA Today*, 1996, 7D).
- ❖ The extras of the customer experience such as real cream and fresh croissants and donuts as well as loaner cars add up, but additional services such as winter tire storage generated $24,000 at a cost of $4,000 which pays for a lot of fresh doughnuts and taxi rides home (Pare, 1993, pp. 23–24).
- ❖ A 5 percent increase in customer loyalty lifts lifetime profits per customer 85 percent in bank branch deposits, 85 percent in publishing, 84 percent in auto and home insurance, 81 percent in auto service, and 75 percent in credit cards (Seller, 1993, p 57).
- ❖ The 1980s renaissance of the Inner Harbor in Baltimore catapulted Baltimore from a drive-through location between New York City and Washington, DC, into a substantial tourism base that draws 7 million visitors per year (Goodfriend, 1997, pp. 7D).
- ❖ According to the Bureau of the Census, estimated annual sales at hardware stores in the United States have risen from $10.73 billion in 1986 to $14.2 billion in 1994. This figure does not include the large building supply stores such as Home Depot and leads some experts to conclude that in addition to growth in the do-it-yourself market, the personalized service of the small, old-fashioned stores pays off at the cash register.
- ❖ Five of the best small cities located on beaches and ski slopes drew new residents at twice the national average between 1990 and 1994 with places like Bozeman, Montana, and Hilton Head, South Carolina, growing 15 percent and 12.5 percent respectively (Heubusch, 1998, p. 48).
- ❖ Hotels, ski lifts, and boardwalks increased retail trade as evidenced by per capita sales in Traverse City, Michigan, reaching $11,700 and in Carson City, Nevada, reaching $12,700 in 1992, far above the national median of $7,400 (Heubusch, 1998, p. 48).

Continued on page 288

Bottom Line continued

❖ Attractive vacation spots raise per capita income through tourism dollars and the affluent residents they attract. Per capita incomes for 1995 were above the national average in Key West, Florida, by 41 percent; Hilton Head, South Carolina, by 22 percent; and Wenatchee, Washington, by 19 percent (Heubusch, 1998, p. 48).

❖ In a poll conducted by Kurt Salmon Associates, two-thirds of consumers reported difficulty finding clothes that fit well, and 36 percent indicated they would be willing to pay more for custom clothes and shoes (Woodyard, 1998, p. 3B).

❖ It is estimated that the Mall of America attracts 40 million visitors a year which is more than Disney World, Graceland, and the Grand Canyon combined with an economic impact of $1.5 billion (Abrahamson, Meehan and Samuel, 1997, p. 97).

❖ More than 400 of the 697 General Motors car dealers in California, Oregon, Washington, and Idaho have adopted GM's Buy Power program in which customers don't have to haggle over prices on certain vehicles (Eldridge, 1998, pp. B1–2).

❖ The Christian Booksellers Association changed its name to CBA in 1996 as the sales of Christian gifts, music, and cards overtook sales of books. This $3 billion-plus industry reported a 12 percent sales increase between 1996 and 1997 (Grossman, 1998, p. D1).

❖ CarMax believed that buying a car should be no more trouble than grocery shopping with transaction time approximating a lunch hour. Its approach to selling low-mileage used cars with a fixed price has earned CarMax a 98 percent customer satisfaction score 30–35 points higher than more typical car dealers (Peters, 1997, p. 281).

Action Agenda

Remember, every experience provider can learn and grow from reviewing the ideas and adapting the successes from other segments within the industry. Consider taking a close and imaginative look at the experience you provide in light of:

• Mix it up with combinations—take a look at other products or services that could be packaged with your current offering to turn it into an experience.

• Walk in your customer's shoes—try to get beyond the more obvious or tangible reason that people use your product or service and find out what psychic or inner needs come into play.

• Turn the radio dial, and as you do, try to imagine the ways in which your product, service, or experience could be changed or marketed to meet the listeners of the various stations.

• Do a face lift—brainstorm a list of ways in which you can update your product, service, or experience to meet the current and future definition of a preferred experience.

• Brainstorm a list of ways in which your product, service, or experience could be redefined to create an environment or provide for ways in which to entertain, educate, or otherwise engage your customers and the other important people in their lives.

Transition Tracking

From   To

Experience infusers have changed a great deal over the past few years. A few of the major shifts include:

- *Outer to Inner*—Buying a car, wearing sneakers, or carrying a particular credit card is no longer about the more tangible, obvious benefits or qualities of the product or service. A car is no longer just transportation, it's a form of self-expression. Sneakers are no longer functional. They aren't even fashion statements or status symbols anymore. They're reflections of people's inner voices. Products and services will re-create the design, delivery, and advertising messages to reflect what people are thinking, feeling, or dreaming about.

- *Purpose to Pleasure*—A host of products and activities that were once regarded as necessary may still be required components of daily living but have been reconfigured as pleasant pastimes. We don't just go shopping. We venture to the mall or the bookstore to climb walls or meet friends. We don't expect the jaunt to the car dealer or the repair place to be tedious but rather comfortable, convenient, and maybe even entertaining. Banks are no longer places where we go to transact serious business; they have been repositioned to provide opportunities for travel, dining, and living.

- *Our Way to Your Way*—How do companies, big and small, define or design their product or service? They don't; they leave that privilege up to the consumer. You don't have to take the same vitamins as your spouse or neighbor. You certainly aren't expected to wear clothing with a cut or color that's not just right for you. Unless these accommodations are made in a way that works for you, you probably won't be purchasing. Television stations solicit input and let viewers decide the fate of favorite characters. Life will never be the same. Let the Gateway Computer approach that solicits information over the phone in order to design a computer based on the specific requirements of that customer and delivers it in a timely fashion direct to the door serve as a model for how you envision your product, service, or experience.

services long before the consumer even realizes he or she has the need or preference for changes. Just like the human life cycle, the life cycle of a product or service and its popularity needs to change to keep it alive and well.

Sears paid a price by resting on its success and allowing Wal-Mart and others to usurp its place in the closets of middle America. Retailers of men's clothing who ignored the changing preferences of Baby Boomers and the trend towards more casual attire in the workplace were left holding the three-piece suits and wing tip shoes. General Motors, Ford, and Chrysler stood by and watched in amazement as motorists chose to drive away in Japanese cars with specifications that the big three auto makers believed weren't important to customers.

We couldn't talk about thinking outside of the box and discovering a totally innovative way in which one connects with one's customers without mentioning Weekend Warriors. Weekend Warriors was dreamed up and started by Skip

Maggioria at his music store in Sacramento. The idea was subsequently licensed by the National Association of Music Merchants (NAMM) and has set up locations nationwide.

What exactly is Weekend Warriors? It's a five-week program that operates out of music stores across the country where bored, musically undernourished, current or potential customers with regular jobs come together to form a band. The band practices for a month under professional supervision and then gets its own show at a local nightspot. It resembles a dating service for would-be or former musicians who no longer have the time to get the gang together in the garage. The end result is to rekindle interest in music while creating a new revenue stream for music stores (Bernstein, 1998, p. F1).

Another innovation, thinking outside of the box approach to experiences, brings us to Robert Shepard, a part-time contractor and farmer in Buxton, Maine. When his farm wasn't paying off as it should, he transformed a cow pasture into Barn Yard Golf where golfers and nongolfers use tennis balls with a tractor serving as a hazard (Collins, 1996, p. B7).

Sources

Abrahamson, V., Meehan, M., & Samuel, L. (1997). *The future ain't what it used to be.* New York, NY: Riverhead Books.

Bernstein, Matthew. (1998, February 15). Retailers hope to strike a chord in a generation past. *The Boston Globe.*

Clifford, Hal. (1997, December 28). Disney-fying Santa Fe. *The Boston Globe.*

Collins, Rachel M. (1996, September 30). Putt out to pasture. *Boston Sunday Globe.*

Davidson, John. (1998, March). Times square revival. *Working Woman.*

Eldridge, Earle. (1998, March 11). One-price deals save time, hassles, but not money. *USA Today.*

Eldridge, Earle. (1997, December 26). Dealer turns showroom into automotive showcase. *USA Today.*

Fletcher, June. (1996, September 4). Insect marketers want to wrap small things in better packages. *The Wall Street Journal.*

Goodfriend, Anne. (1997, September 19). Bicentennial Baltimore harbors a rich diversity. *USA Today.*

Green, Nancye. (1997, December 1). Environmental reengineering. *Brandweek.*

Grossman, Cathy Lynn. (1998, March 12). Stores have strong faith in sales soaring to heaven. *USA Today.*

Hays, Constance L. (1998, March 10). Be true to your cola, rah! rah! *The New York Times.*

Heubusch, Kevin. (1998, January). Small is beautiful. *American Demographics.*

Horowitz, Bruce. (1997, June 2). Marketers get in line for extreme sports. *USA Today.*

Jacob, Rahul. (1993, Autumn/Winter). How to retread customers. *Fortune.*

Jurkowitz, Mark. (1998, February 1). At the top of their game. *The Boston Globe Magazine.*

Keedle, Jayne. (1998, January 22). ESPN goes for bigger gold. *The Hartford Advocate.*

Klein, Alec. (1998, January 31). Cigar smoke screen. *Hartford Courant.*

Mohl, Bruce, & Wen, Patricia. (1997, October 12). Stones ticket offer has Sprint long-distance service soaring. *The Boston Globe.*

Pare, Terence P. (1993, Autumn/Winter). The tough new consumer winning companies. *Fortune.*

Peters, Tom. (1997). *The circle of innovation.* New York, NY: Alfred A. Knopf.

Peterson, Karen S. (1996, October 1). Mike Lafavore, the life force of *Men's Health. USA Today.*

Ransdell, Eric. (1998, December–January). Adventures in retail. *Fast Company.*

Roberts, Paul. (1998, December–January). Kinko's—The free-agent home office. *Fast Company.*

Rubin, Sal. (1996, April 3). Off-road now means two wheels. *USA Today.*

Seller, Patricia. (1993, Autumn/Winter). Keeping the buyers you already have: The tough new consumer winning companies. *Fortune.*

Taylor, William C. (1998, April–May). Permission marketing. *Fast Company.*

USA Today. (1996, August 30). Giving canals new life.

Washington Post News Service. (1996, September 20). Designers on scent of new market. *The Arizona Republic.*

Wells, Melanie. (1997, March 3). Nike swooshes in to sponsor Olympics-style event. *USA Today.*

Woodyard, Chris. (1998, February 16). Mass production gives way to mass customization. *USA Today.*

Woodyard, Chris. (1997, December 23). Stores court customers with theme park fun. *USA Today.*

Signs of a Shift

Do you remember when hospitals were sterile, unfriendly environments for sick people who were admitted and seemed to stay for an eternity? Can you recall when theaters, churches, museums and libraries meant a quiet, hands-off setting? People whose grandparents were thrilled to have an automobile now board airplanes with children and sporting equipment in tow without giving it a second thought. (This transportation shift also parallels a time when people organized their own closets, stayed at home with infants and toddlers, and lived in neighborhoods with a natural sense of community.) Change has certainly accrued for the community and personal service providers.

Sterile delivery rooms have given way to living room–like birthing centers. Hospitals and churches are now almost as much fun as community recreation centers. Spas and health clubs are not just for the wealthy "leisure" class. Newborn babies go to day care followed by preschool and summer camp. The senior class in college is just as apt to consist of 70-year-olds as 22-year-olds. Community pools are increasingly more experiential with zero depth entry, lap pools, and wave generators replacing the standard Olympic-sized competitive pools. Airlines and rental car companies attract repeat business with frequent customer award programs and preferred treatment for regular customers. Community planners are just as likely to be employed by a public agency trying to create an environment where people will become less dependent on cars as they are to be working with Disney and other planned community designers to turn a housing development into a communal, friendly place to live.

The industries that make up community and personal service providers have made a grand leap into experience marketing. Churches already design services specifically for singles, teens, and families. Art providers reach out to a variety of groups not only the older, more affluent population historically targeted. Hospitals conduct almost as many tai chi and yoga classes as they do operations. Golf communities are designed as much for people who don't know an iron from a putter as those who hit the links regularly. Camps can still feature nature, crafts, and color wars, but they are just as likely to specialize in computers or weight loss. Museums actually encourage and expect people to make noise and touch things.

The rate of change among experience enhancers goes through the roof as people turn to community and personal services that provide

Continued on page 294

Chapter 12

Experience Enhancers

As we move into the Experience Economy, we are
commoditizing services by wrapping them in experiences for
the customer.

Joseph Pine II

The How, Who, and What of
Experience Enhancers

The arena of personal and community services has escalated to new heights with
the proliferation of enhanced experience strategies. These segments of the experience industry are continually challenged to provide comprehensive yet specialized services to create the appearance and feel of individualized care and attention. Experience-enhanced industries are often viewed in the eyes of the consumers as examples of how such facilities and services ought to be. This often
results in a series of mixed metaphors in the world of real competition. Catering
to every individual need, understanding the aspirations and endeavors of customers, and replicating an experience for the sake of remembrance, enjoyment,
or self-actualization are essential to those who pursue a comprehensive, attractive approach for their service portfolios.

Health & Wellness Industry

If there has been an industry that has changed substantially during the last decade by enhancing the experience marketing mix for its consumers, it's healthcare. How does one define the healthcare industry today? It is becoming increasingly more difficult to know where medical care starts and wellness-related health
services end.

Today the emphasis in medical care is on prevention rather than treatment.
The cost of medical care in the United States has soared. The very way health and

**Signs of a Shift
continued**

service and support that enhances their personal lifestyles. As a result, these industries meet the needs of individuals trying to balance their responsibilities and preferences for what life should and could be for them.

well-being are perceived has also undergone a paradigm shift. Doctors and hospitals are not only being rewarded financially for making sick people well but also for trying to keep people well and to prevent them from becoming ill in the first place.

The ever-rising cost of healthcare coupled with the advent of competition within the healthcare industry has resulted in vast opportunities for growth in marketing. Healthcare marketing expenditures were $235 million in 1990 and rose to $800 million in 1996 with projections to $1.6 billion by 2000 (Galuszka, DeGeorge, Palmer and McCann, 1997, p. 86). The race is on to see who can attract the most members to his or her managed healthcare plans, hospitals, and even health clubs as the amount of money spent on the ever-expanding area of health continues to escalate.

These changes in healthcare are not only about money and insurance; there are other factors at work as well. The aging of the population, the obsession of the Baby Boomers with staying young, the changes in attitudes toward authority, and the ease of access to information via technology have resulted in a groundswell of support for wellness as a segment within the health arena. Wellness, with its focus on the whole person and not just the physical condition, has its emphasis on living well by empowering people to become more involved in their own health. Wellness has expanded the service continuum to include a number of new specialties including acupuncture, aroma therapy, and reflexology that have only recently become an accepted part of mainstream treatment.

All of these changes acting in concert with one another have resulted in the blurring and blending of the continuum of services within this industry. More surgery is performed outside of the hospital than in. Many hospitals now resemble community centers with coffee clubs and classes. Fitness clubs have almost as much monitoring equipment and technology as hospitals. Holistic health centers which blend vacation, rehabilitation, and spa into one are gaining in popularity.

The "being sick" and the "getting well" experiences have changed significantly, resulting in plenty of opportunities for experience marketing.

Community Resources

Why do people live where they do, or what makes certain locations attractive places for businesses to locate? These questions elicit a variety of different responses based on the perception of the quality of life issues in a particular community or region. While a number of factors enter into the definition of quality of life, the majority of those factors incorporate the presence, availability, and the quality of community resources and amenities.

Who are the providers of community quality of life? Community resources can include everything from aquariums to zoos and generally don't include services such as sanitation and infrastructure but rather nonregulated resources.

The list is actually quite substantial and includes a variety of public and nonprofit service providers including parks and recreation, libraries, museums, living-history sites, concert halls, theaters, as well as special services for children or senior citizens.

These providers truly enhance the quality of life within a community or region. They often serve as nearly invisible strands of the fabric of life in an area. Imagine what a community would be like without parks, recreation, or libraries? What would life be like without books, ball parks, and places for the birds to flock? Think of how most people take for granted the American Red Cross or airports? These community resources make a significant difference in key life experiences. They enhance daily life for people in demonstrable and sometimes in obscure ways.

Not only do these community resources make a difference in quality of life, but they do so in ways different from the past. Libraries have story hours and play rooms. Museum exhibits such as the da Vinci at the Boston Science Museum and the Lego Marine Exhibit traveling around the globe come complete with a hands-on, interactive exhibit that results in noisy, sometimes messy experiences in the once hallowed halls. Theater hasn't been left out of this interactive approach either. Participatory theater was born years ago with the off-Broadway performance of *Tony 'n' Tina's Wedding* and the ever-popular murder mysteries which let the audience become a part of the production.

Community resources, most especially the arts, have taken a different approach by attempting to become more attractive and accessible to more segments of the community. Local symphony orchestras feature big name artists, and high-profile, art exhibits which include selected works of Monet or Picasso serve to draw new audiences. Orchestra Hall in Chicago emphasized public access in its recent renovation. It was renamed the Symphony Center, and a sky lit rotunda was built that can be used for receptions and small concerts as well as free noontime programs featuring local choir groups. A restaurant along with lobby areas on each level of the building which enhance the public interaction before the curtain rises, during intermission, and after each performance complete the package.

The economic impact of community resources is not to be overlooked. Many local chambers of commerce often create or sponsor events to draw shoppers or customers to area business districts during periods of slow or reduced traffic. Convention and visitor bureaus work hard to showcase the amenities and attractions of a particular area and attempt to facilitate arrangements for group travel or conventions as a source of additional revenue for a city or a region.

The desire for enhanced community experiences has resulted in an upsurge of such services in the private sector as well. The growth of planned communities and second homeowner communities attest to this preference which takes on a variety of forms. Second homeowner communities within driving distances of large urban areas have sprung up around lakes, rivers, and mountains. They provide a variety of amenities all designed to enhance the weekend experience and are often centered around a particular theme or purpose. Golf communities are popular as are communities specifically designed for mature adults.

Planned communities can be quite diverse in nature and include examples like Disney's Celebration, Florida, and the Cambridge, Massachusetts, Co-housing project. Celebration brings together upper middle-class families and retirees and provides them with a built-in sense of order, security, and community. Cambridge Co-housing provides for greater socioeconomic diversity as 85 residents come together in 41 condominiums complete with communal dining, play room, kitchen, and living rooms. Community members, as the residents are called, are united by a common commitment to a new way of life. Community planners are just as likely to work in the public sector trying to refurbish neighborhoods as they are in the private sector trying to turn housing developments into profitable ventures.

Once regarded as niceties, community resources and the amenities and ambiance they bring are rapidly becoming necessities as people seek to enhance their lives on a daily basis.

Learning and Growth Industry

From Outward Bound to Spanish immersion programs or from cooking school to learning vacations, never have so many wanted to learn so much. Babies learn to swim, toddlers tackle tumbling classes, and those things are just a start. Kids go to camps and colleges but so do adults and grandparents. There appears to be no end in sight to the learning curve.

A combination of factors fuels this growth. The aging of the Baby Boomers with their incessant need to continue to bloom and grow plus the downsizing of the work force which sends people scurrying to acquire new skills contribute. The competition among colleges to fill classrooms and residence halls with the smaller Gen X cohort has put the spotlight on the education of the upcoming Millennial Generation.

Most of these learning and growing providers have expanded their target markets by going after nontraditional consumers. Adults go to camp, and kids go to camp at colleges. These providers have extended their traditional "season" to generate additional revenues. Colleges are just as busy in the summer as they are in September. Camps hold special weekend events in the fall and winter months and there are also more options available. Parents can elect to educate children at home or send them to a specialized magnet school outside of their neighborhood or to private schools.

One of the biggest strategies of this industry segment is the infusion of enjoyment and entertainment into education. College catalogs include page after page of pictures of social happenings and dining and exercise facilities with few students actually shown in a classroom setting. The Disney Institute infused a big dose of fun into adult learning. This segment of the industry has been radically reshaped by merging fun and facts together.

Transportation

Transportation has undergone a number of changes in this past century. Early on there was heavy reliance on mass transportation, most especially the railroads.

Cars and then planes began sounding the death knell for trains as people could afford to own cars, and airlines took over the bulk of passenger transportation.

The need to move people from one place to another for work or play and the variety of modes to do so has heightened competition in this industry which has in turn sent consumer expectations skyrocketing. There is competition among various forms of transportation. For instance, Southwest Airlines, the industry leader for value, maintains that it doesn't compete with other airlines on price but rather on other modes of transportation such as buses and cars. Mass transportation competes with the convenience of individual cars as economics and environmental impact of dependence on individual automobiles has shifted the emphasis to commuter trains and buses.

The airlines and the rental car companies don't so much compete with cars and trains as they do with one another. They use a variety of experience marketing techniques. Loyalty programs such as upgrades and frequent customer programs abound as do varying levels of options that make a concerted effort to create a customer-centered experience. Price is long gone as a variable that either industry could use as a competitive advantage. Once price is eliminated as a source of competition, experience marketing comes into play in a big way.

Religious Providers

The world of organized religion underwent dramatic changes in the late twentieth century. Only one-third of Americans acknowledged that they were religious, and with fewer than 40 percent attending church regularly caused churches to explore marketing alternatives as a matter of survival (Spiegler, 1996, p. 24). One such example is the U. S. Episcopal Church, a maturing denomination that has lost more than a million members in one generation going from a high of 3.6 million in 1965 to 2.4 million slipping below one percent of the U. S. population for the first time in its history (Renner, 1998, p. F1).

New churches recognize that they need to understand what business they are in and to know who their customers truly are and how they want their needs addressed. Kenton Beshore, senior pastor of the Mariner Church in Newport Beach, California, describes his church's strategy as "giving them what they want and giving them what they didn't know they wanted—a life change" (Truehart, 1996, p. 44).

Knowing the needs and preferences of today's would-be worshipers can result in congregations offering day care for young families or recreational activities for older adults. Traditional churches are experimenting, exploring, or engaging in enhanced religious experiences with music, classes, special interest groups and communication strategies to satisfy the interests of various target markets. The actual physical facility of the place of worship has undergone dramatic changes as well.

Churches have become adept at creating varying alternatives such as faster-paced worship services, modern-language Bibles, casual attire, celebratory services with practical sermons, louder sound, and more modern music.

Personal Services

For a time there has been growth among individuals and businesses who provide personal services for their customers or clients. People who lack the time, the talent, or the inclination to perform any number of commonplace or special tasks for themselves are fueling this increase. There are many aspects to this growing area of industry. There are personal chefs, veterinarians who make house calls, and personal concierges who help people accomplish routine tasks in a more time effective manner. There are other personal service providers such as hairdressers and trainers who help their clients reach their personal best in a number of different ways.

In addition, there are other personal service providers such as Mother's Matters in Reston, Virginia, who accompany a new mother and her infant home from the hospital and provide the kind of support and assistance that people once received from mothers, sisters, or friends. Personal service providers can also include those people whose focus is on creating an experience for the client or the client's family, friends, or business. While these purveyors of catered experiences provide such services at a price, there is also a small but growing group of people who facilitate experiences for themselves and others on a volunteer basis.

Whether one would like to have a new version of a baby shower, fiftieth birthday party for a spouse, well-crafted corporate press conference, or a big bash to launch a new product or to raise money for a charity, there are party and event planners that can make all the arrangements at a price. An entire industry has grown around the desire to have events that are big or unique and come off without a hitch.

There are also providers of more personal kinds of services that enhance lives. There are closet organizers and personal trainers. There are personal coaches and pet trainers. There are professional organizers who will clean out our attic, rearrange our closet, run our yard sale, and put together our scrapbooks. This list of experience providers that enhance experiences is growing rapidly.

While the other categories of experience enhancers mentioned in this section require or relate to the personal presence, involvement, or perception of

Fast Facts

❖ The United States Personal Chef Association indicates that the number of people using personal chefs increased from 5,000 in 1995 to 30,000 in 1998 (Armour, 1998, p. A2).

❖ Circles, a matchmaking service in Boston, Massachusetts, for people who are looking for people or companies to help them clean closets, organize yard sales, or wait for delivery men, began serving 200 to 300 customers per month in its first year of operation (Armour, 1998, p. A2).

❖ Membership in the National Association of Professional Organizers has grown 16 percent a year since 1992 and now has over 1,000 members (Armour, 1998, p. A2).

❖ LesConcierges of San Francisco experienced a doubling of its client base in 1996 and has continued to grow at a rate of 25–50 percent per year (Armour, 1998, p. A2).

individuals, they don't fit the mold of personal service providers. The personal service category differs because personal services exist to support the personal lifestyle, interests, needs, and habits of their customers. The rate of growth in this area continues to escalate as people become too busy to carry out certain life tasks or are accustomed to a level of expectation or expertise that can only be met through the personal service provider.

Many hairdressers have redefined their role or mission in their customers' lives and have expanded their services to incorporate nail and skin care as well as tanning beds and massages. Many of them provide makeup and fashion advice by helping today's professional person put his or her best foot forward. Some takeout food providers have expanded their services by becoming the family meal and nutritional supplier. These people plan, prepare, and deliver meals that cater

❖ *Titanic*—The Exhibition showcased at the Florida International Museum advertised itself as a "feeling you won't forget" when the museum retooled its facility to enable visitors to stand on the deck and feel as if they were on-board.

❖ Wolf Trap, the National Park Service's premier outdoor performing arts facility in Virginia, has a theater that embraces the natural environment and provides blanket seating for picnics or social affairs at the crest of the amphitheater which creates a perfect venue for the Washington Symphony to play backup for the Moody Blues.

❖ Mount Sinai Hospital in New York has 19 suites where fresh flowers and high tea in the library are daily experiences along with private baths, showers, and sitting rooms.

❖ The Salon of Ian North (SIN) in Sarasota, Florida, encourages its patrons to experience their visits and does so by providing settings that resemble an intimate art gallery or private library, and provides a glass of wine or cup of herbal tea, and classical music.

❖ Visitors from Europe flock to Harlem's Baptist churches on Sunday mornings to experience a form of Christianity much different from their own.

❖ The Florida Gulf Coast Railroad Museum schedules a great Western train robbery so that people can experience the thrill as the good guys battle the bad guys.

❖ The government move to ban cars from the Grand Canyon, Yosemite, and Zion National Parks and replace them with shuttle systems reduces the haze from car exhausts and enables visitors to walk, hike, or bike the parks.

❖ Virgin Airlines competes with the other airlines flying from the United States to London using video screens for each passenger for amusement en route.

❖ Educational Institute, a training laboratory for many of the country's hotel works, has retooled its videos and CD-ROMs to feature upbeat music, interactive technology, and MTV-style pacing to provide "enter-trainment" for would-be bellmen, front desk clerks, and housekeepers.

❖ Karen Brody, a minister and wedding planner for Teton Mountain Weddings, puts together weddings that occur on river rafts, backpacking trips, horseback rides, and even dog sleds.

to the individual preferences of various family members while trying to squeeze those right nutrients into the daily food allotment. It's not just about haircuts or pizza delivery anymore, it's about uniqueness and how to create or adapt a service that meets the needs of those lifestyles.

There are also individuals or small groups of people who have come together to use existing resources to create experiences for themselves. There are all levels of organization and affiliation associated with this approach, but the opportunities for experiences are usually created by the potential participants themselves. There are some people who gather every New Year's Day to plunge into the icy waves of the ocean. The Adrenaline Junkies Club is a loosely formed network of

Close Seup

Griffin Hospital, a 160-bed acute care facility in Connecticut isn't the picture of a traditional hospital. Based on the Planetree Model established in 1978 by Angelica Thierot, an Argentinean who was appalled by her dehumanizing hospital experience in the United States, this model traces its roots back to Hippocrates and ancient Greece. The three central tenets of this model include widespread patient access to health and medical information, active involvement on the part of patients in their care and treatment, and the involvement of the patient's friends and families in the process as well.

The Planetree Health Organization has 25 affiliated hospitals in 11 states as well as in Norway and England. Griffin Hospital became the first United States affiliate in 1992 with the addition of a new wing to the hospital.

The actual design of the facility resulted in the following:

- an L-shaped room with the bathroom placed in the middle to serve as a natural divider between roommates;
- care-partner rooms with sleeper sofas for the patient's spouse or significant other;
- fully equipped and stocked residential kitchens where patients and their families can cook their own meals;
- a piano lounge on each floor;
- a 200-gallon saltwater fish tank filled with exotic fish in the quiet lounge;
- an intensive care unit that provides for 24-hour visiting hours as well as ease of access for treatment teams; and
- a birthing center with specially designed double beds and a Jacuzzi for mothers in labor.

Adherence to Planetree's philosophy related to patient education and involvement in treatment has resulted in patients (Grandjean, 1996, pp. 39–41, 101–109):

- reading their medical charts;
- having breakfast at noon;
- eating whatever they like providing it meets dietary recommendations;
- being assigned a primary nurse who serves as their advocate;
- having access to a Resource Center with nearly 4,000 health-related books, audiotapes, videocassettes, magazines, scientific journals, and computers; and
- being able to play cards, write letters, or get their taxes done thanks to PRS (Patient Room Service) staffed by volunteers.

500 people of all types and ages living somewhere in New England who get together to bungee jump, whitewater raft, hang glide, skydive, or play Paintball. The recent upsurge in investors' clubs and book clubs and the rebirth of things such as quilting bees attest to growth of this aspect of experiences.

A more unusual example that underlies the serious needs that can be addressed through experiences are the laughing clubs in India. In a country known for both its seriousness, overcrowding, and plight of poverty, middle-class men and women come together at the beginning of their day for 20 minutes of forced laughter. Laughing clubs are described as a mix of mysticism and the Marx Brothers, but more important, a chance for people to experience a brief respite from the sadness and poverty that surrounds their day. It is estimated that 150 such clubs exist in urban areas throughout India (Los Angeles Times, 1998, p. A15).

Reducing stress, gaining quality time, making something good or special happen for significant others, feeling special or even indulged are all reasons why the personal industries are a valued commodity that will continue to grow as they integrate additional aspects of experience marketing into their approach.

Parameters of the Experience

That first P in the experience marketing mix, parameters, incorporates a number of factors related to the attributes of an experience. Factors within the parameter of the experience include the actual dimensions and attributes of an experience. Components within these parameters include the actual experience, need(s)

As has been mentioned before, the needs of people change. The range and type of changes within this category of experiences has resulted in significant changes to experiences as well as the creation of entirely new ones:

- The Omega Institute is often referred to as an oasis for soulful living and learning. It offers winter workshops on St. John, July trips to Bali, and April and June "vision quests" in Utah's Canyonlands for people looking to change their inner selves.
- "Experience the fun" is the slogan of the Virginia Beach, Virginia, Park and Recreation Department as part of the effort to promote the benefits of living and playing in that city.
- Discovery Channel's Eco Challenge Adventure Race answers the "before you can win you've got to survive" drive for extreme competitors.
- At the Dogpatch in Los Angeles, people drop off their dogs so the dogs can spend the day painting or making ceramics.
- The Promise Keepers, a national men's ministry, attracted thousands of men whose inner needs were not being met by mainline religions.
- Ocean Challenge is a different kind of summer experience for teenagers who learn to sail the *Roseway*, a historic tall ship.
- Martin Gray, a photographer and anthropologist, maintains a Sacred Sites Web site for a cyberview and visit to spiritually altering spots.
- Doctors refer patients to medically supervised health clubs for aquatic rehabilitation and strength training.

- Cigna Corporation's healthcare unit hired Asian-American staff who can speak a total of six dialects and have printed bilingual publications to reach ethnic markets.
- Camp Timberlock in New York's Adirondack Mountains offers family camping in a rustic, old-fashioned camping setting with wood stoves, gas lanterns, midnight canoe trips, farm-style meals served on a covered porch, and sing-alongs with the lodge's player piano.
- Precept Group, a consulting firm out of Costa Mesa, California, does demographic and psychographic analysis for its clients by surveying a geographic area identifying important issues such as changing religious preferences, views on crime and community, family needs, and lifestyles.
- The Cooper Fitness Center in Dallas goes beyond simply designing exercise programs by using a behavior assessment test to determine the readiness and willingness of individuals to exercise.
- The Buckeye Hall of Fame Cafe opened in Columbus, Ohio, to attract and generate revenue from visiting alumni through T-shirt and other merchandise purchases that placed the Ohio State University's logo on everything.
- Diet programs with a spiritual connection such as Weigh Down, First Place, and Step Forward are being offered in churches throughout the country.
- The Akron General's Health and Wellness Center created KidStyles programs including Dive in Movies, KidFit, After Prom, and several different lifestyle camps for kids.
- The Omega Institute for Holistic Studies added a Celtic Christmas retreat and an annual New Year's celebration expanding its season beyond the summer.
- The Surfer's Chapel in Huntington Beach, California, holds services on Saturday night that don't interfere with Sunday morning surfing. The dress code is "knock the sand off your shoes" although many people attend barefoot.
- Lifetime living facilities establish a number of separate residences within one establishment including independent living, assisted living, and long-term care.

being addressed through the experience, the other people involved in the experience, and the role and relationship with the provider of the experience. Community and personal service providers have enhanced a number of these components into their overall marketing strategies. They have placed particular emphasis on the relationship between emerging needs and changes to more traditional types of experiences.

There are a variety of different personal and community service providers that have altered various dimensions of the experience to heighten the experience for the customer. The San Diego Zoo, known as an environment primarily created for its residents, augments the visitor experience with enhancements such as heated rocks that encourage the lions to venture out on colder days, delighting the visitors. The Vancouver International Airport built a $200 million terminal meant to mimic the British Columbia countryside. The floor-to-ceiling glass walls frame the mountains outside so that arriving passengers immediately get the feeling they're in British Columbia complete with the numerous man-made babbling brooks and the tree-like support beams.

❖ Freedom Village, a retirement community in Bradenton, Florida, offers continuing care with 510 independent apartments and villa homes, 135 assisted living apartments, and a 120-bed skilled nursing center on a 36-acre campus. It provides nightly meals in the Revere Dining Room, rides to and from doctor's appointments or shopping trips, and recreation and social activities.

❖ The fresh flowers, scented candlelight, soft and relaxing music, the glass of water, cup of herbal tea, or goblet of wine make Spa Radiance in Glastonbury, Connecticut, a retreat for a few hours or a full day.

❖ The Jewish Home of Central New York has an Alzheimer's wing in Depression-era decor with vintage furniture and accessories as therapy to help calm and reassure residents. This environment of familiar things helps their long-term memory function better.

❖ The special exhibits such as the da Vinci program at the Boston Museum of Science requires advance purchased tickets for reserved patron time slots.

❖ The Kripalu Experience of Lenox, Massachusetts, enables people to take advantage of peaceful surroundings, simple accommodations with an emphasis upon yoga and nutritional eating.

❖ The $30 million student center at George Mason University in Virginia features a movie theater, bank, food court, library, and classrooms.

❖ An expansion of the Miami Airport includes some special touches of Florida including sensors that, when set off by moving passengers, activate chimes and an Everglades symphony of birdsong, croaks, and alligator roars.

❖ The new Oakdale Theater in Wallingford, Connecticut, comes complete with corporate boxes, baby-sitter stubs on the tickets, and an expanded number of rest room opportunities for women.

❖ The Guggenheim Bilbao, one of the world's best branch museums, is described as a futurist sculpture, an art castle in Spain, and a great sailing ship, as the shining titanium and honey-colored stone is as much an art form as the art exhibited within the museum.

❖ United Airlines installed air filters on all its jets to bring cabin air quality up to the highest possible standards in an attempt to insure the health of frequent fliers and flight attendants.

❖ Forever Young Health Club in Green Island, New York, has a Body Barge anchored in the river that allows club members to exercise outdoors seven months of the year.

❖ Fisherman's Wharf Aquarium takes the visitor underwater in a glass contained tunnel that takes him or her into the bay where via the conveyer belt he or she becomes a part of the natural habitat and gets a sense of what it feels like to be a sea creature.

❖ Northwest Trek Natural Habitat Zoo in Tacoma, Washington, puts the visitors in vehicle "cages" so they can then experience real life in the wild.

When *Tony 'n' Tina's Wedding* came to off-Broadway a number of years ago, the theater experience changed radically by giving birth to interactive or participatory theater in which members of the audience are actually part of the production. This production led to others such as *Grandma Sylvia's Funeral*, Blue Man

❖ The Tampa Children's Hospital has a computer outlet in each hospital room allowing parents to stay connected to the work world and a playground where visiting siblings can work off some excess energy.

❖ Virgin Atlantic Airlines offers business class passengers drive-through check-in at Heathrow Airport in London and Newark Airport in New Jersey. These fliers even get a limousine ride to the airport, and the chauffeur calls ahead to the airport to let the airline know how many bags to expect. Preprinted luggage tags and security checks are ready and waiting upon their arrival.

Group in *Tubes*. People can come dressed to the theater as if they were attending a wedding or a funeral. They are not forced to take part in the actual festivities, but can elect to play the part of a long-lost relative claiming an inheritance or dancing the "Macarena." Variations on this theme include murder mystery plays in which participants are given acting parts with clues to the murder or plays where the audience members are polled to determine their preference for the play's conclusions with the actors then giving them their definition of a "happy ending."

*Close*Seup

The 15 years of planning and four years of construction brought cultural legitimacy to Los Angeles in the form of the J. Paul Getty Museum. Inspired by the acropolis of ancient Athens, the 110-acre campus is surrounded by an additional 600 acres of Getty-owned open space. The museum has one million square feet of building, 54 individual galleries, two full-service restaurants, two cafes, a 750,000 volume art research library, and 1,200 parking spaces.

A visit to the Getty is truly an experience in itself. Admission is free, but parking costs $5 with reservations required. Museum visitors reach this acropolis by spending five minutes aboard driverless electric trams. The view from the top stretches for miles and makes one feel as if one is living in the clouds. Permanent and changing collections are featured in the galleries with color and fabric including red corduroy and brown wood gabardine. Skylights and domed ceilings create natural lighting in the galleries.

The extent and variety of nature rounds out the experience. Thousands of native oaks and plants line the tram route to the museum. These native trees double as fire protection since they are resistant to wildfire and provide erosion control. The gardens surrounding the museum include a natural ravine, reflecting pool, fountains, casual seating, and more than 1,000 species of plants. Tours of the gardens are offered daily as well.

There is one additional peripheral that impacts on the experience. Architects eager to protect the priceless art collection from broken water pipes decided to include only a few rest room facilities at the site.

 There's nothing like the selection of fitness and exercise classes and programs that reflect the ways in which peripherals are connected with the variety of needs and interests of people:

- The Mindful Body in San Francisco offers classes in Bikran Basics, Somatic Exploration, and Creative Visualization.
- The Chelsea Piers Sports and Entertainment Complex of New York City offers pre- and postnatal classes.
- In Philadelphia, the Market West Athletic Club offers "aerofunk" classes that combine aerobics with funky music.
- Brick's Women's Health and Fitness Club in Baltimore includes a Breast Wellness Center.
- San Fran Club One offers aerobic classes called "street jam" as well as Latino salsa classes.
- The Bath & Racquet Club of Sarasota, Florida, offers Basic Training Boot Camp for six weeks of military style training with certified personal instructors.
- At Fitnois in San Francisco, members work up a sweat without moving a muscle during the 45-minute visualization workout.
- The Old Texas Barbell Co. in Lockhard, Texas, takes a back-to-basics approach. This "old-style" gym and iron-pumping museum has iron weights and benches along with no heat or air conditioning. No music is allowed.

The experience of attending a performance of the Blue Man Group, an interactive performance art where three blue performers backed by a rock band make music on plastic tubes, splash paint, have food fights, and satirize the society and most particularly the information age starts as soon as people enter the theater with many of them being handed plastic raincoats to wear as protection during the performance. The electronic communication board spotlights specific members of the audience by name for five seconds of fame and recognition by fellow theatergoers. Right before the show starts, the ushers pass out strips of paper streamer for people to wrap around their heads indicating they are ready and eager to participate in the performance.

The participation part of the experience is just that. It has a heavy reliance upon participation from the audience. The audience is invited to read from three different sets of poster board and electronic message boards. Some people even get to take to the stage and paint a personal portrait. The performance culminates with all members of the audience pulling on paper from "toilet-paper like" rolls to the tune of blaring music and strobe lights and wrapping themselves and the rest of the audience in one giant paper mountain.

After the performance, the postexperience kicks into full force. A lucky few people can purchase (for $25) the actual paintings created in the performance they attended. The rest of the attendees can walk out of the theater and receive personally autographed "blue" kisses from the three blue men awaiting them on the sidewalk. The fun of this performance has resulted in productions in New York, Boston, and Chicago and has created a Rocky-Horror-ish cult following as well.

❖ "St. Francis Care Today—Where Health Works" is a television program created by St. Francis Hospital and Medical Center to promote health and explain disease.

❖ The nonprofit education group, Aish HaTorah, conducts seminars worldwide portraying Judaism as offering spiritual fulfillment and a sense of belonging.

❖ The downtown churches in Concord, New Hampshire, open their sanctuaries every New Year's Eve to serve as event sites for the community's First Night Celebration.

❖ The Synergy Health and Fitness Center in Boulder, Colorado, gets the word out about its rehabilitative services by offering brown bag lunch lectures at local corporations and high schools.

❖ The Scribes of St. Peter founded by Benedictine monk Brother Woodworth produce spiritually-oriented Web sites to keep people in closer contact with the word of God.

❖ The Joselin Clinic sponsors Live 'n' Learn Cruises to help diabetics learn how to live with their disease even while on vacation.

❖ The San Diego Zoo holds a Roar and Snore and the zoo in Asheville, North Carolina, has the Zoo Snooze as both facilities use fun-filled sleepovers as ways to reach the family market.

❖ University Community Hospital in Tampa, Florida, held a full-day celebration for seniors complete with health screenings, lectures, a craft show, a luncheon, and door prizes that culminated with a senior prom, a semiformal affair with big band era music and special guest Debbie Reynolds.

❖ The Museum of Fine Arts in Boston put a 500-pound gorilla on its door step, gave away promotional baseball caps and let everybody under 17 years of age in for free as a way to engage the younger market.

❖ HIP Health Plans gave out free, prepaid 10-minute phone cards to anyone requesting information during its enrollment period.

❖ James Broughton, the mastermind behind the mega-exhibits that started with King Tut, had great success taking curator shows like Ramses the Great, Catherine the Great, Napoleon, and the Splendors of Ancient Egypt on the road to medium-sized communities.

❖ At Kids Fest sponsored by the Aurora, Colorado, Parks, Recreation, and Television Services Department, the local branch of the postal service set up an outpost office on site and manned a crafts booth where children could design postcards to send to relatives. The event logo was used as a special cancellation stamp.

❖ The Florida Aquarium stocks and maintains two large aquariums in the baggage area of the renovated Tampa International Airport introducing arriving visitors to their presence.

❖ St. John Siegfried Health Club and St. John Medical Center in Tulsa, Oklahoma, air "Get Cookin'," a weekly television spot, on the local station on Fridays during the early news segment. The show features the St. John wellness dietitian and the executive chef of the medical center highlighting recipes that are quick, easy, tasty, and healthy.

People

The second P of experience marketing is people, and as with other organizations and companies in the experience industry, the role of people, their patterns and

Integrating important gender, age, and cultural aspects from the second P, people, with a lifestyle marketing approach is critical to the success and profitability of the healthcare industry. A few examples of such approaches include (Jeffrey, 1996, p. 9):

- The office of Oxford Health Plan in New York City's Chinatown has a Cantonese speaking receptionist who can greet patients in their native language when they enter.
- Mexican Americans use the word *rayos* when referring to x-rays while Cuban Americans call them *placas.* HMOs are making those type of subtle adjustments in their marketing materials.
- A Cigna Corporation clinic in Phoenix, Arizona, schedules a bilingual, female gynecologist for Hispanic women one day each week.
- A Cigna-owned hospital in Albuquerque, New Mexico, has relaxed its policies on visits to the intensive care unit to allow Hispanic patients to visit longer with their family members.
- Managed care plans across the country are setting up bi- or multilingual customer service phone lines, recruiting ethnic physicians, and training staff to be culturally sensitive.

preferences, is critical to the success of experience marketing techniques for the enhancers. The 4Cs of this P are core, culture, choice, and change. These coordinates include an entire range of people-related variables including age, gender, cohort, household, values, attitudes, life stages, life events, and seasons or cycles.

The vastness of variety inherent within this P of the experience marketing mix make it a significant component within the overall marketing strategies for personal and community service providers. As these providers look to enhance the lives of the individuals and groups they serve, they need to know who they are and what they want out of life and life's experiences.

Experience infusers employ the full range of the 4C of people to revise their experiences to better meet the requirements of each consumer group or as a means of specifically designing services for particular particle markets. A number of churches have added basketball leagues, mentoring programs, new fathering classes, and programs for divorced and single men as a way to attract them to their congregations. The Wang Center, a theater in Boston, sponsors a drama club for teenagers, workshops for teachers and the Young At Arts community outreach program targeting high-school students as potential art lovers.

Willow Creek Community Church started life in a converted theater in Palatine, Illinois, in 1975 where Bill Hubels preached to a congregation of about 100 people. Twenty-plus years later that same church is a super church with a 145-acre campus in South Barrington, Illinois, that draws 17,000 attendees every weekend. How has this church managed to grow in this way? One of its secrets is that it doesn't treat all churchgoers the same. Right from the beginning, Bill Hubels realized that he had to hold two different types of church services— one for believers and one for what he calls seekers. Hubels believed that he couldn't create a service that met the needs of both those who already believed in God and those who weren't sure about the whole concept of God.

❖ The Fitness for Her & Day Spa in San Diego has a New Member Motivator program, a 30-day trial membership to make sure people are getting exactly what they want.

❖ Responding to requests for unique events, aquariums, zoos, and museums rent their facilities to groups for parties, fund-raisers, weddings, and other community celebrations.

❖ Colleges and universities hold alumni parties in different regions of the country to create ongoing connections with people who hold promise for their ongoing viability.

❖ Fitness networking systems which include cardiovascular and strength-training machines are connected to a central kiosk and function as an automated personal trainer. Exercisers register their PIN and machines automatically set up for a customized workout.

❖ Alamo offers Quicksilver service for its frequent car rental customers. A personalized file is activated by the customer's credit card at the kiosk so that preferred customers don't have to wait in line. It also does double duty by profiling the service preferences of those preferred customers as well.

❖ The Pampered Professional is a concierge-by-phone service that shops, delivers, makes reservations, and much more all with one toll-free call.

❖ Responding to the preferences of their customers, Amtrak is adding more business-club cars to its fleet with computer power sources, telephone lines, and meal services. It is even adding smoking cars for some of its long-distance routes.

❖ Quest, a peer-learning community for older adults held at City College of New York, has 140 members who with the assistance of one paid administrative assistant runs and teaches over 40 courses. Classes include a variety of topics such as short stories, American musical theater, the philosophy of Plato, and recreational math.

❖ Spinning, an indoor cycling program, invites participants on a journey of the mind and body that takes people on an incredible 40-minute workout where the customer climbs mountains or moves across deserts in an effort to maintain participation and motivation in exercise.

❖ To expedite travel which is part of its promise to its customers, the Dulles Toll Road in Virginia used FASTOLL, a credit card payment system that let users zip through special computerized lanes on the road. Ironically, the name FASTOLL was so successful that it led to higher than warranted driving conditions and had to be changed to SMARTPASS.

❖ The Tampa, Florida, airport was ranked number one in a passenger survey recently completed by Plog Research, Inc. Tampa rated highest in five of the eight areas important to travelers: quick baggage delivery, close-in parking, easy-to-reach gates, available ground transportation, and understandable signs (Huettel, 1998, pp. 1, 6).

The seeker services at Willow Creek Community Church are different from the services for the believers. These services are more anonymous, nonparticipatory experiences that include art, drama, multimedia, dance, and video. These services often focus on important issues of the day such as parenting, marriage, relationships, or concerns of the workplace which are discussed in a auditorium devoid of any religious symbols. Additional variations for the seeker services include Saturday night services with topics, music, and drama specifically tar-

How do you define outdoor recreation? Is it bowhunting, horseback riding, golf, or hiking? There are a variety of definitions for outdoor recreation that are based on differences in customer's perceptions and preferences. The Ohio State Park system features a variety of outdoor recreation experiences to meet the variations in these definitions. The 207,000 acres of nature includes 80,000 acres of water for summer recreation pursuits such as fishing, boating, and swimming. Winter provides a setting for sledding, cross-country skiing, snowmobiling, and ice-skating.

The actual facilities and amenities within those facilities vary as well. There are eight resort lodges featuring full-service accommodations and conference facilities that include championship golf courses, indoor pool and sun deck, exercise room, whirlpool and sauna, dining rooms, and lounges. At the other end of the amenity spectrum are natural sites treasured for their lack of the basics such as electricity and flush toilets.

Even camping has different definitions within this park system as evidenced by the different types of rental packages offered such as:

- Rent-A-Camp, which includes a lodge-style tent, dining canopy, cots and sleeping pads, cooler, propane stove, and a lantern or lamp;
- Rent-A-RV, which treats campers to the comforts of home with a travel trailer equipped with a refrigerator, stove, microwave, color TV, AM/FM radio and cassette player with stereo, furnace, air conditioner, and private bath with shower;
- Rent-A-Teepee, complete with an 18-foot teepee attached to a wooden platform; and
- Houseboat Rental, for a unique experience that features a boat with a galley equipped with a sink, refrigerator, stove, microwave, TV, VCR, stereo system and other amenities.

geted for Generation X members as well as a new ministry called "seeker small groups" targeting the upsurge in loneliness and alienation among people (Webber and Row, 1997, p. 130).

Peripherals

The third P of experience marketing, peripherals, refers to those factors and variables related to and involved in the entire process. Peripherals add substance and definition to the experience by incorporating factors such as place, price, packaging, policies, public image, patterns of demand, and popularity cycle into the entire experience itself.

Experience enhancers are continually trying to serve and support the ongoing lives of their customers, patrons, or residents. Their efforts to sustain their lifestyles, meet their personal needs and expectations to enhance the overall quality of their daily lives often result in changes within this P. These changes can be subtle or more sizable and visible, but the end result is usually a significant impact on the experience.

Experience infusers have pumped up peripherals as a way of making personal and community services more appealing and convenient. Australian Body

Pueblo West Total Fitness won recognition as the State-of-the-Art, Fitness-Only Health Club from *Fitness Management* in 1997 because of its customer matching efforts. Prior to designing or building the facility, the owners of the 14,500 square foot facility clearly identified people who are deconditioned as their target market along with the specific needs that such a group brings to a health club. In addition, it decided to eliminate amenities offered by competing health clubs and in doing so created a facility that was a "fitness-only, customer-service-oriented center that appeals to the deconditioned population."

The $620,000 facility spent the majority of its construction dollars on features and layouts designed to increase member satisfaction. The building includes high ceilings for an open feeling, independent shower stalls and changing areas for privacy and comfort, natural lighting, and air conditioning. The service focus incorporated the full range of medical, nutritional, exercise, and holistic specialists.

The facility opened in the summer which is traditionally the slowest season in the industry and surpassed membership projections in less than three months (Nova 7 Finalists, 1997, p. 26).

Works set up space in a grocery store to bring fitness to locations people frequent and find convenient. At the University of Nevada at Reno, students can live in three-bedroom, two-bathroom suites with a living area, kitchen, thermostat control, and wiring for computer technology. West View Health Club in New York City renovated its facility to take on a more spa-like setting converting its kiddy pool to a rock garden with waterfall while Better Bodies Club in Los Angeles includes art as part of its workout space.

Graceland Chapel in Las Vegas is not affiliated with Graceland of Memphis, Tennessee, but with its blessing, puts together wedding packages. The Rev. Norman Jones will dress in a black, beaded jumpsuit upon request. The bridal couple can rent the chapel which seats 120 people for $55 with an additional $40 for limousine service if desired. Married couples renewing their vows receive a copy of Elvis' original marriage license, a renewal certificate, and a ceremony that ends with a sing-along recording of "Viva Las Vegas."

PerInfoCom

PerInfoCom, the P of experience marketing that replaces the traditional approach of promotion, is a challenging aspect of experience marketing for the enhancer industries. Mass transportation, hospitals, and community resources generally need to attract the interest, attention, and participation of entire communities, especially diverse groups of people. They have had to create innovative approaches to reach out and connect with these different groups. Personal service providers generally are able to focus on a narrower segment of the market or to target their service on a particular need or preference, but in those instances it is critical that the message and delivery match the needs and desires of potential customers for whom the service has been developed or designed.

❖ Now people can have it all, good health and splendor and comfort, when they enroll in the Pritkin Longevity Center at the Lowes Santa Monica Beach Hotel. The luxury of this four-star beach front hotel is combined with physicians, dietitians, exercise physiologists, and lifestyle counselors who encourage and aid guests to create the lifestyle changes needed to live a healthier life free of heart disease and diabetes.

❖ Northwest Airlines limits most coach passengers to one carry-on bag with the exception of their WorldPerks Gold members who can carry on two bags.

❖ St. Elizabeth's Hospital in Beaumont, Texas, developed a fitness center that has the requisite 50 classes but goes beyond that with team and individual sports to create an atmosphere where people can meet friends and reach for a higher quality of life.

❖ TWA allows passengers who pay full fare into its airport Ambassador Club the day they travel, a privilege normally extended to first-class and business passengers only.

❖ *Harvard Magazine* runs personal classified ads for alumni and faculty helping them to make a match that's truly in their league.

❖ United Airlines implemented a priority rebooking policy that rebooks passengers, when an United flight is canceled, in descending order of how much they paid for their flight.

❖ Dr. Stanley Turecki who runs the Difficult Child Center in New York City visits families on their home turf to see how the family really interacts and functions with the terrible teen.

❖ Several new exhibits as well as a new display for the Hope Diamond resulted in a record-setting attendance year for the Smithsonian that attracted more than 27 million visitors in 1997, a 23 percent increase over 1996 (Hainer, 1998, p. 7D).

❖ The Good Samaritan Hospital and Medical Center in West Islip, New York, responded to the area's high rate for breast cancer by opening a Breast Health Center that provides access to early detection, education, screening, and treatment support.

❖ Old Army and Navy buddies and former sweethearts are among the people reunited through Old Friends Information System that locates people who have been lost to one another over time, and after securing the permission of the newly rediscovered person, releases the information to the searcher.

❖ When is a taxi more than a taxi? When it's the Ultimate Taxi, the brainchild of Jon Barnes of Aspen, Colorado, who cruises the streets while passengers experience the mirrored disco ball, laser lights, party supplies, and surf the Net. Live pictures of his passengers show up on his home page.

❖ Meetings Connections was formed in Maine to secure the assistance of its residents in encouraging and persuading the groups and organizations to which they belong to consider Maine as a convention or conference site.

There are a wide variety of options within this experience marketing variable which the experience enhancers have actively pursued. Personal service providers and community resource providers are dependent for their very existence on the ability to reach people in need of their service. In addition, they need

At one time the Sears Tower was the tallest building in the world and as such attracted more visitors and tourists than its nearby neighbor the John Hancock Center which was 14 floors shorter. Both buildings towered over the city of Chicago and offered not just a view, but the history of the city also. When the Petronas Towers in Kuala Lumpur, Malaysia, was completed in 1996, Sears lost its world's tallest status, and Chicago was left with just two tall buildings and no world title.

The Hancock building decided to undertake a major renovation to update its 25-year-old approach and to compete with the Sears Towers for people interested in gaining a view of the city. It set about to create an experience that would surpass the usual approach and clearly differentiate itself as the more desirable community resource and attraction.

U. S. Equities Realty brought together MRA International, Edwards Technologies, and Lexington Scenery & Props who created three mini-experiences, Quicktime, Soundscope, and the Skywalk. Quicktime takes the visitor on a virtual tour of the city complete with specific information about the identified attractions. Soundscope involves talking telescopes that can describe the sights of the city in four different languages and comes complete with sound effects such as traffic noise, waves crashing, and chirping birds. The Skywalk has traded the glass enclosure for screens that allow the visitor to feel the wind of the Windy City whip through his or her hair.

Not only do these renovations differentiate the Hancock experience from the Sears Tower, they are value enhancing. Why just see the sights of a city when you can hear and feel the city as you gather information to plan your visit. Hancock couldn't change the size of its building, and it couldn't eliminate the Sears Tower as competition, but it could and did use experience marketing to capture the imagination and admission fee of visitors traveling to the city (Kane, 1997, p. 6).

to gain recognition and appreciation from groups of individuals who may not even use their services.

There is no end to the challenges of communication for businesses and organizations who attempt to enhance experiences. The University of Massachusetts used famous alum Bill Cosby, wearing a baseball cap and sweatshirt, to inform prospective students of the successful people who attended the institution. Pictures and comments from other alumni including basketball legend Julius Erving, Boston Celtics coach Rick Pitino, astronaut Catherine Coleman, and John Welch and John Smith, CEOs of General Electric and General Motors respectively, round out the commercial.

Experience infusers go to great lengths and make use of PerInfoCom options in an effort to do exactly that—infuse elements of an experience into their service. The Treasure Coast Blood Bank in Fort Pierce, Florida, offered round-trip, one-day cruises to Freeport on Grand Bahama Island to anyone donating a pint of blood during its slow months. D. C. Chartered Health Plan gave away Thanksgiving and Christmas packages to new members during its open enrollment period. Mount Sinai Medical Center in Miami Beach works year round with condo developers to attract new patients by forwarding welcome packets through referrals from the builders.

A number of factors such as growing demands being placed on the local tax base, the advent of charging fees for its facilities and services and the increase in alternative service providers created a positioning challenge for public parks and recreation. This sector of local services had long been providing programs and services for preschoolers up to senior citizens as well as natural areas and facilities such as ball fields, hiking trails, and community open space that would not have existed without its stewardships.

When more and more of the public began to picture the industry as just for kids and sports, the National Recreation and Park Association took on the goal of repositioning this public service from a nicety to a necessity. It created a project and program called *Putting the Pieces Together—The Benefits of Parks and Recreation.* The immediate outcome was both internal and external. It provided people working within this field a chance to rekindle their sense of purpose, value, and worth as a community resource. In addition, it gave the providers of this community resource marketing information to communicate clearly to the public. Crafted by Leisure Lifestyle Consulting, Inc. it brought together research information as well as actual examples in order to remind the public what parks and recreation does for individuals, the community, the economy, and the environment.

Making Customer Matches

Making the right kind of customer matches may be the overriding challenge to this segment of the experience industry. It answers the perennial question, "How does one make important aspects of life more comfortable, convenient, accessible, and personal for the variety of people each provider attempts to serve?" This is not an easy challenge. Hospitals, museums, and park and recreation departments must attempt to serve all groups residing within a community. Fitness clubs and public transportation providers face similar challenges in trying to change the behavior of people when they are perfectly content with the status quo. Other providers such as airlines and planned communities must zero in on the exact needs and preferences of their customers.

None of these is an easy challenge to address, but attempts at doing so are greatly advanced when organizations make a concerted effort to provide what people want. How do they define comfort, convenience, and accessibility? What changes are taking place in the behavior patterns and preferences of people these organizations are trying to attract?

In a number of instances, close attention to the changing or emerging needs of people has resulted in the creation of new businesses or entire new industries. Personal trainers got their start because people had different exercise and fitness needs and required a convenient way to add this activity to their already busy lives. Closet designers got their start when people were unable or unwilling to organize that particular aspect of their lives.

Enterprise Rent-A-Car has grown more than 25 percent a year for the past 11 years and has done so by identifying a need that people had that the other rental

❖ The Rev. Charles Henderson, formerly a Presbyterian minister, is the founder of the First Church of Cyberspace, an interfaith, virtual sanctuary with sermons, movie reviews, Christian art and music.

❖ The Columbia Miami Heart Institute opened a Center for Alternative Medicine and Longevity, the first hospital-based alternative medical center in the United States that brings together the traditional medicine of the West with the holistic approach of the East. The center offers 30 different alternative approaches to treatment including therapeutic herbology, Chinese medicinals, Ayurveda, and energy medicine. Entering patients are examined by an internist who then makes recommendations to the medical board comprised of both traditional physicians and alternative medicine professionals.

❖ Bilbao, a rapidly deteriorating industrial city of Spain with a serious public relations problem, decided to use culture as a way to counter its bleak, industrial image and did so by joining in a unique partnership with Guggenheim Foundation of New York to construct a "branch" museum that provides the city with the same sort of identity as Sydney with its opera house.

❖ Baptist Hospital and Health Systems in Phoenix, Arizona, redefined itself and now operates three hospitals, a long-term care apartment building, and a home health agency as well as a Wellness Connection in two area shopping malls where shoppers are given coupons for tests and screenings to be conducted at one of its hospitals.

❖ When Greyhound Bus Lines bought Trailways, it maintained the corporate policy of providing return transportation home for runaways.

❖ Franklin Memorial Hospital in Farmington, Maine, established a barter system to assist the underinsured patients for whom it provided services. Patients without insurance can work off their hospital bill by providing the hospital with their time and talent.

❖ Airport Fitness Centers, health clubs conveniently located at airports, was the brainchild of fitness enthusiast Michael Michno who spent numerous hours in airports. For $11.25 the traveler gets use of treadmills, stair climbers, and weights as well as free shampoo, soap, deodorant, and other toiletries. Shoes, T-shirts, and shorts can be rented for an additional $3.50.

❖ Organ transplants, the next frontier of healthcare, joined with technology resulting in Xpedite, a pilot program of the Virginia Organ Procurement Agency that beats the clock on organ matching by transmitting donor information electronically to all participating hospitals.

❖ Some of the more innovative private learning companies and human resource consultants are adding or expanding on experiences as part of the education. Outward Bound–type experiences have been supplanted by corporate executives visiting Civil War battlegrounds and learning important lessons in leadership from long dead generals.

❖ Lakeland Regional Hospital in Florida broke up its 897-bed hospital into 40-bed minihospitals with self-contained labs and admissions. These minihospitals were further broken up into microhospitals where Care Pairs, a registered nurse and technician, performed 90 percent of the pre- and postoperative requirements for five to seven patients (Peters, 1998, p. 128).

 **Slice of Life** Urban centers are undergoing great transformations some of which are rather challenging. These changing urban conditions impact on a number of colleges and universities located in these urban areas in less than positive ways. Less than desirable neighborhoods, unsafe streets, and competition from rural and suburban campuses for the same group of students has forced many institutions to turn their attention to their relationship with their community. Some of the transforming choices and changes that these institutions have made include the following (Marklein, 1997, p. 11D):

- Yale University, situated for nearly 300 years in the center of New Haven, Connecticut, has launched a number of community initiatives including the design and construction of a home in a nearby, low-income neighborhood by architectural students; providing mortgage assistance for employees who agree to purchase a house in the city; and converting a dilapidated building into a home for the Yale School of Arts.
- University of Illinois at Chicago combines child-care training for people who provide day-care services for employees of the University.
- Clark University in Worcester, Massachusetts, became a true neighborhood partner when it started a secondary school for neighborhood children and developed a light industrial park to bring jobs to the area.
- Trinity College in Hartford, Connecticut, brought together community activists, private investors, nonprofit groups, and local government to revitalize the area marked by empty storefronts and boarded up houses which has resulted in a $2.9 million face lift. This initiative will create a 14-acre Learning Corridor near Trinity's campus that will be made up of Montessori, middle and high schools; day-care services; a home for the arts; and a science and technology center.

companies seemed to overlook entirely—the local replacement market. In fact, this market that previously had been barely noticed now accounts for 40 percent of the rental car market. Enterprise grew and prospered by becoming the spare car that customers didn't have to own as it delivered cars to people whose cars were in for repairs or were too small or too unreliable for an upcoming family trip. A survey conducted by Enterprise found that 63 percent of people would rather do without a phone for a day than without a car. The pick up and drop off is a key aspect of this service. It seems so obvious, but it took this company to realize that if a customer needed to rent a car, there was a good chance he or she didn't have transportation to go over to its location to pick it up (Jones, 1997, p. 13B).

These pieces of information are critical to completing the puzzle that eventually results in the creation of experiences that both meet people's needs and work harmoniously with their lifestyles. The necessity of connecting with patients or patrons at the point of first contact is crucial to making them lifelong supporters and participants with an organization. The more progressive hospitals are recruiting care partners—friends or relatives of the patient—who are willing to work through the procedures and the recovery period as a member of the health-care team while two of the largest hospitals in the country, Parkland Hospital in Dallas and Catholic Medical Center in Brooklyn and Queens, have changed their policy to allow "family presence" in the emergency room. The Department of Psychiatry at Massachusetts General Hospital uses voice mail to let people conduct their own screening system for depression, providing them with privacy and convenience. At the end of the screening, people are given a rating for the level of their depression along with suggestions for corresponding courses of action.

Marketing Changes

The individual needs, interests, and desires are continually changing, and customers have now come to expect that organizations will automatically incorporate these new priorities and preferences into their experiences. Such an expectation on the part of the consumer requires organizations to recognize and act on emerging marketing strategies. At one time people were comfortable allowing doctors and hospitals to tell them what to do and how to deal with their health problems. They were content to enroll in a fitness program for a few months to lose a couple of pounds at the start of a new year or before bathing suit season. Those approaches have changed as people now want, actually insist upon having, more control and involvement in the services that involve them personally.

Competition has also made a difference. The airline industry is a good example of the impact of competition. What happens when most of the flights leave at approximately the same time for the same destination at exactly the same price? What's an airline to do? Southwest responded by offering the best price and adding a personalized feel for the customer. Delta decided to launch Delta Express, a lower-priced, no frills operation to some destinations with a great deal of competition. United Air Lines went with the business traveler and re-

Close **Seup**

US Airways, formerly US Air, decided to reinvent itself by changing its name, but it went beyond that by starting a new low-fare airline division as well. Nothing incredibly earth-shattering about that since both United and Delta had made the same kind of move earlier. The real excitement about this new airline division was the way in which US Airways used its human resources for this start-up effort.

It pulled together employee teams from throughout all levels of the company—mechanics, flight attendants, reservation agents, pilots, everybody—to spend four months working on this project. Much of their time and attention was directed at ways to address Southwest Airlines' venture into US Airway's East Coast markets.

Michael Scheeringa, the coach of the team, rallied the union employees, hourly workers, managers, manual workers, and professionals together with a game plan that called for pairing team members up and sending them out to work in other US Airways jobs as well as flying on other airlines. Armed with lists, stopwatches, cameras, and questionnaires, this team took on decisions and choices both big and small that needed to be made about this new airline division.

It then made decisions about coach seating, boarding procedures, and a variety of techniques for getting an airplane "turned around," unloaded, cleaned, fueled, catered, boarded, and headed out again. US Airways not only got a new airline, but it also created an airline that reflects the knowledge, expertise, and enthusiasm of its most important resource, its employees (Wall Street Journal, 1998, pp. B1, B7).

tooled its operation to meet his or her needs. American Airlines responded with world travel partners to create a global network.

Terms such as value-enhanced, mass customization, and share of the experience are critical in this part of the experience industry as experience enhancers strive to reposition themselves in an ever-changing world. The Children's Corner,

Bottom

Line

❖ At the Landings on Sidaway Island in Savannah, Georgia, half-acre wooded interior building lots go for about $40,000 while half-acre lots on the golf course cost $90,000 to $120,000 (Dugas, 1997, B2).

❖ Before the outreach program for men at Resurrection Lutheran Church in Roxbury, Massachusetts, 80 percent of the church's new members were women. Due to current efforts nearly half of the new members are men (Ribadeneira, 1998, p. A5).

❖ The National Center for Educational Statistics reported that 40 percent of Americans participated in adult education in 1995 which was an increase from the 32 percent participation level in 1991 (Henig, 1998, p. 13A).

❖ It is estimated that the average conventioneer spends $210 per day on hotel, food, and miscellaneous items. The city of Las Vegas alone draws 200,000 people to conventions a year with an annual $280 million boost to the economy (Berner, 1996, B1).

❖ The "Get Cookin'" television spot created by the St. John Siegfriend Health Club and St. John Medical Center of Tulsa, Oklahoma, reaches 75,000 people in the Tulsa area and has resulted in the publication and sales of a *Get Cookin' Cookbook*. What's even more impressive is that the cooking spots which would have cost between $200,000 and $250,000 cost the hospital nothing except staff time (Nova 7 Finalists, 1997, p. 31).

❖ As soon as an Enterprise Rent-A-Car site grows to 150 cars, it opens another outlet a few miles away. The company indicates that it is now within 15 minutes of 90 percent of the U. S. population (Jones, 1997, p. 13B).

❖ *The Guide to Cooking Schools* had 604 listings in 1992 and increased more than 30 percent to nearly 800 listings in 1997 (Henig, 1998, p. 13A).

❖ Since Trinity College in Hartford, Connecticut, joined with its community partners to create a Learning Corridor, applications to the institution have increased 34 percent between 1995 and 1997 resulting in more selective admission rates going from 57 percent to 43 percent (Marklein, 1997, p. 11D).

❖ The Frogs Athletic Club in Encinitas, California, expanded its children's programming and while doing so increased its annual revenue base by three percent (Loyle, 1996, p. 32).

❖ Educational Institute, a subsidiary of the American Hotel and Motel Association, with its "enter-trainment" approach to education trained personnel at 16,000 hotels in 1997 with an estimated income of $7.5 million (Alexander, 1998, p. 8B).

❖ A Meetings Connections approach to attracting conventions to an area was implemented in Cleveland, Ohio, and resulted in bringing 90 meetings worth $36 million to the community in its first year (Collins, 1996, p. B11).

❖ As a result of its changes based on "patient-focused" care, Lakeland Regional Hospital in Florida reduced the time of routine tests from 157 to 48 minutes, reduced the number of employees that a patient encountered in a multiday stay from 53 to 13, and raised satisfaction levels among both patients and physicians (Peters, 1998, p. 130).

a day-care center in Ridgefield, Connecticut, installed a video system that allows parents to check in on their kids during the day via the Internet. For $25 a company called Complain to Us will write the letters, work the phones, and climb the corporate ladder to fight for unhappy consumers who are unwilling or unable to take the time and effort to challenge corporations over a problem transaction or purchase.

Organizational Change

Change is the keyword in this aspect of experience marketing. There are a number of aspects of change included in this category such as the shift from management to leadership and organizational change in use of resources and their definition of competition. However, probably one of the biggest changes for experience enhancers is how they change their mission, vision, and delivery to ensure

Action Agenda

All players within the experience industry can benefit by taking a look at marketing options practiced by other experience providers. This applies to techniques and strategies developed and utilized by experience enhancers as well. Try to imagine how some of these approaches can work for your part of the experience industry:

- Take a trip to your local hospital or interview someone who has been a patient at one recently and borrow a page from its new medical manual, especially ideas that blend together the best from high-tech and high-touch.
- Turn back the hands of time and recreate a visit to your local library. Be sure to look around and recall the specifics of the peripherals, the facility, the staff, and the ambiance. Take your "old visit" list and compare it to ways in which today's libraries function. In what ways does this suggest possible changes for your product, service, or experience?
- The next time you have the opportunity to take a train or plane, take a small notebook with you and jot down all the ways from beginning to end that your trip could become a more customer-centered experience.
- Examine the lives of three family members and friends, and brainstorm personal services not currently in the marketplace that would make their lives easier, happier, or more enriched.
- Sometimes people just get together and informally or with loose organization create opportunities for an experience that particularly draws them. Can you think of any such experiences that could be transformed into a business opportunity for your organization or as a new venture?
- Make a list of the tasks or daily life experiences that you personally find boring, too challenging, or just don't have time to undertake. What can this list tell you about people's needs and possible preferences for new products, services, or experiences?

future success and long-term viability. This is probably the marketing aspect with the greatest potential impact.

Such changes can be relatively small, such as finding a new way to generate additional revenues or to identifying a very different kind of service organization for use in benchmarking. It can also be much more encompassing as when an organization reenvisions who it is and how it might go about serving people or is being perceived by its partners or customers. Columbia Medical Center in Phoenix used the pizza delivery guarantee as its benchmark for emergency room services. Now if a person coming to the emergency room has to wait more than 30 minutes, his or her visit is free of charge.

Whether the change is small and incremental or larger in scope, these changes in how experience enhancers view themselves and their customers, patients, visitors, or patrons is critical to their future. Better Bodies Club in Los Angeles treats patrons to an art gallery as part of the gym motif. The selected works include painting and metal art priced at $2,000 and up and the club retains 30 percent of each sale.

The College of the Ozarks in Point Look, Missouri, admits students who are primarily from Midwestern farms or families who have worked overseas as missionaries and are not afraid of hard work. These students pay no tuition but work

Transition Tracking

From   **To**

Experience enhancers have changed in a great many ways but a few of the major shifts include:

- *Professionally Powered to Participant Partners*—Giving birth, looking at art, raising children, or growing old was at one time defined by the professionals and experts of the given field. This has given way to people demanding and expecting to define their participation and experience in partnership with the professional provider.

- *Introverted to Extroverted*—People went everywhere or nearly everywhere—to the hospital, the library, the museum, the theater, and even school—with the admonition to be seen and not heard where now noise, voices, and laughter are an integral part of most of these experiences.

- *High-Tech or High-Touch to HighTech&Touch*—There was a time when people wanted the transportation or the medical care choice that had the latest technology available. There were other aspects of the industry where one-on-one, face-to-face contact was a requirement. The more that technology and scientific advances invaded hospitals, homes, classrooms, museums, and libraries, the more personal presence created a hardship for overburdened members of society, and a balance between the two, high-tech and high-touch, has been struck.

- *From a Nicety to a Necessity*—Access to a reputable medical center, parks and open space, the arts, and public transportation are just a few of the amenities that people have come to expect when deciding where to live, work, play, or retire.

15 hours a week on the 930-acre campus building classrooms, raising cattle, and running the college's fire department, airport, and restaurant. Room and board can be worked off as well by taking summer jobs on campus. This college withdrew from the federally insured college loan program to discourage students from accumulating thousands of dollars in debt before going out into the work force (Associated Press, 1998, p. A18).

Sources

Alexander, Keith L. (1998, March 24). Firm entertains while it trains. *USA Today.*

Armour, Stephanie. (1998, June 3). Personal services no longer a luxury. *USA Today.*

Associated Press. (1998, February 15). Nestled in Ozarks, college of hard work. *Boston Sunday Globe.*

Berner, Robert. (1996, October 1). Space glut intensifies cities' battle over conventions. *The Wall Street Journal.*

Collins, Rachel M. (1996, October 6). Pitching Maine as a convention state. *Boston Sunday Globe.*

Dugas, Christine. (1997, January 18). Gated living makes fairway fashionable. *USA Today.*

Nova 7 finalists. (1997, December). *Fitness Management.*

Galuszka, Peter, DeGeorge, Gail, Palmer, A. T., & McCann, Jessica. (1997, December 8). See the doctor, get a toaster. *Business Week.*

Grandjean, Pat. (1996, August). This is a hospital. *Connecticut.*

Hainer, Cathy. (1998, February 13). Smithsonian halls filled with more visitors in 1997. *USA Today.*

Henig, Robin Marantz. (1998, March 2). Adult-ed groupies grope for "aha" moment. *USA Today.*

Huettel, Steve. (1998, February 17). Passengers again rate TIA top airport. *The Tampa Tribune.*

Jeffrey, Nancy Ann. (1996, February). Breaking down barriers. *The Wall Street Journal Classroom Edition.*

Jones, Del. (1997, November 24). Enterprise rides on "spare car" niche. *USA Today.*

Kane, Gregory. (1997, August). Make it worth my while. *What's New for Family Fun Centers.*

Los Angeles Times. (1998, March 15). Laugh for no reason, and India laughs with you. *The Boston Globe.*

Loyle, Donna. (1996, February). Kid's programs and services. *Club Industry.*

Marklein, Mary Beth. (1997, November 12). Universities clean up neighborhoods. *USA Today.*

Peters, Tom. (1997). *Circle of innovation.* New York, NY: Alfred A. Knopf.

Renner, Gerald. (1998, February 2). Ailing churches placing faith in demographics. *Hartford Courant.*

Ribadeneira, Diego. (1998, February 16). Churches reaching out to men. *The Boston Globe.*

Spiegler, Marc. (1996, March). Scouting for souls. *American Demographics.*

Truehart, Charles. (1996, August). Welcome to the next church. *The Atlantic Monthly.*

Wall Street Journal. (1998, March 29). New airline planned from bottom up. *The Tampa Tribune.*

Webber, Alan M., & Row, Heather. (1997, October–November). How you can help them. *Fast Company.*

Signs of a Shift

Remember when birthday parties meant party games in the backyard and going on vacation meant two weeks at the beach or touring regional attractions in the family station wagon? Recall when all that ski resort operators needed to know was how to groom trails or that golf course operators just needed to know how to grow grass? Well, those days are over.

Going to the movies used to mean balancing overbuttered popcorn and candy while trying to find a seat in a row without a tall person in front to obstruct the view and attending a concert used to involve standing in long lines to go to the rest room, but no longer. These two aspects of the entertainment business have had to respond to customers' changing needs due to competition from entertainment options such as HBO, video rentals, and CDs.

Eating at a restaurant, staying at a hotel, going on vacation, or going out to the ball game have all taken on new meaning in the 1990s. Eating out at a restaurant can include munching in the midst of a rain forest, watching the kids tumble in the soft play area, or spending more on sweatshirts and souvenirs than on food. Hotel choices include specific benefits whether we are seeking good value, a good night's sleep, or a location that can double as an office. "Take me out to the ball game" now goes way beyond balls and strikes as fans can dine, shop, or sunbathe at the old ball park.

The days of basic amenities or activities have been replaced with the creation and provision of customer-centered experiences. The slope of the mountain or the green as well as the menu choices and the size of the hotel room are secondary to the ambiance, accouterments, and the pampered, intentional catering to the personal and inner needs of people that are utilized today to attract and retain patrons. Even professional sporting events share the spotlight with carnival-like contests at halftime with such innovations as souvenirs being projected via slingshot into the crowd, and scoreboards that tell fans when and what to cheer. Experience makers are continually redefining experiences as part of their marketing mix.

Chapter 13

Experience Makers

It's about immersing people in an experience that is entertaining and making them want to take that away with them in as many ways as possible.

Scott Adelson

Who, How, & What of Experience Makers

Who are experience makers? They would include everything from an individual owner of an unique bed and breakfast to major corporations such as Marriott or Disney and all types of operations and alternatives in between. Experience makers are not new to society. The ancient Greeks had their Olympics, and the Romans filled the coliseums for bread and circuses. People's desire to be entertained is as old as mankind itself.

There are a number of categories of enterprises that make up this segment of the experience industries. Included in these categories are the hospitality, travel, amusement, entertainment, sports, and products or enterprises that exist solely to create an experience for its participants. Hospitality refers to that ever-growing number and variety of eating and dining establishments as well as hotels or resorts. The travel industry which now includes cruises, tours, events, and destinations is growing at an incredibly rapid rate. The amusement and entertainment segments of the industry have spilled over into eatertainment, shoppertainment, and edutainment, but these industries still continue their strong viability as providers of experiences just for the sake of the experience. Amusement parks, water parks, family fun centers, casinos, and a variety of pastimes for kids of all ages are just a few of the alternatives within this segment of the industry.

- Music lovers spent $1.3 billion on concerts in 1997 (Associated Press, December 29, 1997, p. 23A).
- According to *Amusement Business,* a record 177.2 million people visited the 50 most frequented amusement parks in North America in 1997 (Associated Press, December 31, 1997, p. B1).
- Disney negotiated to pay the NFL $9.2 billion for eight years for the rights to three Super Bowls, every Sunday and Monday night game, the Pro Bowl, and the league's college draft (Meyers, 1998a, p. C1).
- A Roper Starch Worldwide survey found that 56 percent of Americans gambled at least once a week in 1996 (Heubusch, 1997, p. 35).
- The Tourism Works for America Council reported that in 1995, domestic and international travelers spent $421.5 billion in the United States with this amount soaring to approximately $1,017 billion when induced and indirect expenditure are added to the tally.
- A 30-second ad in prime time for 1998 Winter Olympic coverage in Nagano, Japan, sold for an average of $500,000 (Wells, 1998, p. 1B).
- Statistics from the Travel Industry Association of America reveal that 92 million Americans have gone on a soft adventure trip since 1992 (Reed, 1998, p. W5).

Hospitality

Two of the biggest drivers of the growing global economy are the travel and hospitality industries. Since people generally travel to a particular destination or for a specific reason, there is a close interdependency between these two industries and this travel creates the subsequent need for the hospitality extended by hotels and restaurants.

Many restaurants and dining settings have turned into experiences within themselves. At the Century City, California, restaurant, Dive! every 45 minutes or so, the lights begin to flash and the commands to "prepare to dive" and "flood torpedo tubes" booms through the restaurant. Ever since McDonald's added playgrounds and the first Hard Rock Cafe opened in London in 1971, restaurants plunged into the experience maker category.

Some refer to it as eatertainment or foodertainment, but regardless of what it is called, people are being attracted to restaurants not only on the basis of culinary delights, cost or how fast the food arrives, but also on the experiences afforded the diner. Trendy urban restaurants offer fusion foods that meld two or more ethnic cuisines into their menu and decor. Places such as Hard Rock Cafes and Planet Hollywood restaurants serve average food at somewhat inflated prices but have waiting lines for the chance to dine surrounded by memorabilia. The T-shirt and sweatshirt sales make the food almost a sideline.

Hotels have been impacted by the growth of experiences as well. The overnight accommodation options include a variety of experiences. There are value-oriented national motel chains, charming one-of-a-kind bed and breakfasts, as well as establishments that have designed or modified their rooms and amenities to accommodate differing target market groups and needs. Whether one is looking to spend the night in an igloo or prefers a good night's sleep in a predictable setting, this segment of the industry can accommodate.

Resorts round out this category. They are both different from and yet similar to restaurants and hotels. They do provide sleeping and eating facilities, but at resorts, these experiences are designed and specifically constructed as a vacation destination. There is great variety within this category as resorts can be simple or luxurious, remote or in the center of it all, leisurely or filled with non-stop action.

Travel

Travel and tourism is the third largest retail industry in the United States after automobiles and groceries. In addition to contributing to the economic well-being of local communities and the global economy, travel both provides and creates a vast array of differing experiences for people.

The variations in motivation and approaches to travel as well as industry specific responses to these needs are substantial. While there are different categories within the travel industry such as tour companies and cruise lines, and destinations created and events scheduled primarily for the purposes of attracting tourists, the number of different experiences inherent within this category defies simple categorization. What spells a vacation or fabulous trip to one person sounds like sheer drudgery to another. There are limitless options to travel experiences.

Recall the traditional image of cruising complete with hordes of gray-haired, fairly well-off people sitting and watching the world go by while they ate and ate and ate. Make way for a revised image. Cruise lines have done a superb job of changing the peripherals of the experience from food to destinations to activities while including the ship itself remaking cruises for the ever-evolving variety of would-be passengers.

There's a baseball field in the heart of Iowa's farm country that underlies the accuracy of the statement, "If you build it they will come," and come they do as people by the hundreds, thousands, and hundreds of thousands flock to destinations, fairs, and expositions, throughout the United States and the world. Building experiences around destinations or creating experiences at these destinations spells increases in business revenues and tax coffers alike at these places and events.

When it comes to this category of experiences, what is your preference? There is ecotourism, adventure travel, heritage tours, and a host of other options. People can take to the highways on their own or use wholesalers who can make travel arrangements, or they elect small tour companies to book unique tours and trips for them.

Amusement & Entertainment

The bread and circuses of ancient Rome and the medieval fairs of yesteryear are nothing in comparison with where experience makers have taken the amusement and entertainment industries. Sports bars with television sets in the rest rooms, movie theaters that serve drinks and dinner, and swimming facilities that resemble a rafting adventure are all part of the entries in this ever-growing world of experiences designed to amuse, entertain, and exist for no other reason than the pure pleasure of the participants.

Within these categories are a variety of different experience providers such as amusement parks, family fun centers, water parks, bowling alleys, and movie theaters. Newer entries into this category include a greater infusion of experiences into casino gambling as well as the appearance of adult amusement centers.

Sports

Sports have always been a metaphor for the commitment, endurance, challenges, and victories of society. However, professional sports in the United States are being threatened by the greed, defiance, and behavior of super-salaried superstars. The demands of team owners for bigger and better stadiums with the public footing the bill played havoc with their relationship with the public.

The hunger Americans have for the sport experience, however vicarious, has always benefited the purveyors of professional sports who understood the game was for all who would love it; not just for those who would play. Sport offers the spectator the thrill of the ring, court, diamond, or field. While sport has been an expression of our survivability and our enthusiasm for the quest, it has always been entertainment as well.

Professional sports such as baseball, football, and hockey as well as some supporters of amateur participation in golf and tennis are focusing on breathing renewed life into their activities. Baseball is trying to speed up the game because to many it's boring to watch on television. Hockey and football are trying to recruit new fans. The U. S. Soccer Federation has created Project 2010 sponsored by Nike in an effort to recruit and train young players with the ultimate goal of winning the World Cup by 2010.

Purveyors of sports activities or facilities are digging more deeply into their creativity and funding sources to create more authentic, challenging, and appealing opportunities for their participants. Let the games begin!

Experiences

A subtle but growing category within experience makers encompasses individuals or organizations whose sole purpose is to create a particular kind of an experience for their clients. Not since the resounding "De plane! De plane!" from the television show "Fantasy Island" have we been inundated with the variety of experiences that are being created to meet the growing needs of people to experience a different way of life or to take part in a fantasy or dream of their own whether big or small.

There are so many experiences from which to choose. One can take control of a military T-34A aircraft and be part of a simulated dogfight and copilot a real plane after a weekend program at the U. S. Space & Rocket Center in Alabama. One can head to the hills of Wyoming to help with the spring cattle drive and live the life of a real cowboy. Whatever one's dream or fantasy, it's likely there is an experience maker out there somewhere ready to provide it. So whether one wants to relive the Civil War complete with uniform, tent, field training, and a mock battle or join with the other boys of summer for fantasy baseball, these experiences are just a phone call or a weekend away.

Experience Makers Commonalties

Experience makers are unique in that they exist solely to engage or entertain people. They generally hold no pretense of contributing to the greater good of the individual or society as many of the experience enhancers did. While it's true that they may provide opportunities for families to play together, for people to gather and have a good time, they are essentially in place to meet individual preferences for a good time.

Experience makers provide people with opportunities and alternatives for:

- escaping reality for a period of time,
- interacting with others,
- facilitating a sense of belonging to a larger group, and
- meeting inner or psychic needs in a safe and socially acceptable manner.

This group of enterprises incorporates a wide variety of experience marketing tools and techniques in its approach to attracting and retaining customers.

Parameters of the Experience

The first P in the experience marketing mix is parameters of the experience which incorporates the actual dimensions and attributes of an experience. Components within this parameter include stages of the experience, the actual experience, need(s) being addressed through the experience, the other people involved in the experience, and the role and relationship with the provider of the experience.

For experience makers, the stages of the experience are really quite important as the preexperience goes a long way to build an anticipation that actually becomes part of the experience. A number of simulated adventure rides such as the Bermuda Triangle attraction at Sea World in San Diego establish the mood of anticipation for the experience before the participant even enters the attraction. They begin with Hugh Downs, the newscaster, warning of the dangers lurking within the Bermuda Triangle. When the staff dressed in "official" naval-looking uniforms solemnly direct the participant to stand on specific spots located on the floor of the briefing room, the level of anticipation skyrockets. Such approaches raise the adrenaline levels of the waiting participants.

Many tour companies forward their clients a list of recommended readings prior to the trip. Such readings serve double duty by extending the preexperience of the trip as well as heightening what the traveler takes away from the actual trip itself due to his or her securing a better understanding of the history or culture before the visit.

Concerts have become more about experiences and less about the music. The Grateful Dead with its legions of Deadheads who followed them around the country attests to the experiential nature of concerts. Jimmy Buffett fans, known as Parrot Heads, are well known for starting celebrations in the parking lot next

❖ The annual commemoration of the Battle of Antietam, one of the Civil War's bloodiest battles, is re-created with a number of authentic touches such as living-history encampments, a regimental string band, and reenactment of three battles.

❖ "Star Trek: The Experience" at the Las Vegas Hilton transports riders into the twenty-fourth century. Riders start by taking seats in a room shaped like a shuttle, but an incident lands them on a transporter pad aboard the Enterprise where they face a 22-minute mission to find their way back to their real place in time.

❖ LaPiste Debois in Quebec is an Inuit-style village of domed igloos, snow houses, teepees, and wigwams where visitors can simulate a native experience.

❖ Japiur, India, is the home of Oberoi Rajvilas, a palatial spa resort that was once the former playground of the maharajas. The high walls, spacious gardens, and turreted towers also include 14 "luxury tents" where guests have individual bungalows with billowy, pole-supported cloth ceilings.

❖ People can relive the *Titanic* experience over and over again by renting any of several videos, or they can sign-up with Quark Expeditions for a seat on a minisubmarine to venture two and a half miles under the surface of the ocean to view the "real" thing.

❖ The popular Rainforest Cafes have created what they call an environmentally conscious family adventure. They use only recycled paper and plastic goods, soybased inks for printing, and they don't serve net-caught fish or beef from deforested lands. The cafes also feature live and animated versions of animals, vegetation, and a periodic tropical rain storm.

❖ Actor George Hamilton teamed up with Hyatt Hotels to provide little pleasure domes for sipping martinis, smoking cigars, and playing backgammon in upscale lounges at some of the Hyatt resort locations in Florida and California.

❖ AMC Theaters installed "love seats" that give couples the option of lifting the arms between the seats so they can cuddle. This change in the experience complicates the decisions surrounding the first date situation.

❖ Bassless fishing tournaments are held throughout the Midwest in the winter months with anglers casting their lines into indoor swimming pools. A computer then determines whether the bait has been taken by a fish swimming in the location of the cast.

❖ VIA Railway Canada changed the Skeena, a train through the Western mountains to the Pacific, from an overnight train to a two-day train allowing passengers to see the wonderful scenery and wildlife between Jasper and Prince Tupert. The night is spent at a hotel.

to the concert venue days or hours before the Buffett concert. The cheeseburgers and the Margaritas in the parking lot are everywhere with an occasional swimming pool set up in the back of a pickup truck. Once inside the concert venue, fans compete in mock basketball for Buffett T-shirts. They are primed and ready to go by the time the concert starts.

Think of the trinkets, souvenirs, and pictures that are often part of an experience package. These items, like many of the peripherals within an experience,

One of the most popular areas of interest in recent years has been the fascination with the continent of Africa. The variations of this experience as created by experience makers reflect the differences between simulation and authenticity. "Take me to the Serengeti" has become the password of the experience industry as one experience maker after another has jumped on the safari wagon and is riding it to a greater revenue stream.

Spotlight on Success

There are numerous alternatives available for people to experience the Serengeti. IMAX Theaters throughout the country whisk the viewers across the sea and set them down in the plains of the Serengeti just in time to witness the migration of the zebras and the wildebeests that they've likely viewed on the Discovery Channel. The sights and sounds provided by the large, surround IMAX screen makes the viewers feel as if they are actually standing off to the side and can feel the earth shake as the hooves pound by them.

But that's just one of the simulated versions of the Serengeti. Creating an African experience that provides greater realism than a seat in a theater for the millions of people who can't afford or want to avoid the long, costly, and often risky travel to Africa has become the latest trend. The San Diego Zoo spent $7 million to create an African exhibit. Busch Gardens spent a combined $1 billion developing an African-themed attraction.

Walt Disney World, not to be outdone, opened a 500-acre Animal Kingdom where on safaris, riverboat rides, and jungle trails, visitors can observe animals in natural settings, participate in exciting adventures and learn about the dangers facing wildlife throughout the world. A former Florida cow pasture has been transformed into Kenya's Masai Mara complete with rutted roads, acacias trees, and a lagoon.

The thousands of participants who aren't content with the man-made version of a natural environment flock each year to the actual Serengeti to witness the twice a year migration. There are a host of travel companies providing such an experience, and, even then, there are variations to the type of experience with some lodges being located almost in the middle of the migration and with some tours accessing a more close-up look at life in the Serengeti either through luxury tented campsites or hot air balloon rides over the plains (Morris, 1997, p. 27).

serve a dual purpose. In this case, they create a revenue stream for the organization, but they also make memories for the participant while stretching the experience ad infinitum as the joy or excitement of the experience is carried away with the participant to be relived over and over again.

Actually, postexperience is often an important and memorable part of the entire experience. Consider how the size of the fish seems to grow with each recollection of the catch. Recall how friends and families come together and continually refer to those good times they've previously shared. Memories are an integral part of an experience.

The dimensions within the experience are a hotbed of alternatives for experience providers who would like to change, improve, or in some way differentiate their experience from others. Experience makers have incorporated a number of these components into their overall marketing strategies with particular emphasis on the dimensions of the experience itself which includes such factors as

* The Janus Jazz Festival, set in a natural amphitheater in Snowmass, Colorado, brings music to the mountains.
* Thousands of people showed up at Somerset Place State Historic Site in North Carolina for the tenth anniversary of the first Somerset Homecoming where descendants of those who lived on the Somerset Plantation, both the enslaved African Americans and members of the family that owned the estate, came together to share stories and tour the facility.
* Every March from Boston to Chicago to San Francisco, and plenty of points in between, longtime, well-attended garden shows bring a touch of spring to the landscape.
* The Albuquerque Balloon Festival and the Rose Bowl Parade not only draw thousands of visitors but are the two most photographed events in the world.
* Hilton Head, South Carolina, welcomes spring with its annual SpringFest with popular attractions such as a Chocolate Fair, WineFest, and a WingFest.

whether or not experiences are natural or man-made, real or virtual, customized or mass-produced, commonplace or unique.

Many experience makers have gone the distance when it comes to using parameters within the actual experience to address specific needs of people, to simulate exciting new experiences for them, to provide unique or unusual opportunities, and to enable them to interact and connect with other people in meaningful ways. Falling into this strategy would be the sizable number of festivals, fairs, and events that dot city landscapes and the countryside alike. Some places or events occur naturally such as the sunshine of Florida and Arizona attracting vacationers and retirees during the winter months, or the return of the swallows to Capistrano or solar eclipses. Other places and events have been created by man to bring people to a particular location. Few people ventured to the desert of Nevada or the wetlands of central Florida before legalized gambling or the advent of Disney and fewer still would show up in Pamplona, Spain, without the annual running of the bulls or West Springfield, Massachusetts, without the Big E every fall.

Fairs and expositions, be they local, state, or regional, have experienced great success in the late 1990s as they have managed to connect the old and more traditional ways of life with the new world. These fairs manage to have something for everybody, and the attendance proves it. Recent annual attendance figures approach 152 million passing through the gates of 3,238 fairs in North America (Shriver, 1996, pp. D1–2).

One year the Texas State Fair, the best attended fair in the country, had a tribute to Duke Ellington and a production of *Miss Saigon* as well as its legendary Texas Star Ferris Wheel. While the carnival and entertainment aspects of these events continue to grow, fairs remain the last vestige or outpost for rural America. The New Mexico State Fair features a Native-American village, and the Topsfield Fair in Massachusetts boasts the All-New-England Giant Pumpkin Contest. It's amazing that the cow barns and the pig pens are able to coexist with ostrich burgers and Internet demonstrations.

Clos seup

Bob Dowdell, a director and producer of fantasy baseball camp experiences for "maturing" would-be athletes, is a consummate experience provider. Making good use of the various stages of the experience, Bob sends along preseason workout recommendations for campers. Bob's efforts serve double duty as they not only work on building the excitement before camp but also help to reduce the number of injuries during the camp itself.

Paying close attention to the actual camp experience itself, the baseball fantasy camp incorporates many authentic and transforming dimensions within the experience. Would-be big leaguers play their games on the actual spring training fields used by real major league teams. The authenticity is heightened by the inclusion of regulation uniforms as part of the experience. A focus on the individual is very much a part of the package. Campers get their own lockers and have their names put up in lights on the scoreboard and get to hear their name called out over the loudspeaker system as they take the field or come up to the plate.

The fantasy camp experience has a substantial focus on roles of participants. Retired major league baseball players are a big part of this experience. Campers get to meet them, receive instruction from them, and actually play against them during their fantasy week. There are also a variety of roles that campers can assume. In addition to becoming baseball players for the week, people can elect to assume the roles of coaches, umpires, or in one case, the official singer of the national anthem before the big games.

Fantasy baseball camp may actually last for only one week in the spring, but the experience stays with a camper for a lifetime. The Dowdell organization not only provides photos of the campers with former greats such as Carl Yastremski of the Boston Red Sox, but it creates a tape of the experience that these older boys of summer can replay for years to come reliving their week at the big show for ever and ever.

Festivals are even more numerous and popular than fairs and expositions. If you can dream it up, people will show up. Some festivals like the Cheyenne Frontier Days have been held for over 200 years while others like the Japanese Cultural Festival held in Dallas, Texas, that featured kabuki theater, an exhibition of important Japanese art, and a parade are a one time occurrence. Festivals are so important to the tourism industry that the American Bus Association annually names a list of the top 100 events for the coming year as a way to promote trips.

People

Recall that the second P of experience marketing is people. Naturally, there would be no experiences without the participation of people. This P of the experience marketing mix is an essential component of the entire process. Factors within this variable include age, gender, cohorts, household, values, attitudes, life stages, life events, and, of course, seasons and cycles.

The vastness of variety inherent within this P of the experience marketing mix makes it a significant component within the overall marketing strategies of most industries within experiences. Two overall approaches that have worked well for successful experience makers are a clearly delineating focus on a particular particle market along with changing or expanding the experience as the needs and preferences of these particle markets evolve.

Resorts are good examples of how experience makers focus on a particular element within the 4Cs. Resorts have tended to focus on a particular lifestyle choice whether it's skiing, golf, tennis, gambling, or escape. Some resorts turn these activity choices into particle markets by including an additional element. Beaver Creek Resort in Colorado and Smuggler's Notch in Vermont are two ski resorts that have positioned themselves as family-friendly getaways. Golf resorts have added amenities and attractions to position themselves for the nongolfing member of the household.

Resorts in the Caribbean have made moves to attract families as well. Club Med has designated some of its locations as family friendly with day care for the little ones and plenty of activities for older children. There are even a few resorts that provide the guest families with their own personal nanny. Still there are other sun and fun resorts that limit their guests to couples or singles.

Women are targeted by casinos who gear their promotional programs to make the most of gender differences. Slot machines were originally installed as a way to keep the ladies occupied while their male companions hit the tables. Slot machines are now promoted as a party or social experience where women can sit side-by-side enjoying one another's company. Older women are targeted with bargain rate bus packages that include transportation, meals, and sometimes overnight accommodations. Other gender inspired promotions are points programs or clubs where, win or lose, the gambler is rewarded with coupons or points that can be redeemed for meals or merchandise. Women like the personal aspects of the clubs such as the birthday cards or postcards and are accustomed to the coupon concept. An emerging technique is to offer high-roller female gamblers hospitality packages with spa or salon services included.

Many resorts are taking psychographic profiles into consideration as well. Marriott publishes an attractive brochure called *Serious Guide to Fun*. This publication helps people to select the resort that is right for them by blending benefits with psychographics in the following categories: brilliant sun spot, treasure islands, busy bodies, making waves, American dreams, second homes, world-views, and swingers' paradise. By the way, in this case, swingers refers to golfers.

The other strategy that successful experience makers embrace is growing or changing with their market. What happens if fans stop coming out to the ball park because they've grown older and have other responsibilities? What happens if season pass holders have traded in their skis for sun? Remember, without people there is no experience so the industry employs techniques to ensure they either retain, regain, or recruit some new fans or followers.

Ski resorts once reluctant to welcome snowboarders to their slopes have faced up to the reality of changing demographic and psychographic profiles and the subsequent impact on the bottom line. Disney World, realizing that households without children were the fastest growing segment of the population, began to reposition the Disney experience for footloose and newly "children free" older couples.

Whether it be by age, gender, household, ethnicity, life stage, health, or lifestyle, there are a number of ways in which experience makers incorporate elements of people into their overall marketing approach:

- Carnival Cruise Lines launched a spin-off line called FiestaMarina that caters to Spanish-speaking passengers with other Latino twists such as later dining, tapas, salsa club, and Spanish, Cuban, South American, and Mexican cuisines.
- Elderhostels and Eldertreks are just two unique travel options available for mature travelers who want to venture into new geographic and intellectual areas.
- Regency Cruise Lines gives a nod to the makeup of the changing American family with new fare schedules for single parents.
- Grandtravel, a travel company of Maryland, specializes in trips for older travelers accompanied by their grandchildren.
- Historic tours commemorated the fortieth anniversary of the King's arrival in Germany by providing serious Elvis fans with a six-night tour including a cable-car ride over vineyards just like Elvis did in *G. I. Blues* and a visit to the barracks where he lived.
- Total spa programs for the health conscious are offered on Carnival, Costa, Crystal, Diamond, Holland America, and Seabourn cruises just to mention a few.
- A number of bars and nightclubs in urban areas are holding "alternative" events on slow evenings such as Mondays or Wednesdays and are attracting a whole new group of customers, the gay and lesbian market.
- The *MS Fantasy*, which packs 217,000 passengers on 100 cruises a year, is just one of the quintessential pleasure ships that sail for three days of sun, fun, and hedonistic delights targeted towards singles.
- Holiday Inns launched KidSuites where kids find their own beds, space, and entertainment in themed, fun hotel rooms.
- Serenity Trips provides year-round sober vacation opportunities with trips ranging from a Jamaica singles week to a foliage outing to a New Year's party in Mexico as well as sober spring break trips for college students.
- Canadian Mountain Holidays creates travel packages for solid intermediate to expert skiers at 11 areas in British Columbia where participants are afforded heliskiing powder experiences.
- LeBoat, Inc. markets more than 400 barges including those with wheelchair accessible barge grips throughout the Burgundy region of France.
- Sarah McLachlan organized Lilith Fair, a summer music festival featuring only women artists. It earned $16.4 million in 1997 (Associate Press, December 26, 1997, p. 23A).
- Spa Adventure offers packages for the adventurous types who don't want to give up a bit of luxury by combining hiking, rafting, and biking with gourmet meals and deluxe overnight accommodations.
- Interhostel is a study-learning travel program for people 50 and over that provides people with a group travel and learning experience that the independent traveler would have trouble duplicating on his or her own.
- Kim Reichhelm's Women's Ski Adventures in Crested Butte, Colorado, targets women of all skiing abilities from first-timers to experts.

Slice of Life

The cruise industry is composed of both small and large operators, but collectively they have changed over the years to create destination packages for increasingly smaller particle markets:

- The Champlain and Erie canals, part of an inland transportation system developed over 150 years ago in upstate New York, are now a cruising opportunity.
- Marine Expeditions takes people for a two-day, one-night look at ice caps in the Arctic.
- The Royal Caribbean Cruise Lines became the first mass-market line to offer cruises in the Far East on a year-round basis.
- The Orient Cruise Line added a helipad to the *Marco Polo* so that passengers could fly over the fjords of New Zealand or scout icebergs and wildlife in Antarctica.
- The six-day crossing of the Atlantic afforded by the *Queen Elizabeth II* still remains a more leisurely way to start or complete a European vacation.
- The Orient Lines is packaging "surf and turf" vacations for people who want both land and sea trips. They combine tours of the Greek Islands with extended port stays in Athens and Istanbul.
- Freighter Cruise Lines books passengers on freighter cruises from North America to Europe and worldwide destinations for people interested in hopping a slow boat to China without faxes, fancy food, and floor shows.
- Windjammer Cruises out of Maine and the Caribbean attracts a group of sailors interested in a more authentic sailing experience complete with trimming the sails and helping the cook.
- Attempting to attract an upscale but informal group of Baby Boomers, *Star Flyer* and *Stay Clipper*, four-masted schooners holding 170 passengers, have pools and a piano bar but no formal evenings or themed dress parties.

Closeup

Major league baseball fell from the public's grace during the 1994–95 season with a strike-shortened season that resulted in the cancellation of the World Series. This game, once called America's pastime, was also falling out of favor with younger would-be fans who found the action of the game to be too slow. To address these attitudes, professional league baseball has refashioned its stadiums, pricing packages, schedules, and experience strategies. Celebrating history and heritage, numerous franchises have leveraged their special anniversaries with events and activities to attract a broad cross section of fans. Kids are the ticket!

In Chicago, the Cubs distributed 10,000 Cubbie Beanie Babies and held an All-Star Kids Clinic. The Philadelphia Phillies coordinated a Phillie Phanatic Pajama Party on the mascot's birthday. Numerous other teams have promoted "run the bases" days to attract younger audiences and nostalgia days to lure wayward fans.

Minor league baseball team owners have responded to this discontent with the pros by repositioning themselves as the real heart and essence of the game. The experience of the minor league game can often be anything but another Saturday at the park with pigs delivering baseballs to home plate, '70s music resounding throughout the stands, and nuns offering soothing massages as is the case in St. Paul, Minnesota.

Slice of Life

The old adage that times change is certainly true, and it's especially true related to how time changes people. The changes that time makes in the lives of people affect their preferences, perceptions, and patterns related to experiences. One such example is New Year's Eve.

New Year's Eve tended to be about parties, drinking, and general carrying on. But that's not necessarily the case anymore as the celebration of this holiday has changed. Guy Lombardo, that New Year's Eve bandleader of renown, joked that when he died he was taking New Year's with him, and maybe he did. Industry surveys showed that many people just stopped going out for New Year's Eve sometime in the 1980s.

Did that mean the end of the New Year's Eve experience? The death knell tolled by drinking and revelry has been transformed into other ways to mark the occasion. In 1976 the city of Boston launched First Night. A group of artists decided to throw a big block party in downtown that would provide inexpensive, alcohol-free, family-oriented cultural events and performances. Since that time, the concept has grown and now approximately 190 cities and towns in North America have rallied civic groups and volunteers to create this alternative to the more traditional New Year's Eve celebration.

First Night isn't the only alternative experience. The Omega Institute, a center for holistic study of health, culture, spirit, and the arts located in the Hudson River Valley of New York, offers weekend or week-long experiences for the new year providing people with an opportunity to reflect, regroup, or rekindle their spirit. Renaissance Weekend in Hilton Head, South Carolina, brings together notables from the worlds of education, business, politics, and the arts to come together and discuss issues and explore resolutions. Groups of friends and family now rent mountain retreats or book cruises so they can celebrate the holiday in a new and different way.

Does this mean that nobody shows up in New York City's Times Square to watch the ball drop? No, but then even New York City embraced the First Night approach in 1991 (Vitullo-Martin, 1997, p. 9).

Football has finally acknowledged that some of its best fans are female. Not only do women pop out of the kitchen to catch the two-minute drill, but they also play the most influential role in deciding what sport their children will play according to Sara Levinson, president of NFL properties. It has been estimated that 40 million women watch professional football, and nearly 400,000 attend games each week. The NFL has responded by creating NFL Flag, a noncontact coed football league, that is being promoted through local park and recreation agencies nationwide. To capitalize on this newly acknowledged legion of female fans, the NFL has licensed a dozen companies to market female clothing with team insignias. The result has been an upswing in sales for products that are sized properly and that suit female tastes.

Peripherals

The third P of experience marketing, peripherals, refers to those factors and variables related to and involved in the entire process. Peripherals add substance and definition to the experience by incorporating factors such as place, price, packaging, policies, public image, patterns of demand, and popularity cycle into the entire experience itself.

What are people looking for when spending a night away from home? If they're looking to sleep in the Jail House Inn in Preston, New Mexico, or the Shoe House in Hallam, Pennsylvania, they won't be disappointed. If they're in need of a place where the kids will not only be accommodated by but also catered to or a room that can double as office space or a home away from home, they will have a range of options and alternatives from which to choose.

The overnight accommodation options include a variety of experiences. These value-oriented national motel chains, charming, one of a kind bed and breakfasts, and hotels or lodges specifically designed to accommodate differing target market groups and needs are the current approach.

A mesh of target market strategies and manipulation of elements of the experience has resulted in concept rooms. No longer limited to the recognizable smoking and nonsmoking classifications, guests can select from a range of options including rest space for a few hours to space more suitable for a two-week stay. Green rooms come with nonanimal tested toiletries, low-flow toilets, water conserving shower heads, air filtration, and unbleached sheets. Business class rooms offer data ports, oversized desks, office supplies, and in-room or on-floor faxing capability.

Hotels aren't the only segment of the industry making substantial changes in the peripherals of their experience. Cruise lines have embarked upon this journey very seriously. New ships are being built, and older ships are being renovated to alter or define the experience for today's passengers. Some of the peripherals they've been controlling and manipulating include physical changes in the ships or cabins themselves, the use of themes, the inclusion of more offbeat

❖ LaQuinta Inn and Suites broke from its traditional reliance on cookie cutter rooms and offered three choices for its guests within it moderately priced facility: regular guest rooms, suites, and extended stay rooms.

❖ Hilton Hotels has created Sleep Tight rooms for guests who have trouble falling asleep away from home. These rooms feature sleep masks, earplugs, better mattresses, tinted windows, thicker carpeting, tighter door seals, "white noise" machines, reading materials on bedstands, and minibars with herbal teas, milk, and cookies.

❖ At Sheraton, "day break" rooms on airport properties enable guests to rent rooms for two hours as a respite after a red-eye flight.

❖ Residence Inns by Marriott advertises its rooms as places to relax with room to work and breathe while Club Hotels by Double Tree suggest that we "get it all" with its club room that it describes as equal parts den, office, and cafe.

❖ The Holiday Inn Express, this chain's scaled down, value-priced version of overnight accommodations, claims it didn't invent the bed and breakfast, that it just brought it up to date.

destinations, new and different niche markets, and alternations in the traditional cruising experience itself.

While some experience providers have been expanding the experiences through peripherals to grow and prosper, others have made use of peripherals as part of survival. Few enterprises have come under fire the way the movie business has. The old theaters with their balconies and the drive-in movie theaters are vanishing breeds soon to become national monuments. There are a number of peripheral alternatives being employed. One involves size with either huge megaplexes or the revival of small intimate facilities. Another one relates to technology and design of the facilities to immerse the viewer in the movie-going experience, and another such approach is creating a different kind of experience entirely. An additional technique is the bundling of peripherals together to maximize the experience.

The megaplexes, the trend towards bigger and better movies theaters, combines the size, technology, and design factors into one major trend within the

*Clos**e**eup*

Manipulation of peripherals by the cruise industry is quite extensive:

- American Adventure Lines provides separate space for parents and children, particularly teens. The underlying idea is to develop a ship for families with enough space and programs so that neither group interferes with the other. *Disney Magic* and *Disney Wonder* are "purpose built" providing areas and activities for three different audiences: children, families, and adults traveling without children. *Disney Magic* offers 15,000 square feet of children's space that is nearly 10 times the area of most other cruise lines.
- Use of available space is being changed as well. Many ships now offer full-sized fitness centers and spas. *The Norway's* 6,000 square foot Roman Spa with Bally equipment features marble columns and sculptures.
- Luxury in a cabin as defined by Silversea Cruise Line includes private dressing area, marble bath and tub, dressing table, writing desk, wall safe, stocked minibar, refrigerator, TV and VCR, personalized stationery, and plush terry robes.
- More ships than ever before are offering private balconies adjacent to cabins for a more intimate sense of space.
- Royal Caribbean Cruise Lines' *Grandeur of the Seas* provides cabins that are 23 percent larger than those of its other ships as a way of differentiating it from its competition.
- Ships are coming in different sizes as well, from gigantic to cozy. *Carnival Destiny* (101,000 gross tons carrying 2,600 passengers) is more like a floating resort. The exact reverse is the cruise lines positioning themselves for people who don't want to vacation with 3,000 other people. One such example is the American Canadian Caribbean Line with vessels that carry 100 or fewer passengers providing access to different locales and an entirely unique experience.
- Cruise lines also avail themselves of that longstanding traditional marketing tactic, pricing incentives. A variety of pricing alternatives include the lowest price and best cabin selections for early booking, last-minute super sales, and discounts and perks for returning passengers.

Slice of Life

Different strokes for different folks certainly applies to the lodging industry. Hotel corporations and resorts are recognizing that differences in preferences and pricing patterns translate into different types and levels of what is essentially the same experience—sleeping overnight in a room away from home. The following are just two illustrations of this range of peripherals:

- Marriott Corporation has expanded beyond its initial Marriott Hotels and now encompasses a number of lodging options that include the following: Fairfield Inn, Courtyard, Residence Inn, TownePlace Suites, Marriott Conference Centers, Renaissance Hotels and Resorts, Marriott Resorts, and Marriott Vacation Club. Fairfield Inn is a more value-oriented set of overnight accommodations with basic-plus amenities. Courtyards are specifically designed for the business travelers while Residence Inns are for those business travelers staying for several nights or even weeks at a given location. The resorts and vacation clubs, of course, don't resemble the others much at all. The price, location, amenities, and the experience itself are quite different.
- Walt Disney World advertises accommodations in every variety and it is right on target. It has five different categories of overnight accommodations: value, moderate, "home away from home," deluxe, and campgrounds. Each of these different levels provides peripherals that vary the recreational, dining, and service experiences which are naturally reflected in the price. For instance, the "home away from home" options come complete with flexible in-room arrangements, fully equipped kitchens and close proximity to shopping. The deluxe accommodations boast larger rooms, luxurious dining and recreational choices, with business, concierge, and room services available. In addition, these peripherals are presented in a themed manner. The Coronado Springs Resort has ranchos, cabanas, and casitas right out of the old Southwest while the Wilderness Lodge recreates the old Pacific Northwest with totem poles, teepee chandeliers, and bubbling spring in the lobby. No matter the choice, it's guaranteed to be an experience.

industry. Megaplex offerings include 20-plus theaters, digital sound, comfortable seats, stadium-style seating, and concessions that offer gourmet treats alongside the traditional buckets of buttery popcorn. These megaplexes generally cost about twice as much to build as the more traditional theaters, but not having to crane one's neck and the sensation of hearing the approaching helicopters over one's shoulder seem to be a substantial enough change in the experience to more than pay for the initial investment. The exact opposite of this trend is the miniplexes that show up in urban areas in the back rooms of bookstores, bars, and coffee shops that generally show everything from classic movies, student productions, and foreign films to low-budget features.

Drive-ins are more than just a faded memory of summer nights piling an entire family or group into the car for a night out. While there are substantially fewer drive-ins than there were in their heyday of the 1950s, they too have changed over time. Car radios are now used for sound rather than those old metal speakers, and first-run rather than second- or third-run movies are shown. Many of them have expanded the experience by offering elaborate concession stands, playgrounds, pony rides, and even Laundromats.

Movie theaters are not the only segment of the experience industry that has been undergoing a dramatic reshaping of its peripherals. Roller-skating rinks, bowling alleys, and a variety of other entertainment and amusement providers have made changes as well. Roller-skating rinks change the music featured during skating hours as a way to attract specific age or interest groups such as preteens or church groups.

Bowling has experienced a comeback as some lanes have remodeled to attract a better educated, more upscale crowd. They've hired designers to revamp the space so it has a more family room–like appeal and they've updated furnishings with more contemporary colors and textures. Food and beverage service has changed as well with pickled eggs and beef jerky being replaced with bagels, tacos, salads, premium beers, and wine.

Other changes to the bowling experience have been even more dramatic. Whether it's called "atomic," "mystic," or "cosmic," the cranked up music, artificial fog, strobe lights, and glow-in-the-dark bowling balls are packing them into bowling alleys across the country on Friday and Saturday nights. Previously boring bowling has become a striking success.

One of the other areas particularly important to the experience industry is the pattern of demand. Everybody wants to head to Six Flags on a long holiday weekend. Golf courses, restaurants, and movie theaters are almost abandoned on Mondays. The kids (and the adults) get impatient waiting in line for almost any kind of food or fun.

How to manage demand so it doesn't negatively impact on the experience itself and how to use those patterns of demand to reinforce profitability are two continual challenges for experience makers. Cruise lines are encouraging passengers to fly a few days early to ports such as San Juan, New Orleans, and

❖ The Screening Room, combined restaurant and movie theater in New York City, has in addition to its main theater two smaller screening-dining rooms where the customer can invite friends over for a Super Bowl party or to show the video from his or her last vacation.

❖ The Cinderella Drive-In in Englewood, Colorado, has a kiddy amusement park with a Ferris wheel, train, and carousel and in Silver Lake, New York, the drive-in has an ice cream parlor and miniature golf course.

❖ Saturday nights at Town Line Ten Pin in Malden, Massachusetts, finds its 46 lanes shrouded in artificial fog and lit up like airport runways as a disco beat accompanies the ball towards fluorescent bowling pins.

❖ The Astro Drive-In in Dallas, Texas, continues its tradition of $10 for everybody in the car on Monday nights.

❖ The Ryan Bowladrome in Boston, Massachusetts, boasts the best sound system in its neighborhood while the Big League Bowling Center in West Roxbury, Massachusetts, has a live DJ for cosmic bowling nights.

❖ Void on Wednesday, a SoHo bar in New York City, has video screens built into the tables to complement the large screen in the bar itself.

Clos**eup**

Bob Sheriden, owner of an Ultrazone laser game franchise in Wisconsin, used peripherals to his advantage for both strengthening the ongoing popularity of this game as well as managing patterns demand. Some of these changes included:

- building three arenas for play with unique themes and elaborate settings making it more maze-like and challenging;
- using the Ultrazone's unique button technology which can make the game more challenging for frequent participants;
- starting a button membership program that lets people create distinctive, fun aliases and career statistics;
- Restricting button membership play to after 8 P.M., a slower business time;
- sponsoring corporate outings and holding special days for service clubs; and
- making Sunday family day with parents playing free when accompanied by a paying child.

Vancouver as a way to spread the demand for flights into the departure cities. Movies have reduced rates for late afternoon or Monday shows. Golf courses throw in free rental of a cart for people playing 18 holes on a Monday. Tuesday may be seniors' discount day at a ski area. Restaurants have early bird specials to reap the revenue of an additional seating. Hotels create special themed packages for times that traditionally experience low occupancy. Hotels have seasonally themed packages such as romantic getaways around Valentine's Day but go even farther by sponsoring contests or murder mystery events to fill hotel rooms at other off-peak times.

That other challenge, how to keep people engaged and entertained while they wait in line, remains a big challenge for experience makers. Disney always displays the waiting time for an attraction to give people a choice about whether to wait or not. The time is usually inflated so people feel better when they didn't have to wait as long as anticipated. While waiting for the Shamu show at Sea World, guests play participatory trivia games on a big video screen where they indicate their choice for a correct answer. Anything to make the time move along. All-Star Steakhouse provides waiting guests with its version of a tailgate party in the bar and summons diners to their table by calling them by the name of their favorite all-star athlete.

Peripherals are an essential part of the experience marketing approach. Peripherals transform ordinary activities into experiences that remain popular and profitable.

PerInfoCom

The experience marketing version for the traditional P of promotion is PerInfoCom, which incorporates the essential elements for informing and attracting participants to experiences in the twenty-first-century marketplace. These elements are personalization, information, and communication. There are a wide variety of options within this experience marketing variable, and this category of the experience industry has made good use of them.

Spotlight on Success

While some peripherals involve slight changes in various elements of the experience, there are a number of instances where entire facilities are being designed and built to create experiences for people. Two recently completed sport complexes illustrate this wholesale use of peripherals.

Look at life in Ericcson Stadium, the $187 million home of the NFL's Panthers in Charlotte, North Carolina. Designed by the same folks that created Camden Yards in Baltimore, Maryland, this facility was designed to be a downtown civic building so the ramps are masked by arches and domes with plenty of landscaping.

The seating is reported to be the best of any NFL stadium but comes with a fairly hefty price tag. Fans interested in spending anywhere from $190 to $600 for season tickets to the 19 home games must first buy the rights to the condo-style permanent seats at a cost of anywhere between $975 to $9,500 depending on location. This technique raised $130 million to offset the cost of the stadium that was not publicly financed.

The amenities are not overlooked in this sports palace either. There are plenty of tasty eats available at the 430 concession sites where FanCash, special stadium-only bank debit cards, can be used. There are also 213 individual unisex rest rooms and six huge sculptures of snarling black panthers at a cost of $600,000 just to remind the fans of the team's mascot (Designer Football, 1996, p. 1B).

Bank One Ballpark with its retractable roof that soars above this 1.3 million square foot new home to the Arizona Diamondbacks is so big that it could hold the America West Arena where the Phoenix professional basketball and hockey teams play eight times over. Not only is it huge but it also resembles the old brick ballparks of yesteryear and creates new experiences for its visitors. The concourses where fans enter have a pastel timeline of great moments in baseball. There's a Cooperstown West museum and an interactive baseball theme park behind the center field stands.

Comfort has not been overlooked. There are elevators and escalators to transport fans, an air conditioning system that can lower stadium temperatures by 30 degrees in under four hours, and expanded leg room and cup holders on the chairs in the lower deck area. Fans may be comfortable, but they won't have to get bored in this stadium. There are picnic areas, batting cages, pitching tunnels, a children's playground, and of course, the swimming pool, Jacuzzi, and waterfall where fans can soak up some sun and cool off while catching the action of the game.

Opportunities for revenue generation have not been overlooked either in this $355 million stadium with $238 million of it publicly financed. The main concourse is divided into 10 zones and each zone has a corporate sponsor such as Miller or Pepsi. There are 61 portable concession locations, 38 fixed concession stands, and 12 novelty stands. Additional revenue producing ventures include three McDonald's, a glass-enclosed Arizona Baseball club restaurant, T.G.I. Friday's Front Row Sports Grill and Leinenkugel's Ball Yard Brewery (Berry, 1998, p. 14).

Two of the most common and exceedingly effective forms of PerInfoCom for experience makers are event marketing and sponsorship. Almost all experience makers create special events as a way to attract customers and fill up seats or empty hotel rooms. Smart experience marketers identify needs that people seek and then create events or promotional packages around those particular needs.

❖ Most of the major hotel chains employ frequent guest programs that provide loyal customers with special perks or free lodging.

❖ Bob Dowdell's Fantasy Camp includes a Hall of Fame membership for any baseball camper that plays ball with his organization 10 times.

❖ Hotels join with airlines to generate rewards for travelers who are frequent guests and frequent fliers.

❖ Disney, McDonald's, and Coca-Cola have joined together to provide one another's products in their various locations.

❖ Volkswagen showed off its new Beetle at the second Winter X Games in Crested Butte, Colorado, with its Drivers Wanted campaign.

❖ The Cracker Barrel Restaurant chains located on or near highways in the Midwest and Southeast rent audiotapes of books at its restaurants that can be picked up in one location and dropped off at another. What a great way to get customers back in for another meal!

❖ Vending machines dispensing T-shirts imprinted with the official full-color movie poster made their appearance with the launch of *Lost in Space*. For $16.96, consumers picked up a shirt in the size of their choice compressed into a 16-ounce can from the vending machine in the theater lobby on their way out.

❖ The Disney Institute sends would-be visitors a video so they can take a firsthand look at the kinds of experiences they might want to select as part of their edutainment program.

❖ Edge, the American Skiing Company's frequent skier card, lets skiers earn points towards free lift tickets at any of the company's resorts, eliminates ticket window lines, and gives great deals on equipment, lodging, and meals.

❖ Adventure World in Prince Georges County, Maryland, extends its season by featuring Hallow Scream! on autumn weekends.

For a time cruise lines have been packaging specific themed events within their cruises as a way to attract a specific target market. Themes can include everything from archeology and ballet to yoga and zydeco. There are bridge cruises where people get to play cards with premier players. Vacationers can join people from Jacques Cousteau's team for a diving adventure. Chefs and winemakers team up to do Epicurean cruises. There are cruises for peanut butter or chocolate lovers. Norwegian Cruise Lines includes several Sports Afloat sailings with Olympic gold medalists or NBA or NFL all-stars. There are even cruises to the spirit world aboard Carnival's Extrasensory World at Sea hosted by a psychic and Majesty's six-night psychic cruises which include tarot card and astrology readings.

Sponsorships are also used extensively by most experience makers as a form of copromotion, lifestyle marketing, and source of additional revenue generation. There is not a golf tournament, college football bowl game, or virtually any other festival or celebration that does not have corporate sponsors. Look at the number of sponsors for just one event. The National Finals Rodeo was sponsored by Coca-Cola, Colt Manufacturing, Coors Brewing, Copenhagen Skoal, Crown Royal, Dodge Truck, Justin Boots, Resistol hats, and Wrangler jeans and shirts.

Slice of Life

What started in 1985 on a San Francisco beach when an artist burnt a wooden man to provide closure for a broken romance has led to the Annual Burning Man festival which is described as a surreal adventure that is a mix of Mardi Gras, Woodstock, and Alice in Wonderland. The makeshift city constructed for the five-day festival consists of art installation–type attractions such as a cathedral of pianos, a life-sized version of the board game Mousetrap, and a papermâché opera house as well as theme camps with motorized sofas and men dressed as nuns.

Although the festival is rather loose and informal, the 20,000 attendees pay $75 for admission which covers site cleanup, security, medical emergency equipment, and portable toilets while camping gear and other survival tools need to be provided by the participants. Press passes for the twelfth annual festival held in Hualpai Playa, Nevada, were inscribed with the following: "This pass entitles you to nothing in particular. Have a beautiful experience of your own."

Naturally, the event concludes with the burning of the 40-foot high wooden man for whom the event is named (Haring, 1997, p. D6).

VISA, McDonald's, Coca-Cola, General Motors, Anheuser-Busch, and IBM are just some of the bigger corporations that provided financial contributions to have their names linked as sponsors for the Olympic games. Kodak won the bidding competition to be the official film for the event as corporations used sponsorship as an alternative way to communicate more personally with current and potential customers.

The experience makers recognize the value and importance of communicating a personal relationship with their participants and employ most all of the PerInfoCom strategies to this end.

Close-up

In the late 1990s Walt Disney World added both rooms and attractions to the resort side of its enterprise. In order to maintain occupancy for these resorts, it created a number of events or special promotions to bring people to its resorts, facilities, and other attractions such as:

- Walt Disney Resort Marathon,
- Chevy Truck Challenge at the speedway,
- Walt Disney World Indy 200,
- Mardi Gras at Downtown Disney Pleasure Island,
- Spring Training Home for the Atlanta Braves,
- U. S. Men's Clay Court Tennis Championships,
- Epcot International Flower and Garden Festival,
- Vibe Live celebrating Black Music Month,
- Latin Fest,
- Jazz Fest,
- Disney's Oldsmobile Golf Classic,
- Epcot International Food & Wine Festival, and
- ABC Super Soap Weekend at Disney-MGM Studios.

Outback Steakhouse, Inc., a Florida-based chain with more than 400 restaurants nationwide, decided to take a nontraditional approach for communicating with its customers. It signed a contract to sponsor sportscaster John Madden's specially designed bus that he uses to commute to weekly football games. Outback Steakhouses are meat and potatoes kinds of places where the emphasis is upon lively, casual fun, and John Madden meets this criteria perfectly.

Spotlight on Success

The bus is decorated inside and out with Outback signage and occasional live shots of the bus turning into the stadium show up on the national broadcast coverage. During a Thanksgiving Day game, Madden repeatedly mentioned the huge turkey that was cooking in the Outback Madden Cruiser. As Madden travels across the country, Outback contacts local radio stations in the various towns and sponsors a Ticket to Ride contest where the winners get football tickets and a ride to the game in the bus.

In addition, Outback also sponsors college football's Outback Bowl, formerly known as the Gator Bowl. Outback management believes that in this day and age of intense competition in the casual dining segment of the restaurant industry that the traditional 30-second TV spots are no longer cost-effective (Reidy, 1998, p. E3).

Making Customer Matches

Due to the highly individualized and personal nature of experiences, it is critical that experience providers are able to make good customer matches. The essential components of making such a match involve finding out what people want and then creating customer-centered experiences around that information. The combination of these customer-centered strategies with the infusion of information create the right kinds of experiences to retain existing participants and reach emerging markets.

Organizations both large and small make use of survey research to detect preferences or trends among customers and prospective customers. In a number of instances, experience makers use intercept surveys when people have completed the experience or are leaving the facility or attraction to ascertain customer satisfaction and feedback. Observation of participants' actual behavior while involved in the experience or their response to a particular promotional package also are ripe with information about how to match customer preferences with experiences.

Information about people's preferences and patterns of participation needs to be infused within the organization so that experiences can become centered on what's right for the customer. This information can be used to adapt services to provide good customer service or customer care, but it can go beyond that in responding to people so that a connection between the experience provider and the participant may eventually result in a collaborative relationship.

A good example of the creation of a customer-centered experience based on knowledge, connection, and collaboration with the customer is Untour. Untour provides two-week vacations in a number of European spots. Untour is for the

Close-up

The hotel and lodging industry has undergone vast transformations in the last few years creating concept rooms and expanding their service line to offer a range of sleeping experiences. Many of these changes as well as future changes are based on what customers tell the researchers they need and prefer. Some changes made on the basis of customer input include (Alexander, 1998, p. 8E):

- Holiday Inn customers indicated they preferred showers to baths and hated the feel of the wet shower curtain around them so bath-shower combinations have been replaced with wraparound showers that don't require a curtain.
- Marriott replaced its traditional hard-back desk chair with an ergonomic, upholstered swivel chair.
- Holiday Inns have designed their rooms above the first floor with windows that open so that guests can have the fresh air they prefer.
- Marriott moved the paintings from the wall above the bed to the wall parallel to the bed.
- Holiday Inn now supplies all of its rooms with coffee makers.
- Marriott installed electrical outlets and telephone jacks on the base of its desk lamps so guests don't have to crawl around on the floor searching for them. They also extended the length of the telephone cord from three to six feet.
- Both Holiday Inn and Marriott have installed brighter lights in response to customers' suggestions, and Holiday Inns makes sure that, during the day, guests never walk into a room with the drapes drawn.
- Marriott added a dimmer switch to one of its wall lamps near the front door to serve as a night light—another request from guests.
- Both Marriott and Holiday Inn have designed desks and chairs that are light enough for guests to move them around as desired.

A recent study conducted by Hyatt Resorts and *Honeymoon* magazine found that:

Fast Facts

- 64 percent of those responding said their lovemaking is better on vacation;
- a third of those surveyed indicated they actually "overindulge" in such activities when away from home;
- nearly 75 percent of couples responding indicated that the amorous feelings kindled or rekindled by a romantic getaway trip lasted up to four weeks after their return home with 10 percent of those couples reporting that the romantic feelings lingered up to six months; and
- more than 8 out of 10 of the respondents indicated they take at least two romantic trips per year.

The Hyatt Regency Maui used this information to create Discoveries in Romance, a computer program that creates romance profiles for individual couples. Once each partner responds to the series of questions, the computer does an analysis and creates a list of recommended activities to meet the romantic expectations of the couple (Farrell, 1998, p. 9G).

Slice of Life

A recent cruise market study surveying adults determined that there were indeed different benefits and psychographic groupings related to vacation patterns and attitudes. These subgroups were as follows (Grossman, 1998, p. 1D):

- Family Folks—in need of assurance that a cruise is an affordable, family-oriented vacation.
- Comfortable Spenders—generally high-income, high-energy travelers who often frequent resorts with activities that can be duplicated on a cruise.
- Want It Alls—vacationers who value top quality shopping, dining, and night life.
- Cautious Travelers—people who spend less than all other groups on travel and who rarely travel abroad.
- Adventurers—well-traveled, intellectual types who fear boredom and want the freedom to do things they like.

type of traveler who doesn't want a packaged tour with the regiment of the tried and true. So what Untour does is essentially provide airfare and an apartment in a foreign town and some advice on how to discover and meet people on one's own. In addition, each vacation package includes someone to meet the traveler at the airport and food and other provisions in his or her accommodations upon arrival. A local representative is also available if needed. Basically, it's an independent tour with a little local help close-by which is just the type of relationship that this type of traveler prefers from the travel provider.

Marketing Changes

People's needs, interests, and desires are continually changing and customers have now come to expect that organizations will automatically incorporate these new priorities and preferences into their experiences. Such an expectation on the part of the consumer requires organizations to recognize and act on emerging marketing strategies. These emerging marketing strategies ultimately result in increased revenues for the experience maker.

Some of the experiences provided in this segment of the industry are either directed towards a particular group of people with a specialized need or interest or, in some instances, lend themselves to participation in a particular season or time of year. Many challenges are included when trying to meet the ever-changing needs of people by responding rather than reacting to the need to keep the experience personal, meaningful, vibrant, and attractive to current and would-be participants.

Since 1959 when Disney unveiled the Matterhorn, the first roller coaster with a steel tubular track, the amusement industry has thrilled audiences with its scream machines. The industry recognized the need to add new attractions to maintain excitement and attendance. Industry figures released for 1997 revealed that while attendance for amusement parks increased 23 percent from 1996, those figures varied for different locations. For instance, attendance soared 14 percent to 2.5 million at Busch Gardens in Virginia where it added an inverted roller coaster, but attendance plummeted 13 percent at Six Flags in Houston

❖ Raddison's Meeting Solutions Program provides toll-free assistance with meeting planners that include on-site specialists, quick fax confirmations, and special amenities for meeting service kits placed in each meeting room that include such things as a stapler, tape, pens, markers, and scissors.

❖ I Need It Now is the Chicago Ritz-Carlton's delivery service program to provide guests with toiletries on a moment's notice. Additional perks for dog owners include free dog grooming, walking and sitting services at its canine spa and a dog room service menu.

❖ The LeParker Meridien Hotel's wellness program includes nutritional counseling and body fat analysis.

❖ At the London Mews Hilton, guests looking for a pet project can sign up to take Pierre, the concierge's dog, for a walk in nearby Hyde Park.

❖ Canyon Ranch, the world renown spa in Arizona, changed its policy for a week-long stay and now allows access to phones and the outside world in response to changes in the work patterns of its clientele.

❖ The National Football League connects with its fans during the Super Bowl festivities through the NFL Experience, an interactive theme park set up in the Super Bowl city offering 50 games, a Quarterback Challenge, the NFL Training Camp obstacle course as well as a chance to meet and compete against NFL players.

❖ The Inn at Little Washington, Virginia, carries its five-star approach into the dining room as diners who are also guests of the hotel receive a small white rose for their lapel to ensure the kind of attention they deserve.

where it didn't add a major new ride (Sloan, December 1997, p. 1D). The experience counts, and today's children, the primary customers of these amusement parks, are accustomed to nonstop action and excitement and attendance patterns bear that out.

Other experience makers, particularly entrepreneurs, have recognized the increased interest in fun and games for children, young adults, and even empty nest households and have responded with a number of new experiences. DisneyQuest and Buster & Dave's are relative newcomers to the experience industry, but the ways in which these innovative marketers have recognized and responded to changing market demands has paid off for them.

Astute and agile experience makers have taken advantage of a variety of techniques to meet this challenge. Whether they attempt to grab a greater share of the experience time or dollar or whether they try to breathe new life into an existing experience, the end goal is the same. Experiences can't stand still or be allowed to become stagnant because participants won't wait for the experience provider to play catch-up.

Organizational Change

Change is the keyword in this aspect of experience marketing, and the biggest change is the shift from management to leadership. Organizational changes inherent within this shift include an overall approach such as identification of vision, precipitation of change, and becoming versatile and virtual. Other aspects of needed change within organizations relate to use of resources and the changing nature of competition.

❖ The addition of golf courses and the subsequent golf schools and special tournaments were popular alternatives adopted by a number of ski resorts such as Mount Snow and Stratton Mountain in Vermont. In addition to golf, Mount Snow plunged into mountain biking in a big way, and Stratton created a prestigious tennis school and tennis center as well.

❖ Elegant Vacations of Atlanta, Georgia, provides adventures in the Costa Rican jungle where guests stay in a resort with in-room Jacuzzis and a golf course.

❖ Other ski areas and resorts built water slides to occupy their downhill terrain in the summer months or developed special events such as food festivals or outdoor concert series as a way to continue to fill up the accommodations.

❖ Classical Cruises retrofitted its ship to sail into adventuresome spots such as the Amazon and the Arctic with designer decor.

❖ Pebble Beach in California created a golf widow package as did the PGA National Resort in Palm Beach Gardens, Florida. Both packages include spa amenities and services.

❖ Aspen, a prime ski attraction in Colorado, has added snowshoeing at dawn and sleigh rides in the early evenings.

❖ The VIP Tour at Disney costs approximately $60 per hour but results in reserved seats at performances and parades, restaurant reservations, chauffeur service for an additional fee, and faster access to attractions due to guides' experience and expertise.

❖ Sports Plus, a multiattraction indoor family entertainment center on Long Island, New York, brings together a variety of attractions including iWERKS Motion Theater, Laser Tron, NHL regulation ice rink, 48-lane bowling center, and an event center for concerts and recitals all under one roof.

❖ Holoword in Pasadena, California, a futuristic family entertainment complex combines themed restaurants with virtual games and a video arcade. There are five alcohol-free restaurants including an Old World saloon, a space alien room and an ice cream bar. The cosmic golf and laser tag maze changes with each game.

❖ Peters Pond Park in Sandwich, Massachusetts, opened in 1932 as a simple campground for fisherman, now features 500 wooded campsites with electric hookup adequate to power central air-conditioning and an indoor game room.

❖ Upscale hotels such as the Ritz-Carlton in Marina del Ray, California, the Omni Royal Crescent in New Orleans, and New York's Waldorf Astoria, have added additional alternatives for in-room services such as pedicures, manicures, makeup consultants, massages, seamstresses, private fitness classes, acupuncturists, and even weekly rental of fitness equipment.

❖ Primal Instincts of Palo Alto, California, provides reduced-risk dangers to average people by helping customers parachute or bungee jump from hot-air balloons, towers, and bridges while maintaining relative safety.

❖ VIP, the very important pet package at the Sutton Place Hotel in Vancouver, British Columbia, brings dogs or cats room service meals served in a porcelain dish with a drinking bowl of Evian water. Turndown service with dog biscuits or anchovy popcorn comes with the $60 price tag as well.

❖ The Blue Goose Restaurant in Newcastle, California, gets more than its share of the New Year's Eve experience market by hosting three seatings: the 6 P.M. seating has an ocean liner theme and motif with dinner guests celebrating midnight out over the Atlantic which is 7 P.M. PST; the 8 P.M. seating replicates Times Square in New York City so the midnight celebration coincides with 9 P.M. PST; and the final seating of the evening at 10 P.M. is the big shebang with dinner, a dance band, and a New Year's celebration at the real midnight PST.

❖ Ziosk, private spaces in public places, are available for hourly rental at airports and train stations. The seven by nine foot cubicles create a private experience for renters who can relax between flights, make private phone calls, or hold small meetings. A true experience maker!

Slice of Life

The importance of tracking demographic, economic, political, or competitive trends can't be underestimated. The changes in steak restaurants attest to the importance of trend tracking. Steakhouses and specialty restaurants were virtually written off during the health-oriented era that arrived on the scene about the same time as the decline of the expense account lunches and dinners, but, the big beef purveyors are back and are packing new perks and experiences as well. Steakhouses have incorporated a number of experience marketing strategies including people, PerInfoCom, information infusion, customer centering, and marketing change into their approach.

The growing market for beef caused three longtime steakhouses, Morton's of Chicago, Palm of New York, and Ruth's Chris of New Orleans, to open chains of their operations. Sales from these three chains were approximately $350 million, and that amount doesn't include the earnings of other less-expensive steak purveyors such as Outback or Lone Star.

All this competition for a target market which is primarily middle-aged, affluent, male business travelers has caused the restaurants to add sizzle to the steak as a means to attract and retain customers. The remaining independent steakhouses such as Chicago's Gene & Gerogetti and New York's Pen and Pencil are cooperatively advertising in airline magazines extolling themselves as the "last of the great independents." Palm in Denver snatched a popular $500 a plate, men's cancer fundraising event away from Morton's. Morton's has invited its big customers to join a VIP club complete with an unlisted phone number for reservations and complimentary cordials after dinner. Palm created a Steak Market Game which is a frequent diner contest with a $20,000 payoff.

The advertisements, contests, and clubs are augmented by a number of ego builders such as private humidors and wine lockers for customers. It adds an entirely new meaning to the expression "where's the beef?" (Jensen, 1997, p. B6).

Close*eup* What's an industry to do as it watches its traditional target market erode and its normal mode of operation fall out of favor? If you're the ski industry, you update your experience to uplift your profits.

Vail's Adventure Ridge, a veritable Disneyland in the snow with its indoor-outdoor complex that features ice-skating, moonlit snowmobile tours, bobsledding, snowshoeing, snow biking, a luge track, night snowboarding, snow tubing, and laser tag, was just the answer to changes in this industry. There are plenty of pluses with this multimillion dollar activity and eating center at the top of Eagle Bahn gondola. It provides options for nonskiing vacationers, new-style after-skiing options for the kids, family evening fun, and something to do during after ski hours.

Adventure Ridge means experiences of varying kinds for most all members of the family. Teens turn it into their own private refuge from parents and young siblings. Kids who just never seem to get tired have something to do besides watching TV or videos. Families have a chance to snow tube or ice-skate as a clan and, of course, there's gourmet coffee and quiet dinners for parents who sit and relax while the kids play (Ogintz, 1998, p. 38).

Organizational change for experience makers needs to focus on the evolution of their mission and vision. Imagine what Disney would be like today if it had remained focused only on providing amusements and entertainment for children. Envision the city of Las Vegas if it had been content to remain a dusty, desert town with one-arm bandits and some poker games. These are two examples of experience makers that didn't confine themselves to one narrow definition of their mission as entertainment or gambling but expanded that mission by virtue of their vision to create experiences for people.

Successful experience makers both recognize and respond regularly to the changing and emerging needs of people for still better and different experiences. For many experience makers it becomes a "think outside of the box" proposition where they need to break through the screen of traditional approaches to long-time popular experiences and come up with something that makes the most of existing or underutilized resources while tapping into the pocketbooks and mindsets of participants.

Individuals, small businesses, and large corporations demonstrate evidence of such an approach. The large hotel chains like Hyatt and Marriott recognized that they were in the hospitality business, but they didn't allow a narrow definition of hospitality to keep them in just the hotel and resort business. They have expanded to provide convention services, second home vacations, and residential care for the elderly. Hilton decided to expand their definition of hospitality to incorporate a strong hold in the gaming end of the experience industry.

The American Skiing Company didn't let the decline in ski enthusiasts and the growth of competition interfere with its vision of change. It brought together under one umbrella ski resorts in Maine, Vermont, Utah, and Nevada. The outgrowth of this venture resulted in a frequent skier card good at all the areas, good corporate sponsorships including VISA, Mountain Dew, Budweiser, Mobil, and Fila, as well as cross promotions through its *Edge Magazine* and vacation packages.

Examples of Disney brainstorms and advances, some large and some small, include:

- On Disney's new cruise ship, *Disney Magic,* dining includes food stations located throughout the ship and rotation dining where each evening guests can enjoy their dinner in a different dining room as they rotate with their waiter and table mates so they can experience the cuisine and ambiance of one of the three main dining rooms aboard.

- At the Animator's Palate, one of the dining rooms on *Disney Magic,* the dining room with its synchronized sound and light show gradually transforms from black and white into full-color as each dinner entree becomes more colorful.

- Disney didn't just build a baseball field as part of its Wide World of Sports; here it created experiences as well. It provides tournaments for youth teams from around the country to gather and compete. Tournaments not only include field maintenance and equipment guarantees but athletic trainers, scrimmage time, and ice water in the dugouts and a chance to play in near-professional surroundings.

- Disney recruited workers from Uganda, Zimbabwe, Ghana, Botswana, Cameroon, and South Africa to work in the African-themed area. This type of recruitment addressed a dual need to answer an employee shortage in the area and lend added authenticity to the experience.

- Disney lights up the night with 66 acres of clubs and eateries including Wolfgang Puck Cafe, Dan Aykroyd's House of Blues, Gloria Estefan's Bongos Cuban Cafe, a 24-screen AMC theater, the world's largest Virgin record store, along with other themed shops. Outdoor concerts and street parties complete this hot spot that incorporates Marketplace, Pleasure Island, and West Side into a 10-block area called Downtown Disney.

- Disney Cruise Lines features open-air massage cabanas on the beach for adults at its private island, Castaway Cay.

- The NFL Experience, the National Football League's playground that is featured on site at Super Bowls, has a permanent version at Disney where fans can test their football ability at various interactive exhibits.

- Americans have bemoaned the lack of community and the decline of public education. Disney heard the call and responded with Celebration, a planned community complete with front porches for neighborly conduct and a school system predicated upon technology and team projects.

- Disney Regional Entertainment brings a piece of Disney World to kids who haven't gotten there yet through DisneyQuest, a form of high-tech playground. Kids can fight virtual-reality duels with Captain Hook, design their own roller coaster ride, and take simulated raft rides down a prehistoric river or make a trip to the moon.

The $50 million of on-mountain improvements and $60 million on hotel improvements during 1996 didn't hurt either. This vision of change is paying off.

Recognizing safety and security issues surrounding children's play led to the creation of the family entertainment industry with Discovery Zones and other similar service providers. Why should kids have all the fun? The creators of Dave & Buster's thought better of it and now have the clubs and revenue to refute the old adage.

*Clos**eup*

The cruise industry set sail for new worlds when it hoisted its sails, raising the definition of the cruise experience. It went into the real estate business when it started purchasing uninhabited bits of the Bahamas. While Norwegian Cruise Lines actually made the first island purchase in 1977, it has only been in the 1990s that cruise lines such as Royal Caribbean International, Princess, Costa, Celebrity, Premier, Holland America, and Disney have begun to play this game.

Holland America's Half Moon Cay is a 45-acre site on Little San Salvador. Holland America bought the 2,400-acre island for $6 million and invested another $10 million to develop it. While most of the island remains untouched, it has created an aqua-sports center, a West Indies–type shopping village, an ice cream store, a post office, and a Spanish-style chapel for wedding and vow renewal ceremonies. Royal Caribbean owns Coco Cay where it built and sank an 84 foot reproduction of a sixteenth century pirate ship to enhance the snorkeling experience of its passengers.

How do such islands change or create experiences for passengers? The list is quite extensive. Private islands provide privacy and safety not always found at regular ports of call. Such islands avoid the oversaturation by cruise ships at more popular destinations and the pressure of native street vendors. These designer islands create a more sheltered, relaxing, pristine experience.

While these cruises are not for all travelers, especially those who value culture, history, and authenticity, they do provide one type of experience for passengers and additional sources of revenue for the cruise line who now reap the revenues from rentals of Jet Skis and snorkeling equipment while profiting from the shopping as well (Bleecker, 1998, p. F5).

There are a number of sport-related visionaries who combine sports and entertainment into one package. The new Bank One Ballpark in Phoenix, Arizona, with its Sun Pool Pavilion, a luxury backyard with swimming pool, spa, and barbecue area, is one example. Tropicana Field near Tampa, Florida, which includes a shopping mall, car dealership, hair salon, brew pub, and cigar bar is an example of another. The Chelsea Piers Sports & Entertainment Complex transformed the sagging waterfront of New York City into a state-of-the-art field house with indoor soccer fields, gymnastic workout areas, outdoor in-line skating rink, heated driving range, a bowling alley, a spa, a brew pub, and upscale stores. As an added plus the facility offers a view of the Statue of Liberty, and the golfers don't have to bend over to put their ball on the tee since it's handled mechanically.

Many people in the experience industry become a bit annoyed by the ongoing success of the Disney organization and the amount of attention it receives in the press. At one time the company had completely abandoned any tradition of vision that its founder, Walt Disney, had established and was on the verge of a takeover. Under its current leadership complete with legions of critics, Disney remains one of the role models for shifting from surviving to thriving and for that reason can't be left out of ongoing discussions of experience marketing.

Disney never stops. It never stops taking the pulse of people and asking itself what does each pulse indicate or what can it become. Disney continues to embrace a vision that includes the continual redefinition of entertainment and how

Slice of Life

The PGA hit a hole in one when it took control of the professional golf experience for both the primary and secondary participants, players and fans with the development of TPC (tournament players clubs). The TPC system facilitates many changes to be made, and all of these changes impact upon the experience for the participants. As the PGA bought or built golf courses, it was able to revamp the courses to build as a challenge for the golfers while providing better vantage points for the spectators through the creation of stadium golf. An added bonus was the development of houses and condos surrounding these TPC courses to offset the cost of purchases or renovations.

This vision of creating a network of TPCs has enabled the PGA to exert greater control over professional golf tournaments. Prior to this time, the PGA was a guest at private golf clubs throughout the country and subject to the whims of these membership driven organizations. While some of these arrangements still exist, most notably the Masters Tournament in Augusta, Georgia, by owning and operating its own courses, the PGA can create its own schedule. This provides a boon to areas of the country who always had to endure the heat of mid-August or the lack of notable golfers due to a tournament being scheduled right before the British Open. The PGA didn't have to take any penalty strokes either when it created the Seniors Tour as a way to create tournament play for the over-50 pro golfers and their maturing but loyal followers.

that redefinition can be transformed into experiences for people—not just children, not just Americans, but for all kinds of people—in different parts of the world.

The potential lying just beneath the surface to respond to the inner needs and dreams of people is largely untapped. Fantasy baseball is just the beginning. The Rock-'n'-Roll Fantasy Camp was first held in Miami Beach and brought together middle-aged wannabes including doctors, executives, housewives, teachers, middle managers, nurses, and truckers. These folk got to interact with the camp's instructors, Rick Derringer, Nils Lofgren, Felix Cavaliere, Clarence Clemmons, Mike Love, Liberty DeVitto, and Mark Farner. Campers attended classes and had jam sessions with their heroes (Spitz, 1997, pp. 93–98). Imagination in this area knows no bounds.

The latest in innovators who know no heights and aim for the stars include Original Ventures, Inc. and Advent Launch Services. Original Ventures envisions a $300 million indoor ski slope for southern Florida. Its plans call for Mount Miami to have two mountains and a gondola to take skiers and snowboarders to new heights. Plans call for a 400-room hotel, a marina, stores, a 1,000-seat aquadrome theater for water ballet and hang gliding between the two peaks. Not to be outdone by the stellar nature of that plan, Advent Launch Services is just one of the companies making plans for space tourism. For approximately $3,500 people are making reservations for space travel. The sky's the limit for innovation in experience marketing!

One aspect of the experience makers is those individuals and small companies who create products that actually create an experience for people. This is currently a small but a growing part of the industry with great potential for the

The Evolution of the Destination Experience: Las Vegas

Spotlight on Success

The City of Lights (North American style, that is) would be one way to describe Las Vegas. The experience capital of the world might be another. Where else could one sail the Nile, spend time in ancient Rome, see a working circus, and visit New York, Oz, and King Arthur's Camelot all in an afternoon? Where else is there a pirate battle four or five times a night? Where else can one see Roman statues come to life and talk on the hour?

It's Las Vegas, that meadow that was discovered by a Mexican scout in search of water in the early 1800s but wasn't really settled until the railroad came through in the early 1900s. Nevada was the last western state to outlaw gambling and became the first to legalize casino gambling in 1931 setting the groundwork for the funding for Nevada's public school system and the growth of one of the country's largest destination resorts.

The Flamingo Hotel opened by Bugsy Siegel in 1946 led to a building boom of the '50s which resulted in the Desert Inn, the Sahara, the Tropicana, and the Stardust among others. The megaresort-type hotels and casinos began to arrive in the '60s with Circus Circus and Caesar's Palace.

Las Vegas was always on the lookout for new niches to tap. It went family friendly in the '90s to compete head to head with Disney World as the nation's top destination. Using this approach, Las Vegas managed to triple the number of visitors under the age of 21 to 3 million between 1990 and 1995 but gaming revenue per visitor dropped from $162.71 to $156.75 in that same time period (Grossman, 1996, p. 9D). Las Vegas will continue to remain family friendly, but it will refocus its main message as "Adults are kids" and continue to build still more experiences for the child in all adults.

All the while emphasis on themes and experiences just keeps piling up. Hotels that have opened since 1989 include Polynesian-themed Mirage; the Excalibur, a Las Vegas–style tribute to King Arthur; the pyramid-shaped Luxor; the MGM Grand Hotel and Theme park; and the Hard Rock Hotel.

Experiences added in the last few years include Stratosphere Tower, the tallest freestanding observation tower in the United States with the world's highest roller coaster; Big Shot, a zero gravity simulator; and the Fremont Street Experience, a 90-foot canopy of a spectacular light show in the downtown casino area. The Fremont Street $70 million project completed in 1995 transforms five blocks of Fremont Street into a color-filled pedestrian promenade complete with sound as well.

New hot spots taking their place in Las Vegas include the Orleans, complete with a French Quarter and Mardi Gras, as well as New York New York with the Manhattan skyline, the State of Liberty, the Empire State Building, and Central Park. New York New York has New York Fire Department boats spouting water in a "river" outside the hotel; yellow stretch limos with the Checker Cab pattern; and people with "New York" accents answering the phones. The Rio Suites, the only all-suite hotel has the only Napa Wine Cellar & Tasting Room. Within this property is a $200 million salute to carnival highlighted by the "Masquerade Show in the Sky," a $25 million interactive entertainment with music and costumes where guests can don costumes and climb on floats, to be part of one of the three Mardi Gras parades featured daily with a choice between Mardi Gras in New Orleans, Venice, or Rio.

Spotlight on Success *continued*

Las Vegas has something for everyone. The Desert Inn is a smaller, quieter, more luxurious experience coupled with gambling. The more exotic experiences can be found at places such as the Luxor, the Mirage, or New York New York. Families can go to Circus Circus, MGM Grand, and Excalibur with their attractions for children, and the senior set can camp out at Boom Town and Sam's Town with their RV parks.

Changes as the end of the twentieth century approaches include reaching a higher socioeconomic group. Las Vegas is going upscale. The Four Seasons joined the Vegas scene as did the Ritz-Carlton with a 560-plus room hotel about 20 minutes outside of the strip catering to a quieter crowd with fine dining, tennis, and a spa as big as its casino. Additional experience hotel-casino venues included the Paris Casino resort with the Eiffel Tower, the Seine, the Opera House and a working French winery as well as French-style gondola rides and Bellagio, a destination resort that recreates a Northern Italian village. Let the experience begin (Carpenter, 1997, p. M12)!

future as people's need for experiences and the personalization of those experiences grows exponentially.

You have to look closely for them, but these products are out there and growing in popularity and profitability. The Boyfriend in the Box includes a photo suitable for framing and authentic-looking phone messages from the mystery man all suitable for the career woman to take with her to the office to deter coworkers with ideal blind date possibilities. The Virtual Baseball Bat with its computerized

Bottom

Line

The bottom line with experience marketing or any other approach to marketing is, as always, examining the ways in which it pays off for the organization. Look at the following:

- The twenty-fifth anniversary marketing campaign undertaken by Disney World's Magic Kingdom resulted in a record-setting 17 million visitors to the park, an increase of 23 percent over the previous year (The Associated Press, December 31, 1997, p. B1).
- Tourism in Las Vegas grew 43 percent in the decade of the 1990s from 21 million to 30 million in 1996 (Sloan, February 7, 1997, p. 9D)
- The 4,000 club seats planned for the renovated Foxboro Stadium, home to the New England Patriots, will cost seat owners $2,500 per year while generating $10 million annually for the team (Cassidy, 1997, F3.)
- According to a University of New Orleans study, the 12-day carnival parade season in New Orleans with its 981 floats and 546 marching bands has estimated crowds of 3.5 million and more than 300 Web sites resulting in expenditures of $929.9 million in 1995 and $810 million in 1996 (McCafferty, 1998, p. 6).
- National Amusements reported that its megaplex movie theater in Lowell, Massachusetts, attracted nearly 200,000 people in the first five weeks of operation who were willing to drive 30 minutes more for the experience (Mohl, 1998, p. A35).
- Each of the 13 Dave & Buster's clubs produce between $15 and $16 million in sales each year with approximately half of it generated from food and beverages (White, 1997, p. D5).

Continued on page 356

Bottom Line continued

- New attractions such as a new water park at Elitch Gardens in Denver and a new inverted roller coaster at Riverside Park in Massachusetts resulted in a 67 percent and 50 percent increase respectively for each park over the previous year (Associated Press, December 21, 1997, p. B4).
- Despite disappointing sales of new albums, the seemingly ageless Rolling Stones brought in $89.3 million for their Bridges to Babylon tour and in a similar situation U2 and Tina Turner generated $79.1 and $24.8 million respectively (Associated Press, December 26, 1997, p. 23A).
- According to *IEG Sponsorship Report*, Olympic sponsorships which are sold in packages for winter and summer have generated revenue figures as follows: Albertville, France, and Barcelona, Spain, in 1992, $195 million; Lillehammer, Norway, in 1994 and Atlanta, Georgia, in 1996, $360 million; and Nagano, Japan, in 1998, and Sydney, Australia, in 2000, $475 million (Wells, 1998, p. B2).
- Fans of the Arizona Diamondbacks bought 35,000 season tickets at prices between $283 and $4,050 before the initial season even got under way (Berry, 1998, p. 14).
- The month-long Sydney Gay and Lesbian Mardi Gras festival attracted hundreds of thousands of partygoers with approximately 3,000 tourists coming from around the world in 1998; an audit in 1993 found that the festival generated more than $10 million for the Australian economy (Associated Press, 1998, p. A23).
- Sales of merchandise at theme restaurants in the United States are growing approximately at the rate of 20 percent a year with sales exceedingly $900 million in 1997 (Horowitz, 1997, p. 1B).
- According to the Travel Industry Association of America, more than 65 million Americans indicated they visited a historic site or museum or attended a cultural event in 1996 with those groups of travelers spending $615 per trip compared to $425 for all U. S. travelers (Sun Sentinel Report, 1997, p. 6).
- Approximately 88 percent of the visitors to Disney's new addition, Wide World of Sports, indicated they made the trip to Florida primarily to play sports (Meyers, 1998b, p. C2).
- Each year, about 1.7 million tourists swarm Gettysburg Battlefield pumping approximately $105 million into the local economy (Pound, 1997, p. 4A).
- Capital Metals Company of Phoenix, Arizona, paid $4,000 to book the splashy, new water section of Bank One Ballpark, the home of the Arizona Diamondbacks, for an employee outing (Walker, 1998, p. W1).

sensors that read the power and timing of the swing and tell the player whether the swing was a home run, hit, or strike out is certainly an experience maker. Ice Breakers, a box of 32 cards with different sayings, some of them insightful and some silly, comes with safety pins to attach to guests so they can wander around the room and get the conversation going at a party. Ice Breakers come in two versions, party and birthday. The CBS Masterworks Dinner Classics that combine music and recipes for a special party or event such as Dinner in Spain or Sunday Morning Brunch are yet another example. Successories is an already successful company that creates a full line of posters, T-shirts, coffee mugs, and plaques inscribed with motivational messages to give to people who have reached success in various aspects of their lives.

Action Agenda

Remember, every experience provider can learn and grow from reviewing the ideas and adapting the successes from other segments within the industry. Consider taking a close and imaginative look at the experience you provide in light of:

- Visit a specialized facility such as a ski area, tennis center, bowling alley, or fun center and identify ways in which it has attracted, amused, and profited from the presence of non- or secondary participants.
- Restaurants have incorporated a big slice of eatertainment in their current menu of offerings. Consider ways you could infuse eatertainment into your product, service, or experience.
- Hotels and resorts figured out that not all overnight guests or visitors are after the same type or range of services. Brainstorm the extent of differences in services that your experience might have hidden within it.
- Cruise lines have done an incredible job of creating themes or specialized approaches that would appeal to small but profitable particle markets. What impact could such an approach have upon your experience?
- Check out what people do immediately before they purchase your product, use your service, or venture to your experience and right after to see if there are ways you can impact the pre- and postexperience while simultaneously expanding upon your experience package.
- Think special event. What kind of unique or interesting event could be incorporated into your experience either to create an entirely new experience or a new group of participants or as a better way to interact and attract current clientele.
- Imagine that your most sizable or profitable target market group was whisked away to Mars tomorrow. With whom would you replace them, or how would you reposition yourself for surviving and then thriving?
- Experiences change over time. Compare the traditional birthday party or family vacation of yesteryear with today's reality. How has your product, service, or experience changed with the times, or has it?
- The best experiences are the ones that truly meet the needs, preferences, and expectations of the participants. Can you list what three things make your experience special for people?
- In what ways could you alter or modify your experience so it could accommodate more than one group of participants simultaneously? Think Disney magic!
- Who is your competition for the same type of experience, for an experience that answers the same or similar need, an experience that addresses a new or emerging need? How can you make the most of this information?
- Check out your down time or your slow time and brainstorm possible needs of people for types of experiences that could be addressed through peripheral changes or repositioning.
- What have you done for your customers lately? In what ways have you added, changed, modified, or done something that updates and refreshes the product, service, or experience for your customers?

Insight and imagination are the only two limits for experience makers. Entrepreneurs and "think outside of the box" organizations can hit home runs in this arena as the demand for experiences grows and grows.

From   ## To

Experience makers have made some rather significant changes in their approaches to marketing over the last few years. Some of these changes include:

- *Activities for Some to Experiences for All*—At one time only those with money got to go to Disney World or off to the Serengeti but now, thanks in large part to technological advances and the economies of mass participation, most everybody is able to go and do just about everything. The technology of IMAX theaters, virtual reality simulators, holography, and the blending of audio-animatronics such as used in Disney's Animal Kingdom makes it possible. It won't just be techno-experiences that flourish but varying levels of realistic experiences as well. People will be able to become a rock star, beauty queen, explorer, or performer. Levels of the experience will vary from karaoke to an actual performance at Carnegie Hall.

- *Turn up the Heat to Cool Down the Risk*—Sky diving was originally a fringe activity done by the fearless few. The U. S. Bungee Association didn't exist until 1990, and taking a trip someplace where one didn't speak the language was considered high adventure. All that has changed as the number of people, the range of options, and the popularity of extreme, risk, or adventure experiences has increased dramatically. People now line up and pay money to jump off cliffs, scale the highest peaks, risk life and limb in the jungles, anything to get the adrenaline pumping.

   The prevalence and preference for adventure-type experiences among the general populace is being tempered by a reduction or softening of the risk and adventure aspects. Experiences are being designed and packaged to minimize actual risk and to "comfortize" the activity or outing for the participant.

- *Me or You to Me and We*—The types of experiences will diverge into two different directions. People are pursuing experiences that set them apart from other people. It is the twenty-first-century version of keeping up with the Joneses. It involves something like "my trek to the Himalayas was longer, scarier, or more expensive than yours." "Me" type experiences will also involve a focus upon needs or desires that directly reflect the state of mind of each individual.

   Almost simultaneously people will start to become attracted to experiences that provide them with a sense of "we." Celebrating special events such as milestone birthdays or special anniversaries of historical events will focus on joining with other people to create a sense of "oneness" or togetherness.

- *From Fun and Frolic to Quest for Meaning*—"Let the good times roll" might have been the slogan of the end of the twentieth century, but the new millennium will put a different emphasis upon experiences. Yes, many of them are still pleasurable, but there is also an underlying sense of purpose within such experiences. People of all ages will be pursuing experiences with the aim of coming to better understand themselves, various cultures, and the world in general. The value of storytelling and dream making will continue to be valuable and important.

Sources

Alexander, Keith L. (1998, March 17). Hotel designers ponder the look, feel of the future. *USA Today.*

Associated Press. (1998, March 1). Gay pride festival's finale draws thousands to Australian city. *The Boston Globe.*

Associated Press. (1997, December 31). Magic Kingdom most visited site. *The Tampa Tribune.*

Associated Press. (1997, December 29). Rolling Stones top concert draws list. *Sarasota Herald Tribune.*

Berry, Walter. (1998, March 29). Bank One ballpark set to make debut in big way. *The Tampa Tribune.*

Bleecker, Arline. (1998, March 15). Cruise lines lay claim to islands. *The Hartford Courant.*

Carpenter, Richard. (1997, February 9). Viva, New York! *Boston Sunday Globe.*

Cassidy, Tina. (1997, October 12). A not-so-instant replay. *The Boston Globe.*

Designer football in Charlotte, NC, as NFL's Panthers christen Ericcson stadium. (1996, September 2). *USA Today.*

Farrell, Brenda D. (1998, February 15). Resorts attempting to woo couples with romantic trips. *Sarasota Herald Tribune.*

Grossman, Cathy Lynn. (1998, October 1). Cruising numbers climb as megaships prepare for sea. *USA Today.*

Grossman, Cathy Lynn. (1996, April 26). Vegas keeps its chips on adults. *USA Today.*

Haring, Bruce. (1997, September 5). Burning man elevates the surreal to an art. *USA Today.*

Heubusch, Kevin. (1997, May). Taking chances on casinos. *American Demographics.*

Horowitz, Bruce. (1997, October 9). New buckeye cafe gives old college try. *USA Today.*

Jensen, Elizabeth. (1997, December 29). Upscale steakhouses are locked in a sizzling rivalry over customers. *Sarasota Herald Tribune.*

McCafferty, Dennis. (1998, February 20). Mardi Gras: Is the party over? *USA Weekend.*

Meyers, Bill. (1998a, January 23). Entertainment giant towers over field. *USA Today.*

Meyers, Bill. (1998b, January 23). Sports' magic kingdom. *USA Today.*

Mohl, Bruce. (1998, February 8). The big picture is movie megaplexes. *Boston Sunday Globe.*

Morris, Jerry. (1997, June 1). Wild time. *Boston Sunday Globe.*

Ogintz, Eileen. (1998, March 22). Kids will get a kick and a slide out of Adventure Ridge resort. *The Tampa Tribune.*

Pound, Edward T. (1997, September 26). The battle over Gettysburg. *USA Today.*

Reed, Danielle. (1998, April 3). Takeoffs & landings. *The Wall Street Journal.*

Reidy, Chris. (1998, January 16). New ways to holler, "Hey, sports fans!" *The Boston Globe.*

Shriver, Jerry. (1996, August 30). An annual pilgrimage back to the heart of America. *USA Today.*

Sloan, Gene. (1997, December 24). Magic kingdom no. 1 in visitors. *USA Today.*

Sloan, Gene. (1997, February 7). Rio Suites stands tall in Las Vegas. *USA Today.*

Spitz, Bob. (1997, December). It's still rock 'n roll to them. *Sky.*

Sun Sentinel Report. (1997, December 26). Cultural tourism rides high. *The Tampa Tribune.*

Vitullo-Martin, Julia. (1997, December 31). New ways to the new year. *The Tampa Tribune.*

Walker, Sam. (1998, March 27). Hair salons, hot tubs, and . . . oh, yeah, baseball. *The Wall Street Journal.*

Wells, Melanie. (1998, February 6). Nagano's remoteness challenges marketers. *USA Today.*

White, Michael. (1997, August 10). Disney announces plans for virtual reality centers. *Virginian Pilot.*

When Henry Ford first manufactured  cars, he maintained that people could have any kind of car they wanted just as long as it was black. When television initially appeared on the scene, the choice of shows was basically Milton Berle or the prize fights. Both the automobile and television are inventions with significant impact and ramifications on modern day life. Try to imagine our world with no suburbs, CNN, couch potatoes, or rush-hour traffic.

The arrival of a new millennium reminds us of the potential changes and the impact they have upon our future—a future that can cause, create, or contribute to significant alterations in the ways we live, work, and play. Charting our course in a new millennium is similar to setting sail for a new world. When Columbus sailed from Spain he intended to locate a shorter route to the Orient. However, his journey led to the discovery of the New World, and this discovery resulted in massive changes to the old world he left.

This experience marketing journey which takes us through the knowledge-based economy may indeed result in the discovery of yet another "new world." Like Columbus we are reaching toward the unknown, and we may discover something other than the riches of the Orient. We may uncover an entirely new way of life.

All aboard for the trip to the New World!

Chapter 14

Creating the Future— Potential and Possibilities

> Industry foresight must be informed by deep insights into
> trends in lifestyles, technology, demographics, and geopoli-
> tics, but foresight rests as much on imagination as prediction.
> To create the future a company must first develop a powerful
> visual and verbal representation of what the future could be.
> To borrow from Walt Disney, what is required is imagineering.
>
> Gary Hamel and C. K. Prahalad

Setting Sail to the New World of Experiences

Borrowing a page from Columbus and his search for the Orient, a boat will serve as transport for this metaphorical journey existing within a discretionary economy. In this instance, it is a new world of experiences. This sailing metaphor was adapted from a concept developed by Robert Holland, a senior fellow at the SEI Center for Advanced Studies in Management at the Wharton School.

As is true with most expeditions, it is highly unlikely that everything will go as planned or intended. There are many factors, circumstances, and conditions surrounding any new venture with the potential and probability for significantly altering the journey and the outcomes. Factors that we need to be especially cognizant of as we embark upon this journey into the new world of the twenty-first century include waves of change, prevailing winds, shoals and sharks, and weather conditions.

Waves of Change—Environmental Factors

Waves of change include those alterations and shifts in the environment in the areas of sociodemographics, science and technology, economics, and politics. The more traditional strategic planning approach acknowledged these forces as individual categories. While changes in birth rates, shifts in the political climate, technological advances, and economic changes individually may continue to be cited, marketing experts will come to view them collectively. These waves of change

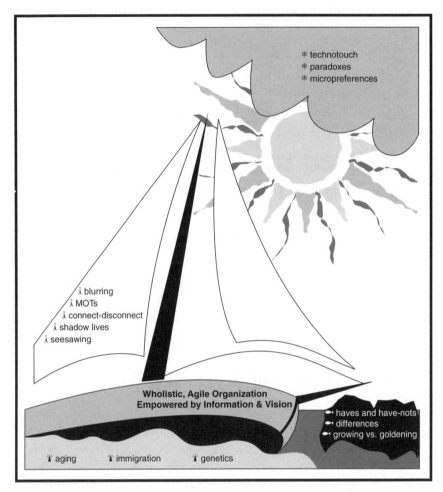

exist in the same framework and the subsequent impact of these factors is really
an integration of the changes and shifts acting in concert with one another.

Prevailing Winds—
Perceptions and Preferences

While waves of change are documented and visible, the winds which serve as
driving forces for the new millennium are less tangible and visible. These winds
are based on perceptions and preferences of people and on the changing practices within organizations. We may not be able to see the winds, but we certainly
see the results of their strength and directional force if we're watching for them.

Shoals & Sharks—Threats

Every journey, including one into the next millennium, includes the unexpected.
Two unexpected elements, in this instance, are shoals and sharks. Shoals refer to
those hidden or partially hidden dangers or obstacles while sharks, on the other

hand, are more visible. Changes in the waves and winds often result in the creation of shoals making it possible to reroute our course around the shoals. Sharks, however, often take the form of competition. These competitors watch and follow our course making them somewhat more difficult to lose.

Both shoals and sharks can be dealt with if mechanisms for doing so become part of our strategy for moving into the discretionary economy.

Weather—The Unexpected

Weather conditions may potentially serve as a threat or challenge to our experience, but differ from shoals and sharks. Changes in the weather are a constant. We know the weather will change. We just don't know exactly where or when and how the particular change will impact upon our experience. This is the land of unintended or unanticipated consequences. Sometimes a change that appears small initially can have significant and wide-ranging impacts often unanticipated. For instance, the discovery of birth control pills appeared on the surface to control conception. But other secondary ramifications of this invention included changes in women's roles, the workplace, childhood, and sexual behavior. Those changing aspects of life subsequently led to the popularity of three-day weekends, expensive children's camps, exotic travel, and a host of other experiences.

Charting the Course

It is virtually impossible to cite each and every wave of change or shift in the wind patterns. It is even more unlikely that every shoal, shark, or weather pattern can be identified or predicted. Rather than attempt the impossible, allow us to provide a preliminary map that incorporates signs to watch and routing suggestions:

ⵜ Waves of Change
- aging population
- immigration
- diversity
- size and distribution of world population
- genetic advances
- longevity
- global economy
- impact of connectivity
- political changes

ⵜ Prevailing Winds
- blurring
- connect-disconnect
- pleasure-purpose
- MOTs (moments of truth)
- shadow lives
- seesawing

⌁ Shoals & Sharks
- differences
- growing versus goldening
- haves and have-nots

✳ Weather Conditions
- technotouch
- paradoxes
- micropreferences

Reading the Chart

Waves of Change

Census documents provide clues as to who we will be in the future. Scientific, technological, and medical publications keep us current with the widespread implications for life and how we experience that life. Make note that each and every potential change will not be pinpointed and described in this section.

While it is helpful for experience providers to read what others have to say about these environmental changes that we have called waves of change, the real value lies in having such an approach become a way of life for an organization. Experience providers need to make wave watching a priority within their organization and to create a place for it within their ongoing operation. Suggestions made in the chapter on infusing information, particularly as it relates to scanning practices, will be helpful for providing insight and direction in this area.

Prevailing Winds

Prevailing winds are shifts in perceptions and practices of people and organizations that impact this trip to the new world. Some of the specific forces within the prevailing wind category with potential for shaping experiences include:

- **Blurring.** Call it blurring. Call it blending. But whatever we call it, we need to stand back and take a look at the number of products, areas, activities, and experiences where we can't tell one from the other. It's hard to tell the young from the old on the basis of behavior. A growing number of families celebrate one or more December holidays whether it's Christmas, Chanukah, Kwanzaa, Ramadan, or the winter solstice. Access to groceries or financial services makes it hard to tell day from night. Cities and shopping malls start to all look alike thanks in part to Planet Hollywood, Starbucks, the Gap, and the Sharper Image. This blurring carries over into what kinds of experiences people pursue and how they prefer to experience them.
- **Connect-Disconnect.** Never before in our recent memories have so many people been intent on seeking, meeting, networking, and in some fashion connecting with people who are friends, spouses, children, family members, colleagues, competitors, or complete strangers. At the same time, people are ardently carving out spaces, time, and opportunities to secure downtime, space, or solitude as a way to disconnect from the pace and patterns of modern day life. Experience providers need to look for ways to accommodate either one or the other of these needs or a winning combination of both.
- **Pleasure-Purpose Continuum.** Experiences were once focused and simple. We either pursued hedonism for pure enjoyment and self-indulgence, or we opted to imbue the experience with a more overriding sense of purpose than just self. Both ends of this spectrum have been pushed to their edges as people want to experience one or the other in the fullest

way possible. An added dimension to this consumer force finds people integrating a little of both into the same experience.

- **Shadow Lives.** Experiences have the potential for becoming the only "real" life people have. Life has become complicated and hectic. Time has replaced money as people's most valuable resource in the knowledge-based economies. Evidence includes the number of people willing to trade a day's pay for a day off. This pattern leads to the construction of two separate lives: the real one and the "other" one. Beautifully (and often expensively) decorated homes lie vacant all day and sometimes into the night. People trek all over the world and tramp through nature preserves and then talk about returning to the "real" world. Children watch the video of the lions playing with one another rather than waiting for the real thing. Facsimile lifestyles are alive and well in today's society.
- **MOTs (Moments of Truth).** To say that the combination of social changes and economic patterns have played havoc with life as we know it would be an understatement. There is not an aspect of life from birth to death that has not been beset by significant change. It's almost as if a trumpet has sounded throughout the country indicating that it's time to stop, reflect, and face some of those issues that have been placed on the back burner or ignored for far too long. This shift in priorities will lead to new experiences and opportunities for providers as well.
- **Seesawing.** To say that people today have their ups and downs and that people also seem to go back and forth on a number of issues would be another understatement. Surveys indicate that even though Americans feel good about themselves and their family, they don't feel good about the country as a whole. Even though the economy is stable, they remain insecure about their financial future. The ups and downs between feeling good and feeling bad isn't the only seesawing going on. People also vacillate between seeking out change while wanting the comfort of the past. There is a continual shifting back and forth between this continuum.

Shoals & Sharks

This category includes factors hiding under the water or lurking in the murkiness. These shoals are not actively out to rock the boat of our experience but can cause trouble if not detected or ignored. The more shark-like elements within this category include any and all factors serving as competitors to our experience. Keep in mind that competition may be a newer form of an experience, but it can also be new and emerging intrinsic needs. Some of those potential factors that could rock the boat include:

- **Differences.** Americans have always prided themselves on their individuality, and today that individuality has translated itself into very different beliefs and behaviors. Gerzon's *A House Divided: Six Belief Systems Struggling for the American Soul* identifies six conflicting belief

The levels and types of differences that will drive wedges between people and nations and will create increasingly fragmented markets have been identified by a number of individuals. There are approaches that reflect differences among Americans as well as differences worldwide. The following provides a capsule overview of two such approaches.

Gerzon's *A House Divided: Six Belief Systems Struggling for the American Soul* identifies six conflicting belief systems that include patria, the religious believers; corporatia, the business community; disia, the disempowered; media, the communicators; gaia, the social action advocates; and officia, government representatives and employees. These groups have very different perspectives on how the country should function and the society should flourish.

Huntington in his book, *The Clash of Civilizations and the Remaking of World Order,* identifies seven major world civilizations whose influence and preference can potentially lead to clashes as follows: the West which includes the United States, the Christian portion of Europe, as well as Canada, Australia, and New Zealand; Orthodoxy which includes Russia, modern Greece, and other countries with an Eastern Orthodox approach to Christianity; Sinic which includes China as well as Taiwan, Hong Kong, and Singapore; Japan, different despite its original ties to China; Hindu which includes India and Sri Lanka; Muslim with its widespread, religious focus; and Latin America with ties to the West with independent traits as well. The definitions and perceptions of experiences among these seven cultures will certainly challenge experience providers in the glocal world around us.

systems that increase conflict among the various groups. The current suggestion to create conversations to resolve racial misunderstandings, and a call in some quarters for the end of affirmative action programs and reductions in immigration contribute to this growing sense of differences. The differences inherent within the United States are not the only ones causing concern. Huntington in his book, *The Clash of Civilizations and the Remaking of World Order,* identified seven major world civilizations whose influence and preference can potentially lead to clashes. Experiences are very much based on cultural beliefs and preferences.

- **Growing Versus Goldening.** Two rapidly growing age groups are children and their grandparents, great-grandparents, and great-great-grandparents. The dilemma is the challenge of using finite resources to provide for the needs of two groups. These groups are at disparate ends of the life continuum, growing up and growing old, which causes them to bring with them very different needs for experiences.
- **The Haves and the Have-Nots.** The growing gap between groups of people who have resources and those who don't certainly influences the world of experiences. Resources, in this instance, refers to a variety of things not all related to wealth. This gap can include a two-tiered level of health, access to technology, healthcare, and a social support system.

Haves and Have-Nots

The terms have and have-nots have been around for a long time, but now their definitions and influence on society and experiences are being substantially broadened. The terms can now refer to any and all of the following:

Haves	Have-Nots
• have their health	• disabled or incapacitated
• have a full-time job	• piece together two or three part-time jobs or projects
• have health insurance	• pray they don't need it
• have time	• have little to none
• have a support network of family and friends	• live on their own with few others to depend upon
• have a "working" relationship with technology	• think VCRs and ATMs are acronyms for foreign corporations
• have "real" experiences that promote growth and self-efficacy	• experience simulations and passive entertainment

Weather Conditions

Despite advances in computerized technology, many weather forecasters still seem to have trouble making predictions that are accurate. The same holds true for weather conditions. The following is a short list of potential weather patterns that may produce bumper crops, disaster, and everything in between for the experience industry:

- **Technotouch.** It may not be the most cybersavvy term to use, but regardless of what we call it, the overriding, ever-infusing impact of technology will invade and touch every aspect of our lives. We will be bombarded with an ever-increasing onslaught of common products and services that have been technologically enhanced. The unknown or unpredictable element of technology is the way in which it eventually impacts our lives in unanticipated ways. For instance, who knew that television would isolate neighbors (and even family members) from one another while conversely, it would provide connections among people living in areas around the world? This touch may alter lives and experiences as dramatically as natural disasters such as floods or tornadoes and can brighten lives as well.
- **Redefined Paradoxes.** Societal shifts, technological changes, and medical advances are impacting every aspect of life and experiences. People are now able to redefine life and the experiences they seek. The interesting part of this redefinition that creates inordinate challenges

for the experience industry is the extent of the contradictions within this approach to redefinition.

People go on vacation yet they take their cellular phone, laptop, and beeper with them. They say they want to spend more time with their children and then they pick resorts with separate programs so they don't have to entertain or interact with them. They indicate they want to become healthy and spend billions on diets and exercise equipment while the stock prices of steakhouses rise as quickly as their cholesterol levels. Everywhere we look we can find a multitude of these contradictions. It will be a challenge to find just the right balance between the paradoxes or to read between the lines to determine the real need behind such behaviors.

- **Micropreferences.** Words such as fast and instant have become the norm in today's world. The remote control permits people to change TV viewing instantly. The number of channels lets them relieve boredom on a whim. The speed at which we can change things and the unprecedented levels of personalization in products and services led to a phenomena called micropreferences. "I want it and I want it now. I want it and I want it my way." The interaction between these two factors will substantially challenge the experience industry like the weather which often provides very little advance warning. It is the growth of micropreferences that signal the start of the discretionary economy.

Sailing 101

When Robert Holland developed his sailing metaphor, he maintained that sailing into the new millennium required two essential elements. These two elements for successful sailing were strong, vision-directed leadership and a pace-setting organization (Holland, 1994, p. 60).

Holland has not been the only individual to suggest what it takes to sail into a new world. There have been others who have offered their insights and suggestions as well:

- Jay W. Forrester, MIT: "The challenge to business in the coming decade will be to operate in a world where trends of the past no longer predict the future."
- Peter Drucker, writing in *The Practice of Management* published in 1954: "Any business enterprise has two, and only two functions, marketing and innovation."
- Hamel and Prahalad, writing in *Competing for the Future:* "foresight rests as much on imagination as prediction."

These insights suggest that there are a number of practices that twenty-first-century experience organizations will embrace to thrive in the new world of a discretionary economy. Vision-directed leadership that monitors change and

Continued on page 374

Signs of a Shift

Signs reflecting the impact of the waves, winds, shoals, sharks, and weather surround those in the experience industries. Just a few examples of these changes include:

Waves of Change

✝ The projected population increase in the United States between 1990 and 2050 is 134 million; 61 percent of that projection is due to immigrants and their descendants raising the overall minority population from 24.3 percent in 1990 to 47.3 percent in 2050. The impact of aging will also be pervasive with the percentages moving from 12.6 percent of the 1990 population to a projected 20.6 percent in 2050 (Dighe and Clement, 1996, p. 89).

✝ According to *Vital Signs 1997*, the gap between the rich and the poor in the world has doubled in the past 30 years with a 30 fold difference between the 1960s and the 1990s. The richest 20 percent of the world's population earned 61 times more income than the poorest 20 percent.

✝ Many of the more than 500 Gold's Gyms worldwide have changed their names to the Fitness Edge to move away from the young, male, bodybuilder image to cater to men, women, and the more mature, health-oriented consumer.

Prevailing Winds

⋏ First the gym became a fitness center, and now it's a full-blown wellness center complete with medical records, free weights, massage therapy, and a whole host of alternatives. It becomes increasingly hard to tell if one is working out, tuning out, or going for a physical checkup.

⋏ The Old Friends Information Services of Orinda, California, helps clients find that war buddy they thought lost forever, that fifth grade teacher who so shaped their future, or that long lost first love from junior high. While 70 percent of the reunions have been successful, about four percent of the located people, when contacted, requested not being found.

⋏ Sprint installed a Communication Center 10,350 feet above sea level in Vail, Colorado, so vacationers could work on their parallel turns and portfolios simultaneously.

⋏ Rosemont, a small suburb in Illinois adjacent to Chicago's O'Hare airport, is home to 4,000 permanent residents but attracts 3.4 million visitors annually boasting the nation's twelfth largest convention center. In 1997, it became the first American town to build a gate surrounding its main residential area. They joined the more than 8 million private communities that are gated in this country. Rosemont appears to want to "connect and disconnect" simultaneously (Grunwald, 1997, A1).

⋏ Halloween has become a $2.5 billion annual industry that now ranks behind New Year's Eve and Super Bowl Sunday as the most popular days for adult parties (Kaufman, 1997, D1).

⋏ Break-Away, a nonprofit group based at Vanderbilt University, helped more than 15,000 college students participate in alternative spring break projects such as tutoring migrant farm workers, building homes in Appalachia, and working with the homeless in New York City (Hellmich, 1997, p. 9D).

⋏ A recent Hyatt Hotel poll found that people want rest and relaxation on a vacation,

Continued on page 372

Signs of a Shift continued

but they also want more than just that. They are seeking what Hyatt dubbed "conspicuous competence," a focus on some kind of self-improvement or soul-searching opportunity.

Å Backroads of Berkeley, California, offers 19 global, multisport trips that provide sweaty and intense activities during daylight hours and more luxurious, pampered evenings. Global Fitness Adventures combines the luxury of a spa with cravings for adventures with trips to exotic locales for mountain biking and hiking complete with massages and fluffy towels.

Å Earthwatch enables people to maintain trails in the Appalachian and Colorado mountains or work alongside archaeologists on remote Southwestern digs. The Global Citizens Network committed to cross-cultural understanding sponsors building projects in Belize, Guatemala, and Kenya.

Å A quick look around the supermarket checkout lines reveals carts filled with Lean Cuisines, frozen cheesecakes, and the latest copy of *Martha Stewart's Living*. Most people live in urban areas but subscribe to country living type magazines. They buy expensive gourmet cooking gadgets and spend more money eating outside the house and decorate houses that sit empty during the day.

Å Ad executives broke ranks with colleagues who created Joe Camel and the Marlboro man by forming an alliance called The Initiative on Tobacco Marketing to Children. They created ads directed to the advertising trade with the tag line: "We can't close their eyes. Can we open ours?" (Brownless, 1996, B1).

Å The National Commission on Civic Renewal headed by former Senator Sam Nunn and former Education Secretary William Bennett is scrutinizing entertainment, politics, sports, and a confrontational legal system, and is compiling "an inventory of hope" to identify promising community and neighborhood efforts to address problems with crime and education (Lawrence, 1996, p. A2).

Å The initial success of Snapple's tea was the resurgence of a traditional beverage that simultaneously infused change and adventure with innovative flavor choices.

Shoals and Sharks

- Census Bureau statistics indicate that, since 1980, the wealthiest one-fifth of the population has experienced 21 percent income growth while wages for the bottom 60 percent of the population have stagnated or decreased (Leonhardt, 1997, p. 82).
- According to a study cited in *The Journal of American Medical Association*, nearly 100 million Americans suffer from one or more chronic conditions including heart disease, diabetes, and arthritis. Such conditions cost $272 billion in 1987, eating away at three-fourths of the healthcare spending in the United States. Researchers estimated that by 2030, chronic diseases will strike 148 million Americans with a price tag of $798 billion (Medical Journal, 1997, p. 67).
- Spending on media (newspapers, magazines, cable and satellite services, books, on-line services and wireless communications) is projected to grow twice as fast as the U. S. economy by 2006 with a growing gap between the media "haves and have-nots" since only about 40 percent of the population will own personal computers and have access to new developments such as wireless phones and digital TV services (Lieberman, 1997, 3B).
- Recent Census Bureau reports indicate that the number of people without health insurance grew by 1.1 million to 41.7 million in 1996 and that the number of

Signs of a Shift *continued*

people living in poverty increased by 4.1 million between 1989 and 1996 (Jones and Belton, 1997, 3B).

➤Retail and service providers in Florida face a current challenge as the nation's preeminent "old" state undergoes a youth transfusion. An analysis of the population estimates for this state suggests that from 1997 until the year 2005 that 23 of the 67 counties will get younger, not older (Nasser, 1997, p. A1).

➤Many phases of the entertainment industry including movies, television, and music are being subjected to clash of value systems as some segments of the population call for rating systems to help parents curtail children's exposure to nonappropriate lyrics, language, and subject matter.

Weather Conditions

✻ In the first quarter of 1997, $50 to $60 million worth of airline tickets were booked on-line (Rosato, 1997, 8E).

✻ One doesn't have to call ahead for an appointment or spend time languishing in the waiting room when an E-mail to the psychologist will produce a response. There are a variety of sites such as Psych Central and Shrink-Link that are providing on-line therapy.

✻ A survey conducted by the Food Network found that on-line shopping services have grown by 73 percent between 1994 and 1996. Home shopping programs are now offered by 40 percent of grocery store operators (Tomorrow in Brief, 1996, p. 5)

✻ John Updike's book, *Murder Makes the Magazine,* was written with a little help from his friends. Updike placed an opening paragraph on a Web site and then selected one additional paragraph each day from writings provided by visitors to that site.

✻ A Michigan surgeon and a NASA computer expert joined forces to create an airline lifeline system that enables doctors on the ground to address in-flight medical emergencies via video camera, laptop computer, and the Internet.

✻ A kiosk exhibit at the National Museum of History in Washington, DC, gives visitors a chance to save the giant Hubbell telescope. They use a remote arm to dock it with the space shuttle. There are time limits to this process, and if would-be astronauts succeed, they get a congratulatory message. If they screwup, an alarm is set off.

✻ Information from the *U. S. Statistical Abstract* revealed that in 1995, Americans spent $8.7 billion on athletic and sports clothing and an additional $2.5 billion on exercise equipment. On the other hand, the *1995 Midcourse Review of Healthy People 2000* prepared by the Centers for Disease Control reported that 60 percent of American adults had insufficient leisure-time physical activities to reduce their health risks.

✻ People claim that they want to return to a simpler, more basic way of living, and the heightened sales of outdoor camping equipment supports that notion. However, Recreational Equipment Inc., outfitters for the hard-core outdoor market, reports soaring sales for such luxury items as large tents with multiple separate rooms and awnings and oversized, folding rocking chairs soared while sales of the more basic backpacking equipment remains flat. This trend in luxury camping gear was born out by L. L. Bean and Coleman Company who reported selling ever-growing amounts of amenity type items (Miller, 1997, B1).

fosters innovation requires a "wholistic" approach to thinking. "Wholistic" thinking will result in experience marketing that sets the trends rather than responds to them. That newly acquired information and knowledge are dependent on organizational imagination and action.

"Wholistic" Thinking

The experience industry is indeed sailing not only into a new millennium but also into an entirely new era with vast potential and unlimited possibilities. What then does it take to successfully make this journey, this transition to an era of experience marketing? Heeding the advice of the aforementioned experts, it seems that organizations, in order to become or remain successful, will need to combine the elements of marketing and prediction with innovation and imagination.

Organizations need to collect and closely monitor data, trends, and information then infuse that newly acquired knowledge with creativity and innovation. The challenge for experience providers is to blend both sides of their cerebral capacity, their organizational left brain with its logical, analytical side and their organizational right brain with its intuitive, creative side.

In order to accomplish this balance between both sides of cerebral capacity, organizations will need to become holistic in three different ways. They need to involve the *whole* organization, the *whole* brain of the people within those organizations, and tune into the *whole* needs of their participants.

Involving the Whole Organization

Not everybody is a marketer, but everybody is "in marketing" (and innovation, too). The experience organization that wants to create its future will make concerted attempts to use the insights and information of everybody in the organization. Remember, it was the housekeeping staff who helped hotels get a slice of their guests' dining dollars by pointing out the large number of pizza boxes they had to discard. Here are a few suggestions for involving the whole organization:

- Manage by playing around. Rather than having another standard department meeting, take the group out to play. They can participate in your activity or some other experience. Over snacks after the "playing around," do an informal debriefing about insights gleaned and new ideas generated. Keep in mind that this activity is not limited to management and supervisory types only.
- Post a challenge or problem area on a bulletin board near an area where staff or customers congregate or pass frequently. Provide colored markers and lots of white space for people to add their thoughts and suggestions.
- Provide guest certificates so your staff can invite a child, friend, or parent to accompany them to your experience or to a competitor's experience. Be sure to ask them for their reactions and observations afterwards.

- Give a small work team an Instamatic camera and have them take pictures of your experience, the location, the staff, the participants, and any peripherals of the experience that capture their attention. See what develops.
- Create a mechanism for regularly soliciting insights employees have gleaned from interacting with participants.
- Create an environment that supports both physical and mental comfort and flexibility.

Involving the Whole Brain of the Organization

Organizations have traditionally valued logical, orderly information and thinking based on facts. This is still important, but experience providers now realize that the challenges of the new world require that they tap into the whole brain of the organization. This means the left part of their brain that is so logical must be stretched to incorporate the right side as well. The right hemisphere of the brain tends to be more intuitive, spontaneous, and creative.

One way to give an organization a whole brain workout is to change the focus of how employees spend their time and energy. Organizations already expend substantial amounts of these resources in meetings and working with project teams. And not all of these activities involve much in the way of innovation and imagineering. There are many techniques for changing those results and here are just a few such suggestions:

- Start meetings with brainteasers or riddles to get peoples' minds pumping.
- Look for multiple solutions to every problem or situation; don't jump at the first possible answer.
- Before a team session, post or E-mail a problem or challenge that will appear on the agenda to give people time to incubate ideas.
- Have staff list five things about your experience that you've always done and then give them time to explore ways to break those rules or patterns.
- Brainstorm as many possible uses for old calendars or improvements to a shower stall to serve as a springboard for innovative ideas to enhance your experience.
- Use props such as toys or gadgets to enhance brainstorming activities or to generate solutions to problems.

Identifying the Needs of the Whole Person

If people go to a hospital for surgery, they don't take only that part of their anatomy in need of repair. When children show up at a family entertainment center, they don't just bring their need for fun and amusement. They bring the needs of their parents with them as well, even if the parents aren't physically present. Gaining insight into the whole person and his or her whole way of life can lead to important changes to an experience. There are a number of ways you can increase the range of your understanding of your whole participant:

- Have employees role-play wearing different shoes or hats that represent various participant groups as a means for better understanding the many aspects of participants and their lives.
- Identify five reasons your participants would not want to return to reexperience with your organization. Turn this list around to generate five surefire reasons they would want to return again and again.
- Talk to kids about your experience, or watch them as they interact with the parameters of your experience. Children have a different way of observing and sharing their thoughts.
- Take a field trip to a hospital, bookstore, church, movie theater, amusement park or some other experience provider and see what you can learn about people and experiences in general.

An entire industry is being built around creativity and innovation. Consultants and trainers are helping organizations incorporate these approaches. The shelves at libraries and bookstores have many volumes on these topics. Read some of them and share either the book or the ideas or both with others in your organization.

Don't overlook the value of this component as it relates to the reinvention and regeneration of your experience. As a post script, Ben & Jerry's has a Joy Gang that meets regularly to generate ideas to keep work fun. An enjoyable workplace houses empowered employees.

IdeAction

All the holistic thinking within an organization goes for naught unless that organization can transform those innovative ideas into action. The second essential

Ted Klauber, whose former title with Foote, Cone & Belding was advertising account executive, does not necessarily spend his day at the office any longer. Klauber spends his days in the field watching families brush their teeth or hang out at urban basketball courts. This form of market research, referred to as consumer ethnography, is proving invaluable as a way to interact and observe real people living their real lives in real time. Foote, Cone & Belding found the approach so effective that it created a global department called Mind & Mood to incorporate these types of activities.

Klauber explains that Mind & Mood involves living with the customer, and it involves real impressions that can then be incorporated into marketing activities. Mind & Mood is about walking in the shoes of potential or current customers. It's about finding out firsthand what their day is like, how they undertake certain commonplace activities, whether such activities are habit or ritual, and the identity of others influencing or involved in the activity (jobtitlesofthefuture, 1991, p. 70).

element cited by Holland for sailing into the new world was an organization that set the pace for others. Setting such a pace requires incorporating ideas and trends that are augmented by organizational imagination. Those ideas then need to be transformed into action.

Action approaches can involve looking at the past, the present, and the future. The next section of this chapter does a bit of both. The section's brief profile of role models takes you back to people and organizations with a track record for combining information and imagination. That bit of history is followed by a list of suggestions in the area of marketing that identify present potential and possibilities. The future arrives with two different "IdeAction" suggestions for the future, a sampler and a set of scenarios.

Role Models

There are a number of individuals and enterprises, large and small, local and global, that have managed to combine imagination and prediction into one package. Walt Disney was the uncrowned king and creator of imagineering. In fact, the legend and the legacy of Walt moves forward today. So it is only fitting that Disney World, one of Walt's last visions, serves as the starting point for this section.

Disney World

When Disney World opened in 1971, the experts predicted that it might someday manage to attract 6 million visitors annually. When it celebrated its twenty-fifth anniversary, the 47 square mile resort drew 30 million paying customers a year. Much of that attendance resulted from adding experiences that the company dreamed up for an ever-changing world.

The Disney experience now encompasses a wide range of diverse opportunities. Fans can witness world class sports competitions in the new $100 million sports complex, paddle a canoe into a Florida swamp, learn cooking and cartooning at the feet of masters, stay at five-star resorts, and celebrate New Year's Eve every night.

But Disney isn't finished imagining new experiences for people quite yet. Disney expanded its Downtown Disney, a pseudo-urban entertainment and shopping district, with a 24-screen movie theater, House of Blues, Virgin Records Megastore, a Cirque du Soleil theater, and a Planet Hollywood. It created a 500-acre Animal Kingdom where guests are taken back 65 million years to the end of the dinosaur era.

Disney continues to practice imagineering with its eye on the bottom line. Jill Krutnik, an entertainment analyst at Smith Barney, comments that "every new piece in the puzzle represents a clearly considered attempt to evolve a visible presence in every conceivable market niche while continually taking steps to protect and preserve the essence of the 'Disney experience'" (Fenichell, 1997, pp. 19–25).

There are others who have met the challenge as well. Some of them are relative newcomers to the experience arena. Many of them are clearly imagineers. It is often said that true marketing innovation involves looking at something commonplace and ordinary and altering it in some way to make it interesting, exciting, or special. Take a look at these experience providers who have done just that.

Martha Stewart

Time calls her one of the 25 "most influential Americans" while *Newsweek* predicts she'll be one of the most important cultural figures of the twenty-first century. How does a former model, former stockbroker, and one time home-based caterer inspire the imagination and loyalty of legions? Martha Stewart is a taste maker as well as a dream fulfiller.

The "queen of how-to," as she is sometimes called, has made a fortune focusing on things people forgot or never knew how to do. Basic, common kinds of things such as folding a flag, making a gingerbread house, or painting a front door are among her specialties. She has been prolific with 20 lifestyle books, a weekly TV show, magazine, and morning CBS appearances. With her alliance with Kmart, Stewart caters to the dreams, hopes, and aspirations of millions of people who can't afford Tiffany's or Neiman Marcus (Yemma, 1997, p. E2).

Her secret lies in the intrinsic needs found within her experiential options. She took the ordinary activities and events of daily life and made them special. She imbued them with meaning.

Jimmy Buffett

On the surface this guy, just another singer with a guitar who makes the concert circuit every summer, may not appear special. But Parrot Heads, as his fans are called, know that he is much more than that. These people of all ages and from all walks of life take the day off from work to make sure they get a good spot in the parking lot before the concert. They need time to set up their grills, coolers, and sometimes even "in-truck" pools to make the trip to Margaritaville. There are few new songs and even fewer surprises. Buffett staffers wander around letting fans play Nerf basketball using a makeshift palm tree as a basketball backboard. Buffett souvenir T-shirts soar through the crowd via giant slingshots. It's the mind-set that these concerts are able to create as people are temporarily transported to Margaritaville, a place where day-to-day cares melt away and are replaced by a carefree love of life garnished with the promise of plenty of good times ahead.

Fantasy Camps

The boys of summer used to be either 10-year-old Little Leaguers or big time professional athletes but not anymore. Bob Dowdell changed all that. Men (and women too) maturing physically but young in spirit head to Florida for spring training and their place in the sun. Dowdell makes sure they get their own locker and professional uniform. However, he provides them with far more than just the physical trappings as these adults, mostly but not all male between the ages of 35 and 80-plus, fly in from all over the world to hear Joe Castiglione, the actual Red Sox announcer, announce their names as they come up to the plate to bat against Fergie Jenkins or Bill Lee. Talk about a field of dreams. Dowdell and others who followed him have created a whole host of fantasies for people to experience. And we thought escapist TV shows like "Fantasy Island" would never become reality.

U. S. Tennis Association

The U. S. Tennis Association launched an ambitious initiative in 1997 to attract more people to play the game of tennis. Acknowledging that the sport had dropped in popularity in recent years, the USTA and the entire industry of tennis professionals, community tennis associations, equipment manufacturers, and allied organizations such as the National Recreation and Park Association designed an integrated marketing strategy to grow participation levels. This initiative represented an unprecedented collaboration between the diverse groups within any major sport activity to grow the market collectively while recognizing that each participating group would benefit from the addition of new players at all levels of the sport.

La-Z-Boy Recliners

Sales of these once low-status chairs have climbed dramatically over the past decade with the Monroe, Michigan, company turning out more than one million recliners a year. How does it manage to bring this once "low-rent, blue-collar, trailer-park Naugahyde chair" back from the dead? It combined the aging of the

- ❖ The Hotel Monaco in Seattle, Washington, offers a temporary pet replacement for its guests. The rooms house complimentary gold fish to help keep the visitor calm and productive during his or her stay.
- ❖ The Ultimate Taxi out of Aspen, Colorado, the brainchild of Jon Barnes, has a mirrored disco ball and laser lights and a keyboard creates an unusual ride home. His Web site features pictures and comments from the famous and not-so-famous passengers of his cybermobile.
- ❖ It's a Wonderful Life is a small business in the greater Boston area that creates one-of-a-kind gift boxes creatively assembled in hatboxes or wire baskets and categorized by theme. The PMS box contains a parfait glass, chocolate sauce, and a hanky.
- ❖ The Fountain, a European day spa in Ramsey, New Jersey, offers a limousine service so that people purchasing a spa package for a friend or significant other can whisk them off for a surprise day of pampering.
- ❖ US Airways added a snacking station to its overseas flights so passengers can get up and grab a munchy whenever they feel like it.
- ❖ Thurston Watts introduced a service he calls "shine and dine" whereby patrons at the Newsroom, a vegan-friendly bistro, exchange their shoes for a clean square of carpet on which to rest their feet while Watts shines their shoes.

Baby Boomers, the retrorage of the Gen Xers with new features such as cup holders, heat, and massage and have virtually given rebirth to a household staple (Wilson, 1997, pp. D1–2).

Not all experience providers jump into imagineering to the extent of those previously cited. However, there is an unlimited number of ways that providers can either create or incorporate in smaller ways to make an experience different, special, or right for their participants.

Marketing Shifts for Potential and Possibilities

There have been a number of marketing techniques, approaches, and strategies included in this book. They form the framework for experience marketing. The few additional approaches cited here are intended to advance the marketing continuum. Such shifts in marketing are intended to help experience providers meet the demands and expectations of the present while preparing for the challenges and promise of the future.

Such marketing and innovation approaches that are crucial for the experience industry today involve addressing current marketing imperatives while transitioning to evolving marketing issues. Experience marketing at the beginning of this new millennium must provide:

Not Only	**But Also**
• Customer's personal preferences and delight	• Emerging 4Ps: promise, power, potential and possibilities
• Reinvention	• Regeneration
• Experiences	• Opportunities and solutions

From Preferences to the Emerging 4Ps

Currently experience providers need to go out of their way to ascertain the personal preferences of their participants. People have come to expect this kind of customization and personalization. Restaurant patrons insist on specifying ingredients and cooking instructions. Fitness club members have come to expect personal exercise specialists, nutritionists, cardiac exams, and rehab equipment.

Personal preference is becoming a given, but it is also being augmented by a growing expectation for the unexpected. People crave the unexpected. It could be an experience provider who gives the extra inch, goes the extra mile, or an unanticipated little extra. The end result is a customer whose experience has been enhanced by the injection of delight into the participation. The attention showered upon a newlywed couple who arrived direct from their wedding ceremony to board a Saturday evening TWA flight was a delight for the couple and fellow passengers alike. The captain sent back a complimentary bottle of champagne, and the flight attendant took their picture before takeoff.

Even healthcare has become taken with the little extras or unexpected extras. Drop a friend off for one of the increasingly more common outpatient surgical procedures, and you will be on the receiving end of a phone call from the surgeon announcing the successful completion of the procedure. On returning home the patient is just as likely to get a good night phone call from the surgeon to check on his or her progress and to reassure him or her if there are side effects.

Personal preference and added delight are part of the present. They are necessary components of experience marketing. However, a shift is on. This emerging shift involves going beyond preference and delight to fulfilling the personal promise sought from an experience, to unleashing the individual power of the participants, and to helping the participant explore the possibilities and reach his or her full potential.

Experiences are becoming the mainstay of the knowledge era and the impetus for the discretionary economy that is currently underway. As the information era leads to substantive changes in how we live, work, and play, experiences will assume a new and growing importance. The sheer variety of those experiences and the diverse nature of the impact that they have on people will fuel the discretionary economy. It won't be just about the experience for the sake of the experience; it will become about providing a fundamental sense of who people are, how they interact with others and the world, and who they can become.

Right now experiences are about possibilities. What are the possibilities for filling up children's time after school or having fun over a long weekend? For a variety of reasons, people will begin to turn to experiences as a way to explore or discover their potential. In this instance, potential may refer to life's work, lifestyle, or life stage. Using experiences as a way to uncover potential will just naturally lead to experiences being designed and promoted as having promise for people. Certain types of laser surgery hold the promise for people to change how they look

---

Clos*eup*

Health Oasis (www.Healthoasis.com), a health and personal improvement–oriented Web site, is a virtual health club as it provides interactive ways for users to take charge of their physical and emotional health. Cyberusers can improve their overall health, lose weight, change their outlook on life, reach goals, make new friends, and find partners with similar goals and interests.

The premium membership costs approximately $40 for the first three months with a smaller fee per month after that. This cyberspace health club lets members create or join specialized teams to work towards their goals. They can interact anonymously using their own personal pen name and private post office box.

This virtual weight loss clinic allows members to find a cyberbuddy, develop a personal commitment letter, become part of a weight loss team, work with nutritional experts, track daily food intake with specialized software, and follow menus created by nutritional experts. A learning annex within the Web site provides updates on health news, a health information library, and a weekly electronic newsletter. Discounts on a variety of health-related products such as vitamins, books, audio and videocassettes, exercise equipment, and personal care products are also available.

❖ Imagine the surprise and delight of guests at LeSport in St. Lucia. This resort caters to both halves of traveling couples, with one half interested in eating and playing robustly and the other half more interested in a spa-like experience. LeSport combines the full range of activity and eating and drinking capacity of a full-service resort with the therapeutic and dietary options of a spa. The resort's slogan, "Give us your body for a week and we'll give you back your mind," plays into the emerging 4Ps of experiences as well.

❖ American Express launched a campaign with its spokesperson, Tiger Woods, sure to fan the fire of delight for its cardholders. It tapped into experiences that people dream of and offered them the possibility of making those dreams come true. Every time cardholders used their card, they were automatically entered in the Blue Box Sweepstakes. Dreams that came true as part of these sweepstakes included some of the following:

- Tiger Country—being part of Tiger Woods' gallery at the tournament of the cardholder's choice plus a half-hour golf lesson with Tiger's dad;
- The Ultimate NBA—seats for every game of the NBA finals plus a chance to meet NBA legends, attend press conferences, and sit in the TV booth;
- Disney Vacation—seven magical days at Disney World for the cardholder and 11 other people of his or her choice complete with an exclusive theme park experience only Disney and American Express can deliver; and
- Designer Original—first-class airfare for the cardholder and a friend to Paris, Milan, or New York to preview the latest fashions with a $15,000 allotment to buy designer fashions.

❖ People sitting in the front seats for World Wrestling Federation special events go home with an added surprise, the logo-laden, cushioned chair as a souvenir of the experience.

❖ VH1 offers the work force in America the chance for the Ultimate Holiday Office Party. An essay of 25 words or less as well as a permission slip from your boss may bring you and your coworkers a party replete with Duran Duran, hosted by Vicki Lewis of "NewsRadio," and sponsored by Sam Adams.

❖ Patients with serious cardiac problems enroll in intensive educational and activity programs with Dr. Dean Ornish or the Cooper Institute and return home able to control their own diet, exercise, health, and lives from that point on.

❖ The Northwest Airlines DreamPerks Auction provides frequent fliers with the chance to bid on unique experiences such as a round of golf with famous professional golfers or highly prized seats at concerts with the proceeds benefiting charities.

and who they think they are and how the world perceives them. Being a Red Sox ball player for even a week will enable individuals to uncover that unexplored potential and transform that potential into a promise for living life more fully.

Eventually, experiences will be about power. The creation and provision of experiences will enable people to seek their own sense of power. Learning institutions who help people "learn to learn" and unleash this newly found power into other avenues for growth are examples of such power. Medical care that provides people with information and opportunities to care for themselves rather than to depend on doctors will provide people with this sense of power.

 ❖ The CardioFitness Center in New York City bills itself as a "no thrills, no excuses" kind of place. Recognizing that 95 percent of people don't like to workout and that many of them are deconditioned, overworked, and overstressed, it created an experience to deal with that. It provides free lockers where members always find their sneakers and workout clothes. Everybody wears the same workout clothes eliminating the sometimes showy or competitive aspect of working out. Members are matched with their own personal physiologist who develops a plan that's right for them, and then this fitness goes a bit beyond. It created an atmosphere where staff and clientele support one another to eliminate the insecurity and stress of not measuring up to the fitness hot shot types. It also doesn't take no for an answer. If members haven't been in for a while, CardioFitness staff call them up. If they don't return these phone calls, the staff try humorous poems via fax. In short, CardioFitness, who provides the in-house fitness services for the Federal Reserve Bank and JP Morgan, does everything within its power to help members reach their optimal level of fitness.

❖ The Freedom Boat Club out of Siesta Key and Venice, Florida, promises just that to its members—freedom. In this case, the time sharing approach to boat ownership means freedom from ownership and all that comes with that including expense and maintenance.

❖ The collaborative filtering offered by some Internet services allows users to supply personal preferences related to books, movies, and music and then based upon the titles or suggestions submitted by other people with tastes similar to theirs, it can present users with films, CDs, or movies they might enjoy.

❖ A new ship, *World ResidenSea,* will let people circumnavigate the globe continually without leaving home because the 85,000-ton, 953-foot vessel will have 250 apartment-style accommodations. *The World* (its nickname) will spend 250 days in port annually staying about a week in most places but longer for more interesting stops such as the Summer Olympics in Sydney.

❖ The Siesta Key, Florida, Chamber of Commerce created a slogan just full of promise and potential for its visitors: "a place for the body to rest and the soul to soar."

❖ Yahoo's Holiday Psychic Gift Guide has visitors answer a few humorous riddles followed by the appearance of one of three fictitious psychics offering holiday shopping tips. Of course, these tips are actually linked to one of the sponsors!

❖ Herds of Harleys roam the desert of the United Arab Emirates as both natives of this country and Western workers there for jobs are members of the Dubai's Harley Owners Group (HOGs) who organize charity drives, Wednesday night rides, and a monthly overnight trip (Associated Press, 1998, p. 8).

The emerging 4Ps of experiences—possibilities, potential, promise, and power—will open a whole new world of opportunity for experience providers and for their participants.

From Reinvention to Regeneration

Currently, experience providers are under considerable pressure to continually reinvent their experience either in reality or in the minds of their customers.

People become bored or complacent with the repetition of the same experience and continue to demand innovation and stimulation. Water park operators know that children are going to expect some kind of new thrill or attraction when the next summer season rolls around. Fitness centers realize that over time members become bored with the same aerobics classes or treadmill and will stray if not rewarded with a more updated version of essentially the same thing.

Changes that fall under the category of reinvention are generally not substantive changes. They usually involve making a small alteration to an existing part of the experience or helping the participants to perceive that something has changed. Reinvention is absolutely essential for most experiences but represents a rather superficial level of change.

The need for novelty that results in reinvention will eventually lead to a higher form of change referred to as regeneration. Regeneration goes beyond revising an experience so it appears new and fresh for the consumer. Regeneration involves renewing an experience. This renewal may include growing the experience so it meets the needs of people as their skill level escalates creating the desire for an experience that is more challenging or absorbing. Renewal of an experience can also incorporate people's growth and transition to higher order levels of need.

Ski areas that are user-friendly for beginner and intermediate skiers run the risk of losing them to more challenging resorts where they can continue to grow and be challenged. Certain group tour experiences may fulfill an individual's initial need for adventure but lose him or her as his or her definition of adventure grows to include conquering new lands independently.

Both reinvention and regeneration create challenges for experience providers, but they are the type of challenges that can lead to new opportunities if addressed correctly and in a timely fashion.

Opportunities & Solutions

This almost invisible transition to an experience economy has taken place gradually and without a great deal of fanfare to date, but all that is going to change. As life becomes more complex and demanding, the benefits inherent within experiences will cause people to take greater notice of the role experiences play, and can potentially play, in their lives.

People everywhere are beginning to take notice that urban areas are trying to transform themselves into entertainment centers and that people are trading big houses for big dreams. As the experience economy becomes a more recognized part of society as a whole, it will become apparent that experiences will be called on to do one of two things. Experiences will either create opportunities for the participants or provide solutions to their problems or challenges. Successful providers of experiences will evolve to serve as the vehicle for these desired opportunities or solutions.

Opportunities

Examples of experience opportunities include:

- Cruise lines such as the Delta Queen and the Holland America encourage "come aboard together" groups to reduce the intimidation or isolation for people traveling alone. They've taken along groups from art leagues, alumni associations, retired airline employees, Civil War buffs, family and class reunions as well as Shriners, Elks, and a host of others.
- Bodegas or stores specializing in Hispanic groceries create an experience that is far more than groceries as they provide a natural support system in the Latino community including such opportunities as a place to hang out, buy a Spanish language newspaper, learn new jokes about Castro and Fernandex, and watch one's favorite Spanish soap opera. Such opportunities are being incorporated by other experience providers into their marketing plan.
- Women's travel providers such as Call of the Wild, Woodswomen or Outdoor Vacations for Women Over 40 provide a chance for women to bloom, grow, and try new things in a supportive, testosterone-free environment (Bly, 1996, 11D).
- Silversea Cruises and *National Geographic Traveler* joined to create an enrichment program with photographers and journalists from the magazine lecturing on board and hosting offshore excursions.
- EFM, a seven-member travel club out of Phoenix, stands for escape from men (marriage, motherhood, monotony, menopause, or whatever) and includes outings such as its Ladies Choice weekend at the Biltmore complete with chocolate tasting, massage, and rental of tear-jerking chick flicks (Bly, 1996, 13D).
- Vacation Getaway Programs offered by the Del Webb Corporation at seven of its Sun Cities communities provides an opportunity for older adults to sample the Sun Cities lifestyles by creating packages that include lodging at a vacation villa or off-site hotel with a round or two of golf, and access to recreation centers.
- The Buckeye Hall of Fame Cafe in Columbus, Ohio, has an exterior that resembles the facade of Ohio Stadium and a interior that includes a giant arcade, four bars, and the Ohio State University logo on everything from menus to bottled water. A sizable part of revenues comes from tourists and alumni with royalties going to the University.
- Libraries have become a community-friendly, full-service place sponsoring sleepovers and magicians for youth and book clubs, concerts, gardens, and coffee bars for the adults.
- Quiz nights at pubs have gained in popularity providing the bar crowd with an excuse to go out of the house, get mental exercise, and have an honest to goodness way to start conversations and meet people.
- Boeing runs intense, two-week training seminars for airline employees from around the world at Boeing U and as the world's biggest builder of airlines helps people make their airlines run more efficiently and profitably. The free classes are an opportunity for Boeing to establish a relationship with potential customers and learn from them as well.
- A company called Ex Marks the Spot created a variety of gift items and packs such as Don't Whine Wine and Don't Dismay, Someday They'll Pay candy coins for people involved in a divorce or broken romance.

Solutions

Examples of experience-oriented solutions include:

- A combination of big brother and dorm mother is found in Smart Date, an electronic message system that enables women to document their dating plans for use by the authorities in case of a problem.
- Hyatt Hotel properties let prospective visitors go on-line to visit various properties. They get to ride the elevators and see the rooms. One Hawaii hotel has a camera mounted on the roof that sends pictures from the beach to the Web site.
- CardioTheater Express by Australian Bodyworks now offers a minihealth club within the Kroger grocery store in Alpharetta, Georgia. Its ultimate intent is to become the McDonald's of fitness by offering nonintimidating, economical fitness in locations convenient for people.
- The Geek Squad founded in Minneapolis, Minnesota, is a high-tech company that specializes in computer support for the fearful and the inexperienced. The 12 special agents wear clip-on ties and white socks, travel in vintage cars and are on call 24 hours a day, seven days a week. They provide supportive, nonthreatening assistance for the cyberly challenged.
- The Web site thetrip.com remembers you. It remembers which airline you prefer as well as seating and meal preferences. It knows whether or not frequent-flier miles are important to you as well as hotel preferences. It factors your travel profile, likes and dislikes automatically into your travel plans and options. This service comes complete with travel guides, interactive maps, weather reports, and actual radar flight tracking.
- The Missouri Department of Corrections, overwhelmed with inmate lawsuits over prison conditions and policies, opened a user-friendly Constituent Services Office for inmates and reduced the number of lawsuits by nearly 70 percent in two years saving the state $2.5 million in court costs (Leonard, 1997, p. D1).
- Classic Residence communities managed by Hyatt in a variety of locations provide Hyatt-style services and amenities along with quality life care. Residents are able to receive supervised, independent living, assisted living, or healthcare depending on their individual health needs all within one operation.
- Mail Boxes Etc. established credit card activated, self-service business centers open 24 hours a day, 7 days a week, in 3,000 stores in a partnership with USA Technologies.
- Choice Hotels International which does franchising for Quality, Clarion, Comfort Inn, Sleep Inn, Rodeway Inn, and Econolodge created Choice Picks Food Courts. These food courts let hotels close restaurants that can be costly to run while allowing guests the choice of brand name foods such as Nathan's Famous, Pizzeria Uno, and I Can't Believe It's Yogurt (Belden, 1997, p. B4).
- Crunch fitness centers in New York and Los Angeles have hypoxic, nine-by-nine-foot, low-oxygen vinyl chambers that simulate conditions at 9,000 feet helping people prepare for treks in the Sierras or skiing in Colorado.
- Air New Zealand has added aroma therapy to help its first-class and business travelers fight jet lag and dry cabin air by providing them with kits containing a half-dozen potions, eye compresses, and facial mist sprays.

Sampler

There are numerous books identifying and providing insights into every trend, emerging direction, activity or experience that appears to be on the horizon for the future. It is strongly suggested that you take advantage of the information and insight provided by such sources. They make invigorating and worthwhile reading.

Rather than provide great detail of such trends and directions, as an alternative a sampler has been created. This sampler features a montage of trends, terms, and target markets with potential for the experience industry.

Scenarios

Forecasting, according to Hamel and Prahalad, combines information, prediction, and imagination. An outcome of these three ingredients can be the creation of scenarios. Creating scenarios is a highly desirable activity for organizations that want to successfully complete the journey into the new world. To help further your journey, we created some scenarios to get your thinking started in that direction.

Postal Suites

There was a time when we were a nation of small towns where post offices served as the center of the community. Neighbors would congregate at delivery time to pick up their mail and of course, the "local news." The post office was the place to see and be seen. Eventually, post offices gave way to more impersonal places where people stood impatiently in line to buy stamps, mail packages, or purchase postal memorabilia.

Of course, that was before technotouch took over. Faxes, E-mail, on-line banking, Federal Express, and home delivery, all conspired to usher out the era of the post office. Post offices are being boarded up in rural areas where the numbers don't support the continued operation and post offices run the risk of eventually disappearing entirely. Who will need them now that we have technology to take its place?

Make way for the new postal suites. The waiting lines will be replaced by comfortable waiting lounges and the stamps for letters will be replaced by the miracles of modern communication. Postal suites will consist of high-tech telecommunication rooms that can be rented by the half hour or leased by the year.

And who might the customers be? Perhaps new parents who want to videoconference with family and friends around the globe to show off their new addition. Work groups will rent these studio suites for teleconferencing with work teams in distant places, visiting with important clients, or holding long-distance holiday parties. Companies that don't need to create an entire office will lease these suites for employees who single-handedly run a local operation. Older people who continue to live on their own much to the chagrin of their adult children will come in once a week for a videoconference. These encounters enable their children to assess for themselves their parent's mental and physical competence to continue living independently.

Sampler

adrenaline rush, alignment, aquarium, anthropology, alternative living arrangements, anti-aging, anthrolineages

bathrooms, biophilia, biochemical solitude, "been there, done that," boomerang parents and exes, Bible resorts, brain salons

casitas, cybercemeteries, cybercampuses, convergence, closure, comfort clothes, comfort TV, comfort zones, Comfort, cosmetic surgery, (personal) concierges, compulsory adult education, corporate wellness, corporate social worker, community marriage policies, Community, conspicuous competence, cultural ethnography, community houses

divorce, dietary diversity, deep marketing, dreams, downward nobility, discretionary economy

emotility, ecopsychology, ethnic ambiguity, ecotourism, edutainment, entereducate, end of retirement, escape, entitlement wars, extreme sports, excessories

familial feelings, frugality, free time, flexible architecture, flexible workplaces, flexibility, food therapy, fountain of youth, financial wellness, fusion foods, fusion everything

generic options, good deeds, "going to the dogs," global identity, grandfamilies, grand gardens, "God forbid rooms," gold-collar workers, generation gaplet

hyperreality, hybrid health, Halloween, healthy pleasures, health anything and everything, hunters (and gatherers, too), healthy pleasures, homophyly

info-relief, incubators, innercise

java, joy, jobs

kids, kids, kids, knowledge economy, knowledge entrepreneurs

longevity, "it's not the years in your life but the life in your years"

medallion choices, minimalism, meditation, multisports, "mild ones," multiple income streams, moderation, mid-youth market, marriage mentors, mediation, myths

nesting sites, NASCAR, niche resorts, nonfamilies, New Age, new age definitions

(adult) orphans, overplaying, office concierge

prescription food, pets, pets, pets, personal coaches, power foods, parascience, personal responsibility, paranormal, portfolio professionals, provocateurs, psychic whiplash

questing, quality of life

reunions, revaluing, renewed attachment, recovery, relative poverty, real-life TV, roommates, the Roaring 2000s

second homes, simplicity, scrapbooks, storytelling, soul, spirituality, self-efficacy, simplicity, studied relaxation, soul-searching

tree houses, the third age, third places, therapeutic tourism, thrivalism

unintended consequences

vitamin counselors, virtual corporations, virtual experiences, virtual relationships, Virtually everything!

waterfalls, women's sports

xcitement, xtraordinary lives

yoga, yesterday, youthfulness

zest, zip

There will be a lineup of people to use postal suites including those who can't afford the latest technology, don't want to be bothered owning that kind of equipment, or would rather not tie up company assets in technology that quickly becomes obsolete.

Mobile Homes

Mobile homes have long been the mainstay for people seeking affordable or compact living accommodations or those wishing to take to the open road. Enter the mobile homes of the new millennium. There will be a big demand for these units.

These mobile homes will be personal cocoons, self-contained with all the necessities and the amenities as well as the personal effects of their owners. Want to live with your former college roommate in Texas for the winter? Want to then move back to the woods and lakes of your childhood Minnesota home in the summer? No problem. There's no need to pack or empty out the refrigerator or in anyway disrupt your living patterns as trailer trucks, trains, and cars easily move these units. The interchangeability of connections enables people to camp out wherever and with whomever they wish to connect.

Who will be in the market for these units? Children who split their time between two or more parents or family units won't have to keep a duplicate set of underwear and toys in more than one place. Migrant workers employed by global corporations can easily relocate without the stress and hassle of actually moving. Older adults who would like to continue ongoing contact with their children but don't want to unduly burden any one of them can commute from location to location on a monthly basis. Childhood friends who have lived apart during their adult lives can now regroup in retirement without having to become joint owners of a new home.

Respitals

"Take two weeks and call me from the sauna." This will become the new version of medicine. As we move from the treatment to prevention model, people will reduce the need and the amount of time spent in hospitals or with physicians. Our doctor is not going to wait for us to develop a serious or chronic health problem; he or she is going to do whatever it takes to head those difficulties off. Physicians will be compensated for how well they are able to keep us rather than rewarded for treating illness.

Many of those alternatives to preventing serious or chronic health problems will result in the physician prescribing a spa-like respite from the stresses of daily life coupled with participation in healthy pleasures. These healthy pleasures may include meditation, walking, hiking, massages, pet therapy, volunteer work, and even parties.

And are we really ready for the good news? Our insurance company is going to pay for the two-week stay and all those good time remedies.

Community Drop-Ins

Make way for the 2000 version of the old-fashioned community center. It may be part bar, part coffee shop, part library, but it will provide a setting where people can drop in, hang out, and connect with one another. The many factors including increased mobility, temporary lifestyles, and the growing number of people working and living home alone will lead to the burning need and desire for a place for people to go "where everybody knows your name." Retired individuals will have a place to go in the morning and read the newspaper. People who work at home alone will have a coffee break spot which can be substituted for chat around the water cooler. People who are temporarily residing in a particular geographic area will drop in to connect with people who may share interests. The growing ways in which our society becomes more disconnected from one another will generate renewed interest in making meaningful human contact.

New World Gauges

How does an individual or an organization gauge those experiences with power, promise, potential, or possibilities for people and their organization. There is no certain answer or one definitive approach but there are two possibilities we suggest: McWatch and Rule of 3.

McWatch is an observation method that can be practice by any individual or by everybody in the organization almost anytime and anywhere. That's what makes it a viable option and opportunity. The McWatch approach starts with McWatch itself but in actuality it is a list of suggestions on how to closely pay attention to what's happening around one as follows:

- McWatch—observing practices and changes at fast-food restaurants or other establishments that attract and serve large numbers of people regularly.
- Go shopping—whether it be the grocery store, the outlet mall, or the warehouse club take a look at the patterns and activities in the retail arena.
- Channel surf—grab the remote, hit the couch, and click round the channels taking a look at the incredibly different kinds of things being offered and ask yourself who's watching what and why?
- Newsstand it—get yourself to the local bookstore or library and wander up and down the vast section of periodicals noting the different types of publications and probable target markets of each.
- Make new friends—since people have a tendency to hang out and spend time with people with similar interests to theirs, make a concerted effort to go places and do things where you will encounter people who are different from you.
- Be childlike—continue to stoke your curiosity and when you encounter things or behaviors that are new and different continue to ask that age-old question, why?

The second suggested method that can identify and launch your ship into the new world is the Power of 3s. Taylor and Wacker in *The 500 Year Delta,* when talking about life stage and its impact upon marketing, make an incredibly powerful observation when they state "build a product that abets the flight, and you will ride it to riches" (Taylor and Wacker, 1997, p. 80). Life stage is just one of those indices that can serve as a takeoff platform for the launch of a new product, service, or experience. Our advice is to act on the Power of 3s. This means that you gauge the forces en route to this new world being ever vigilant for the interaction or collision of three forces. These forces may be demographic, behavioral, or trends but that when and where these three forces come together is the time to ride the flight path of new experiences.

A good vantage point to observe the intersection of these three forces might be to identify critical aspects within either the core or change coordinate of the 4Cs of people which were outlined in chapter 3. The core dimensions incorporate the impact of demographic patterns on experiences. The elements discussed and examined within the change coordinate were life stage, life event, health, readiness, and seasons or cycles. Such elements impact on behavior. If important aspects from the core or change coordinates were then examined in relationship

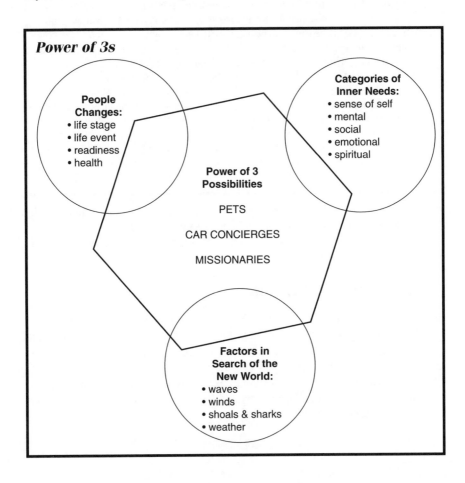

Examples of companies, organizations, or industries that capitalized on the power of three or more factors include:

- For approximately $1,000, General Motors outfits certain cars with OnStar, a satellite-based technology that uses a cell phone to serve as a combination companion, concierge, and caretaker. There's almost no end to what OnStar can and will do. If the car is in an accident that deploys the air bag, OnStar will try to reach the driver by phone. If there's no response, it contacts emergency services. It helps people locate cars temporarily misplaced in a large parking lot or garage. It can tell drivers their exact location and help with directions as well as the location of the nearest bank, ATM, and grocery store. The high-tech of this service is augmented by a heavy dose of high-touch as the service is staffed by a large number of personable individuals who have gone so far as to impersonate an angel by flashing the headlights for a customer's grandchild and searching for song lyrics for a partying customer (Fogarty, 1997, pp. B1–2).
- There are French nuns running soup kitchens in an East Harlem storefront. There is a pastor from Chile who spent a year preaching in United Church of Christ congregations in Massachusetts. Reverse missionaries are in full force in the United States as missionaries from Calcutta and Africa have come to America to feed the homeless and preach the gospel in the suburbs as the poverty of this country, both material and spiritual, continues to grow (Hampson, 1997, p. 17A).
- The Pet Industry Joint Advisory Council indicates that Americans spend $18.5 billion annually on pet care and products. Pets generally join a household at one of two stages of life, the young and growing family or the empty nest. Both of these stages are in full bloom currently and consequently, there is no end to the products and services being created and offered for these new members of the American family. Best Friends Pet Resorts and Salons is just what it suggests, a fast-growing chain of kennels and grooming salons. By 1996, there were approximately 12,000 retail pet stores and almost 1,000 superstores (Ackerman, 1997, p. F4).

to the categories of inner needs overviewed in chapter 2, a preliminary flight plan could be filed. A third element is needed to serve as the fuel to ignite this journey, and often that element can be found within forces cited as factors impacting sailing into the new world.

It's a New World After All

Remember, it is important for organizations to take action. Peter Drucker is quoted as saying "the best way to predict the future is to create it." Think about that for a minute. If you elect to become that pace-setting organization suggested by Holland and if your organization elects to practice some of the principles and concepts within this book, you'll be resistant to the shoals, the sharks, and the weather. You can ride the power of those waves and winds if you have the foresight and imagination to take action now.

Where will the waves and winds take the experience industry? While it's daunting to predict or project, it is possible to share insights and thoughts about experiences in the new world. Some of those ideas include the following:

- Money (within reason) won't matter if the experience is the right one for the individual or a high priority for him or her. People will redirect their resources, time and money, if it targets their needs.
- Growth of "real" simulations as people stay at Port Orleans in Disney World or the Orleans Hotel in Las Vegas and eat in rain forests or rock museums, the enjoyment of authenticity with the convenience of the replication will be a big draw.
- Fueled by the popularity of millennial turning events, there will be increased demand for specialized or one-of-a-kind experiences such as being there for an eclipse of the sun or sunrise at the top of a Hawaiian volcano.
- Experience providers will begin to offer various levels of the same experience with price tags that reflect the exclusivity of the experience. What would people pay to visit the Acropolis at sunrise or sunset before it opened to the general public or the Grand Canyon or Yosemite with only 99 other people in the park rather than the usual horde of visitors.
- Many experience providers will see the advantages of controlling every aspect of the experience from start to finish. Such an approach will

Action Agenda

❖ Create your own map for a journey into the new world by establishing an ongoing mechanism for environmental scanning within your organization.

❖ Hold scanning sessions every six to eight weeks to detect changes in peoples' preferences or the possibility of emerging competition as it relates to your experience.

❖ Review the prevailing wind section of this chapter and brainstorm possible implications for your organization; do the same for shoals, sharks, and weather.

❖ Identify what changes, if any, need to be made in the way your organization approaches information gathering and innovation.

❖ Select one of the activities or suggestions included in the section on "wholistic" thinking and try it out.

❖ Apply lessons learned from one or more of the role models to your experience.

❖ Review suggestions included on the sampler and determine potential and possibilities for your organization.

❖ Take a look at the experiences you provide for people and suggest ways they can be turned into an opportunity or solution for participants.

❖ Create one or more scenarios for your experience. Have a good time brainstorming and dreaming up what function it might serve or how it would need to change for the year 2010.

Transition Tracking

From	To
• Sailing along	• Setting a course
• Customer's personal preferences and delight	• Emerging 4Ps: promise, power, potential and possibilities
• Reinvention	• Regeneration
• Experiences	• Opportunities and solutions
• Old World	• New World of experiences in a discretionary economy

shape the experience for the participant as well as increase the bottom line of the provider.
- Experiences will become more related to individual and societal well-being as evidenced by youth development approaches, the healthy communities movement, and the popularity of wellness offerings.
- Experiences will become a way of life rather than discrete, lifestyle activities as people reorient or revise the ways in which they live, work, and play to create a way of life that just naturally incorporates desirable experiences by their definition.
- Watch for the growth of real "Fantasy Island" experiences as providers recognize the need and profitability of providing people with the opportunity to be prom queen or a rock musician. Get ready to shout, "De plane! De plane!"
- People want to be a star in their own life and experiences will cater to this need complete with fans and groupies.

Welcome to the New World!

Sources

Ackerman, Jerry. (1997, December 28). A businessman's best friend. *The Boston Globe.*

Associated Press. (1998, January 2). Herds of Harleys roam the desert highways of the Persian Gulf. *The Tampa Tribune.*

Belden, Tom. (1997, April 28). Hotels closing restaurants, switching to enhanced food courts. *Hartford Courant.*

Bly, Laura. (1996, November 22). Women-only trips flourish. *USA Today.*

Brownless, Lisa. (1996, November 13). Ad executives break rank over tobacco. *The Wall Street Journal.*

Chapman, Christine. (1998). Making a splash. *Modern Maturity.*

Dighe, Atul, & Clement, Bezold. (1996, July). Trends and key forces shaping the future of quality. *Quality Progress.*

Fenichell, Stephen. (1997, October). Disney world: The next 25 begin. *Sky.*

Fogarty, Thomas A. (1997, November 20). With OnStar aboard, buy a car, get a concierge. *USA Today.*

Gerzon, Mark. (1996). *A house divided: Six belief systems struggling for the American soul.* Los Angeles, CA: Jeremy P. Tarcher.

Grunwald, Michael. (1997, August 25). Gateway to a new America. *The Boston Globe.*

Hampson, Rick. (1997, November 19). Missionaries set sights on American souls. *USA Today.*

Hellmich, Nanci. (1997, March 19). A break from tradition. *USA Today.*

Holland, Robert C. (1994, January–February). Sailing into the millennium. *The Futurist.*

Huntington, Samuel P. (1996). *The clash of civilizations and the remaking of the world order.* New York, NY: Simon & Schuster.

jobtitlesofthefuture (1997, October–November). *Fast Company.*

Jones, Del, & Belton, Beth. (1997, September 30). Median annual income up $410. *USA Today.*

Kaufman, Matthew. (1997, October 24). Grown-up goblins scare up spending. *Hartford Courant.*

Lawrence, Jill, (1996, December 16). Wanted: Good citizens, close communities. *USA Today.*

Leonard, Mary. (1997, November 12). Innovative efforts show government can help. *The Boston Globe.*

Leonhardt, David. (1997, March 17). Two-tier marketing. *Business Week.*

Lieberman, David. (1997, October 10). Consumers to feed growing media appetite. *USA Today.*

Medical journal. (1997, March). *Self.*

Miller, Lisa. (1997, April 11). "Roughing it" now means focaccia on the campfire. *The Wall Street Journal.*

Nasser, Haya El. (1997, April 2). Fountain of youth washing away gray face of Florida. *USA Today.*

Rosato, Donna. (1997, March 25). Cyberscouting the world of travel sites. *USA Today.*

Taylor, Jim, & Wacker, Watts. (1997). *The 500 year delta.* New York, NY: HarperBusiness.

Tomorrow in brief. (1996, November–December). *The Futurists.*

Wilson, Craig. (1997, April 29). All generations relax at home in retro style. *USA Today.*

Yemma, John. (1997, March 23). When Kmart meets Bloomingdale's. *The Boston Globe.*

The Experience Continues

For a good source of more traditional approaches to marketing and service marketing with applications for the leisure industry, please see *Marketing for Parks, Recreation, and Leisure* published by Venture Publishing. Venture Publishing has a number of titles that would help marketers understand play, leisure, people, and their motivation during their free time.

To get in touch with us directly, please contact us on-line at leisurlife@aol.com or visit our Web site at experiencemarketing.com.

Check the Web site regularly for ongoing updates related to experience marketing and leisure and lifestyle behaviors. Feel free to forward your own examples of marketing strategies and techniques and you and your organizations will be cited with the example.

TrendScan is a quarterly publication with an annual fee of $50. It is available by contacting Leisure Lifestyle Consulting, 221 Hollister Way N, Glastonbury, CT 06033. To receive a complimentary subscription for one year, send three scathingly innovative examples that were not included in this book and the newsletter will be yours.

Index

Other Books From Venture Publishing

The A•B•Cs of Behavior Change: Skills for Working With Behavior Problems in Nursing Homes
> by Margaret D. Cohn, Michael A. Smyer and Ann L. Horgas

Activity Experiences and Programming Within Long-Term Care
> by Ted Tedrick and Elaine R. Green

The Activity Gourmet
> by Peggy Powers

Advanced Concepts for Geriatric Nursing Assistants
> by Carolyn A. McDonald

Adventure Education
> edited by John C. Miles and Simon Priest

Aerobics of the Mind: Keeping the Mind Active in Aging—A New Perspective on Programming for Older Adults
> by Marge Engelman

Assessment: The Cornerstone of Activity Programs
> by Ruth Perschbacher

Behavior Modification in Therapeutic Recreation: An Introductory Manual
> by John Datillo and William D. Murphy

Benefits of Leisure
> edited by B. L. Driver, Perry J. Brown and George L. Peterson

Benefits of Recreation Research Update
> by Judy M. Sefton and W. Kerry Mummery

Beyond Bingo: Innovative Programs for the New Senior
> by Sal Arrigo, Jr., Ann Lewis and Hank Mattimore

Beyond Bingo 2: More Innovative Programs for the New Senior
> by Sal Arrigo, Jr.

Both Gains and Gaps: Feminist Perspectives on Women's Leisure
> by Karla Henderson, M. Deborah Bialeschki, Susan M. Shaw and Valeria J. Freysinger

Dimensions of Choice: A Qualitative Approach to Recreation, Parks, and Leisure Research
> by Karla A. Henderson

Effective Management in Therapeutic Recreation Service
> by Gerald S. O'Morrow and Marcia Jean Carter

Evaluating Leisure Services: Making Enlightened Decisions
    by Karla A. Henderson with M. Deborah Bialeschki
The Evolution of Leisure: Historical and Philosophical Perspectives (Second Printing)
    by Thomas Goodale and Geoffrey Godbey
File o' Fun: A Recreation Planner for Games & Activities—Third Edition
    by Jane Harris Ericson and Diane Ruth Albright
The Game Finder—A Leader's Guide to Great Activities
    by Annette C. Moore
Getting People Involved in Life and Activities: Effective Motivating Techniques
    by Jeanne Adams
Great Special Events and Activities
    by Annie Morton, Angie Prosser and Sue Spangler
Inclusive Leisure Services: Responding to the Rights of People With Disabilities
    by John Dattilo
Internships in Recreation and Leisure Services: A Practical Guide for Students (Second Edition)
    by Edward E. Seagle, Jr., Ralph W. Smith and Lola M. Dalton
Interpretation of Cultural and Natural Resources
    by Douglas M. Knudson, Ted T. Cable and Larry Beck
Introduction to Leisure Services—7th Edition
    by H. Douglas Sessoms and Karla A. Henderson
Leadership and Administration of Outdoor Pursuits, Second Edition
    by Phyllis Ford and James Blanchard
Leadership in Leisure Services: Making a Difference
    by Debra J. Jordan
Leisure and Family Fun (LAFF)
    by Mary Atteberry-Rogers
Leisure and Leisure Services in the 21st Century
    by Geoffrey Godbey
Leisure Diagnostic Battery Computer Software
    by Gary Ellis and Peter A. Witt
The Leisure Diagnostic Battery: Users Manual and Sample Forms
    by Peter A. Witt and Gary Ellis
Leisure Education: A Manual of Activities and Resources
    by Norma J. Stumbo and Steven R. Thompson
Leisure Education II: More Activities and Resources
    by Norma J. Stumbo
Leisure Education III: More Goal-Oriented Activities
    by Norma J. Stumbo
Leisure Education IV: Activities for Individuals With Substance Addictions
    by Norma J. Stumbo
Leisure Education Program Planning: A Systematic Approach
    by John Dattilo and William D. Murphy
Leisure in Your Life: An Exploration—Fourth Edition
    by Geoffrey Godbey

Leisure Services in Canada: An Introduction
    by Mark S. Searle and Russell E. Brayley
The Lifestory Re-Play Circle: A Manual of Activities and Techniques
    by Rosilyn Wilder
Marketing for Parks, Recreation, and Leisure
    by Ellen L. O'Sullivan
Models of Change in Municipal Parks and Recreation: A Book of Innovative Case Studies
    edited by Mark E. Havitz
More Than a Game: A New Focus on Senior Activity Services
    by Brenda Corbett
Nature and the Human Spirit: Toward an Expanded Land Management Ethic
    edited by B. L. Driver, Daniel Dustin, Tony Baltic, Gary Elsner and George Peterson
Outdoor Recreation Management: Theory and Application, Third Edition
    by Alan Jubenville and Ben Twight
Planning Parks for People, Second Edition
    by John Hultsman, Richard L. Cottrell and Wendy Z. Hultsman
Private and Commercial Recreation
    edited by Arlin Epperson
The Process of Recreation Programming Theory and Technique, Third Edition
    by Patricia Farrell and Herberta M. Lundegren
Protocols for Recreation Therapy Programs
    edited by Jill Kelland, along with the Recreation Therapy Staff at Alberta Hospital Edmonton
Quality Management: Applications for Therapeutic Recreation
    edited by Bob Riley
Recreation and Leisure: Issues in an Era of Change, Third Edition
    edited by Thomas Goodale and Peter A. Witt
Recreation Economic Decisions: Comparing Benefits and Costs (Second Edition)
    by John B. Loomis and Richard G. Walsh
Recreation Programming and Activities for Older Adults
    by Jerold E. Elliott and Judith A. Sorg-Elliott
Recreation Programs That Work for At-Risk Youth: The Challenge of Shaping the Future
    by Peter A. Witt and John L. Crompton
Reference Manual for Writing Rehabilitation Therapy Treatment Plans
    by Penny Hogberg and Mary Johnson
Research in Therapeutic Recreation: Concepts and Methods
    edited by Marjorie J. Malkin and Christine Z. Howe
Simple Expressions: Creative and Therapeutic Arts for the Elderly in Long-Term Care Facilities
    by Vicki Parsons
A Social History of Leisure Since 1600
    by Gary Cross

A Social Psychology of Leisure
    by Roger C. Mannell and Douglas A. Kleiber
The Sociology of Leisure
    by John R. Kelly and Geoffrey Godbey
Therapeutic Activity Intervention With the Elderly: Foundations & Practices
    by Barbara A. Hawkins, Marti E. May and Nancy Brattain Rogers
Therapeutic Recreation: Cases and Exercises
    by Barbara C. Wilhite and M. Jean Keller
Therapeutic Recreation in the Nursing Home
    by Linda Buettner and Shelley L. Martin
Therapeutic Recreation Protocol for Treatment of Substance Addictions
    by Rozanne W. Faulkner
Time for Life: The Surprising Ways Americans Use Their Time
    by John P. Robinson and Geoffrey Godbey
A Training Manual for Americans With Disabilities Act Compliance in Parks and Recreation Settings
    by Carol Stensrud

   Venture Publishing, Inc.
         1999 Cato Avenue
       State College, PA 16801

Phone: (814) 234-4561; Fax: (814) 234-1651